# DEFECTIVE INSTITUTIONS

IDIOM INVENTING WRITING THEORY

*Jacques Lezra and Paul North, series editors*

# DEFECTIVE INSTITUTIONS

A PROTOCOL FOR THE REPUBLIC

JACQUES LEZRA

Fordham University Press *New York* *2024*

Funding for this book was provided in part by the Helen Tartar Memorial Fund.



Fordham University Press also publishes its books in a variety of electronic formats. Some content that appears in print may not be available in electronic books.

Visit us online at www.fordhampress.com.

Library of Congress Cataloging-in-Publication Data available online at https://catalog.loc.gov.

Printed in the United States of America

26 25 24 5 4 3 2 1

First edition

# CONTENTS

# DEFECTIVE INSTITUTIONS

The I of each is to
The I of each,
A kind of fretful speech
Which sets a limit on itself

Marianne Moore

Never deduce general conclusions from particular instances; nay, it is perfectly illogical to do so; it is a great defect into which those fall who are governed by a party spirit. Thus if some abuses have crept into an institution, it is not thence to be considered that the institution is radically evil.

Victor Doublet

# PREFACE

I began writing these words in spring 2021; now it is summer, two years later.[1] George Floyd's murder was on my mind. Now, as the COVID-19 pandemic wanes and waxes and the noxious political regime the United States endured under the Trump presidency recedes, for the present, I have been reflecting on the failure of governance in the United States. Everywhere I hear calls for strengthening institutions and for defending liberties ostensibly protected by such institutions. The U.S. Supreme Court's decision in *Dobbs vs. Jackson* to overturn the right to abortion sharpens the crisis: *stare decisis*, the doctrine of the authority of precedent, may not survive. Its phantasmatic, habitual, magical authority, the authority of the doctrine establishing the authority of precedent, lay behind the U.S. Senate's willingness to confirm Trump-nominated justices who would later, having cleaved at their hearings to the doctrine's unassailability, having sheltered behind the Senate's apparent belief in itself, in the courts, in the nominees' word, and in the imaginary authority of the doctrine, vote to derogate, if not abolish, that doctrine. *Stare decisis* also implies: *what has been instituted stands*. But *faith* in the standing of decisions; in the authority of antecedent cases and in rules deriving from them; in the coherence, strength, continuity, solidity (etc.) of the institutions that frame and render legitimate these decisions and the rules they buttress; faith (as John Rawls famously put it) that "the successful carrying out of just institutions is the shared final end of all the members of society, and these institutional forms are prized as good in themselves" and that a "well-ordered society (corresponding to justice as fairness) is . . . a social union of social unions"—these will not result in greater democracy, greater horizontality, more equitable living.[2] To the contrary.

In this book I offer an alternative: an aberrant republicanism consisting of defective institutions.

*Aberrant*, because faith in "the successful carrying out of *just* institutions" (Rawls, my emphasis) results in what David Graeber wonderfully called "the game-ification of institutional life" (subjective genitive: "institutional life" is "game-ified" life, life become a "utopia of rules").[3] An *aberrant* republicanism consisting of *defective institutions*, that is, the social form of "materialized utopianism" (Graeber again) consisting in "an anti-authoritarianism that, in its emphasis on creative synthesis and improvisation, sees freedom basically in terms of play" rather than "a tacit republicanism that sees freedom ultimately as the ability to reduce all forms of power to a set of clear and transparent rules."[4]

A few assertions, first off. *Defective Institutions* is a work of academic political philosophy, not (like Graeber's) of anthropology; and it is not a work addressing the sociology of institutions. It urges nonetheless that political philosophy should be nonacademic in three senses. First, whatever sort of institution the *academy* is today, we should recognize that its claims to enable and shelter critical thought and speech are also devices for determining, even policing, just what *counts* as critique: what falls inside academia's walls, what falls outside (but can always be captured, brought within the closure of academic speech, as its *object*). Second, and as a result, political philosophy on my description finds itself neither within nor without academic institutions. It is uneasy as a regime of phrases sanctioned by an institution; neither is it easily an object of such phrases. Third, and putting the first two to use, political philosophy as I imagine it today should work to subordinate the critique of *acts* of institution or of the *substance* of actually existing institutions or political concepts to the critique of their *relation*. Taking on acts of institution or addressing actually existing institutions or political concepts are familiar and familial tasks, congenial to the university frame, to the think-tank frame, and to the more or less smooth transition between the institution of the university and the institutions of political governance. They are tasks undertaken either presupposing or with a view to establishing the fundamental continuity between acts of institution and the substance of actually existing institutions or political concepts, or out of a desire to strengthen actually existing institutions and to clarify their relation to subtending political concepts, thereby producing new and stronger institutions or new and stronger, more coherent political concepts.

The task of critique in political philosophy is other. The integrity of "acts" and "substances" cannot be granted: it is imaginary, contingent. To move between them is to forget that acts have one tense, the present, and substances none. (This is not controversial. When I say, "Yesterday I loved" or "There will be a sea battle tomorrow," I am acting, *now*, to state something. The deictic "yesterday" and the noun "battle," substantive, have no time until I affirm something of them, now, in the present.) Further: today the imaginary, contingent continuity that obtains between acts and substances is the continuity of markets and of universally translatable standards of economic value. Institutions imagined to stand on this continuity and on this forgetting are the imaginary substance of politics today. Instead the task is this: to produce and put into what Sylvia Wynter calls "discursive play" defective narratives, political concepts, and institutions offering to politics, and *as* politics, a different substance and different acts, and a different way of permitting acts and substances to consist.

To tell these discontinuous stories and offer defective political concepts and institutions, the chapters that follow often step outside the walls that traditionally serve to protect and grant legitimacy to thought, as this is imagined in Western societies: the sheltering bounds of given disciplines and of institutions such as the family, the state, the law, the culture industry, and the university. Here and there throughout the first person wanders into arguments where I would never before have let "I" step. This may weaken, delegitimate even, some of the conclusions that *Defective Institutions* will reach, since where I travel you don't follow necessarily, and since it may be that very little that can be generalized is to be found en route or at the end of this road. Recall the epigraph I borrow from Victor Doublet: "Never deduce general conclusions from particular instances; nay, it is perfectly illogical to do so; it is a great defect into which those fall who are governed by a party spirit." But "general conclusions," *strength*, and *legitimacy* are not my goals principally.

To say "I" today, in the many contexts I inhabit, might also, as Roberto Esposito would say, be to obey "the requirement that life be *instituted*": to say "I" would then be to hold *one* life, mine as it happens, responsible for what is affirmed here, if not entirely then sufficiently that noting the fact is necessary; and to determine and institute *one* life, mine as it happens but *all* life possibly, as what can singularly bear responsibility for what can be affirmed about these contexts. So far, we are in the neighborhood of autoethnography, as it was theorized and put into play by feminist and cultural criticism perhaps a decade ago. Still, *Defective Institutions* is not an autoethnography. It rejects—I reject—the proposition that "life," any life, *all* life, is or can be counted as "one." (This is what is entailed in the "game-ification" of life, to return to Graeber's formula.) On, among other grounds, these. Saying "I," as Émile Benveniste famously suggested, is the means for me, some "me," any "me," *all* "me," "to appropriate to [myself] an entire language by designating [myself] as *I*," of "establishing" (Benveniste's French is *installer*) "'subjectivity' in language" and thereby "creating the category of person—both in language and outside of it as well." "Designating" and hence "establishing" are not abstract acts, however, or not *only*. Does "to say" entail "to appropriate"? On what account of entailment, on what definition and distribution of power? Just *who*, just *when*, gets to say, appropriatively, "I," and under what conditions of felicity? Benveniste opens these questions for general linguistics, but they are lived questions for so many who, saying "I," nevertheless are excluded from (that is, they fall outside of what is in practice, historically, designated by or "established" as) "the category of person—both in language and outside of it as well." And I reject the proposition that "life" is or can be counted as "one" on these other grounds, too: just as my saying "I" is both an abstract operation open in principle to any and all speakers of a language *and* an operation that depends on a historically situated power of "appropriation," so too the quantifiers *one* and *all* ("one life," "all life," "life") are both abstract logical operators *and* practical instruments for building and policing concepts and institutions. "I" is amphibian, and "lives" not at all.

*Defective Institutions: A Protocol for the Republic* opens asking why the concept of "institution"—pervasive, fundamental, the very mark of what distinguishes human society from nonhuman animal groupings: packs, murders, flocks, hives, exaltations—proves so hard to define. From this difficulty, and then across and within each of the remaining chapters of the book, follow a number of paths at once, offering a definition and examples—though not just of classic institutions, the (pervasive, fundamental, etc.) ones presumed to work differently from merely instinctual association, but also of the alternative: *defective* institutions wed to the practices and concept of *abolition*.

The book's first path is genealogical. Its chapters move from describing the schema of institution set in place where the West imagines its political origins to lie—at the moment of the foundation of the city, the *polis*—to describing the schema of abolition set in place where that foundation fails or is dislodged, by means of contemporary works that advocate the abolition of the state, the police, the university, and the family. The archive: literary, philosophical, juridical, psychoanalytic, musical. Aeschylus's *Eumenides*, the work of Jean-François Lyotard and Martha Nussbaum, and the U.S. Supreme Court's influential *Marbury v. Madison* decision open the story; James Baldwin, Nina Simone, Sigmund

Freud, Sophie Lewis, and M. E. O'Brien close it. First the chthonic practices of vengeance give way to law, as Athena installs judgment and policing at the city's base. Last, the law and the mechanisms that install and protect it (and that it ostensibly serves to define and protect) are subject to suspension and erasure.

On its second path—simultaneously engaged—*Defective Institutions* concerns itself with the principles of thought that undergird the classic concept of institution: foundation, identity, coherence, composition (the weak "and" in expressions such as "'I' is amphibian, and 'lives' not at all" will be of increasing concern), modality, similitude, quantification. Here the archive opens to include Rawls, Searle, Heidegger, Fine, Moten and Harney, Breton, and Butler. First the "great principle" on which Western philosophy stands, the principle of sufficient reason; then, by means of Proclus and Heidegger and on to Benjamin, Breton and Wynter, following the *insufficiency* of foundational reason (in, for instance, the weak juridical principle of *stare decisis*), to the critique of the logic of identity; to the analytic principle of modal pluralism (in Fine) and its link to "family resemblances," and to the classic European account of the family. (Perrault's "Blue Beard" and Carter's "The Bloody Chamber" are with me here.)

The third path these chapters follow regards the institution of "race," and consists in exploring its deep links to the logics of foundation, identity, and similitude, and to the companion Western institutions of the family, the police, and the state. Wynter's analysis of what she calls the "coloniality of being" guides me here, though I depart from her in my skepticism about the concept of "coloniality." *Defective Institutions* finds its way reading (and listening to) Baudelaire, August Vollmer, James Baldwin, Saidiya Hartman, Frank Wilderson, Nina Simone, and Chico Buarque.

Finally, *Defective Institutions* concerns itself with the *genres* that Wynter's "discursive play" follows (*play* is not without its rules, as Graeber reminds his readers) at different moments and to different ends, and in particular when the end is the abolition of the classic model of the institution and the fashioning of its *defective* alternative. Institutions, too, have their sanctioned genres, preferred literary modes, of course, but also their conventions of expression, exposition, theme, veridification, and so on—and genres are instituted, like the figures of logic I have mentioned, in a circle of reciprocal reinforcement, so that this sort of story or that kind of performance both expresses what an institution identifies as proper to itself, and is itself sanctioned as proper, valued *as* proper to the institution, by the same stroke. (The state's genres range from the national epic to the interoffice memorandum, passing through the formalisms of the law, folklore, and in general the products of the culture industry inasmuch as that industry operates in, and supports, the economic model on which the state subsists.) The drama, poetry, the short story, testimonial narrative, juridical opinion, allegory, the folk tale, the philosophical fable, and finally the operetta (Moten: "the [necessarily musical] theater of objection"), Brecht and Weill's *Threepenny Opera*—these are my references.

A coda allows me to offer a description of the ways in which defective institutions may be weakly coordinated in a radically, aberrantly republican vein.

Something which is defective not merely for me or in my eyes but in itself—intrinsically—has something outside itself which it lacks.

Karl Marx

They all, faces weathered by salty tears, gazes directed upwards from crushed, wooden caves, arms, when still there, imploringly crossed over the chest—who are they?—so unspeakably helpless and protesting—these Niobids of the Sea? Or its Maenads? For they stormed over whiter combs than those of Thrace and were beaten by wilder paws than the beasts, the following of Artemis—they, the galleons.

Walter Benjamin

# INTRODUCTION

## INSTITUTIONS (A FIRST INSTALLMENT)

What is an "institution"?[1] The question is trickier than appears on first blush. Philology takes us just so far. The word "institution" has a verbal origin, from the Latin verb *statuere*, with the addition of the agential particle *in*: to stand up, to set up, to install, to establish, to statute. *Statues*, for instance the Niobids, are set up just so. (Niobe will never be far from my mind.) So is a circle of stones set around a village: brute facts, these stones fall and crumble, and their ghostly symbolic proxies, "institutional facts" as John Searle calls them, come to take their place. The drift, by metonymy, from the verbal form, *to institute*, to the nouns, *institute*, *institution*; from the action to what results from it; is already present in Latin and crops up in Romance languages. The story leading from brute fact to institutional fact is the story of every empiricist philosophy. Both entail an active and instituting "I," a predicative "I" (to use Levinas's language) or a "shared we-attitude," a "joint or collective intentionality" (as Raimo Tuomela has it).[2]

Taxonomies flourish where definitions fail; "institution" has stood for many things since its Latin uses, and against others as well, against "instinct," or "nature," or the nonhuman animal's way of being most notably. At the crossing of political science and sociology there have developed—roughly since 1989, when James Marsh and Johan Olsen published *Rediscovering Institutions: The Orga-*

*nizational Basis of Politics*—three varieties of "new institutionalism": historical institutionalism, rational choice institutionalism, and sociological institutionalism.[3] Just what "institution" means in these contexts is not settled and perhaps cannot be. This is Durkheim, in 1917, at the moment of the foundation of the discipline of sociology:

> The great difference between animal societies and human societies is that in the former, the individual creature is governed exclusively from within itself, by the instincts (except for a slight degree of individual education, which itself depends upon instinct). On the other hand human societies present a new phenomenon of a special nature, which consists in the fact that certain ways of acting are imposed, or at least suggested from outside the individual and are added on to his own nature: such is the character of the "institutions" (in the broad sense of the word) which the existence of language makes possible, and of which language itself is an example. They take on substance as individuals succeed each other without this succession destroying their continuity; their presence is the distinctive characteristic of human societies, and the proper subject of sociology.[4]

So institutions, the mark of humanness, of civilization, of culture, are "certain ways of acting . . . imposed, or at least suggested from outside the individual and . . . added on to his own nature." Durkheim's naturalism persists. Thirty or so years ago, Searle and a social ontologist like Tuomela, despite substantive disagreement regarding both the status of *intentionality* and what Searle calls "the collective imposition of status-functions" fundamental to social institution (just how does it line up with what Tuomela describes as "we-mode collective intentions"?), share Tuomela's view that "social institutions [are] collectively . . . made devices for creating order in a human community, typically society, and helping people to satisfy their basic needs, such as needs related to food and shelter, sexual relations and reproduction, sociality and social power."[5] An institution has been (in Locke's English) a sort of "voluntary" "act" that creates relations other than natural among humans, inasmuch as the relation is "separable from the persons, to whom they have sometimes belonged." This is Locke's full definition, from *An Essay Concerning Human Understanding* (2.28.3):

> Sometimes the foundation of considering things, with reference to one another, is some act whereby anyone comes by a moral right, power, or obligation to do something. Thus a general is one that hath power to command an army; and an army under a general, is a collection of armed men obliged to obey one man. A citizen, or a burgher, is one who has a right to certain privileges in this or that place. All this sort depending upon men's wills, or agreement in society, I call instituted, or voluntary, and

> may be distinguished from the natural, in that they are most, if not all of them, some way or other alterable, and separable from the persons, to whom they have sometimes belonged, though neither of the substances, so related, be destroyed.[6]

Ways of *acting*; an *act*. "Institution" has been *education* and *instruction* (Descartes, in the *Passions of the Soul*: "Good instruction [*la bonne institution*] is very useful in correcting the defects one is born with [*pour corriger les défauts de la naissance*]").[7] The French *instituteurs* and *institutrices* and their Romance language colleagues are teachers and tutors, as well as founders of orders, organizations, or companies. "Institution" is a building intended for instruction, and one intended for housing those who require *institutionalizing*, the mad, the ill. (Guattari, working from and against what he calls a "too restrictive definition" of Oury and Tosquelles's "*psychothérapie institutionnelle*," proposes first the concept of "*analyse institutionnelle*," then, unhappy at the prescriptive, sociological turn given the concept by—for instance—Loureau, Lobrot, and Lapassade, he turns to what he later calls "*métamodélisation*.")[8] "Institution" is a hospital—even the remarkable, experimental treatment centers at St. Alban and Laborde are, to Oury and Tosquelles, "institutions." "Institution" is a handbook or collection of norms, for instance rhetorical or religious (Calvin's *Institutions*, of course, but think also of Quintilian's *De institutione oratoria*, for centuries the core of so-called humanistic education in Europe). "Institutes" are *laws*; thus "institutes" is the conventional Englishing of Justinian's *Institutiones*, though Harris's decisive 1756 translation of the work, which sits at the heart of Western legal systems based in Roman law, is titled instead *The Four Books of Justinian's Institution*.

What is an "institution"? Saint-Just, deploring their lack in the postrevolutionary moment, offers a functional definition: "The object of institutions is to establish in fact all social and individual guarantees, in order to avoid dissension and violence; to substitute the ascendancy of morals for the ascendancy of men" (*Les institutions ont pour objet d'établir de fait toutes les garanties sociales et individuelles, pour éviter les dissensions et les violences; de substituer l'ascendant des moeurs à l'ascendant des hommes*). Maurice Hauriou—writing at the beginning of the twentieth century, in the same tradition—wanted social institutions to be "any permanent arrangement such that, within a given social group, organs with power of domination serve goals of interest to the group, through an activity coordinated with the group as a whole" (*par une activité coordonnée à celle de l'ensemble du groupe*).[9] A contemporary sociologist like Jonathan Turner offers this influential definition: "a complex of positions, roles, norms and values lodged in particular types of social structures and organizing relatively stable patterns of human activity with respect to fundamental problems in producing life-sustaining viable societal structures within a given environment."[10]

Turner's difference with Durkheim is important. For Durkheim, "institutions" are "added onto" human nature, "imposed, or at least suggested from outside"; with Turner, they "lodge" instead "in particular types of social structures." No explicit claims are made about what is natural, or not, in human animals—for instance that they group themselves in "social structures." And yet a social ontology *is* in both cases supposed, even naturalized, explicitly in Durkheim and later in Searle and Tuomela, implicitly in Turner. Here Seumas Miller glaringly embraces it, explaining just why such a "complex of positions, roles, norms and values" "lodges" "in particular types of social structures" (Turner): because, Miller says, "Social institutions are constituted and animated by human beings, and human beings are intrinsically moral agents." That "it does not follow from this," as Miller then says, "that all human beings are moral agents" just means that although "some may not be [moral agents], but, if so, then they would be defective *qua* human beings."[11]

Human beings whose agency does not form the foundation for institutions are then "defective *qua* human beings." In Searle, such "human beings" remain primitively attached to "brute facts." Here is how Searle tells the story; behind it I hear other stories—an Orphic allegory concerning the foundation of a city, or the Rousseauvian story of the origin of private property:

> Consider for example a primitive tribe that initially builds a wall around its territory. The wall is an instance of a function imposed in virtue of sheer physics: the wall, we will suppose, is big enough to keep intruders out and the members of the tribe in. But suppose the wall gradually evolves from being a physical barrier to being a symbolic barrier. Imagine that the wall gradually decays so that the only thing left is a line of stones. But imagine that the inhabitants and their neighbors continue to recognize the line of stones as marking the boundary of the territory in such a way that it affects their behavior. For example, the inhabitants only cross the boundary under special conditions, and outsiders can only cross into the territory if it is acceptable to the inhabitants. The line of stones now has a function that is not performed in virtue of sheer physics but in virtue of collective intentionality. Unlike a high wall or a moat, the wall remnant cannot keep people out simply because of its physical constitution. The result is, in a very primitive sense, symbolic: because a set of physical objects now performs the function of indicating something beyond itself, namely, the limits of the territory. The line of stones performs the same *function* as a physical barrier but it does not do

> so in virtue of its physical construction, but because it has been collectively assigned a new *status*, the status of a boundary marker.[12]

The stakes are high. "Human beings" who fall outside the enclosure, who "may not be [moral agents]," who lack the *symbolic* faculty registering the brute stone as a collectively agreed barrier, are "defective *qua* human beings." Maybe Durkheim will call them "animals." Searle will surely assign them to a "primitive," presymbolic stage of "evolution" (the wall "gradually evolves from being a physical barrier to being a symbolic barrier"). Maybe Miller will call them infants, demented, psychotic, sociopathic, or narcissistic. We have institutions for displaying animals, and for educating or treating such "defective" human beings. If these beings who are "defective *qua* human beings" are determined to be unteachable and incurable, our institutions will contain or remove or exterminate them. (I am remembering just now that "determination," before it is a noun, a substance, is the act of setting up or installing limits, *termini*, for understanding; and that it shares a root with "extermination," which, before it names the worst, means just this: that I set you outside, *ex-*, the *terminus*; that you are to be unthinkable: no term attaches to you any more, no name to grieve, nothing to remember.) The "primitive" we will relegate to Amazons of the mind.

Set aside for now the brutal pathologization toward which the social ontology of institutions seems to take us, at least on the path that Searle, Turner and Miller follow. Set aside too the rigid narrative shape in which we move, it seems, from stony and useful brute facts—a wall enclosing a village, say—to their symbolic proxies, institutions commonly agreed to carry out the same functions. It appears that the multiplication of uses, senses, and domains is not the principal problem we face in defining "institution" but is rather an expression of two others, more complex, less tractable. In the first place, "institution" finds its definition *in* an institutional frame (the law, religion, pedagogy, medicine, psychotherapy, philology). It is this and not that; here and not there; now and not then, depending upon the institution in which "institution" is tagged as a *definiendum*. Of course it is trivially true that any definition of a term supposes and confirms a set of conventions (or more than one), rules of understanding and applicability, sorts of borders, distributions of power, protocols for abolition, even police forces. And it is notorious, as we have seen, that there are contending fields where definitions of "institution" work centrally: sociology, anthropology, political science, management, and social ontology, to name just a few. But "institution" has a slightly different status, in this regard, than some other terms we might seek to define—"apple," say, as defined in the fields of botany or religious symbology, or "botany," or "defect," as defined in philology or in aesthetics. "Botany" is not an object-term in the field of botany; "apple" is, in botany, but it is not a term designating a field, set of conventions, and so forth, in which the naming of things, and hence the creation and recognition of object-terms such as "apple," occurs. "Field," on the other hand, is a term defined one way in the field of botany, another in the field of physics—and it is also a term we use, in the vernacular, to refer to the collective set of conventions, practices, and so forth that conform the disciplines that we call "botany" or "physics." The word "English" can be defined in the language, "English," with no suspicions that doing so renders either the language or the word incoherent. "Institution" is then closer, in its amphibian state, to "field" and to "English" than to "apple" or to "botany," and like "field" or "English," it requires disambiguation protocols whenever it is used, protocols intended to clarify what life it leads. Is "field" used as object-term in the field (say) of sociology, as a *definiendum* of the field; or as its *definiens*, the term *for* the structure of the field? Supplying the disambiguation protocols will be the responsibility of another field or institution; the distinction between object-term and field-designating term, marked in my English by the standard Latin distinction between *definiendum* and *definiens*, introduces a special, even foreign use of English, now able to take itself as its own object. We will assess the felicity or infelicity of this special use according to conventions we find in another field—linguistics, logic, what have you: metalinguistic, metadiscursive *fields*. And we find ourselves threatened by regress.[13]

Here is a slightly different way to come at this regress. Holding that institution's definition depends on the institution in which "institution" is tagged as a *definiendum* does not commit us immediately to wholesale relativism: conventions of generalization and similarity can be supplied that will sew together diverse definitions—sew them together for now, to this or that end, for such and such a group of interpreters of the "institutions" so joined. These second-order conventions *integrate* (to use Talcott Parsons's word) diverse, and diversely defined, "institutions"; they gather them together so that (this is still Parsons) "the complementary role expectation and sanction patterns [are integrated] with a generalized value system common to the members of the more inclusive collectivity." But just what is this normative "generalized value system"? Is it, as in Miller, a "moral" system definitively proper to the "human being"? What status does it have? How is it "generalized"—by virtue of what forces, schools, powers? Can it be presupposed; can it be offered axiomatically? How do we defend its axiomaticity? We might say: the axiom that a "generalized value system" integrates systems of divergent and divergently defined institutions is itself instituted. Relativism has been avoided, but at the cost of installing a norm-giving axiom ("there is a value system, and it is generalized") whose history, conditions, limits, boundaries, means of axiomatization and generalization—whose *institutionality*—we are foreclosed from questioning, perhaps even from understanding. To question them is to take the part of those who are "defective *qua* human beings," and to land in the institutions meant to educate, or cure, or contain, or exterminate them.

"Institution" is hard to define for a second reason. Take Émile Benveniste's 1969 work, the *Vocabulaire des institutions indo-europées*, which addresses economy, kinship, society, power, law, and religion: the classic European social institutions. The *Vocabulaire* treats "institution" extensively. Benveniste writes: "The expression 'institution' is here understood in a wider sense: it includes not only the institutions proper, such as justice, government, religion, but also less obvious ones which are found in various techniques, ways of life, social relationships and the processes of speech and thought. The subject is truly boundless, the aim of our study being precisely to throw light on the genesis of the vocabulary which relates to it."[14]

There are then two ways of approaching the "properly unlimited" concept of "institution." On one hand, insofar as Benveniste's "institution" means what is "outlined" in the anthropological everydayness of social being, the term just serves to designate cases or examples of institutions. And so Benveniste's use of the word *parole* in its technical sense would indicate—his use of "speech" as opposed to "language," *parole* as distinct from *langage*, in Saussure's lexicon. The institutions that Benveniste will define—this is, after all, a *Vocabulaire*—are objects in speech situations, that is to say, they are idiotisms, the factual activity of individuals at such and such a moment. This factual activity does indeed seem to us to be immensely rich, almost impossible to circumscribe, almost "unlimited": there are so many *speakers*, so many *cases* and *examples*, and so many times and circumstances in which each of them speaks! And thus so many possible institutions! Now, this almost lack of limit is a matter of practical means and techniques, not a structural attribute of institutions. For one can imagine a saturated society, a situation of absolute surveillance, a microbiopolitics, a technologization of the disciplinary society, which could indeed seek to account for the vast but not "properly unlimited" or "in itself unlimited" matter of human speech. The "institution" in this sense has only *practical* "limitations." Yes, in principle in every *procès de parole* (which we could translate as "speech act"), in every speech act there would be drawn, in the modality of the possible, another speech act, which could found or refound another institution. The idiotism of speech;

a circumstantial expression—these are practically endless. The infinity they constitute stretches before us: possible speech acts in possible circumstances, like an unbounded set of numbers. For and by every university or family or psychotherapeutic center like Saint-Alban (to give examples), another university, another family, another clinic may be instituted, an alternative, another model, another campus where the home campus can be studied; another home to keep us safe when we are away from home; a La Borde to carry on and expand the work begun at Saint-Alban. Today, the never-ending, ontic logic of the institution intersects with that of modern, reproductive capital, also never-ending—the Jamesian "one more, just one more," one more, one more commodity, one more product or institution, one more university and subdiscipline, or one more family in addition to or in exchange for this one; another, in another place, which would be expressed in the language of that place, and which would incorporate itself, take on body and value, in the language of another market. We soon find ourselves in the lexicons of acceleration and of depletion.

But Benveniste is also serious when he writes that the institution is a *concept* "in itself" or "properly" "unlimited"—as a *concept*, not as a concept's practical instantiation, not as the set of *cases* of institutions that we can build, now and here. The number of speech acts may be vast, even unending, keyed to places, times, and singularities of expression—but they can be compared, submitted to conventions of generalization and similarity, and enumerated, just because the concept "number," and the concept "institution," and the concept "concept," and the operation "is a case of," are in themselves, or "properly," untouched.

The suggestion that the concept of "institution" is immanently unlimited or illimited, the suggestion that it is (as Marx saw in Hegel) *lacking* or *defective*, verges on contradiction. Any institution, let us say, the institution of the family or the university, stands on a principle of identity, of closure, of completeness; it sets in place forms of recognition; it practices sorts of censorship.[15] Every institution, as such, inasmuch as it can be referred to the concept "institution," seeks to rest on immanent self-constraint. A wall of stones surrounds it, then a conventional proxy for this wall of stones. For instance, my families—I have more than one—are effective, unstable compromises between election and determination, decision and consanguinity. In one of my families we agree to recognize that these and only these individuals have elected to form a bond of mutual assistance, care, responsibility, and recognition. I will try to enroll someone else, or will say to another individual: you can elect to be part of our pack; but unless my act of enrolling or my statement of permission is itself antecedently recognized by the members of the pack, they will be infelicitous—they just won't work, or they will be lies. In another of my families I choose to call you my sister or my child. I am speaking metaphorically or literally. You will say that it is the state that guards the border between what I can elect and what is given, between the metaphoric and literal value of my statements *about* you: "You are my child," "You are my sister" (or custom, or religion). But those borders are also guarded by the imaginary form that what counts as my "family" hews to. We agree, in one of my families, in what I will call my biological family, that these and only these individuals (for now) are related among themselves by blood. We have names for degrees and sorts of consanguinity; none of us may, without threatening what we imagine ourselves to be to one another, change those names or what they entail. Social ontologies built by analogy to this image, "resting" on it, will be threatened as well: this is the story of Oedipus.

Take "institution" to refer, today, to this disaggregated field.

## DEFECTS: WHAT AM I MISSING?

> But the indifference I feel when there is no reason pushing me in one direction rather than another is the lowest grade of freedom; it is evidence not of any perfection of freedom, but rather of a defect in knowledge or a kind of negation. For if I always saw clearly what was true and good, I should never have to deliberate about the right judgement or choice; in that case, although I should be wholly free, it would be impossible for me to be in a state of indifference.[16]

What counts as "defective"? How do we judge whether a narrative, a concept, or an institution, you name it, is defective? The Romance languages trace "defect" to Latin *defectus*, from *deficio* (Lewis and Short: "to withdraw, revolt, desert, fall off"; CNRTL: *défectif*, "imparfait, vicieux"; *défaut*: "Absence d'une chose ou d'une personne dont la présence serait nécessaire ou souhaitable [généralement pour former un ensemble cohérent] . . . Perte de la piste de l'animal pourchassé." "Imperfect, faulty" . . . "the lack of a thing or person whose presence would be necessary or desirable [in order, generally, to make a coherent whole] . . . The loss of the trail of an animal being hunted"); Sebastián de Covarrubias in 1611: *defeto*, "falta . . . *Defetuoso* todo aquello que no está cumplido, ni cabal" "Sin que le falte, ni le sobre nada," whatever is not accomplished; neither missing anything, nor having any excess).[17] *Defectus*: the noun and the adjectival form bump up against the verb: *to defect*, familiar from battlefronts and the lexicon of the Cold War, from the Latin *defectus* (Lewis and Short: "defection, revolt; a failing, failure, lack, disappearance") by way of Old French. In Lucretius (and following him), *defectus*, an eclipse; in grammar, a "defective" verb is morphologically lacking: it lacks an infinitive, a tense, a participle, an imperative or a gerund, say. In Castilian Spanish, the verb *abolir*, "to abolish," remains a paradigm of defectiveness, though custom and regulative institutions have tended to supply missing forms through analogy to regular verbs, or to prefer forms that do not produce semantically distressing interferences (for instance, preferring *yo abolo*, "I abolish," to the morphologically more correct **yo abuelo*, which also means "I grandfather").

Romance languages in hand, we understand straight off: something "defective" is discontinuous, disorganized, open, untellable, possibly rhythmic, linked accidentally to *abolition* . . .

Mostly, what is defective is what is lacking—and lacking not just any attribute or quality, but something definitive, even essential. But if this or that thing I buy is missing something essential, something that keeps it from working as it is designed to do or from being what it is supposed to be, is it still *that thing?* What if something I know does not incline my will to act, what if the noun won't draw me toward a verb, toward the event or viceversa—what if I am indifferent? Descartes's remarkable phrase regarding the relation between cognition and the will is strong: "sed tantummodo in cognitione defectum, sive negationem quondam," *defectum, sive negationem*; a defect in, that is, a negation of knowledge. The questions are nontrivial: defects can become negations. ("Can become" takes me partway. I imagine *slight defects* in epistemic situations and in commercial transactions; then more serious defects; then disabling, denaturing ones. Perhaps someone else will take a slight perceptual defect to disable, negate, her judgment. I imagine someone else for whom the color of the paint he has ordered doesn't match, quite, what he wanted—and sends it back. "Defects" lead me close to the intractable relativism of taste.) Take this example, drawn from the German tradition. The young Marx reads Hegel's work, he says, critically—Hegel, whose work was at the time, let's say in 1844, the subject of the most strenuous debate in Marx's circles. (The disagreements among the so-called right, young, and left Hegelians are well known and well-studied, as is Marx's relation to the groups.)[18] When Marx approaches the introductory lines of the "Concept of Nature" section of Hegel's *Enzyklopädie*, in the section of the *Economic and Political Manuscripts of 1844* devoted to the "Critique of Hegel's Philosophy in General," he has Schelling's influence on, and Feuerbach's response to, Hegel very much in mind: that there *is* a *concept* of nature, that is, an abstract determination available to the mind or for Spirit for *thinking*, as if from outside or at a distance or in a mode not identical with the particularity of natural events, objects, phenomena—this marks Hegel's greatest difference from both.[19] Marx will eventually (in *Capital*, for instance) want to understand how this abstract determination is produced; for whom; under what circumstances; to what ends. At the moment, he is just marking what he takes to be the weakness of Hegel's description of the process of conceptualization. He introduces two figures into Hegel's argument: the "abstract thinker" (*Der abstrakte Denker*) and "defectiveness," Martin Milligan's translation of the adjective *mangelhaftes*.[20] (Milligan is not wrong lexically: Kluge's etymological dictionary links "Mangel, from Middle High German *mangel*, masculine, 'want, defect' " to "A Teutonic root *mang*, *mangw*, [which] does not occur elsewhere," but "it may be primitively allied to Latin *mancus*, 'mutilated, powerless, deficient.' ")[21]

This is Marx's commentary on the "Concept of Nature": "The abstract thinker recognizes at the same time that sensuousness—externality in contrast to thought shuttling back and forth within itself—is the essence of nature. But he expresses this contrast in such a way as to make this externality of nature, its contrast to thought, its defect, so that inasmuch as it is distinguished from abstraction, nature is something defective."[22]

"Something which is defective not merely for me or in my eyes but in itself—intrinsically," Marx then says, "has something outside itself which it lacks [Marx's verb is *mangeln*]. That is, its essence is different from [it] itself," or "is a different one than itself." ("Ein nicht nur für mich, in meinen Augen mangelhaftes, ein an sich selbst mangelhaftes Wesen hat etwas außer sich, was ihm mangelt. D.h. sein Wesen ist ein andres als es selbst.") Marx has some trouble—here and throughout the *Manuscripts*—expressing what this something (*Wesen*) that is different from itself or from its being (*Wesen*) *is*. To get at Hegel's stubborn concept, Marx supplies the modifier *mangelhaftes* to render what he takes to be implied by nature's exteriority (*Äusserlichkeit*) to itself for the abstract thinker. (Supplies it, or rather borrows it from Hegel, who—though he does not use *Mangel* or *mangelhaft* just here—leans on the term in the *Phenomenology of Spirit*, and makes constant use of it throughout the *Aesthetics*, centrally in the faceoff between the "essential defect," *wesentliche Mangel*, of natural beauty, and the "necessity of the Ideal," *Notwendigkeit des Ideals*, elaborated in the subsection titled "Mangelhaftigkeit des Naturschönen.")[23] Here, in the *Manuscripts*, Marx says, Nature is defective, it is lacking, *for* abstract thought. And, Marx suggests, this lack in nature is the mark and the effect of a defect *in* abstract thought, which can only conceive of nature's defect as the lack of something that it, abstract thought, possesses, and which is entirely *external* to nature. But why would not possessing something that's entirely external to this or that thing or its concept constitute a *defect* in the concept? Just what would this outside-it be that this being, nature, lacks, if what it lacks is *both* intrinsic to its being, *and* entirely external to it, entirely in the possession of abstract thought? And what would abstract thought then be, if it possesses what is both internal to it and intrinsic to the being of what is external to it, what presents itself for thought as the mere exteriority of sensuous appearing? The topology—in Hegel as in Marx—is lacking, even contradictory: we would want to say that it is *defective*, but we tremble, as this *defect* is necessary. Great motors turn in each, to translate this necessary defect into terms useful to dialectical thought and to the critique of political economy. But never with complete success. European philosophical modernity cannot be separated from the long history of these failures, any more than it can from the colonial character that the simply sensuous, the external, and the natural have for the most "abstract" of its thinkers. And what, finally, is a *necessary* defect?

## DEFECTIVE INSTITUTIONS

> My companion must be of the same species and have the same defects. This being you must create.[24]

Now take the terms together: "defective institutions." It is a coinage intended to excite the imagination in the mode of what is called in psychological literature the "white bear" or the "polar bear" problem. "Try to pose for yourself this task," wrote Dostoevsky in 1863, in a little travelogue called *Winter Notes on Summer Impressions*, "[try] not to think of a polar bear, and you will see that the cursed thing will come to mind every minute."[25] Hence the "white bear" problem. Pose for yourself this task: try not to think of a "defective institution," and the cursed thing will come to mind—a raft of them, every institution you have had the chance or the mishap to encounter. Electoral colleges, supreme courts and judiciaries in general, families, universities like my own. Today, especially today, especially in the context of the response to COVID-19, of the last presidential election in the United States, of the Supreme Court's decision to overturn *Roe v. Wade*, of the Senate confirmation hearings that followed Donald Trump's inauguration, and of the impeachment inquiry in the U.S. House of Representatives, and eventual trial in the Senate; in the context of Brexit, of the crisis of the project of the European Union; in the context of a university-institution in crisis also: today the "curse" of institutional defectiveness is glaringly with us. Indeed, it is hard to think of an "institution" that is not gravely defective, or weak, or misformed. The inverse exercise—offering for you, say, the provocation of the title or the concept "effective institutions," or "strong institutions," or "working institutions," or even "charismatic institutions"—is likely to produce few examples; few will "come to mind," to use Dostoevsky's phrase. Whether in fact what we generally call "institutions" are more subject to defect today than they were (for instance) in 1844 or in 1984; or more subject to defect *here*, more defective here, for instance in the United States or in Bolivia or in Chile, than elsewhere, for example in France or the Netherlands—we will agree, maybe, that today institutions are *represented* as being more defective than at many other times and places. Take this remarkable proposal by the political theorist Corey Robin, recently published in the journals *Jacobin* and the *Guardian*: "The worst, most terrible things that the United States has done have almost never happened through an assault on American institutions; they've always happened through American institutions and practices. These are the elements of the American polity that have offered especially potent tools and instruments of intimidation and coercion: federalism, the separation of powers, social pluralism and the rule of law."[26] Thus Robin. He does not say so but we may infer that a commitment to the *converse* of this proposition has enabled "the worst, most terrible things that the United States has done" historically, and that this commitment will enable the United States to do further terrible thing in the next years. The strong "American institutions" serving to make concrete political concepts such as federalism or the separation of powers will always and as a matter of course resist the assault of skewed, partial, or totalitarian agendas or personalities *because* of their strength—a commitment to this notion *has enabled*, and *will enable*, the worst. *Because* institutions are believed to be strong, because these institutions suffer only minor defects of execution rather than disabling defects of structure, they have historically "offered especially potent tools and instruments of intimidation."

We make judgments regarding the value, coherence, strength, and utility of devices, narratives, concepts, and institutions in different ways historically—ways conditioned by what "making judgments" means socially, for whom, and under what conditions. Today, for instance, I buy a car or a blender. I have in mind something I want it for—I want my car for getting to work, my blender for making soup. If one or the other doesn't work to that end, I will say that it is "defective," a lemon, broken. I trade it in for another that will do the trick. An intentional structure is presumed: I have in mind this end for that device. We can be more or less strict with this conception, but its structure seems irreducible. Let's say, to be a little looser in my "making judgments," that I buy a car and I have in mind more than one end—the car gets me to work, but, alas, it doesn't serve the other end I intended, openly or perhaps even secretly, secretly even for myself—I wanted a car that would help me do what the advertising campaign for this car also promises, to find a glamorous partner and breeze romantically down coastal highways. My Volkswagen Jetta is perfectly good at one thing but perfectly useless at the other. I won't say that it's "defective," since it gets me to work. I will say that I find it a bit disappointing; I may not *know* why, but surely it's in part because my Jetta doesn't also get me a glamorous romantic partner. And now let's say that my therapist gets me, hours into expensive analysis, to disclose to myself why it is that my car, while not defective, still disappoints me. I had another unacknowledged end in mind for the device, and it is not working to that end. An *intentional structure*, even if my intention is or has been secret, still shapes my judgment. Our judgments about the workings of cars and blenders are, to use Kant's lexicon, *teleological*.[27]

Are institutions to be understood in that way today? For not *all* judgments are of this sort, and not all objects of judgment are like blenders or cars: some, for instance, are like polar bears or white bears, or the color yellow, or a sunset. But institutions today are much more like blenders or cars than they are like bears or sunsets or poems. They have ends, and they have use-values. For Robin, political institutions in the United States have two sorts of ends and use-values. Political institutions serve to give shape to the political concepts or fantasies at the heart of the modern secular state—federalism, the separation of powers, social pluralism, and the rule of law; they *also*, as he says, offer "especially potent tools and instruments of intimidation and coercion." This latter may not be an explicit *end* of these institutions, any more than my desire for hooking a romantic partner is when I buy a useful car. But for some it can become so, and in any event when the astute therapist or philosophical diagnostician of current political disappointments reveals the secret, my secret, the institutions' secret, then political institutions can be held to the implicit end of producing coercion and intimidation, and found to be disappointingly wanting or excitingly effective. We might say that institutions today are the political form of use-value, and our judgments regarding the effectiveness, strength, utility, and so on of institutions are not just teleological and technical but are also nakedly expressed in the language of political economy, of efficiencies, excellences, outcomes, customer relations, and so on.

Is there an alternative? Are there ways of conceiving and making judgments about narratives, concepts, and institutions (about their structure, value, effectiveness, etc.) that are not founded on the logics of the intentional structure, the teleological judgment, or the technical a priori? For Kant one answer lies in aesthetic judgments—judgments we form with regard to natural objects (a towering cliff, a beautiful sunset, a polar bear) and (slightly differently) with regard to manufactured objects that we agree to call aesthetic because they have no technical function—works of art, the dome of St. Peter's (which has a function, of course, but which we do not admire *for* its success in keeping the rain off congregants' heads), or even something like a mathematical proof. Such objects appear purposive but lack purpose, or rather, they require of us sorts of judgments that are not determined or given form by the objects' purpose.

A complicating matter: I will say that this or that car is "beautiful," and I may be saying something about its looks or its color. And a blender that may not work to blend may work, in a museum or in my house, as an example of a classically valued design. So an object will unproblematically give rise to different sorts of judgments that need not conflict; it's just a matter of keeping them straight, if possible. But *is* it possible? And on what grounds? The line separating sorts of judgments (for instance, the line distinguishing judgments made in regard of the purpose of an object from judgments made regarding its purposiveness) is not *given* but produced, at different moments, to various ends (some to be described sociologically or politically), by classes of people who have interests in drawing them, for the nonce, *just there*. Such a line is, for instance, the concept of the integrity of "acts" and "substances."

Institutions are *contingent*, *defective* objects—and the judgments we make about them are likewise defective. One "defect," though, does not correspond necessarily to the other, or flow from it, or represent it, or perform it, or serve somehow to resolve it. (We might say: an aesthetic judgment is not *necessarily* an aesthetic object.) A defective judgment regarding a defective object (an institution, a concept, a narrative) is not, by virtue of its lack, discontinuity, disorganization, openness, untellability, or its rhythm, truer to the defective object or a better translation of it than a formally complete, well-formed (etc.) judgment. Contingent not only as pertains to future states or outcomes, but more strangely as pertains to present states (objects may or may not be thus and so, institutions are and are not this or that, and judgments regarding both of these may be purposive and nonpurposive at once) and, most counterintuitively, as pertains to past states. Judgments regarding these special, contingent objects called "institutions" will then depend, for their truth-value and coherence (and, importantly, with Stefano Harney and Fred Moten, for their effectiveness in *falsifying* and in rendering incoherent and inorganic judgments legitimated *by* such special objects-institutions), on what has not yet occurred; on what is and is not in the present; and on what, having occurred, is nonetheless to be thought as radically contingent, that is, as possibly having occurred otherwise or not at all. Whatever such special objects, institutions, are, they are not themselves in any way I easily recognize: they are not necessarily what they are now, or will be, or even what they were. They subject tautology to the solvent of contingency. They emerge aslant the principle of sufficient reason. Defective institutions are heterologous, and judgments concerning them are heterological.

A fully and radically differentiated democratic society stands not only on decentering and disorganizing its political subjects but also on reimagining the concept of its institutions and the schema of institutionalization that sets them in place. The sovereignty of such reimagined, defective institutions is always divisible; the time and conditions of their emergence and persistence are never given in the axioms of their own or other institutions; the narratives they install are generically both over- and underdetermined; the logical shape required of statements about them is unfamiliar. Defective institutions and the wild republics they organize persist and decline according to discontinuous logics and times. They entail regimes of representation, narratives, police forces, pedagogies, rhetorics, and lexicons that do ephemeral work, with often reversible results, transparently. They are inorganic without being, exactly, machinic.

And a further definition. Republicanism in its most radical form, in its wildest and most aberrant shape, in a shape fundamentally incompatible with the logical forms of global capital and of "organic democracy," is the intractable governance of defective institutions.

Worlds are at stake in the ambiguous grammar of that sentence, the subjective-objective genitive expression, *the intractable governance of defective institutions*. Coming up with and setting in practice modes of governance that retain and radicalize this ambiguity—that is the task of this wild republicanism.

## WHEN IS TODAY?

> We must give all the force and chance of an enigma to this today. Where and when is today, the day of today, for the lack in question?[28]

How do we approach this cluster of affirmations today? How do we do as Sylvia Wynter did in 1992, and ask after the specifically, even practically, political outcomes of *radical* institutional critique?

Let's stick with Wynter. In May 1992, in the immediate wake of the Rodney King judgment and the subsequent protests and violent police reaction in Los Angeles (April 29 and the days following), Sylvia Wynter called for her colleagues at Stanford and indeed all universities as such (the "university-institution") to "undo" the "narratively condemned status" of "all the Rodney Kings," of the "starving '*fellah*,' or the jobless inner city N.H.I. [No Humans Involved], [of] the global new poor, or *les damnés*."[29] The gesture is not new for Wynter, though the occasion is perhaps more terrible. As early as 1987, in her "On Disenchanting Discourse," Wynter would hold that the task of the pedagogical elites who have "institute[d] the 'truth'" of social abjection as the "truth" of capital should be to produce "rhetorical motivation systems" serving to "decenter the human subjects whose behaviors enable the stable replication of their own autopoesis as systems."[30] Pedagogical elites would be tasked with "put[ting] into discursive play . . . the [human subjects'] own intentionality and autonomy as autopoetic systems . . . [which] whilst largely compatible with, are not reducible to that of their individual subjects."[31] In 1987 as in 1992, then, those who had wittingly or not "institute[d] the 'truth'" of social abjection as the "truth" of capital were now meant to produce and to institute alternative narratives. This, via critique and by means of critical pedagogies carried out in a rethought university-institution more habitable and welcoming both to (eventually) decentered subjects and to the "largely compatible" but distinctly nonidentical forms of "intentionality and autonomy" that decentered subjects bear as "autopoetic systems." Other regimes of truth, other ceremonies.

Today I approach these questions and Wynter's injunctions lopsidedly. Necessarily so, since the question "What is the university-institution" can only guardedly be posed *in* the university. Take my own, the University of California at Riverside. My university maintains that right here, within these walls, unconditional thinking is encouraged, unconditionally, but on the condition that we respect the institutional integrity, the "proper," the "as such," the basic identity, of the university. The university's "Code of Professional Rights, Responsibilities, and Conduct of University Faculty" thus says both that the university

> seeks to provide and sustain an environment conducive to sharing, extending, and critically examining knowledge and values, and to furthering the search for wisdom. Effective performance of these central functions requires that faculty members be free within their respective fields of competence to pursue and teach the truth in accord with appropriate standards of scholarly inquiry

*and* that

> The faculty's privileges and protections, including that of tenure, rest on the mutually supportive relationships between the faculty's special professional competence, its academic freedom, and the central functions of the University.

On what grounds do we hold that these basic relationships (basic, since "The faculty's privileges and protections . . . *rest*" on them) *are* or *should be* mutually supportive? "Mutual support," like "appropriate standards of scholarly inquiry," hem in, condition, censure me—just where they seek and seem to make my "scholarly inquiry" possible, just where they protect it and me. Say I want to dispute this basic rule, this ground norm, as Kelsen might call it, this rule of association (as Weber perhaps would). My dispute itself—which may take the shape of a program of research intended to "further the search for wisdom"—must conform to the ground norm to be recognized *as* validly, critically, "examining knowledge." Concerning what is basic to the university, there can be no differend argued out *within* the university, certainly not a university that rests on such a "Code of Professional Rights, Responsibilities, and Conduct."

Wynter's approach to the institutional closure, the proper and normative as-suchness of the university, seems different. Here is a characteristically provocative excerpt from Wynter's 2015 essay "The Ceremony Found: Towards the Autopoetic Turn/Overturn, its Autonomy of Human Agency and Extraterritoriality of (Self-)Cognition." These sentences close the introductory section of "The Ceremony Found."

> On the basis of a proposed new and now meta-biocentric order of knowledge/episteme and its correlated emancipatory view of who-we-are as humans (themselves as ones that will together now make possible our collective *turn* towards what I shall define as our *Second Emergence*), we can become, for the first time in our species' existence, now fully conscious agents in the autopoetic institution and reproduction of a *new* kind of planetarily extended cum "intercommunal" community (Huey Newton via Erikson, 1973). And this new kind of community would be one, therefore, that secures the "ends" no longer of biocentric (neo)Liberal-monohumanist ethno-class *Man*(2), nor indeed that of the religio-secular counter-ends of the contemporary westernized imperialist and/or fundamentalist forms of the three Abrahamic monotheisms, but instead superseding them all, *inter alia*, by that of the We-the-ecumenically-Human.[32]

Just what "autopoetic institution" means is not yet clear. Wynter is responding, in 2015, to her own call, in 1984, to seek, in "a science of human systems . . . which makes use of multiple frames of reference and of . . . rhetorical techne," to "attain to the position of an external observer, at once inside/outside the figural domain of our order" from which to "find" ceremony.[33] "We are governed," she says in 1984,

> in the way we know the world by the templates of identity or modes of self-troping speciation, about which each human system auto-institutes itself, effecting the dynamics

> of an autopoetics, whose imperative of stable reproduction has hitherto transcended the imperatives of the human subjects who collectively put it into dynamic play. The proposed science of human systems decenters the systemic subject. Instead, it takes as the object of its inquiry the modes of symbolic self-representation about which each human system auto-institutes itself, the modes of self-troping rhetoricity through which the Subject (individual/collective) actualizes its mode of being as a living entity.[34]

Decentering, then, the systemic, we might say the *institutional* subject. How to do so? In the course of the 2015 essay "The Ceremony Found" Wynter distinguishes (as above) between the verbal and the nominal senses of "institution"—between that which an agent does, the act of *instituting*; and that material and subsisting effect of the act, the *institution*—and she clarifies that her interest lies with the first of these. Both aspects of "institution"—the concept's verbal and substantive aspects—are subject to sociogenic codes "or *Masks*," Wynter says: these are "the indispensable condition of our being able autopoetically to institute ourselves as *genre*-specific, fictive modes of eusocial, inter-altruistic, kin-recognizing kind."[35] "The terms of our eusocial co-identification as humans," she maintains, "can never pre-exist each society's specific mode of autopoetic institution, together with its complex of origin-narratively encoded socio-technologies." Autopoetic institution is then an agent's generically determined act (of institution); because it is concurrent and coterminous with "each society's specific mode of autopoetic institution," it tends to make agents concurrent and coterminous as a class—we the ecumenically human—while *also* instituting them as the retroactive effects *of* the class of "we the ecumenically human."

The ancient problem at the core of the concept of institution, the regressive trap outlined above, seems solved. For an act to found an institution—for an act to "institute"—we saw, it must work in the context of a lexicon and set of protocols governing its interpretation; establishing the conditions for its felicity; guaranteeing its repeatability or the repeatability of subsequent acts it permits; and so on. Every act of instituting thus requires an existing institution, *just as* every institution derives its legitimacy and its coherence from a primary act of institution. Here the formula "just as" expresses the logical-causal impasse that Wynter's term "autopoetic institution" seeks to solve. The solid, almost tautologous architecture of specular acts of institution can become a new "fundament," to use Wynter's term: specular acts of autopoetic institution can become a new fundament for the *second*, substantive sense of "institution," the persistent social device or system instituted to define, collect, guard, classify, and distribute resources among "we the ecumenically human" in what Wynter calls a "lawlikely" manner. What the "institutions" instituted upon this autopoetic institution would look like is left unexamined—the question is not her concern; the "we the ecumenically human" system may well *be* such an institution, the first, the necessary one, prior even to that other "first" institution identified by anthropologists, the family. Other institutions may follow, founded on the fundament of "we the ecumenically human": that is not her essay's brief.

I have been arguing, however, against the proposition that one can move in thought, continuously, from the critical *act* to the political *substance*. I can now add, with Wynter in mind: the continuity of critical *acts* with political *substance* cannot be thought *today* outside a globalizing neoliberal frame that was not yet, in 1984, fully consolidated, its incoherence not yet fully reinscribed and monetized as "risk," its violence not yet rendered correlative with individualism, freedom, property, and other unassailable values. A wholesale rethinking of both the *act* and *substance* of (an) institution is required. Wynter herself is not starry-eyed about the possibility of moving either from the act of instituting to the institution, or genealogically and deductively backward, from actually existing institutions to the field of instituting acts on which they stand. The devices and lexicon that make this movement possible in her work are explicit and remain largely untouched between 1984 and the later essays—on one level, the language of "ceremony" itself; on another, related level, a Girardian account of the "sacrificial" relation at work where the "individual" and the "genre" face each other, as Don Quixote faces the genre of romances of chivalry, and as his "sane" alter ego Alonso Quijano "the Good" faces the confessional conventions of early seventeenth-century La Mancha; on another level still, a conception of the university-institution as comprising collectives of "colleagues" who serve as "institutors" of the confining regime of truth and abjecting social narratives of capital. Finally, for Wynter, moving either from the act of instituting to the institution, or genealogically and deductively backward, from actually existing institutions to the hypothesis of a primal act of instituting, means replacing the concept of "hegemony" by what Wynter calls "rhetorical motivation systems whose function is to bring differing modalities of 'human being' into being, by means of enculturating discourses generated from the grounding premise of an environmentally 'fit' conception of life/death."[36]

What does my skepticism about moving between act of institution and instituted substance get me? Well, it gets me "Defective Institutions"; it gets me devices for guarding and extending, rather than seeking to reduce or render "largely compatible," the radical difference between human autonomy and intentionality, and subjects' "own intentionality and autonomy as autopoetic systems."[37] It gets me a definition of politics as the domain in which that radical difference is negotiated, administered, instituted, and abolished. It may get me devices for coordinating critical acts and institutions that have not been assimilated into, and possibly may not be assimilable to either "organic democracy" and its avatars, or the times and genres of thought offered by the neoliberal globalizing frame.

## FALSIFY THE INSTITUTION

> We owe it to each other to falsify the institution, to make politics incorrect, to give the lie to our own determination.[38]

Let me approach the matter of institutional autopoesis hand in hand with the work of the French philosopher and theologian Stanislas Breton, a thinker a generation younger than Walter Benjamin, one older than Wynter. Breton's extraordinarily rich essay, "Dieu est Dieu: Sur la violence des propositions tautologiques" of 1989, shows that Abrahamic monotheism stands on the proposition "Dieu est Dieu" in a way that is not just exemplary but foundational for the range of tautologies toward which propositional logics tend—"An apple is an apple," "An institution is an institution," even "It is what it is."[39] Like three other great principles of Western logic that stand upon it, Breton suggests, foundational tautology is *violent*. (Breton has in mind the principles of identity, of noncontradiction, and of sufficient reason—the principles subtending the "proper sphere of 'understanding,' language," to lean on Benjamin's words—the primary mode of articulation of reason, *logos*, or speech/thought.)[40] "Violence" here, for Breton, means: tautology installs and depends upon a regime of the identical. (The self-identical; that which can be represented, inasmuch as what represents it will be selfsame *and* will stand for something selfsame; just what Stefano Harney and Fred Moten's view of the undercommons targets: "We cannot represent ourselves. We can't be represented.")[41]

"The university-institution is the university-institution." The claim could be made less broadly, but by using the university-institution I hope to offer something of the order of a meta-example, just as for Breton "Dieu est Dieu" is not *just* one among many examples of tautology. For the university-institution isn't just *any* case. The university has historically been the institution in which the passage from, or between, the *act* of instituting and the *substance* of institution or the instituted substance becomes an object for thought. It is where "liberty" and "autonomy" are defined by, in, and as the domain of thought; and it is the institution concerned with establishing what it is about an example, an instance, a case, or an element, that makes it representative of more than itself. What makes the example exemplary, in short. (Historically as well as conceptually, the struggle over the limits separating the university, the law, and the church is fought on just this terrain: who will be sovereign in determining not just the representativity of the example, but what indeed counts *as* representative in an example. Schmitt: Sovereign is he who determines the example.) The university writes knowledge—and this is why disciplines that it protects and organizes can be charged, as Wynter does in 1984, with "rewriting knowledge." "It is we who institute this 'truth,'" Wynter writes in 1992 to her colleagues at Stanford and beyond—and this is why "we" can be charged with "undoing" the "narratively condemned status" of the "'fellah,' (or the jobless inner city N.H.I., the global new poor, or *les damnés*)." "Critique" is the name that we, yes "we," give to the practices that arrest, disorganize, denaturalize, dehegemonize, the passages that the university-institution builds between an act of instituting and the institution; between the instance and the manifold it represents; between example and exemplarity.

Academic disciplines rest, tendentially, on tautological propositions: a truth in the discipline of history is true according to the protocols of the discipline of history (but not, perhaps, according to those of physics, philosophy, or business). In principle this assertion could be shown to be true for any corporate entity and of any coherent set of protocols, that is, for any discipline destined to produce an object, of any sort, from which it takes its value. The rhythm of a discipline's identity is measured in reference to these tautological propositions. The techniques and the subject matter that we teach, what students learn, the things we and they handle and the objects of knowledge we and they produce—inasmuch as these things and objects are identifiably the effects of our discipline, they also affirm our discipline's identity, and its value as a mechanism for producing such things and objects. Philosophy is philosophy, our tautological disciplinary proposition runs, inasmuch as it produces for inspection subjects and objects that are deemed to be and can be consumed as examples of a philosophical formation. To think unconditionally what counts as philosophical "as such" means granting "as suchness" a normative value, value inasmuch as "as such" tends and attends to closure, to creating and maintaining a border and a *terminus*, to exercising little and great violence. The task of identifying philosophy *as* a discipline, furnished with the usual bag of tools—the vetting of publications, promotions, establishing what counts *as* philosophy (and what can be consigned to parasitic, unserious practices: "theory," or continental philosophy broadly, etc.)—rests, more or less explicitly depending on the degree of good or bad faith of the "philosophers," on thinking (philosophically?) both the "as such" that is proper to philosophy, and the relation that philosophy might have with other ambient practices and institutions, some parasitic and unserious and some not (or less so).

In the academy we thus remark an uneasy reciprocity between the circulation and the processes of valuation and relating of academic things (of things, object, and matter in the academic context), and what the British researchers Roger Brown and Helen Carasso recently called "the Marketisation" of higher education.[42] The thing as datum provides *Homo academicus* and his (!) brethren with value tradable across markets and languages, and transforms the university-institution into a cloistered, autopoetic factory for the production of globally tradable, translatable information commodities.

But this is not entirely what Wynter means by "autopoetic," or by an autopoetic system. She insists, as we saw, on the goal of "put[ting] into discursive play . . . the [human subjects'] own intentionality and autonomy as autopoetic systems . . . [which] whilst largely compatible with, are not reducible to that of their individual subjects."[43] Against the tautology of disciplinarity, then, her task, the task she calls on her colleagues to take on, is *to make use* critically of the nonreducibility of system and individual subjects. The university-institution is the critical frame for this critical use, and should be assessed and thought as such; indeed, providing this frame is—beyond the technical goals of the contemporary STEM university system—the end itself of the classical, liberal arts university-institution. And by saying this, of course, I am reinstalling the logic of teleological judgments at the university-institution's core, since critique, or critical thinking, or the critical use of the nonreducibility of system and individual subjects, or "freedom," become the products, at the second level, of the autopoetic university-institution.

This recursive trap is as hard to avoid as—and is related to—the recursive definitional trap we encountered defining "institution." Brown and Carasso's study focuses on the United Kingdom; the comparable work reflecting on the development of the modern university-institution in the United States (and globally) is Bill Readings's *The University in Ruins*. Readings tracks the effects of the use of the vacuous criterion of "excellence" in assessing research and teaching outcomes. Here is how he describes the state of affairs: "Excellence serves as the unit of currency within a closed field . . . a purely internal unit of value that effectively brackets all questions of reference or function, thus creating an internal market. Henceforth," Readings concludes, "the question of the

University-institution is only a question of relative value-for-money, the question posed to a student who is situated entirely as a consumer, rather than as someone who wants to think."[44] "As an integrating principle," he maintains, "excellence has the singular advantage of being entirely meaningless, or to put it more precisely, non-referential" (22). Disciplines, especially those that took shape in funding regimes inspired in one version of the Cold War (Title VI programs, comparativist disciplines imagined as attending to cosmopolitan rather than narrowly national concerns, the modern humanities), find their standing in the university-institution in question when they appear to fail the test of nonreferentiality. This failure might take one of two shapes, and each would be violent in its way. A discipline might fail to satisfy the conditions of "excellence" by seeking to link the free-floating commodity form of the university-institution to some object or state of affairs outside of it (that is, by producing an object of knowledge that "refers" to an actually existing object or state of affairs outside the closure of the discipline). Let's call this the *transcendent* failure of the university-institution. The value of the "discipline" is then dependent on something it does not produce; the closure of the university-institution is threatened, but only to the degree that this "outside" cannot be reincorporated within the closure of the university-institution—cannot become the object of study for a future, notional discipline. And this inflation of disciplines is just what we see occurring, around the globe. The university-institution-machine is a capturing device, a translating device, I said—so a *transcendent* failure, a *transcendent* critique of the reflexive university-institution value-form will not do the trick. Nothing, really, is transcendent *for* the reflexive university-institution value-form.

But a discipline might fail the test of nonreferentiality in a second way. A discipline might produce, *within* the strangely self-referential value system that Readings imagines the university-institution to have become, excesses or lacks of reference—spots where the closure of the university-institution discourse is threatened from within. (In this case, we would say that the discipline produces "objects" that cannot and could not be valued in the terms given by that discipline or other disciplines—it is an object analytically excessive or defective with respect to them, or both). We will call this a sort of *immanent* failure of the disciplinary machine, just as I referred earlier to the immanent defectiveness of the concept of institution.[45]

Immanent—but are failure and defect then, as I want to think, *necessary*? In what does that necessity consist? (The figure of necessity will keep me company throughout *Defective Institutions*.)

Let's try to understand a little more clearly what it might take to produce this double failure, immanent as well as transcendent, transcendent because immanent and vice versa, within the university-institution, by submitting disciplines built on tautological bases to "translation" and "relation's" absolutization of the not-one; to the *heterologization* of foundational propositions regarding the university-institution. A university-institution is a university-institution, except that the objects of study the university-institution produces, its most intimate result and the condition of its self-intelligibility and of its market value, no longer fall either within the scope of the university-institution or without it. They are, in sum, tautological propositions in a sense unlike the sort to which we are accustomed; impastoral glosses obeying what Breton calls "a new imperative: 'Stop nowhere!,' for He gives you movement in order 'always to go beyond.'" Breton:

> The essential thing here is not to condemn images: rather, to multiply them to infinity, so none of them, fascinating us, succeeds in seducing us. The person of faith resembles a sort of Don Juan, on the search for the eternal feminine. Searching for the eternal divine, he reads in this tautology a new imperative: 'Stop nowhere!', for He gives you movement in order 'always to go beyond.' 'One has to stop somewhere,' we often say: this is, though, an *axiom of laziness*, as every cliché [*évidence*] is.[46]

This imperative, Breton says, describes the form of thinking that he would like to choose—never to allow one function of the tautology of propositions to seduce him, thus allowing him to choose mercy over violence, Pauline humanism over the fundamentalism of the Unique Law. This, he says, is what he *would like*: to retell the story of the Enlightened university-institution, which passes from the theologico-political violence of tautological propositions to the softer violence of instrumental or ancillary pedagogy, always leading beyond itself, as the Augustinian sign always leads beyond itself toward an ultimate, grounding and transcendent sign.

This is one dimension in which the radical critique of institutions unfolds today. Like Wynter's, it is susceptible of capture—it can be inscribed in a sacrificial structure, in the fideistic, Christic structure that she, and Breton, and Girard, and the long legacy of the confessional university share. This dimension of the critique of institutions is theoretical, even spatial: Wynter, for instance, calls on the pedagogical elites to "attain to" and install or institute, as the model of subjectivity that will uninstall the "truth" of capital's abject subject-positions, "the position of an external observer, at once inside/outside the figural domain of our order." For this reason, Wynter's "external observer" of institutions is positioned "at once inside/outside the figural domain of [the] order."[47] Thus, the critical anthropologist, to be sure, but also the university itself—theoretical observers *of* society, but also *parts of* that society; they are religious figures that fall inside the order of human representation, incarnate; and also stand outside, divine. These are paradoxes of position, and they are violently paradoxical *necessarily*, if and only if, either the "external observer" or the "figural domain" is *one*, one *being* at one time positioned in more than one spot; or one being at one time in a spot or position which is itself *not one*. Like the rational impasse to which Breton is led, the decentering of subjectivity we find in Wynter has as its ceremonial outcome the recentering of the subject-structure relation upon a symmetrical and sacrificial figure, in a lawlikely domain: the *one* is maintained, as subject *or* as institution, but each only at the cost of the other. In this higher-order, ceremonial, "figural domain," the "decentered subject" and the institution face off like squabbling twin brothers according to a sacrificial narrative and according to a necessary logic that converts the violence of tautological propositions, the violence that is critique, into the administrative, lawlikely form of noncontradiction. The state so conceived, conceived as the ceremonial figurative-administrative domain in which the One of the decentered subject and the One of the institution face off and exchange the quality of being-One, or in which the One of a particular institution like the family exchanges with the aggregate of similarly unitary institutions the quality of being-One—the state so conceived is *in one sense* Hegelian through and through—it appears purged in the last instance of all defect and all contradiction; it is Christological, universitary, immaculate, teleological.

Breton for his part offers a pedagogical, pastoral alternative emerging, one might say, from a different Hegelianism, from an unpurged Hegel. "Dieu est Dieu" closes on the remark that Breton finds no rational way of choosing between formally identical tautologies (and hence that he rests, or rather that he remains caught, *in* the contradiction, in the defect, in what is not-One), which is a way of saying that he locates in thought itself, in critique, the violence of the choice between tautologies: there is no sphere of thought, as thought, of thought as thought and of thought as thought about objects of thought, that is untouched by violence. No paradox of position this; there is no outside to thinking, no inside; or rather, the relation between thinking and its object, like the relation between the act of instituting and the institution, doesn't fall, for thinking, on one or the other side, on the side of the act or on the side of the substance or the object. Whatever and wherever and whenever it is, the critical, patient remaining caught or forbearing that Breton offers his readers *as thought*, the "as thought" of the language of the defective University-institution, the "as thought" that the defective institution turns on in order to understand, to express, to translate, and also to guard the violence of its theologico-political foundation: this critical "as thought" opens the human animal, for Breton, to the explosive truth of theologico-political foundation, while *also* "falsifying" and "making incorrect" (Harney/Moten) its invariably institutional form.

## DEFECTIVE INSTITUTION, OR "FILTHY CONCUBINAGE"

> Not knowing what a family is, or what the family is, compounds the problem of what exactly to make of its abolition. . . . The abolition of the family would be a generalized restructuring of the material conditions of social reproduction dependent on communization and the suppression of the economy. Communist units of love and domestic reproduction must replace the family for everyone, new institutions explored and constituted through the conditions of struggle.[48]

In *Defective Institutions* I offer an alternative view to the twin Hegelianisms I have attributed to Wynter and Breton. I will argue for defective subjectivities acting, not necessarily in concert and not necessarily intentionally, to constitute defective institutions in a field in which the figure of the domain—the figure of domination by whatever forces determine, bound and order the field—is inconstant, discontinuous, *un*lawlikely, and defective; and to which correspond contingent judgments I have called heterological.

This trebly defective concept of institution defuses the symmetries, substitutions, and mimetisms of the "figurative domain" of the state. Like a car that doesn't work, it probably won't take me where I wish to go; and like the unacknowledged symbolic car that figures my market-driven desires, it goes where it wishes for me—that is, it leads me to what it puts on offer, it builds and hews to the map of my desires. It yields an unfamiliar narrative time (this story doesn't lead from the brute fact of a stone wall enclosing a village, to the symbolic institutions that are that fact's proxy); it yields acts whose substantive effects are not immanently, or transcendentally, derivable from those acts, and substances for which no determining act of institution can be simply derived; substantial institutions the performative authority of whose instituting acts cannot be established—that authority is not unitary; it derives, paradoxically, from a divided sovereignty.

But I have in mind a figure that follows the *abolition* of the state. Will *Defective Institutions*, offering a trebly defective concept of institution, take me where I wish to go—toward the intractable governance of defective institutions, toward "an anti-authoritarianism that, in its emphasis on creative synthesis and improvisation, sees freedom basically in terms of play" (Graeber), and toward a radical, aberrant republicanism close to the sort of philosophical anarchism that Catherine Malabou has recently explored?[49]

I have imagined the university, a sort of meta-example. Now I imagine something prior, the family, the hoariest, most primitive institution; perhaps the first. I remember that in the West the figure of the state and the figure of governance are wed to the family. ("Wed" wants to make explicit the recursive, but also fundamentally ceremonial, constructed, quality of this relation: whatever it is, it is not *natural*. An institution—or many institutions, acting differently, at different levels, enabling and constraining here one way, there another—guards it. Derrida's *Glas* is on my mind just here.)

Take my father's family. It is a bit too odd to be uncomplicatedly exemplary; its recent history perhaps unusual—involving forced migration, exile, return; the languages of Arabic, Castilian, *baketîa*, French, Hebrew, English; involving Spain, Morocco, Latin America, the United States. There is political violence, economic terrorism, illness. I will tell this part of its story in hand with a word, a concept, that seems to govern it allegorically. Other families will have other words; all families may be unhappily alike in tending, for the stories told about them, toward the *monological*.

*Contubernio* is the ugly, single word I have in mind. It would be used to explain officially why my father's family was forced into exile in 1938 by Franco's forces: *el contubernio judeo-masónico-comunista-internacional*, sometimes *el contubernio judeo-masónico-marxista-internacional*, even *el contubernio judeo-masónico-comunista*.[50] By the time the word *contubernio*—which the historian Paul Preston translates, wonderfully, as "filthy concubinage"—started to interest me the immediate wounds to my father, uncle, and grandparents were some forty years cold.[51] The wounds gave my childhood and adolescence a scarred, lumpy shape. We lived in what Franco's regime called "*democracia orgánica*," a form of governance that subordinated the principle of representation to the principle of identity and to the logical figure of tautology—identity constituted in, and expressed by, what were called "authentic living truths" or "authentic life-truths," *auténticas realidades vitales*. The 1933 "*Puntos iniciales*" of *Falange española* lay out just what this "*democracia orgánica*" consists in: a "total," "totalitarian" state unified by a reawakened and hegemonic belief (*creencia* rather than *fe*) in the "historical reality" of the "unity of destiny" (*unidad de destino*; almost better: the "unifiedness of destiny") bearing historically the name "Spain."[52] This hegemonic and hegemonizing belief "unifies" the state administratively as well as ideologically; it is what every element of it must share with every other. Every element, person or administrative unit, participates in the "unity" or the "oneness" of the state, and that is why it is an "element" in the first place: we are in the world of a vulgarized Platonism. Three authentic life-truths form the tripod on which the state stands; three institutions: "A true State, such as Falange Española desires, will not be built upon the falsehood of political parties, or upon the Parliament they engender. It will be built on the authentic life-truths: the family; the municipality; the guild or syndicate."[53]

Insidious, spectral, the *contubernio judeo-masónico-comunista-internacional*—the low alliance of Jews, Masons, Communists, and Internationalists—threatened "organic democracy." It threatened the hegemonizing belief that individuals might have in the unity of "Spain," and it offered an alternate form of association, even of institution. *Contubernium* was the unsanctioned marriage pact between slaves, or between a slave and an owner, in the Roman republic, which only recognized, legally, the *conubium*, the institution of marriage between free Romans. *Contubernium* was also the lowest, smallest unit of accommodation in the Roman legions, the group of six or eight soldiers to a tent. *Contubernium* was by the eighteenth century the name for illicit, extramarital living arrangements. By 1925, the relative lowness, commonness, or servility of its protagonists typically bubbled upward to characterize moral dispositions. For the *Diccionario de la Real Academia de la lengua* published that year it means, figuratively, "*Alianza o liga vituperable*," a despicable, condemnation-worth league or alliance.[54]

The connubial, unitary state seeks to build its ghostly adversary in its image—as a "vituperable" alliance or league of similarly vituperable elements (protagonists, parties, ethnicities, dispositions—levels are crossed, differences erased) united in insidious opposition to "organic democracy." One organism against another. When it is built, determined, in the organic state's image, the contubernial alliance can be eliminated justly by the state—through extermination or through exile. The familiar register of biopolitical determination is at hand: extermination, exile, expulsion, immunity . . .

Now say today is some day in 1938. My grandfather has managed to escape, under threat of execution, from the concentration camp that Franco's forces set up in the seventeenth-century Alcazaba at Zeluán, the first of roughly two hundred camps. He had been interned there, as a Mason and a Jew, since the Fascist uprising in 1936. ("There": Zeluán, Seluán, a nodal point of the Spanish colonial project in North Africa, site of notorious battles in 1910—"la toma de Seluán": Spanish victory over the Berber "Rifeños" who had revolted against Spanish rule—and of the catastrophic loss to Abd-el-Krim, the Berber commander who founded the "republic of the Rif," bloodily taking back the Alcazaba

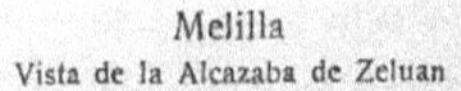

*Figure 1. Postal: Melilla vista de la Alcazaba de Zeluán* (Postcard: Melilla as seen from the Citadel of Zeluán). Photograph taken between 1910 and 1921. Editorial España Nueva.

of Zelúan and routing the Spanish colonial troops in July 1921.)[55] I imagine the frantic packing there. ("There": Melilla, Zeluán.) Take just this, leave that, the car ride out of Melilla (my sick uncle in the backseat), my family's arrival at last in Tangier, the international city in the International Zone where legal, civil, procedural, institutional regimes multiplied and jostled chaotically against each other: French, Spanish, British, Portuguese, Italian, Belgian, Dutch—even the United States had a legation and collaborated in the administration of the Zone.

From where I write, imagining, reading, and remembering, I see three things. I can see that the fantasy of the unitary, immanently and transcendentally "unified" state against which the Zone stood has survived the end of Tangier's peculiar status, in 1956; it has survived the end of Franco's regime in 1975 (and of his direct allies'—the list is long), and I expect that it will survive the end of *explicitly* totalitarian forms of governance.

I can also see that I want to go into that exile with my father's family, somehow—take the hard road toward a radical, aberrant republicanism, maybe to that Tangier of the mind, phantasmatic, colonial, Orientalized. A conceptual, even a political, project sits on fantasies, on recollected wounds.

I can see finally that I have set out to rescue *contubernium* and all that I can make it stand for, all the minimal forms of *apparently* extra-institutional association, the illicit, the nonconnubial; I have set out to rescue it from its specular

LA TOMA DE SELUAN

VISTA EXTERIOR DE LA ALCAZABA DE SELUAN DESPUES DE OCUPADA POR NUESTRAS TROPAS

Fot. de nuestro enviado Sr. Alba

Una de las más brillantes operaciones realizadas en los últimos días de Septiembre por el Ejército de Melilla ha sido la ocupaciónde la alcazaba de Seluán.

A las diez y media rompieron el fuego los rifeños. Disparaban parapetados en la casa construida por la Compañía minera francesa para los trabajadores indígenas. El general Tovar mandó emplazar una batería que pronto dispersó al enemigo. Rehízose éste y repitió el ataque, pero los Schneider le ahuyentaron y tras de nuevos combates, entraron los soldados españoles en la alcazaba.

EL GENERAL MARINA Y EL CORONEL JORDANA EN LA HABITACION QUE SIRVIÓ DE HARÉN AL ROGUÍ EN LA ALCAZABA EXAMINANDO UN PLANO DEL LUGAR DEL COMBATE

EL GENERAL OROZCO, JEFE DE LA DIVISIÓN REFORZADA QUE REALIZÓ LA OCUPACIÓN DE LA ALCAZABA DE SELUÁN HACIENDO SU TOCADO EN EL PATIO DEL EDIFICIO

Fots. de nuestro enviado Sr. Goñi.

*Figure 2. La toma de Seluán* (The capture of Zeluán). September 29, 1909. Actualidades año II (85). Imágenes procedentes de los fondos de la Biblioteca Nacional de España.

capture by the connubial state. Otherwise, I think, *conubium* and *contubernium* and the institutions for which they serve as metonyms will just muddle on fraternally, to this day and as far as we can imagine, wherever hegemony takes the shape of belief in unitary, immanently or transcendentally coherent institutions, and wherever identities bear a relation of shared participation in, or of universal mediation with regard to, those institutions.

Can a project that stands on—is instituted upon—such specific fantasies and recollections be generalized?

*Conubium*. *All* families are subject to fortune—death, birth, estrangement, violence, exile. Yes, and the universal quantifier *all* will be with me throughout *Defective Institutions*: "*all* institutions are . . . ," "for such and such an institution, *all* its elements must. . . ." And *all* classic, connubial families *have* substantive value—see Barrett and MacIntosh's important analysis of "the appeal of the family" and the "familialization of society."[56]

But now add to that the factic, multiply defective quality of "family's" concept *today*: the family is not one (not *all* families are one; different but related, not all *families* are one, since all *contubernial* "families" are not-one)—the family is not the family, and it is never necessarily one; it is not a multiple of individuals related by blood or bond or custom or work or necessity; it can be no model for the organic state's governance. If it can be said to have any substantive value, the contubernial family associating "vituperable" individuals (elements, classes, persons) will be ephemeral, elective; depositional rather than positional; irreconcilable with classic forms of possession; necessarily (with O'Brien, Lewis, and many others) entailing, as O'Brien puts it, "a generalized restructuring of the material conditions of social reproduction dependent on communization and the suppression of the economy." Contubernial "families" are possibly productive, but if at all, autoheteropoietic. No act institutes such a "family" immediately; nor does a multiplicity of acts aggregated according to a common wish, a social desire or need, the ceremony of reproduction, say. In this contubernial "family," genital logic, blood logic, the logic of natality, of possession and entailment, the logic of speciation, the figural realm in which ontogeny and phylogeny stand in solid continuity, even the logic of election that would allow me, sovereign over my decisions, to choose my bond unsanctioned by any ceremony—all these stand deposed: they are abolished. The operators of defection and abolition subject these logics to the divided sovereignty of the heterologics of contingency.

Can I take account of these new heterologics of contubernial association? Not without violence—violence to the family, to the university, to the state, and so on. *What* counts (under certain circumstances, for now, for you, for me, for her, for them, here) as being together, *what* counts as "a relation," as well as who, what, when, under what conditions, for what purposes, for whom, etc.—all these are subject to the mobile, ephemeral aspectuality of differential and *differantial* negotiation and translation.

Republicanism in its most radical form stands on the abolition of the state and on the heterological institution of contubernial association; it is the intractable governance of defective institutions. Coming up with practices of governance that retain and radicalize that phrase's ambiguity is a precondition of the republic. And that *constructive* project—not just a project for thought, but also for storytelling, for imagining and for remembering (for remembering even or especially what has been *exterminated*), a project that generates practices, fantasies and desires and reorganizes or abolishes existing ones—must be the goal of critique *today*.

# 1

# THE SCHEMA OF INSTITUTION

Inaccessible in the depths of the pagan hell, the shadowy trio of the Mothers—and chief among them Nemesis, vengeance—is the guardian of the "schemata," if Mephistopheles is to be believed in *Faust*, Part II. The invisible schemata preside over the fashioning and refashioning—*Gestaltung* and *Umgestaltung*—of the world.

Jean-François Lyotard

The perplexity was very simple and, stated in logical terms, it seemed unsolvable: if foundation was the aim and the end of revolution, then the revolutionary spirit was not merely the spirit of beginning something new but of starting something permanent and enduring; a lasting institution, embodying this spirit and encouraging it to new achievements, would be self-defeating. From which it unfortunately seems to follow that nothing threatens the very achievements of revolution more dangerously and more acutely than the spirit which has brought them about.

Hannah Arendt

A well-constituted court for the trial of impeachments is an object not more to be desired than difficult to be obtained in a government wholly elective. The subjects of its jurisdiction are those offenses which proceed from the misconduct of public men, or, in other words, from the abuse or violation of some public trust. . . . What, it may be asked, is the true spirit of the institution itself? Is it not designed as a method of NATIONAL INQUEST into the conduct of public men?

Alexander Hamilton

A *differend* presides over the fashioning and refashioning of the defective institution.[1] Let's approach it on a bias and ask after *the* differend, as explained by Jean-François Lyotard. Now the definite article is confounding; the legacies of Lyotard's book hang on it. Our way into the *general* schema of institution seems blocked from the beginning by the definite, definitive article.

Are we reading a work that recounts a scene, say from a book titled "The Differend," as we might title a story "The Judgment" or "The Verdict"? Here "The Differend" will be the name of a dispute among phrases, one singular dispute, presented for readers who may judge, one way or another, on the merits of the cases presented by parties to this particular differend, or who—suspending the faculty of judgment, reading for enjoyment or information—learn to recognize "the differend" that is the subject of *The Differend* and forms part of the world outside them. A strange reflexivity is at work. To this point I will have known only about myself. Now, as I judge, as I inform or enjoy myself, a world outside me pronounces definitive judgment upon my innocence and self-involvement. I am, for the world that lay in wait for me, a case.

Or are we reading *The Differend* as a work that builds philosophically the concept of "the differend" and defends its importance to contemporary ethics, political philosophy, even jurisprudence? To any effort to provide a way to envision defective institutions and their aberrant republics? Here Lyotard's book offers a definition of the concept; a description of the world it organizes and a map of the domain it covers: this case of "differend," *and* that case, *and* a further, all individuals collected into the set. *The Differend*, in this case, offers an account of the rules for the use of the concept "the differend." It may provide a genealogy for the term. The regime: cognitive-scientific. I will test the concept, verify the description of its world, verify that one case and another, one individual and then another, are indeed members of the set. I will check the term's uses and its genealogy against its world and against what I took to be mine, then offer a verdict.

I am brought to imagine the differend in this way: Does "the differend" mark the end of my innocence and name the judgment of the real upon me: being definite, privative to a singular scene, being the proper name of a case, does it mark me off from outside me as a case, a finite being, as the world does? If so it condemns me to death: "the differend," reality principle. Or is "the differend" rather a means to determine the world for myself—the means of its description and the determination of its concept, thus its capture? "The differend": a pleasure principle; the form that pleasure in the domination and possession of the world takes. The regime: what is classically understood as the political. We are in the domain of power, even of my will to power.

Need we decide which of these directions to take? I imagine a Cartesian dilemma: if I were dreaming my "or" might well mean "and." According to what rules will I distinguish between what determines me and what I possess or seek to possess? Am I free to decide? Are we?

More is at stake than parsing an ambivalent phrase, more than tracing the legacies of a given book. Lyotard's *Le différend* builds the schema of institution upon the imaginary differend offered by these principles in dispute. I will describe this schema in three steps.

## *INCIPIT INSTITUTIO*

> And louder now the questions rise,
> And, lightning-like, the omen flies
> Through every heart. "Give ear, give ear!
> The Furies' power is witnessed here!
> The prayers of vengeance now are heard;
> The murderer has his guilt confessed;
> Hold fast the man who spoke that word,
> And him to whom it was addressed."
>
> —Schiller, "The Cranes of Ibycus"

Take §92 of *The Differend*. It opens apodictically. The question does not seem to arise, "Is 'the differend' the name of a definite scene, the representation of a case, or the name of the presentation of its concept?" "Reality entails the differend" (*La réalité comporte le différend*).[2] Georges Van Den Abbeele's English translation obscures the phrase's symmetry—two definite nouns, *la réalité*, *le différend*, hung on the peg of *comportement*, here translated as "entailment." It is a disputable symmetry, though. A slightly different way to put Lyotard's phrase is: that there is a "real" entails, comports, the differend; comports, even, that there is the differend. The syntax of *réalité-différend* is built for now on *comporter* rather than (say) on *entraîner* or on *impliquer*, on bringing with or alongside (*com-* suggesting mutuality; we will note the underscoring of this mutuality in Lyotard's verb *convenir*, "*On en convient*," translated as "to acknowledge") rather than on implication or on bringing in train, in sequence, one preceding the other. *Comporter* suggests that both the real and the differend bear, together, the weight of their syntactical yoke; neither trails the other or drags it along, *traîner*. (Van Den Abbeele hesitates on "*comporter*": here it is "entails," as in "Antisthenes," page 37, and in §62 and many others; it is also, however, "Includes" [22, 74]; "accompany" ["Plato," 20]; "borne along" [152];

even "contains" ["Levinas," 112].) Conceptually, though, the arrangement is different, nonreversible, nonreciprocal, hardly mutual; it entails an unexpected ontological priority. The verdict concerning the reality of the real hangs on this contingency: that the differend really be. That there really is something named the differend, however, does not entail the existence of "the real." But what standing would the differend have, as subject of the phrases "The differend is, but not necessarily in reality"? Or "The differend is, but its being does not necessarily comport 'reality'"? Is "the differend" then something like a unicorn, or the present King of France? Like a square circle? Is "the differend" a Meinongian object, given, "absisting" (*gegeben*) but not necessarily really existent?

Here is the rest of §92:

> Reality entails the differend. That's Stalin, here he is. We acknowledge it. But as for what Stalin means? Phrases come to be attached to this name, which not only describe different senses for it (this can still be debated in dialogue), and not only place the name on different instances, but which also obey heterogeneous regimens and/or genres. This heterogeneity, for lack of a common idiom, makes consensus impossible. The assignment of a definition to Stalin necessarily does wrong to the nondefinitional phrases relating to Stalin, which this definition, for a while at least, disregards or betrays. In and around names, vengeance is on the prowl. Forever?[3]

"In and around names, vengeance is on the prowl," *la vengeance rôde*. *Rôder*, "to prowl, to circle," closes the space that "*comporter*" opens. A poetical expression of entailment, *rôder* offers an almost Rousseauvian scene—the enclosure (the wall of stones that keeps Searle's village safe), the protective group, the encampment's fire, faces recognized by name in the flickering warm light, the hearth—and outside, atavistic, bloody, primeval force "prowls." I am watching a film or hearing a story: from here, at my hearth or in the theater, I imagine, outside, the old beast: vengeance. Thus proper names, the mark of property and society, of the hearth and the *oikos*, are encircled by vengeance; it prowls about the hearth of names, and they exclude but comport it.[4] No need for the proper name without the wild from which names rescue us, installing the inside of the hearth, where we know one another's names. The proper name also comports what it displaces but makes it necessary: the regime of the improper, of dispossession; the wild. The phrase regime of proper naming ("That's Stalin") encounters descriptive phrases, that is, the question of meaning or more precisely of the relation between the proper name and meaning, and there, where the question of the proper name's *definition* arises, vengeance is on the prowl.

The time of *vengeance* is not, then, forever, "*à jamais*"—not, at any rate, in the diegesis of *The Differend*. §92 recalls the arc of discussions of the concept: from §35, opening the question of the authority that can be ascribed to the demand for "vengeance," through §§42–44. The sequence goes: "The authority that vengeance may give ought not then to be called a right of law" (*un droit*). "All the same, vengeance authorizes itself on account of the plea's having no outcome. Since one is not able to obtain reparation. one cries out for vengeance." And, definitively, in § 44:

> Vengeance has no legitimate authority, it shakes the authority of the tribunals. it calls upon idioms, upon phrase families, upon genres of discourse (any which one) that do not, in any case, have a say in the matter. It asks for the revision of competences or for the institution of new tribunals. It disavows the authority of any tribunal of phrases that would present itself as their unique, supreme tribunal.

This definitive phrasing echoes in §197: "*La vengeance n'est pas une autorisation (n° 44). Elle montre qu'un autre tribunal, d'autres critères de jugement (s'il en est), sont possibles et paraissent préférables*." "Vengeance" thus shows up early in *The Differend*, offered primitively as "giving" a right (the authority offered by a claim to vengeance first is, then is dismissed as not, a "right"), *un droit*; then as authorized just because reparation for a tort, an injury, a wound, an act is unavailable from the concrete tribunal to which it is addressed; then assigned the formal function of disavowing the authority of *any* superior, unique tribunal; then, absorbed as a formal principle into the structure of judgment, it disappears, no longer treated by name in *The Differend*. Vengeance does its job, the job of showing, shaking, demanding, calling to account, disavowing; the job of calling up and upon the "authority of the infinite" or "were it not so eloquent," the "authority . . . of the heterogenous." Then, like the chthonian regime of vengeance itself, it almost disappears by name from *The Differend* , where it remains just as a "prowling," nameless, formal figure.

Three things.

First, remark how familiar the story is of the not-quite-fading of vengeance and the not-quite-accomplished emergence of the regime of the hearth and the proper name. Familiar, but ambiguous. The story is the very scheme of "civilization" in the Abrahamic West: where there is a proper name, property is comported (and vice versa); you are responsible before the law when I can call you by name and interpellate you, summon you before this or that judicial instance bound to your properties. Before you had a proper name, I took vengeance on you straight off, immediately: pure vengeance, *lex talionis*, except it wasn't law at all. Now that I know your name and can predicate qualities of it and of you in such a way that others will understand them, my "vengeance" has been translated; it resides elsewhere; someone other, beyond us both, has it in hand. To this other we have relinquished the monopoly on violence by agreeing that the bearer of a proper name and the owner of properties can be held to account for actions we can now properly, legally, publicly, ascribe to him or her. (We are calling this the regime of the hearth, and why not; it is the regime of law too.) For the Abrahamic West, the sparest formulation of this anthropological scheme is probably Paul's, in Romans 12:19—famously the epigraph to *Anna Karenina*. "Vengeance is mine, saith the Lord, I will repay," as the King James rendering of the Greek has it.[5] The Vulgate reads *Scriptum est enim: Mihi vindicta: ego retribuam, dicit Dominus*, which Paul introduces with this important clause: *non vosmetipsos defendentes carissimi, sed date locum irae*, or, again in the King James version of the Greek, "Dearly beloved, avenge not yourselves, but rather give place unto wrath." A great deal hangs on the formula *sed date locum*, "but rather give place," from *alla dote topon tē orgē*. We are asked to countenance a sort of metalepsis: *because "ego retribuam," because* "[God] will repay," you should not avenge yourselves. On the promise of eventual retribution, vengeance is translated to the ultimate juridical instance; placed in God's hand; consigned to divine temporality, to the horizon where Lyotard's question "*À jamais?*" belongs. (*Mea est ultio, et ego retribuam in tempore:* Deuteronomy 32:35.) Take the future tense, *retribuam*, as the ground on which you act to give wrath a place; take the subject of that future tense, *ego retribuam*, as the substance and the substantive that guarantees your act. In the language of Pauline theology—this is where we find ourselves—we will say: the avenging subject to whom we translate responsibility for vengeance when we give wrath a place is the hypostasis of the promise that justice will be done, in the form of God's vengeance. In turn, we are reflexively determined as bearers of the proper place of wrath, objects of God's promise, covenanted, its hypostases.

Translation, metalepsis, and hypostasis settle very little. Vengeance, we might say, still prowls in Paul's injunction *alla dote topon tē orgē*, *sed date locum irae*.

Consider. The Vulgate translation leaves unsettled just what the *sed*-operation, the *alla*-operation, which will become the great syntactical operator of Scholastic disputation, amounts to. *Sed* is *syntactical* in Scholastic logic because it serves to coordinate phrasal-argumentative disjuncts, announced by the tag *sed contra*; it corresponds to the subclass of logical conjunctions *per vim*—conjunctions that obtain by force: violently, we might say—commonly called disjunctive conjunctions, including *vel* and *aut*; in English, "either" and "or" and "but." *Coniunctio quae disiuntiva ponitur sentit simul eas esse non posse*, Boethius says, a conjunction that does not allow for the simultaneous existence of what it connects.[6] The *alla*-operation, *sed*-operation is unsettled: the expression *both* conjoins *wrath* and *vengeance* (make a place for one in order to translate the other to the divine instance that will legitimately carry it out: *wrath*, and, and then, *vengeance*) *and* enjoins us to disjoin them (*wrath*, or, privative, *vengeance*).

Say we sidestep, or take as given, the *sed*-operation. Still Paul leaves unsettled what the place is of wrath *after* vengeance has been formalized, assigned to God's time and hand, and the proper regime of the hearth has been installed. And just *whose* wrath is under discussion? The history of the reception and translation of Paul's command unfolds the expression *alla dote topon tē orgē*, Latin *locum irae*, in two not quite reconcilable directions, each implying a distinct phenomenology, perhaps even antagonistic politics. Athens, or Corinth, and Rome are at war here. Aquinas's interlinear comment on "*date locum irae*" is "*iudicio Dei vel ire eorum*," thus "give place unto [*God's*] wrath," emphasis on genitive *irae*.[7] (Note the insistence of the *sed*-operation: *vel*, here—necessarily, forcibly—conjunctive rather than disjunctive: *vel must* mean "*id est*" or "*sive*," that is, "that is," and not *aut*. English would want to say, "God's judgment, or, that is, His wrath," where "or" is the mark of interlinguistic translation in general, or, that is, the mark of the insistence of translation *within* a natural language.) We are asked to make a place for the wrath *of God*. The modernized 1960 version of the classic Reina-Varela Bible is explicit: "*No os venguéis vosotros mismos, amados míos, sino dejad lugar a la ira de Dios* [the wrath of God]*; porque escrito está: Mía es la venganza*." The Latin *requires* Aquinas's gloss, though, because the phrase may also be read indefinitely, with emphasis on *dative irae*. The King James translation of the Greek, however, inclines in this indefinite direction; so does the original 1569–1602 version of the Reina-Valera, which translates from the Greek and Hebrew: "*No os venguéis vosotros mismos, amados míos; antes dad lugar á la ira* [give place to wrath, indefinite]*; porque escrito está: Mía es la venganza: yo pagaré, dice el Señor*." Indefinite, too, is the widely read Louis Segond version of 1910, which works also from the Greek rather than the Latin: "*Ne vous vengez point vous-mêmes, bien-aimés, mais laissez agir la colère; car il est écrit: A moi la vengeance, à moi la rétribution, dit le Seigneur*." *My* wrath may fall into or be given to this place; and yours; and another's, and the law's; and also God's. I remember that the case, *dative*, is the *cāsus datīvus*, the case for giving, in which giving happens. Because the place to which the dative gives is indefinite, what Paul's phrase now gives is not *a case* of wrath, mine *or* God's own, *or* the law's wrath (disjunctively ordered: the *sed*-operation is not given, after all) but rather a series flowing from its *concept*. An additive rather than a privative rule is at work; as when we read the title of a book called "the differend," here I will be able to test the concept "wrath" against my feeling or behavior, and yours, and the law's, and God's.

*Date locum irae*, definite case, indefinite series. The divergent translations of Paul's words (if they are indeed his) repeat the differend concerning the proper place, subject, even the phenomenology of wrath when vengeance has been replaced by the transcendent instance, and time, of the law. *Locus irae*: the unlocalizable affective shape of the differend.

Second. Let's note again how disorganized, how indefinite, even how *defective* is the operation that Van Den Abbeele renders (in §92) as "entailing." Let's say we wanted to mark out the edges of the semantic field it designates; here Van Den Abbeele's loose synonymy is helpful. We would be mapping out the concept, additively. *Comporter* and *impliquer* and *entraîner* and *suivre* and *résulter* (94), and even *rôder* (and perhaps others) gather into the domain designated and held together by the thematized term *enchaîner*, "to link onto" (Van Den Abbeele). (And . . . and.) This is Lyotard's first question: "A phrase 'happens.' How can it be linked onto?" (*Une phrase "arrive". Comment enchaîner sur elle?* [10]).[8] Just how are the terms I have listed *linked*, though? I have made them follow one another; some may be said to *prowl*, *rôder*, in the neighborhood of others; what "follows" may be said to be "brought along" or in train by something else. A phrase formed around one "happens," and we look for a term to designate how another phrase happens to link to it, or to be comported or implied by, or followed, or entailed, or prowled by it. The amphibian quality some of the terms have—meaning that they describe the relation of the terms in the field, and are themselves *part of* the field; that they have a syntactical quality, as well as a semantic one—offers a useful double lexicon of terms that serve as object and theory, and which may then be said to be *performing* the concept as well as describing it. The quality isn't universal, though. The borders of the concept *enchaîner* include cases of terms that designate and perform the linking together of its cases, and terms that do not. Just how these cases are linked—the cases of those terms possessing an amphibian, metatheoretical quality and the cases of mere object-terms—is not given according to a rule; they *happen* to coexist.

Note, third, that where I have specified that what is in debate in §92 is the "proper name," Lyotard just says *le nom* or *ce nom*. He is following the three-way distinction just outlined, in §91 and leaning on Wittgenstein, between ostensive, nominative, and cognitive phrases. "Reality plays itself out [*se joue*] in the three families that have just been named [ostensive, nominative, and cognitive phrases], but also in all the other families of phrases (which are nonetheless untranslatable into the first three as well as into one another)" (91). (Phrases link onto each other, then, so as to form "families." Just what order a "family" institutes, just what a "family" is, other than the common name for a set of linked phrases, is left untouched. We will return to it in the chapters that follow. Already, though, we know to distinguish between connubial and contubernial families. How will this distinction affect the sorts of "families" formed by regimes of phrases?) The question of the proper name's definition is remarkable just because proper names are not properly speaking definable: they are not concepts (the French "Stalinien" is a concept; "Staline" is not). French is less clear on this point than English. *Le nom* or *ce nom* name both proper names (Stalin) and common nouns (a ship, a book). To translate a proper name into a common noun or into a concept means installing the name "on different instances," where the French *instance* much more clearly evokes the institutional frame in which the language game of "defining" is acknowledged to be in effect: a different jurisdiction, a different court, a different regime of veridification, and a different protocol for the enforcement of rules than in the world, or language game, in which naming and "acknowledging," *convenir*, are in effect. A necessary wrong is committed here, or rather a wrong, a tort, is necessarily committed when we translate among phrase regimes and between institutions. For one thing, the usual regress found where a common idiom goes wanting is here on display: the translation from one instance or jurisdiction to another, from proper name to concept, takes place according to a regime of veridification and a protocol for the enforcement of rules of translation, which will be different still from the regimes of "proper names" and of "concepts" (though we may be able to give it a name and a definition). How is this institution that regulates the translation of terms between proper naming and defining instituted? (And the institution that regulates the translation from "naming" to that mediating translation—and so on.) Do the regimes of "proper name" and "concept" acknowledge its jurisdiction? Do they do so in the same way, according to a shared idiom, in the same time and at the same time? Consensus obtains if so, in the last instance and as the last instance: a tribunal of phrases presenting itself as the unique, supreme tribunal deciding on the translation between "proper name" and "concept."

Lyotard circles these three matters carefully. Something wild still prowls here, where regress threatens; a wrong will be committed; the place of wrath will go undetermined in the history of translations; there is a necessary betrayal. Neither wrath nor vengeance has been entirely banished, or forgotten, or consigned to its proper place. Indeed, the place or places they occupy when you and I meet in disagreement, or when the city seeks institutions to mediate and decide upon such disputes, remains in dispute. The term that Lyotard uses to describe the irreducible dispute where the differences of definite-indefinite, proper-common designation join those regarding the places of vengeance and wrath is "untranslatability."

Untranslatability persists where we move (by metalepsis, by translation, by hypostasis)—from a case or an event to a law; from a law to judgment in one court; an appeal, on formal or other grounds; the resolution of the dilemmas of interpreting the constituted law (the law as it is written). In brief, the scheme of institution is the scheme of translation; untranslatability is the internal border of that scheme.

Lyotard describes in two ways how the translation-institution between (proper) naming and conceptualizing occurs: first, as "*Des phrases viennent s'attacher à ce nom*," then as "*L'affectation d'une définition à Staline*" (Phrases come to be attached to this name; The assignment of a definition to Stalin). There is a great deal of play in the hinge between these two descriptions. To say that phrases "come to be attached" to a proper name is to lay stress on what Lyotard has just called "the negation implied [*impliquée*] in the modality of the possible that reality entails [*comporte*]"—that is, to stress that descriptive and definitional phrases attach, not necessarily but possibly, to the proper name; they may attach, and if they do it's not on account of a necessary connection to the name. Indeed, the "negation" that is implied when phrases come to attach to proper names is the negation of their necessary comportment by the proper name. Take the name "Stalin," Lyotard's example. "That's Stalin, here he is. We acknowledge it. But as for what Stalin means? Phrases come to be attached to this name." The instance, institution or genre that affords and determines how meaning-bearing, definitive, and descriptive phrases "come to be attached" to "Stalin" works wildly.

Here is how one phrase comes to attach to "Stalin." I remember of course that battles are fought over the place of "Stalin" in Europe; I remember that the Socialisme ou Barbarie group to which Lyotard adhered as early as 1953 was specifically and militantly *anti*-Stalinist.[9] I also recall this scene, and I cannot offer you a well-founded rule to value it less highly than the phrases I recall that link "Stalin" to "Lyotard" by means of Socialisme ou Barbarie: "Suppose, for example, I see a vessel on the stocks, walk up and smash the bottle hung at the stem, proclaim 'I name this ship the Mr. Stalin' and for good measure kick away the chocks: but the trouble is, I was not the person chosen to name it (whether or not—an additional complication—Mr. Stalin was the destined name; perhaps in a way it is even more of a shame if it was). We can all agree (1) that the ship was not thereby named; (2) that it is an infernal shame." Lyotard, who does not cite Austin's *How to Do Things With Words* in *Le différend*, might have read Gilles Lane's French translation *Quand dire, c'est faire* (1970):

> Supposons, par exemple, que j'aperçoive un bateau dans une cale de construction, que je m'en approche et brise la bouteille suspendue à la coque, que je proclame "Je baptise ce bateau le Joseph Staline," . . . L'ennui, c'est que je n'étais pas la personne désignée pour procéder au baptême (peu importe que Joseph Staline ait été ou non le nom prévu—ce ne serait qu'une complication de plus; l'affaire serait peut-être même plus regrettable, en un sens, s'il s'agissait du nom prévu). Nous admettrons sans peine: 1) que le bateau n'a pas, de ce fait, reçu de nom; 2) qu'il s'agit d'un incident extrêmement regrettable (56; note the shift from "The Mr. Stalin" to "le Joseph Staline").[10]

Austin socializes us: "we can all agree" that the boat was not named by the infelicitous speech act; that "I name" uttered by someone not designated or agreed or chosen to name does not accomplish what the same utterance, on different lips, might. What logic attaches Austin's example of a misfire or an infelicity to Lyotard's example, "*C'est Staline, le voici*"? Does Austin's phrase define or determine Lyotard's? It's tempting to assert that something like a common philosophical idiom must exist, an institution mediating between *Le différend* and *How to Do Things with Words*—and that the figure of accidental recollection, the small story of my recalling one use of "Stalin" in a canonical (uncited and unacknowledged) work spurred by an ostensive exemplary gesture simply refers the matter to that common court or instance. The fantasy then becomes that what Lacan once called *l'universitas litterarum de toujours* directs the phrase to "the destined name," directs for any bien-pensant, sufficiently educated reader Austin's Stalin-phrase (an example of my own wayward and inappropriate action) toward Lyotard's Stalin-name, where it attaches as one of many others, heterogenous as to their origin and descriptive-definitional import.

A number of societies face off here, as a number of terms did in the semantic field designated by *enchaîner*, as they did in the divided questions where wrath's place would be assigned, and just whose wrath it is that survives the translation of vengeance from culture into God's hand and time. That these societies do not take shape on the same level of analysis means that the differend among them cannot be adjudicated in a still superior instance. (They cannot, precisely, be consigned to a superior "tribunal of phrases that would present itself as their unique, supreme tribunal.") They include: Austin's "Stalin"-society, the society of those who "all agree [*nous admettrons*] (1) that the ship was not . . . named; (2) that it is an infernal shame"; the Lyotardian society of those who "acknowledge" [*convenir*] that "*That's Stalin, there he is*"; the society, the "we," comprising those who recognize that one "Stalin" "comes to attach to" the other; the "society" of those excluded from the institution or the society, from that *universitas litterarum* (the institution or the society, if it is one, of those who do not recognize the value, history, and philosophical genealogy of a name when it is offered as an example: here an aristocracy is implied; ivied walls, or at any rate the hearth and the *oikos*; an inside and an out; the civilized and the wild; society, culture, and law on one side, vengeance on the other). And then, of course, there are the disputing societies claiming their identities from either the process of memorialization that values "Stalin's" role in Socialisme ou Barbarie above its role in *Quand dire, c'est faire* (that "Stalin" has a political meaning is more relevant than the name's having the meaning or meanings conferred by being a philosophical example).

The outcome of the wild faceoff I am describing is that definitive phrases are *assigned* to "Stalin." (And to "God," who now has the definitive property, that he holds vengeance in his hand; and to *me*, inasmuch as I am determined as the subject who, giving wrath its place, is the object of God's covenant.) We have been translated to the world of common names; of events become common names, or concepts; of determination; of possession of properties. Now we predicate something, defining or a definition, of what was itself a predicate, "assigning" or *affecter*: *"L'affectation d'une définition à Staline,"* Lyotard writes, *"fait nécessairement tort aux phrases non définitionnelles relatives à Staline, que cette définition, pour un temps au moins, ignore ou trahit"* (The assignment of a definition to Stalin [or to God] necessarily does wrong to the nondefinitional phrases relating to Stalin, which this definition, for a while at least, disregards or betrays). How has the translation from the fragmentary and embattled scene of "attachment" to the scene of events become common names happened? What has been left untranslated, and why? What wrong has been committed? And why does vengeance still "prowl," *rôder*? Hasn't it spent itself with modernity—hasn't it done its old job, shaken the authority of the tribunals, called upon idioms, upon phrase families, upon genres of discourse . . . asked for the revision of competences or for the institution of new tribunals? Having "disavow[ed] the authority of any tribunal of phrases that would present itself as [the] unique, supreme tribunal," isn't the job of vengeance accomplished, *done*?

## SANCTUARY

These questions lead back to *Le différend*'s reflection on the instituting of the schema of institution.

It is an old and familiar, famililal, story, older even than Paul's ambiguous version of Abrahamic civilization, and like that story it is inextricably bound to fantasies of progress, enlightenment, philogenetic and ontogenic therapy, and modernization: the job of the primitive drive, *accomplished*, can be consigned to history. (A place is made where the primitive drives, fear, terror, vengeance, can be consigned, regulated.) Here is the classic example. The subject of Aeschylus's *Eumenides* is the founding and organization of the *polis* against and in response to the wild, telluric forces of anger and mere vengeance. Let me recall it. (Aeschylus's work is surely to be found in the *universitas litterarum*, and "we" recall the scene when "we" adhere to that institution, which is our common idiom, the instance of culture that will separate "us" from the barbarians.) Athena

*Figure 3.* Python (4th c. BCE), *Theatre Scene on a Vase Painting: The Eumenides.* In John Morris Roberts, *Kelet-Ázsia és a klasszikus Görögország* (East Asia and Classical Greece) (Budapest: Officina Nova, 1999).

presides at the trial at which Orestes is acquitted of his ancient crime. The Furies demand the traditional punishments: vengeance, wrath, blood for blood. Finally wounded and defeated at the verdict—a tie, Athena declares, acquits Orestes—they decry the insult to the ancient laws and promise the new gods that they will unleash their wrath upon the city, *io theoi neōteroi, palaious nomous kathip-pasasthe kak cheron helesthe mou*. Athena institutes and affirms the city's laws, places the value of persuasion (specifically, civil and judicial rhetoric) above that of force, and responds to these desperate, wounded, and devastating threats from the Furies by famously declining to *exclude* the Furies from the city's enclosure and promising instead "most sacredly that you will have a cavernous sanctuary in a righteous land [a cavernous sanctuary, *keuthmōn*, in full: *hedras te kai keuthmōnas endikou chthonos*], where you will sit on shining thrones at your hearths, worshipped with honor by my citizens." If the Furies are to be brought into the city's walls they must do so according to the laws Athena has instituted. They will be honored, but supposed, enshrined, afforded their own hearth [*es-chara*] but confined to it as well. They agree; the ancient gods, translated, find their place in the city; new gods [*theoi neōteroi*] and new institutions prevail; the Furies become the Eumenides, the Semnai; their appearance changes—no longer hideous and bestial, they now appear as reverenced women; the regime of the new, of "modern" institutional governance, replaces the ancient, violent dispensation.

This old story persists. Martha Nussbaum, for instance, opens her 2014 *Anger and Forgiveness* with a characteristically salvific retelling. "Unchanged," Nussbaum writes,

> these Furies could not be part and parcel of a working legal system in a society committed to the rule of law. You don't put wild dogs in a cage and come out with justice. But the Furies do not make the transition to democracy unchanged. . . . All of this, needless to say, is not just external containment: it is a profound inner reorientation, going to the very roots of their personality. They have become women, rather than beasts, and "resident aliens" in the city. Their very name is changed: they are now The Kindly Ones (Eumenides), not The Furies. This second transformation is just as significant as the first, indeed crucial to the success of the first. Aeschylus suggests that political justice does not just put a cage around anger, it fundamentally transforms it, from something hardly human, obsessive, bloodthirsty, to something human, accepting of reasons, calm, deliberate, and measured. Moreover, justice focuses not on a past that can never be altered but on the creation of future welfare and prosperity. The sense of accountability that inhabits just institutions is, in fact, not a retributive sentiment at all, it is measured judgment in defense of current and future life. The Furies are still needed,

> because this is an imperfect world and there will always be crimes to deal with. But they are not wanted or needed in their original shape and form. Indeed, they are not their old selves at all: they have become instruments of justice and welfare. The city is liberated from the scourge of vindictive anger, which produces civil strife and premature death. In the place of anger, the city gets political justice.[11]

What are the limitations of this entirely compelling account of the modernization of violence, and the subordination of the principle of vengeance, to a principle of measured judgment and ultimately of political justice? Can the Furies be, indeed, instrumentalized, simply by changing their name and their substance? What is entailed by accepting—as I have done—the topology and ethnonational fantasy that places the Furies in the position of the supplicant or the immigrant at the gates, whose avenue to citizenship is changing his or her name and changing her or his substance or disposition—acceding to the hegemonizing order of reason, rationality, humanity, like the barbarian who must not only learn the Athenian's language but also learn to be Greek before crossing the walls into the city?

For Nussbaum's answer to the question, "Why does vengeance still prowl?," might then be that it *does not prowl*—not, at any rate, under the name "vengeance," and not possessed of its old attributes. The "wild dog" has been translated into something quite other, "something human." Three "human" things, really. "Vengeance," in its ancient chthonian shape, is incompatible with reason, with calm, with deliberation and right measure: it must be reduced, coercively if need be. (Athena does not fail to remind the Furies that she "alone of the gods know[s] the keys to the house where [Zeus's] thunderbolt is sealed."[12]) "In the place of anger, the city gets political justice," and the Furies—because, after all, "there will always be crimes to deal with"—are the city's police force, the armed instrument that political justice wields, deliberately, toward maintaining just measure. For fear, within bounds, is required "among mortals" for them to steer clear of the worst. Thus Athena: "Neither anarchy nor tyranny—this I counsel my citizens to support and respect, and not to drive fear [what is terrible or fearful, *deinon*, also what is marvelously strong] wholly out of the city. For who among mortals, if he fears nothing, is righteous?" (*Eumenides* ll. 674–675).

Hence the police. (*The Eumenides* is a source for claims about the purview of the ancient police, or its cognates; thus Athena's lines, 690–693, after instituting the perpetual Court of Athens on the Hill of Ares, "on this hill, the reverence of the citizens, and fear, its kinsman, will hold them back from doing wrong by day and night alike"; as well as the Chorus's reference at l. 160 to "the cruel, the very cruel chill of the executioner's destroying scourge." Would Nussbaum agree that her argument is a brief for instituting the police? Perhaps not.) But, Nussbaum says, the Furies *also* "have become women, rather than beasts, and 'resident aliens' in the city" (3). "And," Nussbaum writes—as if the additive principle indicated synonymy, *et, vel sive*, or, remitted to a single concept resolving, adjudicating, and bringing differences into order or policing their relations. Here we are to consider the difference between the "police" (that is—and taking our cue from the *Eumenides* and its reception, including, though not explicitly, Nussbaum's *Anger and Forgiveness*—the fearsome, if sanctioned, arm of the Eleven, the magistrature of the *polis*); the "resident alien" (the *metic*, *metoikos*, under the surveillance of the city's laws, and always subject to the police); and the "woman." What rule of likeness or synonymy allows Nussbaum to link these three figures? Historians have insisted on their differences, which are manifold: among others, no woman could form part of the Athenian "police," though she could be *metic*. Perhaps from the Olympian perspective of the free, male Athenian these differences appear vanishingly small: it is *his* reason that prevails and makes a common place, however confining and incoherent, for the three figures. The three-part role that Nussbaum offers her Furies from this vantage is evidence, then, that something other than abstract, universal reason, or even "political justice" embracingly conceived, prevails; or it is evidence that it prevails under conditions that may make it unacceptable or contradictory; evidence that the translation of the Furies is forced; that the reasonable position of the free Athenian male cannot confine what is fearsome without violence; that the brutal cage in which wild dogs were kept has become the rational housing into which a superior form of police that I am referring to as "the Olympian perspective of the free, male Athenian" fits, as into a cell, the police, the "resident alien," and the woman. Or at least it provides evidence that in this case, in one case, an embracing idea of "political justice" founded in claims to abstract, universal reason, prevails where, even *because*, differences of class, gender, and social function are ignored.

"Ignored" is too weak. Imagine I say, "Colors are red and blue and green." I am claiming nothing more about "red" and "blue" and "green" than that they are elements of my concept set "colors." You understand, because you know what "colors" means and can follow the rule of listing that is entailed by the phrasing "Colors are . . .", that I am asking you to ignore the terms' connotations, though not of course *à jamais*: you can hold in reserve, for determination of a different concept set, say the political connotation of "red" and "blue" and "green." You will set aside, not forever, internal differences that might allow you to order "colors" into subsets, for instance of "primary" colors (blue and red, according to one scheme—but just what colors *are* primary is a matter of controversy) and "secondary" ones (yellow, for some). Following this rule, you will be able to add elements—"brown," "purple," "fuchsia"—and exclude others ("house," "entropy"). When I say "Eumenides are 'police,' and women, and *metic*," I am doing something different. There is nothing *to* "Eumenides" *before* my phrase: I am instituting the identity, thus the rule, by virtue of the phrase. There is no rule that I invoke, properly speaking, concerning the phrase "Eumenides are . . ." *before* I utter it, so the rules of "ignoring" or relegating to a different space, not forever, not *à jamais*, just for the time it takes to phrase this—these rules are improperly applied here, unjustly, even violently. You will not know (and cannot imagine) what can be added to "Eumenides are . . ." or what can be excluded. You will not know whether all the elements I have asked you to imagine have the same standing—are some of them syntactical as well as semantic?

Let's polemicize and call by name Nussbaum's argument for renaming, transforming, and instrumentalizing anger and a fortiori furious vengeance: it is the Protestant ethic of modernity otherwise expressed, the iron cage (as Parsons notoriously translated Weber's *stahlhartes Gehäuse*) of liberal reason in which the city shutters the heterogenous regimes of the police, and the alien, and the woman (and . . . and . . . and: the violent nominalism of the concept). It is the place to which the abstract citizen consigns the heterogenous affects and phenomenologies of fury, and fear, and wrath, and vengeance. And it is the schema of institution that improperly translates to a proper-improper name, "Eumenides," the listing attributes of a precedent phrase regime, the phrase regime of indicative set-element listing. (Like "Colors are . . . and . . . and.") As if they were equivalent, or rather as if they could, in a specific historical, socioeconomic institutional regime, be made so. (The Spirit of Capitalism . . .)

Evidence, though—for whom? What that is untranslatable insists here, vengeful still, threatening the schema of institution? Would we be right to generalize Nussbaum's case, her gesture, and to make the ignoring or the erasing of differences of this sort the cost, even the condition, of "political justice" *in general*?

## "A RIGHT IS . . . THE HYPOSTASIS OF A PROPHECY"

I have been arguing that the schema of institution emerges from (is entailed, comported, implied, performed by) the differend between the privative reality principle of the case and the additive pleasure principle of the concept. To understand what the argument commits us to, let's return to the gesture that sets the machine in motion. Eventually, the name "vengeance" will be erased from the sphere of dispute; first, though, Lyotard will advance, then discard, the primitive claim that the victim's call for immediate redress, or vengeance, has the authority of a right (*un droit*)—natural or socially granted.

Lyotard sets the scene. He has been recalling the testimonial aporia that the Holocaust most acutely presents (there is no reliable witness to extermination, since by definition—or according to the juridical regime in which such wrongs are to be denounced—anything other than first-person witnessing is hearsay, thus unreliable; so only the exterminated voice could raise itself, in an impossible speech act: "I who have been exterminated bear witness to my extermination, and on this point of singular first-person report we can move to the broader case, to the concept or the collective cry, as *a* differend can become the concept covering *many*").[13] Just this aporia summons, from the future, the figure of the *historian*, charged "with avenging the people" (35) (Lyotard cites Vidal-Naquet, citing Chateaubriand). The Holocaust's testimonial aporia, suitably weakened, can be generalized. A surplus of singularity, of this-case-ness, of what the medieval or Peircian semiotic tradition would call *haecceity*, makes my claim my own, marked among others similar or somehow related to it. Vengeance is immediate and immediately mine: when I seek it I express the surplus of first-person, this-case-ness, in my I claim that you (extensive . . .) have done me wrong. But the law recognizes and acts upon my claim only to the degree that it is similar to other claims, or related to others. Responsibility for the redress of my wrong is then displaced. When I transfer or translate to the tribunal (to the institution: law, court, judge, police, executioner, Constitution) my desire for vengeance I accept that my claim bears, as if stamped under my signature, the general signature of the case. What is in evidence is my sacrifice, the sacrifice of a right to a social norm, of my right to vengeance or immediate redress to a regime of mediating phrases, protocols and decisions—to bureaucracy. Bureaucratic proceduralism is the *hypo-stasis* of the singular cry for redress.[14]

Here is how Lyotard puts it, in § 42:

> The justice which the victim calls upon against the justice of the tribunal cannot be uttered in the genre of juridical or forensic discourse. But this is the genre in which the law is uttered. The authority that vengeance may give ought not then to be called a right of law. The plea is a demand for the reparation of damages. addressed to a third party (the judge) by the plaintiff (addressor). The avenger is a justice-maker. the request (the cry) is addressed to him or her (the addressee) as to a judge. It is not transferable to a third party, even for its execution (idiolect), its legitimacy allows for no discussion. it is not measured distributively because its referent, the wrong, is not cognizable.

Lyotard's argument flexes around two points: the status of the phrase "The authority that vengeance may give ought not then to be called [*ne doit donc pas être nommée*] a right of law," and the distinction between justice, law [*le droit*], and what van den Abbele translates as "a right of law" (*un droit*). The latter distinction is muddied superficially by the homonymy of "law" and "right" in French—*le droit, un droit*; but the muddiness goes deeper still: is *un droit* conferred by *le droit*, or does the natural possession of rights give rise to a regime of laws? As to the former, the status of the phrase concerning "The authority that vengeance may give . . . ," the phrase subjects the practice of *naming* to a further sort of obligation, an "ought" (*devoir, ne doit donc pas*) that is not of the order of justice, law, or right but also is not of the order of what can be determined analytically ("The justice which the victim calls upon against the justice of the tribunal *cannot be uttered* in the genre of juridical or forensic discourse," *ne peut pas s'énoncer*). Manifestly we *can* give the "name" "a right of law" to the authority that vengeance may give, but we *ought not*, even *must not*. The same more than superficial muddiness obtains here: does the obligation, *devoir*, the "*ought*," spring from a quality possessed by "vengeance," "authority," the "tribunal," the regime of phrases? Is it analytically determined—that the victim's cry for justice, offered against the justice of the tribunal, *cannot be* uttered in the language of that tribunal *entails* (*Comporte? Implique?* How strict is this implicature?) that the victim, and we, "ought not" to name the authority of the claim to vengeance a "right of law"?

There is play throughout *The Differend* whenever Lyotard addresses by means of translation, hypostasis, and metalepsis the primal question, "A phrase 'happens.' How can it be linked onto?" (*Une phrase "arrive". Comment enchaîner sur elle?*). I have said these phrases that designate the right to vengeance, then partially withdraw it (by *instituting* it as the condition of the hearth-economy that supersedes it), are "muddy"; I have said that they "flex." It would be better to say that where the question, "How can a phrase that 'happens' be linked onto?" is addressed, something that is not of the order of "happening" or events, or of relation or "linking," makes itself felt, a location we didn't map out before, a place where wrath is being consigned—but *à jamais*?

I am tempted to call this—place, order—the order of *political institution*. It is an order—a place, a topology—where "happens," and "must," and "ought," and the different orders of necessity in conflict among "entailment," and "implicature," and "comportment" operate, according to rule regimes whose compatibility and coherence are endlessly in dispute. And among which no principle of translation obtains. Calling it the order of *political institution*, I will be echoing but perverting Nussbaum's description of the emergence of *political justice* from the supersession of the chthonian regime of vengeance. I will be doing much the same with the closed, reflexive hypostases between God and subject that we find in Paul's letter. I will be laying stress on the *untranslatability* that characterizes relations between the regime of subsisting names like "colors" and the names I institute, like "Eumenides" or "political justice" or "the rule of law."

This is what the order of *political institution* might look like.

It is a matter, say, of determining (or of imagining) on what authority the act of institution is accomplished—of determining whether such acts are legitimate *because* they are analytically necessary, or just, or legal, or natural.

A case comes before me. It was decided by a lower court, but that court's verdict and, more, its standing to interpret the law or statute have been *impugned*. Two branches of government are parties to the case. It is 1803, early days in the new American republic, and the hegemony of the "rule of law" has not been established.[15] Congress has passed a law *expanding* the Supreme Court's power, my court's power; I am now being asked to use that new power to determine whether the Judiciary Act, which delegates to the Supreme Court the right to issue writs of mandamus, was an improper expansion of the court's original jurisdiction as defined by Article 3 (which was written just months before the case is decided). My decision will not only bear on this case—let's call it, for convenience, Marbury's case—it will also determine the authority that different governmental institutions can claim in expanding the power of (notionally coequal) branches of government in interpreting and enforcing the law. I am asked to decide my court's standing as an arbiter of interpretations of legislative acts that set the boundaries of my court's brief.

This last, my court's standing to determine the *ultima ratio legum*, is not given in 1803. How will I establish it? What is the order I must follow, conceptually—*first* to establish that I do, indeed, have standing, uniquely, to decide *what counts* as law (under the Judiciary Act), thus what counts as a case, what counts as an interpretation of the law or statute, what counts as the relation between law and case; and *then* to decide whether Marbury's petition for a writ of mandamus directing Madison to deliver Marbury his judicial commission is formally correct and thus can be acted upon by my court? Where does that "must" come from? Must all the parties, from Marbury on up, agree to the first, before I can move on to the second? On what grounds am I proceeding? I want to exclude regress; there is no court or instance to which either of these two gestures can be appealed. I can seek guidance from cases like Marbury's, from decisions like the one I am currently reviewing, from other standards of interpretation otherwise attested and sanctioned, and from other institutions similarly dependent on establishing the authority of a last interpretative instance. All of these I will judge according to the standards under which I find that I am operating; they will provide guidance and context, but no foundation more solid than that. With them in hand I offer an interpretation of the document that institutes the different instances of government, the Constitution.

This is too weakly put. I offer more than *an* interpretation, one of many competing ones, of the instituting document: rather, I identify and name what is uninterpretable, hence unimpugnable, about it, and establish *that* as the ground on which stands my court's authority to sort out competing interpretations of the instituting document. Now, on the wings of this act of naming and identifying, armed with the register of *necessity*, with the heft of "must" in hand, I will decide what counts as a case, as an interpretation of a law or statute, as their relation, as my power to act and institute. (*Mandamus*: the Latin for "we command." Marbury's case, on its face requesting the supersession by my court of a lower court's decision, goes to the sovereign authority my court has generally to *command*.[16]) Now Marbury's case before the court can be decided. Now the scheme of institution is definitively *founded*.

Now it is 1997. This is how Paul Kahn describes matters:

> *Marbury* is a self-conscious effort to constitute an American political order characterized by the rule of law. This is a much larger project than the doctrinal defense of judicial review that is often seen as *Marbury*'s primary contribution to American law. Judicial review is the power of a court to declare a statute void because the court believes it violates the Constitution. Important as this function may be, it is hardly a complete account of the rule of law; it is only one institutional role. It does not even exhaust the role of the courts under the rule of law. The rule of law, not judicial review, is the central idea of the constitutional order. . . . The rule of law as a particular construction of American political meaning—one within which we continue to operate—traces its origins to a conception of the courts and of he conflict between law and political action that first appears with clarity in *Marbury*.[17]

Justice Marshall's opinion—whose elegant and consequential steps I need not lay out here—hangs on this stipulation:

> That the people have an original right to establish for their future government such principles as, in their opinion, shall most conduce to their own happiness is the basis on which the whole American fabric has been erected. The exercise of this original right is a very great exertion; nor can it nor ought it to be frequently repeated. The principles, therefore, so established are deemed fundamental. And as the authority

from which they proceed, is supreme, and can seldom act, they are designed to be permanent.[18]

"An original right to establish." Whence does this right proceed? What does it mean for "the people" to "have" a right? How is the right's "originarinesss" established? The opinion offers no answers directly, but does, perhaps, otherwise. Take the characterization "a very great exertion," a consideration limiting the exercise of the originary right of "establishing." In 1803 the expression would have seemed much less abstract than it does today: the Constitution had been ratified, fretfully, in March 1789—just two years before the dispute at issue in Marbury. Marshall and the whole bench had lived through that exertion and through the revolution of 1776, and had, it seems likely, no great taste to see the "original right to establish . . . principles" of government exercised again, by force of arms or constitutional debate. Hence the "permanence" with which the "principles" of government are imbued—in this case, the articles of the Constitution—and the *basic* quality of the "original right to establish . . ." War, revolution, constitutional assembly: these are "great exertions" indeed; imagining them, perhaps just as much as remembering them, serves to constrain. (They are the limits of a world.) And yet it does not follow, or not *necessarily*, of the "great exertion" that "nor can it nor ought it to be frequently repeated." Jefferson, notoriously, maintained the contrary, though he did not prescribe the frequency with which "The tree of liberty must be refreshed from time to time with the blood of patriots & tyrants. It is it's [*sic*] natural manure."[19]

Marshall insists, though. "Nor . . . nor," "Nor can it nor ought it be repeated." The rhetorical translation of "can" into "ought" works strangely: if something, for example an originary act of establishment or institution, or a war or revolution, *cannot* happen often, then why stipulate that it *ought not* happen often? "A phrase 'happens.' How can it be linked onto?" The phrase "The exercise of this original right is a very great exertion" *happens*. Another "links onto it": "nor can it be frequently repeated." Then another: "nor ought it to be frequently repeated."

The *can/cannot* register, which remits to the world of analytic necessity or to the world of physical possibility and impossibility, is not the same as the *ought/ought not* register, the register of obligation, responsibility, morality. (Recall the Humean distinction between *fact* and *value*.) Rather than keep the registers separate, though, Marshall's complete phrase (but is it complete? is it *a* phrase?) clothes the second, the moral register of *ought*, with the authority and indefeasibility of the first, the register of analytic or natural necessity. A "basic," "fundamental," and "principial" right is *necessary*, *necessarily so*: it may even be, as Oliver Wendell Holmes says, "the hypostasis of a prophecy—the imagination of a substance supporting the fact that the public force will be brought to bear upon those who do things said to contravene it."[20] Steps follow in Marshall's opinion and beyond—a strict path leading from this hypostatized image to *Marbury* and beyond, to the "constitut[ion of] an American political order characterized by the rule of law," as Kahn observes (11). But Marshall's translation between the registers of necessity and obligation works according to a rule established or instituted by neither of these, an *imaginary* rule for both constraining and unbinding; entailing strictly and contingently following. Like the "fact," in Holmes's famous definition, that violence will be "brought to bear" by a public force, Marshall's translation between the registers of necessity and obligation is supported by the *imagination*. As in Holmes's phrase, though, just whose "imagination" installs the schema of institution and at what cost is not determined. (But it will be high: the schema of institution is installed imaginatively at the cost of necessarily occurrent deinstitutionalization, or of abolition, or of what Arendt deplores as "recurring revolution"—terror, even the Terror.) Jefferson's violent objections to installing the Constitution as "a lasting institution, embodying th[e revolutionary spirit] and encouraging it to new achievements" (this is Arendt's characterization) are raised precisely against the constraints that what is intended to "last" and what "embodies" place on the occurrent imagination. When the schema of the city's institution replaces fury with the law the question "at what cost?," like the question whether "the imagination" should be understood verbally, as an *event* or someone's *act*, or nominally, as the substantive ("the imagination"), subjective or objective genitive—these and their *terrors* are matters the abstract citizen consigns to extramural spaces, walled away and rendered voiceless by histories of established decisions. *Stare decisis*, the abstract citizen maintains; *stare decisis*, the court affirms. A decision installs and institutes; its perdurance protects the city from the occurrent imagination, the spot where the city dreams, that is, the domain of radical potentiality on which the differend's laws founder.

Writing that tells stories is easy, narration is easy, and philosophy, despite appearances, has never dispensed with it. The point is to break with the philosophical novel, and to break with it radically, not to give rise to some new novel. The philosophical novel, philosophical narrative, is, of course—but not only—the history of philosophy as a doxography that narrates, reports, collects and unfolds the series of philosophical systems. "Telling stories," in philosophy, is, for Heidegger, something ever more profound and which is not as easily denounced as doxography. The Novelistic [Romanesque] we need to wake up from is philosophy itself as metaphysics and as ontotheology. What does this mean?

Jacques Derrida

# INSUFFICIENT GROUND: THE INSTITUTION OF REASON

On what ground do I lay the foundations for defective institutions? A city—Athens, say—will want its Parthenon and its agora, a church its rock, a state its constituting documents. Stepwise, from these, I and you build the grid on which our pleasures, desires, pains, energies, stories, beginnings, and endings are mapped and administered, by ourselves as well as by others. What do I require of my ground and my grid—solidity? Coherence? Extension in space as well as time? Imperviousness, indivisibility? If I follow the conventions of axiomatization, then yes—just these. It's the rational way to proceed. But these are not my conventions, not yet.

A brief story haunts the history of Western philosophy.[1] It tells of what befell the first man who made public the limits of reason, and it provides a lasting, although sketchy and symptomatically knotty, definition *of* reason. At the hand of one nameless, perhaps mythic figure, and on the wings of the newly disclosed relation between what can and cannot be thought, what may and may not be thought, and what may or may not be expressed in public *about* thought and thinking, reason expressed as *logos* (*logos* expressed as reason) begins the slow drift into forgetfulness that becomes the *principle of reason*. In Heidegger's translation the story establishes the ground for modern metaphysics: this is the path toward the "principle of sufficient reason." But it is not quite right to call this story—or any other—just the means, the *technical* means, by which that principle, or any of the great metaphysical principles, is instituted. Heidegger distinguishes in *Being and Time*, in 1927, between one thing and another, writing and thinking storywise about beings ("to report narratively about *beings*": Stambaugh's translation), and thinking and writing so as to grasp beings in their Being, "it is one thing to give a report in which we tell about entities, but another to grasp entities in their Being" (*ein anderes ist es, über Seiendes erzählend zu berichten, ein anderes, Seiendes in seinem Sein zu fassen*).[2] What will be required to break with this story "radically," without just telling in its place another philosophical story? What will happen to break with the principle that philosophy may concern itself with storytelling about *beings*, and the history of philosophy concern itself with telling stories regarding such beings as philosophers are, and such things as their philosophies? Heidegger suspends these questions in 1927. The parallel formula, *ein anderes ist . . . erzählend zu berichten* on one hand, *ein anderes . . . zu fassen* gives us no grammar, no storyline, no thought form for proceeding from one to the other. How then should we imagine reasoning *from* the age of stories *to* grasping the Being of beings? (In my question already two faculties uncomfortably, agrammatically, bump up against each other: imagination, reason.)

I am asking this question at a moment when circumstances—environmental, biological, political, economic—so far exceed the grasp of reason that *crisis*, that *ultima ratio* of the Enlightened mind, lies on every tongue. It is the last story, the last account; and a crisis, like a story, always announces the next; it is generic. But my vocabulary is dated, the jargon of reason, Being and beings, axiom and foundation, exhausted. Approaching today's crises through it or with Heidegger's work will seem at best anachronistic, at worst obstinate to the point of provocation.

Putting matters this way immediately courts paradoxes. Let's pursue and exacerbate them: let's seek in these paradoxes principles for imagining how reason might work past the crisis of its sufficiency, or for reasoning regarding the image of the crisis of reason's sufficiency.

What remains and presses more urgently today than ever is the question of the *principle* of reason's sufficiency that writing and thinking storywise institutes.

The story I open with concerns and institutes the *insufficiency* of reason. We encounter the story in Greek, told by the Neoplatonist philosopher and scholiast Proclus, who is probably working from a slightly different account found in Iamblichus's *De vita pythagorica*; and it crops up as well in an Arabic translation by the great tenth-century translator Abu Uthman al-Dimishqi of a lost Greek work by Pappus of Alexandria.[3] The tale concerns the school of Pythagoras. Here is Proclus's version.

> It is well known that the man who first made public the theory of the irrational (*al-ogon, ana logon*) perished in a shipwreck in order that the inexpressible and unimaginable should ever remain veiled. And so the guilty man, who fortuitously touched on and revealed this aspect of living things, was taken to the place where he began and there is forever beaten by the waves.[4]

And here is the version we find in al-Dimishqi's rendering of Pappus's lost work:

> A saying became current in [the school of Pythagoras], namely, that he who first disclosed the knowledge of that which does not hear and does not speak, and spread it abroad among the common herd, perished by drowning: It is fitting that they meant by this, in the way of a riddle (*lughz*), that everything within totality that is deaf or does not speak or cannot be visually imagined ought to be veiled (*sitr*); and that every soul which by error or heedlessness discovers (*takshaf*) or reveals (*tazhar*) something of this kind that is in it [in the soul] or in this world, will wander [thereafter] hither and thither on the sea of non-identity [more literally: a sea of nonsimilarity], immersed in the stream of coming-to-be that has no order.[5]

The story has not remained unchanged over the centuries. The discovery of additional manuscripts and changes in editorial conventions pertaining to the reading of these new attestations as well as of the earlier sources have shifted the outlines of the story considerably. Its sense and the pathos that infuses it, what the story is understood to tell and to what effect—these have also changed, in and out of time with these shifts in editorial practice. The bibliography on this fable focuses for the most part, when scholars are not concerned to speculate on the identity of the authors of its different attestations, on the different historical puzzles it offers. What *did* the unfortunate Pythagorean disclose? Was it the construction of the dodecahedron? The irrationality of the square root of the number 2 (the diagonal of the square)? Or was it rather a larger principle of mathematical irrationality that would put paid to the Pythagorean world order broadly speaking? Would the Pythagorean school indeed have sacrificed one of its members in this way, even if he betrayed a secret? Did the school treasure such secrets in the first place? Is the story to be read as allegory or parable, as history, or as something else entirely?

In this story, something until now called *logos* catches the first light of mathematical reason, and first encounters what will limit it in a way that can itself be thought: an internal limit. From this point on, reason will express itself as the limit of *logos*. Reason as the thinkable limit of *logos* will emerge, complexly, from within *logos* (reason is the expression of the immanent extension of *logos*), but reason will also be given outside of *logos*, inasmuch as it will designate an outside *for logos*. There are things, sorts of things in the world and in thought, that cannot be thought reasonably; but *that logos* as reason *has a limit*, this can be thought by reason, and when it cannot be thought rationally, it will be imagined, or represented allegorically by other companion faculties. At the same time, however, the limits that reason marks for *logos* are not settled as to how they exist—as to their way of being. Are they then subject to reason, when their not being subject to reason does not, precisely on these grounds, fall within the limits of reason that are immanent to reason or outside of reason, as the brute fact of contingency that is not amenable to reason?

The mystery that the treacherous Pythagorean reveals hangs on an accident. What *is* this bit of information, this deadly secret? The editorial tradition has handed down two answers. The preferred reading of Proclus's story—preferred since the first quarter of the nineteenth century—concerns not what is inexpressible or irrational in general but much more specifically the incommensurability of the measurements of the diagonal and the side of the square—that is, the irrationality of the square root of two, $\sqrt{2}$, revealed by the proportional construction (*ana-logon*) of the geometric figure. On this account—which is bolstered by the observation that the form *alogon* would be out of place, grammatically, in Proclus's text—what founders on the story will merely be a particular subbranch of early mathematics.

On the strong, metaphysical reading that both Proclus and Pappus appear to endorse, however, what is at stake in the story is the disclosure of the unthinkable, the unthought, the inexpressible or inconceivable—*ton alogon*. On this reading, the traitor in my story (who may be Hippasus of Metapontum) threatens to bring about what one critic calls, perhaps hyperbolically, "the sudden collapse" of the "rational, ordered vision of the world set in place by Pythagoras."[6] For Pythagorean cosmology, in the definitive versions we find in Iamblichus, in Porphyry, and in Proclus, tends toward numerical "rationalism." Here is Proclus: "Pythagoras, being asked what was the wisest of things, said it was number. . . . But by number, he obscurely signified the intelligible order, which comprehends the multitude of intellectual forms: for there that which is the first, and properly number, subsists after the superessential one."[7] The metaphysical version of the story produces a paradox. Properly *irrational* numbers, if that is what *alogoi* are in this story, and if the texts do indeed intend *alogon* at this juncture, both belong and do not belong to the "intelligible order," inasmuch as they occur within it but are not part or members of this order; they are and are not intelligible. If "number" "signifies the intelligible order," however obscurely, then our unfortunate Pythagorean philosopher bears us news of something that is and is not a number, and which is unintelligible both in lying outside the order of the intelligible and in violating the twin logical principles on which intelligibility in general stands, the principles of identity and of noncontradiction. Condemning the bearers of such news to eternal, Promethean suffering, over and over, at different historical junctures and under aspects that differ according to how "intelligibility" or rationality are marked, defined, or valued—this seems not only just, but philosophically constitutive, constitutive of the discipline of philosophy, in its long history. Philosophy, understood in part as the study of the extension of reason, of its principles of coherence and application, of its limits and possible worlds, is born where the limits of *logos* are tendered to thought by reason as objects of thought that peculiarly resist being understood.

Miraculous births of this sort persist in the registers of national history and of national mythology, where they then acquire surplus values, catch the pleasures of audiences clothed in sublime bodies of different sorts, die and are reborn splendidly. In the register of philosophical inquiry, something similar may be said to obtain.

A great deal happens between 1927 and 1955–1956, my bookends, the publication dates of *Sein und Zeit* on one hand and of the collection of lectures that Heidegger devotes to Leibniz's "principle of sufficient reason," published as *Der Satz vom Grund* on the other.[8] A great deal happens, in the long eclipsing of European global hegemony, a great deal in the national histories of middle Europe, and in the history of peoples, the Jewish people, the Germans, the Poles, the Spanish. A great deal too, in the history of modern philosophy, where small legions of heretical figures challenge the School on many fronts, disclosing the insufficiencies of one or another orthodoxy, often at great cost: here we witness the emergence and eclipse of psychologism in phenomenology, a momentary consolidation of Hegelianism, the eclipsing of the project of mathematical logic initiated by Frege. These small legions of treacherous philosophers include figures such as Russell and Whitehead, Husserl, Wittgenstein, Gödel, and of course Heidegger.

The "principle" of sufficient reason, generally attributed to Leibniz but found in Spinoza and, inchoately, earlier and elsewhere in the history of philosophy, stipulates that "Nothing is without reason," or, in an expanded form, "Nothing exists whose sufficient reason for existing cannot be rendered." Heidegger's controversial, beautifully argued lectures show how the "principle" of sufficient reason, following a long "incubation" period, comes after Leibniz to underwrite the designation of the human animal as *animal rationale*, and in consequence as what Heidegger calls "the creature that requires accounts and gives accounts" (129). The thinking that is particular to and definitive of this "reckoning" creature, Heidegger says, "brought the world into the contemporary era, the atomic era." But does the "determination that humans are the *animale rationale* exhaust the essence of humanity," Heidegger asks? ("Determination," or "definition": in 1987, the *Gesamtausgabe* published Heidegger's Freiburg lecture notes for the course that becomes *Der Satz vom Grund* as *Zur Bestimmung der Philosophie*, in English generally translated as *Towards the Definition of Philosophy*; *Stimmung*, a musical *tone*.) And if not, "Are we obliged to find paths upon which thinking is capable of responding [*entsprechen*] to what is worthy of thought instead of, enchanted [*behext*] by calculative thinking, mindlessly passing over what is worthy of thought? That," he writes, "is the world-question of thinking. Answering this question decides what will become of the earth and of human existence on this earth."

Here Heidegger is at his most enchanting. The stakes of his question could not be higher: their very magnitude, their hyperbolic, Hyperborean air wants to enthrall. Our time and our world may have lost the anxious dread that informs the Cold War expression "the atomic era," but not because the question that Heidegger poses has been answered, or because the question has been forgotten. The contemporary era is no longer the "atomic era." It is the era of catastrophic global warming, of pandemics, of manifest racial injustice, of environmental depredation, of massive, increasing social and economic inequity linked closely and complexly to all of these. The question whether the "essence of humanity" is "exhausted" (*Erschöpfen*, *erschöpft*) is not particularly or necessarily tied to a concrete existential threat to "human existence on this earth," whether this particular threat is nuclear war among superpowers, environmental disaster, or a pandemic spread on the wings of those aircraft that so enchanted Heidegger. It *is* tied to the way in which thinking imagines, or thinks, "the essence of humanity." If the "essence of humanity" is among those things that are indeed "worthy of thought," Heidegger is saying, then, like all such things, "the essence of humanity" is not to be reckoned with. What is worthy of thought takes shape poetically and in the form of poetic expression, as a *Sprechen*, to which Dasein then responds, noncalculatively. The principle of sufficient reason is enchanting, it casts a spell, not because it is wrong—this is the wrong way to imagine the principle of sufficient reason—but because it establishes or determines, *Bestimmung* is the word constantly at work—because the principle of sufficient reason determines as the principle of thought, as the ground, what the principle *reveals*: that being and reason have a relation, that they can be thought to hang together. When this hanging-together of being and reason is thought as a *principle*, then "the essence of humanity" can only be reckoned with. When, however, we learn to attend once again to what is worthy of thought, then we have rethought, or rather we have disclosed "reason's limiting of *logos*" *to logos* rather than *to thought*. To the limitations of the Leibnizian formulation of the principle of sufficient reason, Heidegger opposes the archaic sufficiency of *logos*.

But who are "we" in all this? Heidegger's "we," his time and world are not neutral spaces or substances; I for one have just the place there of what falls out of his world's *terminus*: the ex-terminal, the exterminated. Can Heidegger's "we" and his impersonal "one" be shorn of their neutrality, and can they serve rather to unsettle the unity of his "world" than to confirm it? This seems a catastrophic way to frame the question. My story seems to depend on installing, on instituting, the ex-terminal as a principle for thought.

So, at any rate it seems—so it would be if the ex-terminal amounted to what the principle of reason could think as its exterior and as its condition of sufficiency. But this is not the story.

If there *is* a "principle" of *in*-sufficient reason, or just of insufficiency, it will be ex-terminal and disenchanting in ways that cannot reasonably be reckoned, and the philosophical stories where it makes its appearance will be novelistic in ways entirely unthought on the grounds provided by the sufficiency of reason and of *logos*. A principle of insufficient reason will reawaken a now-dormant aspect of the old, Pythagorean story (thinking is now, in part, just this reawakening), by stressing again that the limits of the extension of reason are not sufficiently established within the field of reason—and that the field of reason is never, for this and other reasons, identical with itself. (Reason has violently axiological dimensions.) A corollary: the limits of the extension of the discipline of philosophy cannot be established philosophically.

This is the foundation on which *defective* institutions stand.

## DISSATISFACTION

Will a principle of insufficient reason help us to ask the sorts of questions that Heidegger wants us to ask, that is, "world-questions," *as* questions bearing upon the way the "world" can be thought as a world?

If there *is* such a thing, the principle of insufficient reason should allow us to ask "world-questions" while avoiding two sorts of outcomes. On one side, I would like to think that a principle of insufficient reason will avoid the pitfalls into which the later Heidegger seems to me to fall—a chthonian naturalism, linguistic essentialism, different forms of quietism. This side of Heidegger's thought too quickly allows his "world-questions" to become global questions, questions regarding the reach of empires and markets, the flow of commodities, languages and products. These are urgent matters, but when based upon an unexamined notion of the "world" they limit their scope and quickly become proxies and devices for installing the very sorts of power and resource inequities they seek to diagnose, and to change. On another side, I would like to avoid the deflationism of much contemporary Anglo-American philosophy, which rules out certain sorts of questions because they seem misformed, in the sense that they overreach: on this description, "world-questions" clothe themselves in sublimity when, and because, they venture outside the rather small, conventional fields in which the pertinence of questions can be assessed, their claims and consequences reckoned—when they abandon philosophical "realism." The Anglo-American tradition asks questions that concern states of affairs in "worlds" in which those particular questions can be asked and in which, and for which, they can be answered: the "world" in question is reflexively defined by the questions it permits us to ask and answer concerning states of affairs in that world. But such a "world" is not a state of affairs "in" the "world," and so asking "world-questions" must mean asking questions about, and within, a "world" in which particular "worlds" become states of affairs with respect to one another and to that higher-order "world." A poisonous regress threatens—and worse. For "state of affairs" substitute "individuals," for "world" substitute the word "set," and you have described nothing other than the intractable paradox that Russell hit upon in his efforts to mathematize the field of philosophical logic at the turn of the twentieth century.

Both of these outcomes seem to me undesirable. Thinking through the defectivenes of institutions stands on a principle of insufficient reason. And this "principle" as I imagine it, and as I will sketch it out briefly, has an uncanny similarity to a term discarded for the rather bad company it has kept historically—the concept of *mediation*, always to be found where the roughest of trades are practiced, dialectical materialism, critique, psychoanalysis.

Let's rough the terms "insufficiency" and "mediation" up even more. "World-questions" are and should remain ungovernably and incalculably over- and underdetermined. They are conceptually *insufficient*, and they are and remain so because they are always wildly and *in*determinately mediated. In what this "wildness" and "indeterminacy" characterizing both "insufficiency" and "mediation" consist are questions to which I will return at the conclusion of this chapter.

But why should we want to ask "world-questions," wild or tame, determined or indetermined, in the first place? Isn't it possible for human animals to address economic inequity, climate change, pandemics, and other existential threats, in other ways? To address them more narrowly, with greater focus, more realistically? Our lexicon here would include terms like "know-how," "enterprise," and craft; we would be speaking the horribly familiar language of "precision," "targeting," and "outcomes." Our ethics would be consequential rather than deontological; our aesthetics, serviceable. Here Heidegger seems to me indispensable, since he allows us to see that this "narrowing" of the focus, this greater "realism," the more "practical" or technical approach to these questions, begs the question in a most disturbing, but predictable way. It will turn out that these ways of approaching the catastrophe, and the whole lexicon we deploy in this narrowed field, are themselves, in the most important way, the disaster. To the extent that we address circumstantial threats from the perspective of calculative reason, as threats to ourselves imagined as *animales rationales*, Heidegger will suggest, we will have already consigned what he calls "the essence of humanity" to the domain of reason alone, and hence to the disaster of the camps' efficiencies.

On the other hand, I have no interest in "the essence of humanity," nor, I think, should any other human animal. My aim is not to recover such a thing, or to discover it or to invent it if it isn't there to be recovered. Indeed, I think it's a surprisingly silly concept, even a dangerously silly concept in Heidegger in most ways. In most ways, but not—and here is where I really set out—not as a logical operator. What Heidegger calls "the essence of humanity" is what I propose to call the "principle" of insufficient reason, of wild or indeterminate mediation, on which thinking through the defective institution stands.

So let me begin again. The principle of sufficient reason, I remember, joins the other great principles—the principle of contradiction or identity, and the principle of the excluded middle—at the heart of Western logic, a stable tripod on which the metaphysical tradition stands.[9] It is the first two—the principles of identity or of contradiction, and the law or principle of the excluded middle—that are in some measure Heidegger's opening target in *Sein und Zeit*. What can be said minimally and emptily of every other thing or object, whether it is or is not an actually existing object in our world, namely, that it is itself, this cannot be said of Being. And what can be asserted minimally of every statement, namely that it must be either true or false, this cannot be asserted of statements concerning Being. Aristotle puts the first of these principles, the principle of identity ("the firmest of all principles"), in this way, in *Metaphysics* Book Gamma: "For the same thing to hold good and not to hold good simultaneously of the same thing and in the same respect is impossible (given any further specifications which might be added against the dialectical difficulties) (1005b, 18–22)."[10] The fuzziness of Aristotle's expression can be clarified if we say instead that no thing can both have an attribute and not have it, including (or perhaps, as Plato's *Parmenides* argues, beginning with) having or participating in the attribute of being *one*, one thing; of *being* determinable as one thing. Accordingly, one can say that a table is a table, or even that every table is a table; or one can say that Martin Heidegger is Martin Heidegger: but one cannot say that Being is Being, or even that Being *is*, not because such statements would not be true, but because they would be circular. They would not be statements; they would not be true or false; they would be empty, *in a peculiar way*. Similarly, it would seem to be analytically true that it is either true or false that a table is round or square, or that this window is open or shut. I say "analytically," because it would *seem* to be the case that the old principle of bivalence applies, whether the object to which a proposition refers actually exists or does not. This principle is often attributed to Aristotle as well, or its most lasting and discussed formulations are, which Russell himself picks up—namely, in Russell's words, the "proposition stating that 'all propositions are either true or false.'"[11] So we say that it is true, analytically, that the statement "This table is round" is either true or false, or, to put the matter as a problem of ontology, we may say that a table either is or is not round, or that a unicorn either exists or does not, and that it either has a single horn or does not. This sort of statement is true even though we could imagine square as well as round tables, and these sorts of statements are true although we can imagine worlds with and without unicorns, and aberrant unicorns with two horns (this would be a superunicorn, a bicorn, but still it would be a subspecies of unicorn) or horsey unicorns with no horn, a wannabe-unicorn, a sorry excuse for a unicorn, a shamefully castrated unicorn, but still a member of the subclass of those things we call unicorns. But in precisely the same way that we could not imagine a table that is both round and square, or a circle that is also a square, we could not imagine a unicorn that both did and did not have a horn simultaneously, and we could not say that the statements "This unicorn has a horn" and "This unicorn does not have a horn" can *both* be true, when we stipulate that the phrase "this unicorn" is the same in each of the two phrases. (By putting it this way I do not commit myself to saying that either of these phrases "refers to" a unicorn or to anything else, and that it is this referent that really keeps me honest. What is "real" in this case is the identity of the phrase "this unicorn," not any unicorn to which the phrase might refer at one or another time or any world in which a unicorn might or might not exist.) I recognize that I am using a bit of shorthand here by inserting the operational verb "to imagine," when in fact what I am describing, the law of the excluded middle, has nothing to do with the actual imagination: it is a principle of the well-formed statement that it is either true or it is false, at least according to Aristotle's bivalent logic, and by a kind of extension an ontological principle: either a thing is or it is not, and of no thing can it be said that it is and it is not. But it is not analytically true to say that it is either true or false that Being is, or that Being is Being, or that Being is a unicorn, or indeed to say anything or to predicate anything *about* Being. Here again the reason is not that it would be *false* to say that anything that is predicated of Being is either true or false, but rather that it is not established that we can say what would be minimally required for such predications to be either true or false, that is, that it is not established that "Being is" is the sort of thing about which we can speak, in part because "Being is" is an expression that, according to Heidegger's reading of the Principle of Identity, remains, again, *peculiarly empty*.

I have twice used the expression "peculiarly empty." For emptying-out—the emptying-out of a particular philosophical lexicon, of the great pillars of the metaphysical tradition—emptying-out is just what the opening paragraphs of *Sein und Zeit* set out to do—to clear out, even to destroy the defensive misconceptions of a tradition that has obfuscated, displaced, translated, and forgotten the question of Being since the pre-Socratics. Only *after* this clearing-out has been accomplished does it become clear that the question of Being lay before us all along, but was also the condition of this clearing-out. This before-and-after movement and discipline on which *Sein und Zeit* opens, if it is a movement or a discipline, is not a psychological principle or a psychological discovery, but rather a structural one. What the clearing-out of the two logical principles achieves, the clearing-out of the principles of identity or of contradiction, and the law or principle of the excluded middle, is a kind of askesis, the disclosure of a clearing into which what lay before us, the question of Being, can be gathered. In the 1953 lecture on Heraclitus's fragment 50, "Logos," the way in which Being lies before us to be collected is indeed called "logos," rather than "reason" or reckoning. But can Logos, as the way or shape of the recollection of the question of Being that lies before us in the disclosure of the clearing-out of the two great logical principles I have outlined, can *Logos* become a ground for propositions or statements (*Sätze*) *about* Being?

This is a very tricky question indeed, inasmuch as it is also a question of method, even of methodology. We might say that the reason that *Sein und Zeit* cannot come to a conclusion is that it has not posed this question to itself satisfactorily or sufficiently. This might be because Heidegger does not have at his disposal yet the means he will require to pose it: he lacks in particular what *Der Satz vom Grund* provides, that is, a nontechnical understanding of the third of the great logical principles, the principle of sufficient reason. The principal tool that he *does* have at his disposal in clearing out the two other great logical-metaphysical principles is an account of the structure of logical propositions taken from a productive but also quite limiting spot—the field of mathematical logic. Reason's ground becomes sufficient, in Heidegger's early writing, in a shape he takes from Gottlob Frege's work.

Let's look at this suggestion in parts, then. Toward the end of his 1956 lectures on the "principle of sufficient reason," Heidegger casts his eye back across these terrible years to light on *Sein und Zeit* from the perspective of a different question from the one he had posed for himself in 1927. The thirty years that separate *Sein und Zeit* from *Der Satz vom Grund* have not passed in vain, but the works are part of the same moment of thought, aspects of a modernity whose world is the world of the *principium reddendae rationis*, the principle that Leibniz most clearly articulates and whose importance Heidegger had insufficiently understood, we gather, at the time he was writing *Sein und Zeit*. The thirty years between the two books may mark a change in the history of thinking, Heidegger says—his own thinking, of course, but also, by implication, in the history of thought—but it will be nothing as momentous a change as the ones he tracks in *Sein und Zeit* and in *Der Satz vom Grund*. We are, he says, in an "atomic age," whether in 1927 or in 1956, in a "calculated world [that] still remains and everywhere includes humans in its reckoning inasmuch as it reckons up everything to the *principium rationis*."[12] *Now*, he tells us in 1956, now he can describe how things stand for us in this way: "We are the ones bestowed by and with the clearing and lighting of being in the *Geschick* of being, and accordingly the same ones that being touches in and by its withdrawal." (86) *Then*, in 1927, "in the crude . . . and awkward language of the treatise *Sein und Zeit*" ("crude . . . and awkward" is Lilly's translation of *noch unbeholfeneren und vorläufigeren Sprache*, the "still-awkward and preliminary language"), back *then*, in *Sein und Zeit*, *then, at that time*, the proposition that "we are the ones bestowed by and with the clearing and lighting of being" was expressed by Heidegger and understood by his readers to mean that "the basic trait of Dasein, which is human being, is determined [*bestimmt*] by the understanding of being." (86) This retrospective description of *Sein und Zeit* that we find in the 1956 *Satz vom Grund* tells us something of importance about the arc of Heidegger's thought—that for Heidegger, the earlier work's "crudeness" or "provisionality" is to be linked with an inadequate treatment of the way *in which*, or even *whether*, the understanding of Being may be said to *determine* human being, or Dasein. Now, in *Sein und Zeit*—where it is a tricky, miscegenated term for a tricky, mixed function, hailing from Hegel in part, in part from the field of mathematical logic—"determination" or *Bestimmung* renders and follows the structure of the principle of sufficient reason. That Dasein is determined by the understanding of being means that the reason that can be rendered for the being of Dasein is the understanding of being. More strongly put, too strongly put: Heidegger neglects to displace Leibniz's great principle in *Sein und Zeit* because he cannot (yet) do without it, without a concept of founded and founding determination, in his efforts to shake loose the other two legs of the metaphysical-logical tripod. (Some sort of economic principle, even a kind of calculation or reckoning, is at work: keep *one* of the three metaphysical-logical principle so as to shake loose the *two* others. Purchase *two*, at the cost of retaining *one*. A little market is imagined here.) Without a sufficiently developed account of what "reason" might be, and of its relation to being, the logic of *Sein und Zeit* cannot do without retaining and deploying, as a tool of destruction, the principle of reason's sufficiency, the productive haziness with which "determination" plays the role of "sufficient reason."

Let me try to be clearer. Heidegger is aware of this haziness, certainly, by the time that he prepares for publication the lectures of *Der Satz vom Grund*. "Here," the Heidegger of 1956 tells us, making explicit an argument found less overtly in *Sein und Zeit*, "here," and by this he means "here in *Sein und Zeit* as I now understand it," "here [in *Sein und Zeit*] understanding of being never means that humans as subjects possess a subjective representation of being and that being is a mere representation." (86) *Then*, in 1927, what was at issue was a thinking concerned with, or perceived to be concerned with, determination and definition, *Bestimmung*. Thus the three introductory propositions or observations of *Sein und Zeit* concerning Being—that the question of Being is the first; that Being is undefinable; and that Being is a, or rather *the*, self-understandable or self-evident, *selbstverständliche*, concept—these three are taken, together, to clear the ground for the formal way of posing the question of Being that follows. *Now*, in 1956, Heidegger says, he can see that *then*, in 1927, he was providing "nothing other than an interpretation, thought through from the point of view of the question of being, of the old definition of human nature: *homo est animal rationale*; humans are the creatures endowed with reason." But *now*, in 1956, the history of thinking has moved beyond the crude and preliminary shape in which *Sein und Zeit* found and left it. *Now*, in 1956, Heidegger is able to ask the earlier question differently, or he is able to *translate* the earlier preoccupation into a different language: "The question we are faced with by the principle of reason is this: To what extent," he asks, "'are' being and *ratio* the same? To what extent do grounds and Reason (*ratio*) on the one side, and being on the other belong together [*zusammengehören*]?" (104) (*Inwiefern "sind" Sein und ratio das Selbe? Inwiefern gehören Grund und Vernunft (ratio) einerseits und Sein andererseits zusammen?*)

There is much to ponder in this expression—not only the status of Heidegger's "we" (is "we" some general identity to which you or I, any I, any you, could belong equally? Not inasmuch as I am a concrete subect who can be included in, or excluded from, this or that place, identity, term, experience: I, and you, are liable in this sense to ex-termination) but also whether "the question we are faced with" is or is not a single question, as Heidegger claims. Pause for a moment on the difference suggested by the two logical functions corresponding to each of these questions, one ascribed to the "crude and preliminary" idiom of 1927, the other to the mature position outlined in *Der Satz vom Grund*. The first places on one side the function of determining or defining, *bestimmen*; and on the other, the association of identity, the bracketed "is" of the expression "Being and ratio 'are' the same." The two questions—which are supposed to be one question—are arranged chiasmatically, according to the figure called, not surprisingly, *ratio* in Latin rhetorics, or *analogon* in the Greek: "To what extent 'are' being and *ratio* the same? To what extent do grounds and Reason (*ratio*) on the one side, and being on the other belong together [*zusammengehören*]?" Now ask: how, beyond the chiasmus, does the first expression "hang together with," cohere with, the expression that seems if not a repetition then a translation of it, since they are something like the same question? To what extent do Ground and reason on one side and Being on the other, to what extent do they go together? This seems to me to mark one way in which Heidegger's project has changed, from 1927 to 1956. The logical shape of the argument moves from a critique of determination, as a way of clearing out the two great logical principles of identity but providing only an interpretation of a definition, to something no longer "preliminary," something that has to do with the way in which these two questions hang together, and both are and are not synonymous, are and are not one question. They are called by a single name but they are not the same question—that is, they cannot be determined to be the same, or, to be entirely clear here, they are one and not-one at the same time.

We have moved from an interpretation of a definition, an interpretation of *Bestimmung*, to the posing of a single-as-double, inside of which two things hang together. (Or are heard together: *harmony* is the playing and hearing together of notes related, or not: discord, according to a *ratio*.) In what way are these two questions *not* the same, single question? Or rather, to what extent, *inwiefern*, are they not the same question? The syntax at least suggests a certain symmetry;

the chiasmatic arrangement, the difference that a mirror makes, or the persistence of a *ratio*: "To what extent," Heidegger asks, "'are' being and *ratio* the same? To what extent do grounds and Reason (*ratio*) on the one side, and being on the other belong together [*zusammengehören*]?" A conceptual symmetry should follow: "being-the-same" *should mean* "belonging-together," or "being-heard-together," to stress the "hearing" in *Hören*, as if the motif of listening and attending to were to be heard here alongside the register of logical predication. "Being-the-same" *should* both "be-the-same-as," "mean-the-same-as," and "belong-together-with" or "be-heard-with" the operator in Heidegger's *second* question, the operator "mean-the-same-as" and "belong-together-with" or "be-heard-with." That is a bizarrely convoluted expression, but I think necessarily so. Heidegger, the Heidegger of 1956, is showing how far, to what an extent, *inwiefern*, one question does not hang together or harmonize with itself. (Recall our discussion of Lyotard on entailment: here the troubled Lyotardian question of how a phrase attaches to another, or one regime of phrases to another, has been posed as the fundamental ontological question.) *Inwiefern*, to what degree, how far, does or does not the question of the relation between *ratio* and being constitute *one* question, or hang together or harmonize with itself—this may or may not be a question for any and all questions, though it is hard to see how this strange not-hanging-together-with-itselfness applies to questions that do *not* pertain to the relation between *ratio* and being. Questions such as "Is Martin Heidegger the author of *Sein und Zeit*?" "Do unicorns exist?" or "Is the round table round?" may well hang together, but even in this case they do so with an uneasiness that is radicalized extraordinarily when we ask after terms that are not proper or common names, but the terms *ratio* and being. We would say, for instance, that "Martin Heidegger" "means the same as" "the author of *Sein und Zeit*," and thus we would truthfully answer "yes" to the question "Is Martin Heidegger the author of *Sein und Zeit*?" But the name "Martin Heidegger" also names other things as well ("Martin Heidegger" is also the author of other works, including works critical of the "preliminariness" of *Sein und Zeit*, and "Martin Heidegger" does other things, many other, than write works of philosophy). These other senses of the name "Martin Heidegger" "hang together with" and "are heard together with" the sense "is the author of *Sein und Zeit*," but they are not the same as, and do not mean the same as, "is the author of *Sein und Zeit*." Before I read the "Black Notebooks" I would have said that "Martin Heidegger" "is heard together with" or determined reciprocally by one set of phrases, that "Martin Heidegger" is "heard" or determined reciprocally by someone; and after I read the "Black Notebooks" I would say that I and others now "hear" "Martin

Heidegger" "together with" another set. Both sets of phrases have a relation to the expression "is the author of *Sein und Zeit*," but the relation is different, and so is the way of relating, too: *determination* has changed; the tone, *Stimmung*, is different between the two. I intend—the question becomes an ethical one—to leave open the possibility that other phrases still will come to attach to the name, changing its tone further.

To get a sense of the trickiness of these questions and of the ethical register they suddenly open, consider what happens when you say, as if they were synonymous expressions, that "Martin Heidegger was the author of *Sein und Zeit* and was a member of the National Socialist party" and that "being the author of *Sein und Zeit* 'means the same as' being a member of the National Socialist Party" or as "being rector of Freiburg University" at a certain period. The discomfort we feel at the confusion of these sorts of assertions of identity when what is at issue is a proper name, the name "Martin Heidegger," is a manifestation of the structural problem that the Heidegger of *Satz vom Grund* is embedding into the description of the question he can *now* ask, in 1956. He can *now* ask it, though not as *a* question, or not as *one* question, inasmuch as the being-one of the question presupposes the being-one of the object of the question, and although *ratio* may be construed as being-one, as depending on the possibility of saying, of *one* being and *of* being, that it is one, that it is one being and that being is the One—this is something that, presumed in *Sein und Zeit* to some extent, is by 1956 no longer the case.

*Inwiefern*, to what extent, how far can we go, how far can we go in asserting that Heidegger's two questions in *Satz vom Grund* are one question? Or that they can be made to harmonize according to a musical *ratio*? How far can we go in asserting that Heidegger's not-quite-one question in 1956, when he has moved beyond the preliminary and crude formulations of *Sein und Zeit*, how far can we go in asserting that one question does not hang together as one, but is always at least two, is always to be heard, not as a single tone but at least as a doubled one? An overdetermined tone? Recall the submerged market strategy, the embedded reckoning and calculus that trades retaining the *one* logical metaphysical principle for displacing the other *two*. Now, in 1956, one question, the question of the relation between *ratio* and being, is and is not one. What sort of economy can be founded, what sort of calculus and market-value reckoned, when the self-identity of the one number is open to question? To what extent will reason, *ratio*, ever be sufficient to determine or define, *bestimmen*, what is called "one question," when it is *ratio*, the formal structure of reason, that divides the question into two identically structured, apparently synonymous but different questions, and holds the difference, guards it, *thinks* it?

I am asking the questions in this way, laying stress on Heidegger's adverbial phrase, "to what extent," "how far, "*inwiefern*," because I find it so peculiar—because, I want to say, it is here that insufficient reason, that the *insufficiency* of *ratio* and of *logos*, spectacularly enters the work. The lexicon of distance and extension is not, or not only, the lexicon of mathematizable or even of physical space, space to be reckoned or measured. *Inwiefern* suggests a strange empiricism—how far can I go out on the thin ice without falling through it? Such questions, when they designate, are tested in the event; they can be reckoned in advance, but only approximatively. They have a strange propinquity with rhetorics of persuasion, with pedagogies, with counterfactuals, with the imagination. I no longer am asking myself, "Is my argument true? Are my claims and assertions true?" but rather I am asking myself: "How far can I take my argument, before it becomes acceptable or unacceptable to my audience? How far must I go, before my argument becomes, or reveals itself to be, convincing, to me, to my audience? I wonder what will happen if I state this or that. Let me find out," I say, and then I proceed to pile hyperbolic claim upon hyperbolic claim until (imagine!), exhausted or enraged or convinced, my audience says, "Ah no, we've had it, that's enough, that's *sufficient*," meaning in one part of the audience that they're satisfied with the argument, they're convinced—and in another part of the audience that they've heard enough to be sick of it, they are unconvinced and unpersuaded, even unpersuadable, and they're leaving, as when we say in French *ça suffit!* and mean something like "Enough already!" Adverbial expressions of this sort are also, and indeterminately, symbolic and rhetorical functions. When Cicero asks, in the first of the Catiline orations, "when," "for how long," "to what extent," *quo . . . quam . . . quem . . .* Catiline will try the patience of the Senate, he is not asking for a reckoning, but establishing a limit, a political limit. Less colloquially, more formally, you might put it this way. The criterion of "how-far-ness," of "sufficiency," that is introduced by Heidegger in *Satz vom Grund* is *either* an ontic, even empirically testable, or an *imaginary* one. The mode of reckoning it invokes is not mathematical (even or especially musical *ratio*, as the Pythagoreans understood, was mathematical), perhaps not even mathematizable. It is ultimately pragmatic.

"The question we are faced with by the principle of reason," writes Heidegger in 1956, "is this: To what extent, *inwiefern*, 'are' being and *ratio* the same? To what extent, *inwiefern*, do grounds and Reason (*ratio*) on the one side, and being on the other belong together [*zusammengehören*]?" The questions might have been asked differently; Heidegger might have asked, "'Are' being and ratio the same?" and "Do grounds and reason on the one side, and being on the other belong together?" The adverb *inwiefern* calls for an answer that works aslant the domain of judgments regarding the *formal* truth or falsehood of statements, including statements about being; that moves away from a rational relation with the metaphysical ground installed by stories; away from the domain of sufficiencies; and is to be articulated instead in judgments or propositions—or stories—characterized by insufficiency and formal defectiveness.

Do these entailments help us imagine reasoning *from* the age of stories *to* grasping the Being of beings, or do they rather make explicit what holds us, perpetually tossed, at the lip?

Here in 1956, where he structures the logic of insufficiency around an adverbial phrase that opens onto the practical as well as the formal domain, Heidegger revisits old concerns. Here, where he is dismantling/disclosing the destructive/preserving function of *ratio*, Heidegger takes up the project that *Sein und Zeit* envisioned, in 1927, with regard to what, in 1912, a very young Martin Heidegger had called "a universal theory of the concept," a metaphysical and mathematizable theory of the concept through and through. The phrase "a universal theory of the concept" is taken from a review essay Heidegger published under the title "New Research in Logic," dedicated to Gottlog Frege's "overcoming of psychologism in principle." Heidegger discusses in particular Frege's works on "Sense and Meaning" and on "Concept and Object," which, Heidegger says, although they "cannot be disregarded by any philosophy of mathematics," are also "equally valuable for a universal theory of the concept." There is very little trace of the *mathematical logic* of Frege in Heidegger's own work, of course, but what Heidegger does take from Frege is a way of construing as yet unsatisfied predications. These, which pertain in the first place to the relation between "argument" and "function" in Frege ("I am concerned to show that the argument does not belong with the function, but goes together with the function to make a complete whole; for the function by itself must be called incomplete, in need of supplementation, or 'unsaturated.' And in this respect functions differ fundamentally from number"), are "equally valuable for a universal theory of the concept."[13] Now what Frege means by "incomplete, in need of supplementation, or 'unsaturated' . . . functions," his translator Max Black tells us, is "such fragmentary expressions as '—conquered Gaul' or 'the capital of—,'" in other words, incomplete predications whose truth, falsehood, or even standing as statements making one sort of claim or another is deferred until the advent of the name or token that completes, supplements, or saturates them: until that arises which will make them, you might say, *sufficient*. Remark the similarity between this *unsaturated* structure and the project that opens *Sein und Zeit*—a clearing-out of the great metaphysical principles intended to make it possible for the question of being to step into its proper place, to give itself, or, in the event, to arrive (if, indeed, it has such a "proper" place). The project of *Sein und Zeit* might be construed, then, as the "saturation" or "satisfaction" of the emptied proposition "—is being," a project of saturation whose "satisfaction" is achieved by means of (rather, *in*) *Sein und Zeit*.

This remains a problematical way to proceed. Frege's term *ungesättigt*, unsaturated, is drawn not from the formal but from the physical sciences, where it designates a molecule which "is ready to form additive compounds," in the preliminary definition given by Matthew Muir, in his 1884 *A treatise on the principles of chemistry*.[14] "Definitions so indefinite as 'readiness or unreadiness to form additive compounds,'" Muir notes, "do not help us to understand the apparently precise formulae . . . in which these definitions are expressed." (129) Muir is intervening in a debate that would have been familiar to Frege in its German form, and that took focus in the work of Johannes Wislicenus, whose decisive 1887 paper on "Über die räumliche Anordnung der Atome in organischen Molekülen und ihre Bestimmung in geometrisch-isomeren ungesättigten Verbindungen" was translated into English in 1901.[15] Frege borrows the term *ungesättigt* for his description of not yet satisfied or not yet saturated functions in order to differentiate functions (which may or may not be "saturated") from numbers. He has in mind *both* the aspect of the term that bears on the not yet applicable truth or falsehood (we can't assess the truth of unsaturated propositions: we don't know whether "—is the author of *Sein und Zeit*" is true or false until a name or a token has been supplied, although that truth value as it were awaits, lies before us as we provide that name or token, or number); *and* the aspect of the term that has to do with the still unsettled question of the physical principle according to which compounds are indeed added to molecules until the point of saturation is reached. Muir's sense of "indefiniteness" captures both these—both the formal, logical state of indeterminacy or attentiveness, not even a being-toward (since the substantive is the retroactive product of what arrives): a towardness, *un à-venir*; and the "readiness or unreadiness" of molecules to "form additive compounds," a possibilist state of physical affairs that tells us precisely nothing about how such compounds will eventually be formed. (Just as the shape of Lucretian atoms and their laminar flow tells the observer, shorn of the verbal or dynamic, but aleatory, principle of *declinatio*, just nothing about the formation of bodies; and just as the proposition that one regime of phrases follows or links onto another, in Lyotard, finally tells us nothing about the necessity of that following or linking.) *Inwiefern:* "to-what-degree-ness," "how-far-ness." A characterization of the event. Without quite giving it its proper name, Heidegger calls the form of insufficient, defective judgments *about* the unsaturated, insufficient, cleared space opened in metaphysics by the name *of* that cleared, insufficient space.

## FROM INSUFFICIENCY TO DESATURATION

This is still not enough. I opened affirming that today's crises pose urgently the question of the *principle* of reason's sufficiency that writing and thinking storywise installs. "Today's crises" is a baldly historicist formula, but I have been offering throughout a mixed answer to the question in the form of arguments with mixed formal and historical shape and content: the story of Heidegger's development, from 1912 to 1927 to 1956 (and "these terrible years . . . these disastrous years"; an "atomic age"); the lurid fate of our nameless Pythagorean; the story of the passage from the metaphysics of storytelling to our grasping the being of Being; the satisfaction or the saturation of unsatisfied propositions; the barely sketched story of what I hear with "Martin Heidegger" in the after-tones of reading the "Black Notebooks." The principle of insufficient reason that I have been at the same time arguing for, describing, and instancing passes again and again through lexicons that it cannot saturate, that it cannot map entirely, whose limits fall within and without it. In this sense the principle of insufficient reason is indeed kin to the figure of mediation—though mediation of a special sort. Mediation here is *principial*, in the sense that it antecedes but is not the sufficient condition for the emergence and constitution of the terms to be mediated: being and beings; story and Being; and so on. We will say that insufficient reason is the narrative "principle" of our old, Pythagorean and anti-Pythagorean stories. To this degree, and to return to this chapter's epigraph from Jacques Derrida's early seminar on Heidegger, these old stories are precisely *not* the sort of "novel" that the philosophical tradition has never denied itself. Still stories, still narratives, they are not the sorts of *romans philosophiques* with which Derrida wishes to break radically. They are, I think, signs that that break *occurs*: they are allegories of its occurring.

In what sense? The stories I have in mind *do work.* They are lurid; over time they gather and shed cultural values, whether they concern Pappus or a certain Martin Heidegger. They work parabolically not to *saturate* a field, a compound, or a proposition (by supplying an eventual predicate that will make a statement true or false, or just complete it), but to *desaturate* it. *Desaturate* now means: disclose how far every term that satisfies us, every name we can settle, every object we map upon the grid offered us, hangs together with what unfinishes and incompletes it, and makes it count as other than one. None of philosophy's stories, and not even *all* (all? For isn't "all" a figure of saturation?) or more than one of them, will counts as or install *an* event, a founding, self-identical event. Imagined as I intend to, these stories are no longer machines for sanctioning the coherence, intelligibility, and values of other phrases, regimes of phrases, or stories. Instead, it, they, desaturate: they fall out of al-Dimishqi's tale; it, they, fall out of the path of epic return, of *nostos*, and "wander[s] [thereafter] hither and thither on the sea of non-identity." Its—their—Promethean heroics must appeal, must repel: the disclosure of the mystery; the betrayer who bears philosophical fire (who bears the fire of the camps); the secret he discloses that democratizes knowledge, or renders it again a sacred cult tended by hierophants; who extends *philosophia* and not just geometry into "the form of a liberal discipline, seeking its first principles in ultimate ideas, and investigating its theorems abstractly and in a purely intellectual way," *ton peri auton philosophian eis schema paideias eleutherou metestisen*, as Proclus writes of Pythagoras.

My stories' contradictions are signs, I suspect, of conceptual and historical compromises. To note that the gods, outraged at the revelation that *ratio* discloses the limits of *logos*, brought about the traitor's death is to exonerate the school, and in the same stroke to make the school's mysteries matters of divine concern. To draw an analogy among the various mysteries revealed—the construction of the dodecahedron, the discovery of the irrationality of the diagonal (the incommensurability of the diagonal with the sides of the square: *analogon*), the discovery of the irrational, of *ton a-logon*—to do this is to betray the historical record, which insists on the particularity of each mystery; but it is also to establish the commensurability of these singular events, to bring them under the measure of a single scheme, or to bring—violently—two schemes into contact. Is this a mistake? Can I deliberately, intentionally, make a mistake? Is it rational to claim to do so? Imaginable?

To read the desaturating stories I have been telling as allegories, parables, or riddles is to place veils before them, to be removed by initiates in possession of esoteric knowledge. The allegorical mysteries revealed thereby amount to this: that esoteric knowledge must be kept veiled. (Hippasus revealed that there *is* a school, a discipline; he publicized the scheme of disciplinarity.) Whether in their hyperbolic or in their more restricted shape, though, the stories desaturate: they tell also, allegorically, parabolically, the story of the violent foundation of philosophy, and of the costs entailed in moving from an esoteric mystery cult toward *paideia*. The history of *lectiones* of Proclus's *scholium* seems the record of a parallel circuit: moving from an anecdote regarding a cult whose extreme limit is the *alogon*, what is deprived of the *logos*, reason, enunciation, articulation; to a discipline concerned instead to settle the internal paradoxes of the commensurable and the proportional, *analogon*. (The consolidation of Lachmannian method in the positive, technical discipline of philology, another school might say.)[16]

What do we achieve by installing principial mediation, that is, desaturation, something like the story of nonsimilarity (al-Dimishqi), where the principle of insufficient reason also stands? That mediation is principial means that no self-similar terms exist to enter, from outside or from before it, the "sea of nonsimilarity" or of "non-self-identity." That reason is insufficient means that "reasonable" judgments concerning states of affairs—call these "today's crises"—only *by mistake*, *violence*, or *heedlessness* remit to, posit, discover (*takshaf*), or reveal (*tazhar*) its principle. But they do so not by a *leap*, that other, sacrificial-heroic figure that keeps guard over Heidegger's story, and Kierkegaard's, and Kant's, but by a fall. If, indeed, the two can be told apart—the question that Derrida's last gloss on *Der Satz vom Grund* raises:

> This may appear to be both a provocative formulation and just common sense: that which grounds cannot be grounded. That which grounds, the grounding, is necessarily ungrounded, without ground. One could, as I for my part do all the time, draw countless consequences from this obvious fact: the grounding of anything whatsoever, for example, a state, a constitution, an institution, is never grounded, legitimate, legal, since it grounds. The founding of a state is always violent, as is the institution of a principle or a law. The positing of something, for example, a state—this is, of course, not one of Heidegger's examples—or a law or a constitution, this "positing," this position [*Setzung*, if you like] is a leap since it is a matter of positing what was not there, and this by means of a gesture that is necessarily inaugural, violent, without prior justification, whence the relation of affinity between the *Setzen*, positing, positioning, and proposition [*Satz*] but also the leap [*Satz*].[17]

"Today's crises," the catastrophe, the state of affairs. I want to list what counts for me. I look out my window; I imagine worlds, beings, and ecologies without me, for others, for you, across plastic seas. In what languages, in what untranslatable frames, do matters force themselves on us, on others none can imagine? Just how?

Imagine unsatisfied, unsatisfiable worlds. (The contradiction between the terms is profound: a "world" is *always* "satisfied," or it is something other than one "world.") Pause where instituting, allowing to be instituted, and refusing institution coincide. Dwell where a leap and a fall must but cannot be distinguished. Tell in unreckoned ways counterallegories of philosophy. Install (or attend to, *bear*), in the *concept* of disciplines that address or administer today's crises (and in their corresponding practices), principial mistake, violence, and heedlessness. Perhaps like this.

# 3

# THE OBJECT OF ALLEGORY

I needs must fear for heav'n, lest he who took
Hell captive should be master of the skies,
And snatch the scepter from his father's hand.
He seeks no quiet pathway to the stars,
As Bacchus did, through ruin he would make
His way, would govern in an empty world
Tried strength he boasts, by bearing up the sky
Learned that he might have gained it by his might :
Upon his head he bore the world nor bent
Beneath the burden of its mighty mass;
Lightly upon the neck of Hercules
The vault of heaven rested.

Seneca

Let us speak of the leaders; for why should anyone talk about the inferior philosophers? The leaders, in the first place, from their youth up, remain ignorant of the way to the agora, do not even know where the court-room is, or the senate-house, or any other public place of assembly; as for laws and decrees, they neither hear the debates upon them nor see them when they are published; and the strivings of political clubs after public offices, and meetings, and banquets, and revellings with chorus girls—it never occurs to them even in their dreams to indulge in such things. And whether anyone in the city is of high or low birth, or what evil has been inherited by anyone from his ancestors, male or female, are matters to which they pay no more attention than to the number of pints in the sea.

Plato

I imagine worlds, beings, and ecologies without me, for others or no one, for you, across plastic seas.[1] In what languages do matters force themselves on us, on others none can imagine? Imagine telling the stories of unsatisfied worlds.

We will have to understand what it is that makes these stories such that I can tell them, if indeed I can. (What I called "principial mediation" is also a principle for *unsettling* storytelling, in ways that will become clear and in the special sense of "settling" that links the term to colonial extractivism.) What institutions allow the worlds that I imagine to become and remain stories or phrases or tellings, *logoi* or *Sätze*, that I can tell today so that they are understandable to you? My stories pertain to the objects "world" and "worlds," but I have also been telling them otherwise. I have picked up a figure, a stone circle, from Searle; a red car or a family story from my own experience; Athens and the *moirai* to tell the story of the schema of institution; the story of Marbury (and other legal stories to follow: the story of the Supreme Court's decision in *Dobbs* vs. Jackson Women's Health Organization); the old story of the treacherous Pythagorean philosopher as a way to discuss the schema of foundation. These are examples, of course, but they are something more: stories about concepts' relations, infights, limits, here and now—they are allegories. Is there a relation of kin or convention that draws thinking about the objects I am calling institutions particularly close to the world of allegory?

I will need to be clear about what I mean by "object," "story," and "allegory." I will want to show just what counts, today, as an allegorical object; and about the dynamics I intend.

A story concerning the secret limits of reason, I said, haunts Western philosophy. The story holds that secret close, where only the elect or the instructed understand it. The topology is familiar: under the city where we come and go, trafficking in thought and objects, recognizing in each other a citizenship based in deliberation and representation, under the streets of Athens and the *polis*, the Moirai wait, unconverted; vengeance and the telluric passions slumber; you and I and others are excluded or included, judged, impoverished, enriched, identified, determined and undetermined by figures and procedures secret from us, acting where we don't know; the unconscious of the political, even the political unconscious. These figures of constant division unground what seems shaped, most settled, instituted. The story of reason's secret and divisive limit is an allegory: haunted by the *agora*, the forum, the public assembly, and concealing what the *agora* holds as its secret other, *allos*, allegory has an old relation to the speech on which the city is built, and on the secretive topology that marks *any* institution based in political representation. These observations then just unfold what the Greek couplet of *allos* + *agorein* tells us: not just that allegory means speaking otherwise than is spoken in the forum, but that there is another forum, another scene, where a different representation is set before different audiences, and where different, if any, practices and protocols of representation prevail.

For the institution of political representation is allegorical, in the strongest sense of both "politics" and "representation"—that is, in the sense of the terms that goes to their complex roots in the violences of association and exclusion: to their *differend*.[2] We might let *this* individual stand for the attributes he or she bears; or we might let the name of the class of individuals bearing those attributes *stand for* whatever individual of the class; or we might let *this particular* sign, or term, or name stand for *that general* concept, or *this* concept for *that* class of objects. We might work on a different level; we might allow the concept of a "class of objects" to stand in place of a principle of ostensible similarity relating these "objects." Each of these assertions marks an episode in the story of sacrificial substitutions in which allegory's kinship with the institution of political representation unfolds. Political representation and the object of allegory are things wrought; they enter into circulation, acquire value, are consumed, transformed, and traded together. Together, they bear second-order values not dissimilar to the second-order value that accrues to the concept and practices of "translation," the value of designating the processes by which value accrues to produced objects in circulation. Different moments in different modes of production will produce differently configured couplets for consumption at the time, and in later years, and under other constructions of value, production, circulation, consumption, and so on.

Say we try to spell out, historically and formally, this reciprocal relation. Say we do so *today*—that is, at a time when political representation enters into profound crisis in the United States. We soon find ourselves in regressive dilemmas that affect, or should affect, our sense of what it means to be part of the forum, the *agora*. Take the dyadic Scholastic formulas for the sign, *Aliquid stat pro aliquo* and *Supponit aliquid pro aliquo*: "something [that] stands for something else" or "something [that] serves to refer to something else," or "denotes something else," or "stands in place of something else." *This* thing stands in place of *that*; but of course not every thing can stand in place of a particular other thing; a chair, manifestly a *thing*, does not stand in for or stand in the place of an apple. Or perhaps it might, under circumstances we would have to stipulate, and for a group of people who might understand the convention and who would recognize themselves *as* a group, partly because they share a relation to these conventions and to the objects, *aliquid* and *aliquo*, whose relation of standing-for is governed by these conventions. Perhaps we might want to say that "standing for" and "referring" or "denoting" imply a third party or cluster of functions to "fulfil the office of an interpreter, who says that a foreigner says the same thing which he himself says," an office affirming and legitimating the claim that this expression *denotes* or *refers to* or *stands for* that, or that his person or that herself *stands for* the "same thing" as another—what Charles Sanders Peirce called an "interpretant" or (in the course of a long career in which the term acquires and loses senses and domains) "interpretants."[3] This *third* can determine that yes, indeed, *Aliquid stat pro aliquo*, under such and such conditions and to this or that end; or for whom "this" stands for "that." We imagine a *third* as an addressee or a witness to our designating, even just for ourselves, *this* as an object for which something else can stand, to me and to you. And that *third* becomes an object to be referred to, interpreted, *for* another third; and so on. Peirce accepts the infinity of this regress.

Peirce calls the figure of the *third*, I said, an "interpretant": a translator, whose confirmation that "a foreigner says the same thing which he himself says" then becomes an object to which a sign attaches, requiring a further translator, and so on. I am grossly simplifying even Peirce's earliest semiotics, since the *regressive* shape in which the "interpretant" appears has this remarkable limit: "Here, therefore," Peirce explains in his Lowell Lecture XI, of 1866, "we have a divine trinity of the object, interpretant and ground. . . . The Interpretant is evidently the divine Logos or word."[4]

"The divine Logos." Nothing could be less "evident." Peirce is being jokey, but he is underscoring the far from trivial function that the interpretant, and the translator, share: to establish, decisively, by decision (even if it's just for now, for us, and here), *a* translation; *an* interpretation. Let's try giving Peirce's mysterious and polyvalent figure a more specific name, though: the "interpretant" decides; it installs; it institutes and is itself an institution. Perhaps the existence of the figure of the *institutional interpretant* entails the (prior) work of protocols that serve to establish just *who* (or what group, or agency or institution) serves felicitously as an institutional interpretant; and the (eventual) work, performed by another or by the institutional interpretant at a different time, establishes that *what* the institutional interpretant takes to be a relation of standing for is indeed that thing, a thing, *aliquid*, for the institutional interpretant. Or perhaps the existence of the figure of the institutional interpretant will be taken to be axiomatic, and the eventual work clarifying the norms that figure establishes will be consigned to an episcopate. As the standing-for that relates *aliquid* to *aliquo* becomes something that we or some institutional interpretant might be able to designate, it will stand before us, for someone else again, as a thing that can stand, for me or for another, *pour moi*, for the ways in which *aliquid* stands for *aliquo*. Finally, *today*, a conflict between institutions and principles—call these the electoral college and the principle that popular votes count equally—intervenes to disaggregate the figure of the institutional interpretant; to delegitimate it; to strip institutions and principles in conflict of whatever natural or axiomatic authority we have granted them.

One way to tell the story of the relation between the institution of political representation and the object of allegory concerns the emergence, the characteristics, and the eventual fate—the dissolution, the catastrophe—of the institutional interpretant, the norm-providing *third*, the "divine Logos," the *institution* that openly guards the secret of our recognition, of our relation, of our citizenship. The controversial rhyming of modernization and secularization soon shapes our approach: faith in the "divine" figure of the institutional interpretant wanes; the episcopate charged (by whom, after all?) with administering the norms that govern translation and interpretation, what will stand for what, or in relation to what thing, loses its ground and its brief. This is the history, often bloody and always discontinuous, of secularization. When those institutions in turn disclose their contradictory, violent incoherence, a further compensation occurs: desecularization, the return, renaturalization, extraction and commercialization of the allegorical repressed, the *logos*; the disclosure of a long-obscured object, *quo*, eclipsed in modern prose's shop-worn *quid*—"America," made "great again."

Let's adapt Walter Benjamin's schema: the institutional interpretant as *flaneur*, "standing on the threshold of the metropolis as of the middle class," an embodiment of the "intelligentsia" that "sets foot in the marketplace—ostensibly to look around, but in truth to find a buyer. In this intermediate stage, in which it still has patrons but is already beginning to familiarize itself with the market, it appears as the *bohème*" ("Baudelaire" 10). Benjamin concludes: "To the uncertainty of its economic position corresponds the uncertainty of its political function" (10). When the aura of its hermeneutic privilege fades, the intelligentsia, the interpretant-episcopate, hands off its authority to compensatory institutions. Liberalism in the long Millian tradition acknowledges this handoff and calls these compensatory institutions (in English) "situations" or (in Castilian Spanish) "circunstancias." The subject of rights and liberties is *situated*; it is *circumstantial*, *positional*; it a *local*, even *deictic* thing now imagined to emerge and nest at, and to serve to give a transcendental sense and continuity to, the point of crossing of social and historical circumstances.

"The long Millian tradition" means a line of thought regarding individualism that Anglo-American political philosophy associates most often with political science in the wake of Dewey—mostly pragmatic, mostly utilitarian. When the "transcendental sense" of emergent situational subjectivity is instituted through relatively self-aware acts of the will, we are in soil tilled by contemporary scholars like Richard Flathman. When emergent situational subjectivity is ascribed to human *animals* as such we are in the domain of the psychology of situated cognition. Let's stress instead the link this account of "situated" or "circumstantial" subjectivity has with the phenomenological tradition. Here is Ortega y Gasset:

> Man reaches his full capacity when he acquires complete consciousness of his circumstances. Through them he communicates with the universe. Circumstance! *Circumstantia!* That is, the mute things which are all around us. Very close to us they raise their silent faces with an expression of humility and eagerness as if they needed our acceptance of their offering and at the same time were ashamed of the apparent simplicity of their gift. We walk blindly among them, our gaze fixed on remote enterprises, embarked upon the conquest of distant schematic cities. Few books have moved me as much as those stories in which the hero goes forward, impetuous and straight as an arrow, towards a glorious goal, without noticing the anonymous maiden who, secretly in love with him, walks beside him with a humble and suppliant look, carrying within her white body a heart which burns for him, like a red-hot coal on which incense is burned in his honor. . . . Individual life, the immediate, the circumstance, are different names for the same thing: those parts of life from which their inner spirit, their *logos*, has not yet been extracted. . . . I am myself plus my circumstance, and if I do not save it, I cannot save myself.[5]

The history that the *uncertain* intelligentsia tells today, or that some members of that class tell *about* that class (that object), is at base heroic, as Ortega's allegory is. It invites the all too focused Cartesian Subject-Knight, "gaze fixed on remote enterprises, embarked upon the conquest of distant schematic cities," to extract instead the sense, the *logos*, of his situation, his circumstances. (Our allegory is unmistakably gendered, unmistakably racialized: beside the Knight rides not Sancho but his proxy, "the anonymous maiden who, secretly in love with [the Knight], walks beside him with a humble and suppliant look, carrying within her white body a heart which burns for him, like a red-hot coal on which incense is burned in his honor.")

Can allegory labor, can it work in the age of its desecularization? Ortega's *Meditaciones del Quijote* gives us an answer, allegorically. Desecularized allegory does four sorts of work. (Hercules and Andromache, together, rather than don Quijote are our emblem here, as we will see: their *labors*, their work of installing, shouldering, bearing, and deposing worlds and authorities.) First, allegory does explanatory, consoling work—the work of mourning: it allows us to grieve for the interpretant institution. It works, second, to determine the task of the "situated" or "circumstantial" subject to be the identification, renaturalization, extraction and exposure of the secret sense, the *logos*, of the circum-stantial, of what stands about *him*. It works, third, to show how this task of transcendental synthesis *is allegorical*: it is thought as allegory. Fourth and finally, desecularized allegory, the allegory of the extraction of *logos* from our situation, institutes *circumstance*, *situation*, where the authoritative institutional interpretant once stood firmly.[6]

Thus Ortega; thus the line of transcendental phenomenology. But thought as desecularized allegory does other work as well, at cross-purposes with these four labors that reinstall me, "I," as transcendental synthesis of my circumstance. I am tempted to call this work *circumstantial* as well, though I intend it in a different sense from Ortega. Thought as desecularized allegory does wild, unproductive work to open the concept of concept to the also opened circle of phenomenological determinations (the *circum-* of *circumstance*, the circus, the cirque, the circuit of deictics, of here, now, and this). The story of this breaching is too long to tell in full. In what follows I make not so much an argument, that is, a sequencing of necessities, as a discontinuously narrativized collection of what Benjamin calls thought-images, *Denkbilder*, intended to illustrate it: I will be offering my own desecularized allegory.

## CARDINALITY

> History repeats itself, arbitrariness and patchwork are the transversal axis in migration policies. Resources for welcoming migrants are still lacking; death still keeps immigration company [*la muerte sigue acompañando a la inmigración*]. Young people, adults, babies, teenagers, men and women are part of a marine cemetery that extends throughout the Mediterranean because Europe and the capitalist system that governs the world offers no livable alternatives to this endless human tragedy. A migration policy focused on control will not dissuade anyone who has decided to emigrate to find a better life in another country. No route is definitively closed. We may not know their names, nor the age of all these dead: still, just one of them deserves all our efforts, our commitment and our firm intention to ensure that migration policies are based on respect for life and dignity, that they are inclusive and respectful of diversity, and that they seek above all to put an end to human suffering.[7]

I am trying to get my bearings. What do I see, what direction am I facing? Where I am standing will have some effect, perhaps a determinative effect, on what I see (this is perspectivism at its most brutal), but will it have the same, or any, effect on how I conceive? A mountain may not be a mountain, if I am standing where planes stretch out before me endlessly and I am pointing to what in a rugged region, say to my north, is barely a hill. "Blue" is one segment of the visible spectrum, by convention, here, where we respect that convention, out of convention. It is a different segment there, and another to those who stand just *there*, and so on. But these positional considerations are circumstantial, you'll say—and you will have Kant's essay "What does it mean to orient oneself in thinking?" in mind. (Kant does not use "circumstantial," but "accidental," *zufällig*. To set aside the mere inmixing, *Beimischung*, of the concept with the image, *Bild*, is the first gesture of his essay, which then moves from considering orientation in physical space to orientation in thought, inverting the spontaneous priority that appearing has over thought.)[8] For, you will say, I have the intuition that an object like a triangle is a triangle whether I bring it to mind in Madrid or in Dakar—just so long as I don't mean one that I can point to here and now, occupying this or that concrete position in space and bearing properties that strike my senses. *Where* I am, like the substance on which I might draw the triangle, are circumstantial, situational; my intuition as regards the inmixing of that circumstance with the triangle that is always and everywhere a triangle, is however *not* circumstantial, though "the circumstantial," and even my circumstances in specific, are in part what it regards.

What would it take to argue successfully, and against Kant, that concepts are produced and thought positionally, or prepositionally? That their inmixing, *Beimischung*, with image is not *only* accidental or circumstantial, but necessary? I want to follows another intuition, which runs across the one that Kant offers: the intuition that (as Ortega maintains, though in a mystified register) "circumstance," *situation*, *position*, and the image, are not without violence unmixed from my conceiving. Violence, though? Now I remember Machiavelli. *The Prince* opens mapping political ontology onto a landscape. He provides a famous image: the view from the mountain is the Prince's view; the view from the plain, the subject's. Not thought, not birth-right, but accident, *Zufälligkeit* or Fortuna, determine which of the two positions I will occupy. And I wait for the passing years to disclose the kinship between Kant's term *Beimischung* and the racial, ethnic, and religious *mixings*, the *Mischlinge* that the National Socialist regime regulated, interned, and exterminated.

To ask how we might argue for *defect* is to argue that the inmixing of image and circumstance are indeterminately definitive of the concept of concept, and that whatever concept of thinking we want to offer is inextricably circumstantial as well. The argument is awkward for at least three reasons. First, concepts are the sorts of objects I can fashion across the compass and not just in this or that spot, so what is it about them, in fact, that is circumstantial? Kant refers to concepts' "abstract" nature. Since they are produced or manufactured across specific markets and spaces, a quite specific form of abstraction is entailed today: concepts are not the ore or forest native to my country, to just this little patch of land, but commodities whose stuffs I can poach anywhere (given sufficient force); whose production is outsourced in the global scheme of extraction and production; and whose abstractness, value, and sense are determined both locally and globally. Too, in the global market of markets in which "concepts" circulate; in the market of epistemologies; the "concepts" I make entail, stand on, and produce differential access *to* markets, resources, and means and scenes of production. "Concepts" com-port "migration policies focused on control." They *com-port* them and the institutions and violence, state and local, with which they are enforced; "concepts" make and take migration policies along *with* them on the long roads of exile and economic displacement.

The claim that concepts are objects produced and thought circumstantially, positionally, or prepositionally, is awkward for a second reason. If I ignore my first qualms and still claim that concepts—by virtue of their prepositionality, by virtue of anteceding both posing and position—*can* be produced "anywhere," then am I not granting them a sort of universality? Am I not subtracting from (say) "the South" (and its cardinal cousins North, East, and West) their specificity, their locality, their ecology, their proper resources? My extractivism becomes universal. And in universalizing subtraction and extractivism, am I not making it impossible to orient myself in thought, as Kant puts it? At least I am making it impossible to think, or represent, thought *just* cardinally.

Finally, the claim that concepts are circumstantial objects produced and thought positionally, or prepositionally, is awkward for a third reason. Say I further ignore my worries that the claim entails that the locations or directions to which concepts may attach—here or there, now and then, or "South," "North," "West," "East," or "Oriental" or "Western"—are not cardinal modifiers, as it may, also worrisomely, inmix the universalization of subtraction and extraction. I will try to argue against the notion that concepts are circumstantial, "Northern," or "Southern" (etc.), inmixed with posing and position. I will find that my counterargument, the argument from abstraction, hangs on a rhyme, or on a parallelism, between the fashioning or "production" of concepts; their use as objects *of* thought—we "think" concepts; and their use as the means *of* thought (we think about objects of thought in and with concepts). The strict rhyme or organic syncopation, or—best—the *synthesis* of production, objectivation, and instrumentalization of and in the "concept" constitute the integrity of the classic concept of concept. But this synthesis is obscure, obscurantist, as materialism insists, not the dialectical or mechanical sort but Marxian, and in its longest phase, Lucretian materialism. That thought is circumstantial, "positional," or "prepositional," is not a concept we are likely to have encountered *outside* (another prepositional marker!) of this tradition; not a familiar concept, and in fact the proposition that thought is circumstantial, image-inmixed, "positional," or "prepositional," may not be a concept at all: not "Northern" or "Southern," but also not Oriental, and so on.

## MELANCHOLIA AND THE INSTITUTIONAL INTERPRETANT

Focus now on other circumstances: on a shift that seems to occur roughly in the second half of the nineteenth century, both in Charles Sanders Peirce's United States and in the European metropolis, thick with the wealth of the colony and with the violence of industry: between 1861, when Baudelaire published the second edition of *Les fleurs du mal*; transiting through 1866, Peirce's Lowell lectures at Harvard; and 1917, when Freud published *Trauer und Melancholie*. That this period and this shift are my focus is dictated in part by *our* circumstances *today*: by the circumstance that the simultaneous crisis of credit capitalism and the reconfiguration of the nation-state around global oligarchic networks *produces* a history for itself, rooted in the first articulations of industrial capitalism with a recognizable, post-Renanian concept of "nation"; by the catastrophic emergence of electoral fascism in the United States, in Israel, in Brazil. This crisis-reconfiguration shapes the languages at hand to offer images of thought (it lies behind my qualms and worries about abstraction, universalization, extraction, and subtraction in the production of concepts). This crisis-reconfiguration instructs, it polices, it produces; it is the institutional frame that configures how thought is thought.

"Le cygne" is Baudelaire's *cogito*-in-verse: it bears on what *penser-à* means; on thought's objects; on the timing, the rhythm, of thought; on the circumstances in which "I" engage in whatever-it-is the poem calls "penser." Benjamin remarks in the *Passagen-Werk* (*Arcades Project*) that the poem "has the movement of a cradle rocking back and forth between modernity and antiquity" ("Baudelaire" 356).[9] (Not all cradles rock happily: think of the answer Whitman's poem gives, to the rhythm of the cradle's rocking, in the exactly contemporaneous "A Child's Reminiscence," better known as "Out of the Cradle Endlessly Rocking": The sea,

> Delaying not, hurrying not,
> Whisper'd me through the night, and very plainly before daybreak,
> Lisp'd to me the low and delicious word death;
> And again death, death, death, death" [165–69]).[10]

This is Baudelaire. Let's attend to the back-and-forth movement that his verse gives to its thought's allegorical object:

> Je vois ce malheureux, mythe étrange et fatal,
> Vers le ciel quelquefois, comme l'homme d'Ovide,
> Vers le ciel ironique et cruellement bleu,
> Sur son cou convulsif tendant sa tête avide
> Comme s'il adressait des reproches à Dieu!

Here is Richard Howard's excellent translation:

> I see it still, inevitable myth,
> like Daedalus dead-set against the sky—
> the sky quite blue and blank and unconcerned—
> that straining neck and that voracious beak,
> as if the swan were castigating God![11]

"I" tells the poem's reader that it sees a swan sign; the poem designates it. What "I" sees is first a strange, fateful myth (Howard: a "still, inevitable myth") and then—as though to disclose the register in which this direct identification of the swan sign with the myth occurs—"I" sees this "myth" at the uncertain juncture of a double simile ("like Daedalus . . . as if . . . castigating"). By this point, it is not obvious what it means for "I" to *see* an object, or if it is one, since what "I" sees is not only a bird but also the acoustic echo of a sign in another sign *(le signe, le cygne)*, as well as a myth. And since whatever it is that "I" sees can both be seen for what it is (whatever that is) and seen *comme*, like or as, something else, it is likewise hard to tell just what sort of thing the *aliquo* of our Scholastic dyad, this "I" that can see, or conceive, or imagine, in this way, will be—is the lyric "I" something of the nature of the swan, or of the sign, or of the myth, or of what can be seen under the aspect of a similitude? And who is it, or what—what third—is it that witnesses or constructs this strange scene? ("To the uncertainty of its economic position corresponds the uncertainty of its political function" [Benjamin, "Baudelaire" 10].) Gayatri Spivak first shows the constructive-destructive role of Andromache, "condition and effect of the fertilization of Baudelaire's memory," and then shows that granting her this position—after all, a muse's role—"perform[s] a blindness to the *other* woman in the text," the African "*negresse*" who, Spivak shows, serves as a screen—an abstraction—for the figure's "original" (Spivak's quotation marks), "a textual palimpsest of the 'original' of the agonist of 'A Une malabaraise,' one of two women Baudelaire encountered in Mauritius and the island of Reunion respectively."[12] However we tell the story that the poem tells, we will have moved uncertainly away from the sign, the swan, "*le cygne*"—rocking, perhaps.

Toward what and by what means? At some point before 1917, as the object in which "I" invested affection was lost to "me," the "shadow of the object fell upon the 'I'," and, Freud says, "the 'I' could henceforth be judged by a *special* agency *as though* it were an object [*wie ein Objekt*], the forsaken object" (*Mourning* 249; emphasis added).[13] Mourning, the social expression of grief and object loss, disclosed its kinship to melancholia, private and endless, shadowy and seemingly objectless. Up to this point, "New palaces, scaffolding, blocks of stone, / Old quarters, *everything*," every object, "becomes for me [an] allegory" (Baudelaire 91)—that is, every object that I, Baudelaire's *moi*, and Metropolitan Europe's "I," as well, every object I turned up as such or could regard with affection, becomes allegory: objects made or unmade, objects single and atomic as an event, or the vision of an escaped swan, or objects aggregated of other things and objects, like a palace or a scaffolding. Every thing, every object—stony and heavy and material things, or ephemeral and conceptual ones like a rhyme; a name we allude to; a concept like "economic class" or "nation," or whatever abstract object a word refers to, everything—becomes *an allegory*: every object I turned up when I walked in the city alone or alongside you; everything became grievable for me and for you.[14] Everything was at hand, where we could see and hold it in public, and where you and I could lose it. And any *this for that*, *aliquid pro aliquo*, becomes, "*devient*," something or everything for someone, *pour moi*. Whatever it is, a rule or an agency or a convention or a contingency, that governs this *becoming* derives neither from the side of the dyadic sign nor from the side of the institutional interpretant. Whatever it is emerges and lodges with us in the forum, in the *agora*: a part of the city, but foreign to it as well—extimate. But from this point forth—sometime after 1917, after the violent shadows of decolonization and world war fell on the European metropolitan class and on mere mourning, and "I" stood in the light of the unconscious—the "I" began to wind its way, solitary and self-forsaken, judged by a *special* institution, agency, or instance, *Instanz*, that it generates for the purpose and carries with it.

Just how the rocking fall into, then out of, mourning *allegory* happens; *to* what it happens; and *for* whom—these are obviously *literary* questions in the mid-nineteenth century. Less obviously, they are sociological ones; and much more obscurely, they are questions that pertain to political economy. Let's pause with Baudelaire to understand first the hinge that I am suggesting obtains between institution, *Instanz*; mourning; objects; and allegory. Say that sometime between 1857 and 1861, "allegory" was the public loss of objects publicly recognized as losable. What I understand by the becoming allegorical of every such object, by its *devenir allégorie*, will be tied to the sense of the terms that surround my definition: what was "loss," then, as France's colonial power reshaped itself under the Second Empire's particular dispensation? What did the "public" mean in the time of Baron Hausmann? And to whom? What were "objects" under the regime of mass production and of industrial capitalism? What was "everything," *tout*—since it is not just this or that discrete thing that has a historical way of being, but also the collective concepts into which we group them? And perhaps most complexly, what did it mean, when Baudelaire was writing "*le cygne*," for something "to become," *devenir*? I will want, for every object that I affect, that it should lose, in its becoming allegorical, a specific anchor to the circumstantial, historic object that it is; it will lose this or that scaffolding on a building on that street or this. Every object I affect to lose will gain, will have to gain—according to an economy we would again have to examine in the philological context in which the *Fleurs du mal* are published—generality and exemplarity. Objects become representative; they become, *ils deviennent*, stand-ins for classes of objects, bearers and revealers of the concept of which they are instances. For an object that I affect, a grievable object, to become allegory means that it has shed its here-and-nowness and assumed, for you and me and as a part of a general lexicon, the recognizable form of its conceptuality. The stone or swan I see becomes a sign we read as we pass, or a sign that I make to you in this poem I call "Le cygne," "The Sign," or "The Swan." The allegorical sign is marked and enriched by the loss of its *ob-ject*, a loss recollected in and repaid by the concept that the object, phoenix-like, becomes. We recognize that allegory is in mourning, and you and I emerge from mourning it.

Now let's return to Freud's *Mourning and Melancholia*. Sometime around 1917, ostensibly comparing what he calls the "normal affect of mourning" with the "pathological condition" of melancholia, Freud allowed himself to tell the little story we just heard. "The shadow of the object," he writes, "fell upon the 'I'"; it fell just there at a certain moment in the subject's normal experience of object loss, with pathologizing effects.[15] We are inclined to be indulgent with Freud's little story. The psychic system can only be referred to tropically; it is properly, that is, literally, unrepresentable. We can analogize it to writing pads; its dynamics seem to us like the work of agencies or *Instanzen*—it works like the prehensile hand—or we may compare the apparatus to a hydraulic system or a battleground, or call it an "apparatus"—but it is none of these. And when the characters in our stories *act*—when the hands, or writing pads, or agencies, or objects we refer to tropically *act* over time—in ways that are also unrepresentable and are also referred to tropically, then we are squarely in the world of narratively extended metaphors or, classically, of allegory. For no shadows are cast by the sorts of objects Freud has in mind when he says that "the shadow of the object fell upon the 'I.'" No sun lights the corners of the psychic apparatus; the "I" is not a surface on which shadows can fall. Even the verb tense in Freud's famous phrase is, in one of its senses, allegorical. It may well be that at a certain point in the progress of a case whatever it was that we call or called, allegorically, the shadow of the object, *fell* upon the analysand's "I": a discrete event in my description of the development of a pathology; an event followed by certain symptoms—by melancholia. But the melancholic cannot put *in the past* that *falling* of the object's shadow; she or he cannot experience it, the falling of the shadow of the object, *as* past. What Freud calls the "work of melancholy" does take place, first becoming (so often) a form of mania linked to "my" regression into primary narcissism, and then becoming a recollection of the melancholic condition—but this pastness-as-regression and futurity-as-recollection is not something the melancholic can look forward to. Freud's "little story," his sentence-long story, is not only an allegorical rendering of the unrepresentable *falling* into melancholia of normal grief at object loss, and of the emergence of psychic *special agencies* that will manage that fall; it is also a sentence-story about the representability or unrepresentability of mental objects in general, and about the *Instanzen*, the (minimally social, minimally political) institutions or professions like psychoanalysis or like poetry, that arise when we either seek to represent such mental objects, or seek to grieve the loss of well-known but mistaken ways of describing or of mourning them. "The shadow of the object fell upon the 'I', and the 'I' [can] henceforth be judged by a *special* agency as though it were an object, the forsaken object" (*Mourning* 249). A fantasy, an allegory of the genesis of psychoanalysis as the melancholic agency, the *Instanz*, is tasked to judge, *beurteilen*, the "I." A fantasy, an allegory of the special status of the languages of psychoanalysis, whose *objects*, the objects and dynamics of the psychic *apparatus*, are always only spoken of *as though*, *wie*, they were forsaken objects, lost objects—that is, doubly removed, let go of, or forsaken [*verlassen*] and spoken of *as if* they were forsaken.

We are social, even political, animals, to the extent that we share a disposition toward objects: we take them to be, indeed we fashion them as things we can possess and openly lose, mourn, grieve for. For a thing to be a thing, another must know that I possess this thing or that it can be possessed, or grasped, or fastened on to; another recognizes that I can lose it, or that I can be dispossessed of it. Grieving and mourning concern the public loss of objects publicly recognized as losable: I am not mourning if you don't know I am, or if you couldn't know that I am, or if what I have lost is not the sort of thing one can lose. It is because we both can lose this object, this ob-ject cast before us as losable, as grievable, that we recognize in one another a likeness, a common quality, a kinship, even a form of fraternity: we *fall* under the same concept. The mother, of course, is our first object; part of what we express, violently, in wishing her death, is the desire that she *be* losable, that she *may* be at our disposal in the way that other objects are, as such, like bobbins or tops we can fling off, away, *Fort*, and recover as we will. And the father is, again of course, the sign we erect in place of our desire for the mother's death. It, too, like all objects, becomes allegorical—becomes allegory—for us to lose. The band of brothers that loses and sacrifices the common father, sadistically and sacramentally sharing his body or tokens of his body, falls together in consequence. This band of brothers is, in allegory, theologico-political society: it is society built upon an Oedipalized fashioning of the object, upon an object we understand to be allegorically sacrificeable. We are all children of the object.

So far, so good. You will have heard echoes so far of other works by Freud and works of Jean-Luc Nancy. But when Freud discloses melancholia's kinship to mourning, we *lose*, publicly, that common disposition toward, and filial relation to, the object. We lose our likeness in respect to the object—an object we imagined as grievable, as what is cast out for anyone to seize or lose. We appear to *gain*, correspondingly, two *private* qualities. The first is a shadowy objectality: the "I," in the shadow of the ungrievable object, can now be lost, as well, to itself. As an ungrievable thing, as something potentially lost in the shadow of its objectality, the "I" is already wounded, its narcissistic integrity already unmade. It's hard to count this *as* a gain, but without this unmaking of our primary narcissism, there would *be* no objects for "I" and thus no world. The second is that "I" gain a *special* agency or instance for judging "myself," for judging my "I" objectively (*beurteilen*): "I" gain a faculty, an institution, an *Instanz*, capable of seeing "I" *as if* it were cast out into the world of grievable ob-jects—*as if* it both were a member of the class of objects and entertained no likeness at all with every other object.

But our loss goes deeper still. When I, or the "I," fall under the shadow of the object, or when the object's shadow falls upon me, then "I" may be *losable* to myself—but this condition will not be the source of "my" identification with you. You may well suffer from melancholia, as well; I may look across the Parisian street and read in your face a sign of misery that mirrors mine; you may become for me an allegory of object loss, as I become it for you. But I will not derive, from this seeming likeness to you, kinship, the sense of association that structures public mourning, the public face of allegory. Melancholia is not just radically individualizing; it marks the outside of collective representation, the outside of the representation of the collective as an object we share.

Yes, something happened in the sixty-year period between the composition of *Les fleurs du mal* and the publication of *Mourning and Melancholia*. Whatever it is bears on the political status of the mode of *allegory*: it bears on its objects, on allegory's disciplining relation to its objects, and on how the public, collective aspect of representation comes into crisis. Over these years, allegory's object has *become*, for me, ungrievable. Whatever its object, it is I, the "I" inasmuch as it or I can be lost as well as, or as easily as, any ob-ject that I affect; it is this "I" that I, the melancholic, lose after I, too, come onto the scene *as* an object. Or rather, it is when and because I come onto the scene doubly that I cannot grieve for myself as I would, say, for my dead mother, or for the father I have killed, or for the passing of the republic.

When we pass from mourning to melancholia—when we lose mourning's public object and come instead under its mere shadow—we fall into a time when political identities and institutions must be reconceived under the shadow of the loss of the loss of the object. The logic of melancholia cannot be squared with classically understood social practices, and perhaps it cannot be squared with any form of communitarian imaginary.

The logic of melancholia: sometime around 1917, I came before myself in my *likeness to* another object and thus as a member of the *class* of objects that I am *also* instituting, by means of a disposition, or a *specific agency*, or an instance, *Instanz*. I institute this class of objects by separating them apart or cutting them apart originarily from other ob-jects: *be-ur-teilen*. I am, at this moment, a member of the class of objects that I can lose, as well as the dynamic principle of similarity that constitutes them as that class, distinct, cut apart from other objects. I am a member of that class; I am ob-jected from it as its principle.

It is this double logical status—as member of *and* principle regarding or principle of relation, or principle of axiomatization of—that I cannot share with you.

I cannot be *like* you in this, alike though you and I may be in being members of the class of grievable objects. And this is the *time* of the melancholic. It is not time in any recognizable, phenomenological sense—not time we can experience, not the time of grieving or mourning, which will always fall to our past or characterize a future we dread—but the condition of belonging to what you are at the same time constituting as a class.

The full story, which is complicated, long, and thrilling to tell, has a number of crossing (jostling, contradicting, rhyming) plotlines. You will have heard me trying to capture some of them more less explicitly. Echoes of others may have sounded as well. Each of these stories will have to be told in two times and according to two narrative procedures: in the time of mourning, in the time of allegory as mourning, and the logico-structural *time* of melancholia.

One of the stories thus doubly told clusters about the battles regarding the formalization of the notion of a class or of a set in philosophical logic, in the period from the last quarter of the nineteenth century to the publication of Wittgenstein's *Tractatus*. Here, for instance, the equivalence I have been drawing between the notion of the "individual" and that of the "object" would be fundamental. Here we will be concerned with the possible reality or nonreality of so-called abstract or conceptual objects. The main figures in our story are Mill—whose *System of Logic* is a reference point for both Freud and Marx—Cantor, Frege, Meinong, Russell, and Zermelo.

A second plot *also* concerns classes and individuals, but in quite a different sense: it regards Marx's articulation of historicism with structure; it turns on the absorption of Marx's critique of the objectality of objects, and on the conception of *ideology* that flows from it. After Marx's critique of Feuerbach, objects cannot be lost or mourned, and commodities cannot be cast off—they cannot be ob-jects alone, because they are always part of us and are always casting their objectness upon us. The main figures in our story, on this side, are Mill, Marx, Lukács, and Althusser.

A third plotline concerns the conceptualization of institution under the figure of *administration*, even *bureaucracy*. The allegorical form—that is, the political instance—of melancholia is modern bureaucratic administration. Here the main figure of our story is Weber.

There will be more such stories: they will have different intensities; they will have discontinuous and uneven relations to their two narrative frames. We might refer to the tangle of intensities that unravels from Baudelaire's word *devenir* as the historical *dynamics* of the object of allegory.

## THE AFFECT OF EXTRACTION

For the first time in my life I neglected a human being for a thing.[16]

But how do we live this tangle of intensities? I think the double status that I've described is what we also call our "exemplarity": to be at once case *and* norm, members of *and* principles regarding or principles of relation, or principles of axiomatization of. The political consequences of instituting the loss of the loss of the object become, *deviennent* (to adapt to this level of the argument the word in "Le cygne," and to bring along with it the analytic of contingent occurring I outlined), the crisis of the lack of a communitarian imaginary. But what are they for us, day to day?

Here, for example, is a story. I asked earlier whether a project that stands on—is instituted upon—specific fantasies and recollections can be generalized—how, to what degree. This story, like the story of my father's family sometime in 1938 or so, comes to me circumstantially, unnecessarily, involuntarily. It has to do with a direction I am taking; with what and how I saw and felt, and with how I now regard what I once saw; and with the limits of thought. (Maybe just *my* thought.) "Limits" here is a modal notion: it means that my story has to do with what may or may not be thought ("may," conveying what is given as possible/impossible for thought); with what may or may not be thought (now contingent "may"—conveying what is not given *yet* as possible or impossible, but could be either); with what necessarily is or is not thought (conveying *necessity*); and, inhabiting all these limits, my story will also have to do with the sorts of power, institutions, expectations, and so on that *enforce* these limits, and tell us, now and then, what *may* or *may not* be thought. My story begins—though I don't know it then, when I'm experiencing what I will tell you now—with the *institutional* shaping of my circumstances.

This is my story. I'm traveling south. The slow night train from Madrid to Algeciras takes a turn at the end of its run, at sunrise, in Andalucía. The couchettes are on the train's left, east-facing side. I remember mountains out those windows. An aisle runs the length of the coaches on the western side, and we gather at the windows when the track curves to look across the straits. It's been an interrupted night, as train nights are: stations lumbered by, bells clanged, the rails clacked. The Mediterranean is still hidden: all we see, suddenly, is the African mountain range rising beyond the hills of olive groves on this, the European, the Spanish side. We see the Rif—every time, a wash of sensations lighting the landscape. What are they? Did you share them? Did you feel something sufficiently kin, or just determinately different enough, to refer to, standing by me at the noisy, moving window then or today? Nothing I can *think* explains what we see or what we feel when we're returning to Tangier—not because I don't remember something, and not because the hills, the hidden Strait of Gibraltar, and the Rif beyond haven't been thought for us before, many times: rather because I do and they have, and what I feel has been thought for us settles on the landscape and shows it otherwise, allegorical.

(But is "settling" the right verb? Perhaps if I intend "settling" as appropriation, claiming, with a view to extraction: as when we speak of "settler colonialism." But predicated of what subject—of *everything* I see, *tout*? As to the first, to what *act* this "settling" of emotion, value, and sense on what I see corresponds: Baudelaire's famous line—*tout pour moi devient allégorie*—which I just glanced at, becomes in Howard's English "but in sadness like mine / Nothing stirs. New buildings, old / Neighborhoods turn to allegory." Yes, Howard's "turns to" subtly catches Baudelaire's rather submerged double senses—*devenir* as mere headless becoming, *and* as the intentional assuming of an identity—but it also turns the verse from the first toward the second. The line's first Castilian translation, Marquina's in 1905, reads "*todo para mí vuélvese alegoría*"; Santayana's more recent one is "*para mí, todo se torna alegoría.*" Castilian's reflexive construction captures and twists the strange, displaced agency of the verb *devenir*, settling it closer to the active, subjective sense that French subtracts: we say, in Castilian, "*me vuelvo hacia la costa, hacia las montañas,*" and we mean that we choose to turn and face the coast and the mountains. Today my thoughts turn somewhere else: inasmuch as this and that and the other thing I see—the train window, olive groves, the Rif—conform *à tout*, they are "for me." I wonder about the *for-meness* of what I saw, and now see myself seeing then: for at the same time—or maybe better, correlatively—this "I" possessed of the conformed *tout* is just that, the collection of its, my, circumstance.)

What did I feel, what do I see, how do I think about the object that lies before me? Franco made his way into Spain across this stretch of sea, and at school in Madrid we have learned the story of King Rodrigo, the faithful-faithless Count Don Julián, and his daughter, *la Cava*: a grand tale of the political consequences of an act of royal betrayal and rape, leading the insulted, outraged father to conspire with the invaders, open the doors of the citadel, fling wide the Mediterranean passage from the Kingdom of Fez to Hispania. The Muslim invasion of the Iberian Peninsula in 711; eight hundred years of the great Umayyad caliphate—all laid at the feet of one story. One of the *Romances* we learn goes:

Cumplió el rey su voluntad _ más por fuerça que por grado.
La malvada de la Cava _ a su padre lo ha contado,
que es el conde don Julián; _ el conde muy agraviado,
de vender a toda España _ con moros se ha concertado.

> The King had his way, more by force than by her will. Wicked Cava has told her father, Count Don Julian. The Count, greatly offended, has arranged with the Moors to sell all of Spain.

All this and more, the trace of other times and other stories, of other summers and others' wishes, pleasures, and worries, fringe the mountains for us, beyond the sea. I am eight, or maybe I am ten. Because I have been taught my circumstances by institutional interpretants, by institutions I cannot enumerate (my family, the state, my school: what else?), the South—South of Spain, South of Europe—secretly produces in me, but not where I can properly *think* it or such as I can think properly, a synthetic image.

Today, as I write these words, other stories intrude. Jean Genet travels from the Andalusian seaside village of San Fernando to Cádiz, down the coast from Algeciras. This is what he sees. It is evening:

> San Fernando is on the sea. I decided to get to Cadiz, which is built right on the water, though connected to the mainland by a very long jetty. It was evening when I started out. Before me were the high salt pyramids of the San Fernando marshes, and farther off, in the sea, silhouetted by the setting sun, a city of domes and minarets. At the outermost point of Western soil, I suddenly had before me the synthesis of the Orient. For the first time in my life I neglected a human being for a thing. . . . I thought about Tangiers, whose proximity fascinated me, as did the glamor of the city, that haunt, rather, of traitors.[17]

The *prestige* of the city; the "synthesis of the Orient." ("Glamor" is quite off: it connotes transitoriness, ephemerality, meretriciousness, in a way that "prestige" does not.) "Prestige" speaks of social value; it is perhaps what Ortega's self-involved hero seeks, "embarked upon the conquest of distant schematic cities," intent and blind to his circumstance.

In what does it consist, this *synthesis of the Orient* produced, in Genet's narrator and in me, differently, "at the outermost point of Western soil"? What did, what does, the sight of the Rif across the veiled Strait offer me, him? I would like to say, first off, three things; I'm trying to think through their relation. I am offered (but is this the right verb?) a sense, a throng of emotion; I am offered *a concept*; and I am offered the frame, the circumstance, of their appearing—involuntary, accidental; foreseeable (I have been on this train before); eloquent and, as Ortega says, "mute." Both *what* I see from the train and what I remember now, and *that* I see and *that* I remember, are violently unsettling. Genet—one of my proxies, along with Baudelaire, Spivak, and others I don't recognize—gazes across the Strait. The ghost of sacrificial violence *suddenly* appears: I recognize in and as a synthesis the neglect of a "living being," of *un être*, for things, *choses*. Europe is Africanized (there are now pyramids of salt in San Fernando, on the Spanish side of the Straits); Tangier is Orientalized: "a city of domes and minarets," *une ville de coupoles et de minarets*. In both scenes *prestige* and *neglect* hold hands, life and death, value and its lack, sensefulness and senselessness, the port of return and the first port of exile: the pyramids, vast monuments, vast tombs, records of wealth, of enslaved labor, of death; Tangier become a city "of domes and minarets," to which all else that a city might be or contain (a city, that city, is also a crowd of things and beings, *êtres* and *choses*) is reduced, abstracted. (Right now I am seeing another scene and another city as well. I see it suddenly, involuntarily, accidentally. Another school, later in my life, offers it me—and offers me its context, its circumstance: it is, why not, the primal scene of the European Romantic imaginary, the lone male poet gazing, with wonder and surmise, out at a newfound, old object, off a peak in Darien, in the Alps, over Caspar David Friedrich's shoulder, or from a city bridge. For whether I want to or not, I see, or I remember, Wordsworth's traveler, pausing at dawn on Westminster Bridge on September 3, 1802, gazing at the City. The eponymous city; a City within the metropolitan city, London. "Silent, bare / Ships, towers, domes, theatres, and temples lie / Open unto the fields, and to the sky." "Open" means: both "open" to gather in all that nature, fields and sky, can offer, generous, colonial, embracing; and "open," a city in ruins, Piranesian, roofless, a record of past, lost, grandeur. Not just a city, or a City, even an Eternal City such as Piranesi perhaps imagined, but all that each image stands for, all that is inmixed with "Ships, towers, domes, theatres, and temples": the concepts of trade, colony, extraction, religion, art, and so on. What Wordsworth's traveler sees is the open, defective *synthesis* of ruin and generosity, of "ship" with "trade," "tower" with "glamor" or "prestige," "theatre" with "art," "temple" with "religion," and of each of these with the others, their contours simultaneously hard and well-defined, and inmixed.)

Now, I have said that these "traces"—including the trace of Baudelaire and Genet's stories, which I borrow, which my eight- or ten-year-old self borrows, from this year, here and now, as I write to you; of Wordsworth's apocalypse—that these traces of allegorical stories "settle" on the landscape; they "fringe" it. "*Tout pour moi* devient *allégorie*," we heard Baudelaire say. Wordsworth uses the verb "to steep." I say I "light" the Straits with the figure of return, with the aura of return. (I translate "aura" from Benjamin's lexicon into my own.) But these are the wrong verbs and the scheme, consisting of a landscape or a cityscape onto which other symbolic forms supervene after and independently of them, or which just *becomes* other, is off as well. Genet is in one sense right, and now the arrow of extraction, the unsettling arrow of settlement, has switched direction: Tangier, *synthetic*, takes every thing from me. Every story installed on that landscape reminds me, now, as I look out the window of the train in Andalucía or in Chicago today, or in Los Angeles, or in Paris where I am writing these words, also of theft, treachery, inequality, violence, rape, extraction, exile; as does every story that things and the landscape install, for me and for others. Every thing lies *open* and everything *is opened*, ruined as well as wholly welcoming. This is in part because the circumstances that steeped, settled and still settle, instituted and still institute, those stories on the thing, the object, the land, the city, and on my experience; because the institutional interpretants that shape phenomenologies to allegorical forms and circumstances, things, and land to both, now seem to me violently founded in and irreducibly inmixed with inequality. My progressive school teaches me don Julián's legend (in the halls of that school I often see doña Ángeles, who runs it with doña Jimena: Ángeles Gasset de las Morenas, José Ortega y Gasset's first cousin, and Jimena Menéndez Pidal, the daughter of the liberal philologist Ramón Menéndez-Pidal); the fascist state; the historiography of exile and diaspora; the economic base of my family's summer travel; the global university-conceptual market in which, today, we trade these words; even the cardinal orientation of the train's rails, north to south. I remember that Moroccan laborers, in economic exile in Belgium, France, and Germany, take that train back to Tangier as well, every summer. Institutions, I think, don't only make their things, their subjects, and their objects; they don't only make me and my circumstances: institutional interpretants install upon things, subjects, and objects other senses than those that others give them. I saw with schooled eyes then, and today I see with other senses, schooled otherwise. Institutions and institutional interpretants, I think, are synthetic machines, allegorical machines; so, reciprocally, are the things that allegory takes from us, so are objects, so is the land, if such things exist any more than—say—a palisade of stones surrounding a village.

I am eight or ten; I travel north to south on the rails of petit-bourgeois tourist desire. Every *thing* I see, every object, everything I recall I light up with the synthetic figure of exile and return. (Return—to my grandparents' flat! But also: to the city of my father's exile! To the first port the Sephardim touched, perhaps, leaving Spain on being expelled, centuries ago!) I give the synthetic figure, today and for me, the aura and the smack of value, the allure, the prestige, of the example.

But now look over from the other side, across where the Mediterranean and the Atlantic meet. Still other stories, installed by other institutions, shape the mountains that my train travels through, the Strait I don't yet see, my eyes at the window. (And who am I to ask that you stand just there, on the other shore, and borrow or extract *local* eyes? Isn't this just what generations of Northern observers, tourists, writers have done—Bowles, sheltering his theft of Mohammed Choukri's words behind the mantle of translation; Gide; Sarduy?)

Here are two views.

It is 1970, about when I am traveling south from Madrid to Algeciras and Tangier. Juan Goytisolo places, as an epigraph to his novel *Reivindicación del conde don Julián*, the line from Genet's *Journal du voleur* I cited earlier: "*Je songeais à Tanger dont la proximité me fascinait et le prestige de cette ville, plutôt repaire de traitres*" (I thought about Tangier, whose proximity fascinated me, as did the glamor of the city, that haunt, rather, of traitors). Gazing across the Strait, South to North, Goytisolo and his narrator have in mind, among other things and beyond the "vindication" of the ostensibly treacherous Count don Julián, to think through just what the allegorical *synthesis* of phenomenological frame and sacrificed *chose*, thing, object, or land consists in. Not just think it through, but, having produced its concept, to *reject* it. "*Tierra ingrata*," Goytisolo's novel begins,

> harsh homeland, the falsest, most miserable imaginable, I shall never return to you: with eyes still closed, it is there before you, enveloped in the blurry ubiquity of sleep and thus invisible, but nonetheless cleverly and subtly suggested, foreshortened and far in the distance: with even the tiniest details recognizable, outlined, as you yourself admit, with such scrupulous accuracy as to border on the maniacal: one day, another, and yet another: ever the same: a predictable sharpness of contour, a mere cardboard model, in reduced scale, of a familiar landscape.[18]

The emergent "familiar landscape" of Spain seen from the South, across the Strait, has, Lane's translation reads, "a predictable sharpness of contour, a mere cardboard model, in reduced scale, of a familiar landscape." Goytisolo's Castilian Spanish makes a different point. Lane writes "a predictable sharpness of contour." Goytisolo's "*la nitidez de los contornos presentida*" offers, rather, "*presentida*": "foreseen," stress on the subjective temporal experience of the narrator rather than on the objective quality of the emerging, nebulous "cardboard model." She writes: "outlined, as you yourself admit, with such scrupulous accuracy as to border on the maniacal." Goytisolo: "*dibujados ante ti, lo admites, con escrupulosidad casi maniaca*," a sentence in which the interjective "*lo admites*," "you admit," could also be taken to antecede "*con escrupulosidad casi maniaca*," an amphiboly that makes the narrator's *admission* the subject that "*escrupulosidad*" modifies. And most startlingly, Lane writes: "with eyes still closed, it is there before you," it, the coast of Spain seen from Africa, from Tangier. But "it is there" is not there in Goytisolo; his phrase makes no existential claims about its object, about what the narrator "sees" with eyes still closed, other than to offer a list of aspects and modifiers of some object whose "it *is*," either the existential *ser* or the circumstantial, positional *estar*, is sacrificed, withdrawn, subtracted. The object, the northern thing, is perhaps "*presentido*," intuited or foreseen or taken for granted, but its existence is never affirmed. Translation here—that great South-to-North machine, that economic machine that brings the language of the South into the market of the North, that machine that moves the novel, and us, from Castilian into English—translation works to make the edges of Goytisolo's prose clearer, its senses starker, its objects and subjects less nebulous, less emergent, less *foreseen* and more seen; emplaced. Lane's English opens allegorical eyes that Goytisolo's prose keeps closed; where Goytisolo subtracts, she adds. Goytisolo's prose occludes and obscures the "ungrateful" North (not "harsh": Spain is withholding what, out of gratitude, it should offer; and Goytisolo's narrator holds back, withdraws—as if in response, as if taking revenge, as if vindicating himself—the being of the object that his eyes merely "foresee"). Lane's English offers Spanish, and Spain, back its "it's there." She translates melancholia into object loss, into mourning.

Now it's 2006. This is what Tahar ben Jelloun's character Azel sees, looking North across the straits. Ben Jelloun's novel, *Partir*, has just been published; it is winter in the novel, dawn, and the sea is already filled with bodies.

> In Tangier, in the winter, the Café Hafa becomes an observatory for dreams and their aftermath. . . . Leaning back against the wall, customers sit on mats and stare at the horizon as if seeking to read their fate. They look at the sea, at the clouds that blend into the mountains, and they wait for the twinkling lights of Spain to appear. They watch them without seeing them, and sometimes, even when the lights are lost in fog and bad weather, they see them anyway. . . . As if in an absurd and persistent dream, Azel sees his naked body among other naked bodies swollen by seawater, his face distorted by salt and longing, his skin burnt by the sun, split open across the chest as if there had been fighting before the boat went down. Azel sees his body more and more clearly, in a blue and white fishing boat heading ever so slowly to the centre of the sea, for Azel has decided that this sea has a centre and that this centre is a green circle, a cemetery

> where the current catches hold of corpses, taking them to the bottom to lay them out on a bank of seaweed. He knows that there, in this specific circle, a fluid boundary exists, a kind of separation between the sea and the ocean, the calm, smooth waters of the Mediterranean and the fierce surge of the Atlantic. He holds his nose, because staring so hard at these images has filled his nostrils with the odour of death.[19]

Everything distinguishes what I see, waking on the train and gazing South sometime around 1970, from what Ben Jelloun's Azez sees; the dissymmetry seems unbearable, obscene. Ben Jelloun's character looks south to north, to the North. His way is barred by seas that, obscured for now, just promise me passage, in 1970. To seek to cross to economic opportunity means for Azez a night journey, illegality, exposure. It is not return to *al-Andalus* that he contemplates, nor the treacherous invitation offered by don Julián, but the luck of the *patera*—barely boats, rafts: unstable, deadly in the roiled waters of the Strait. (The rescue organizations Andalucía Acoge and Fundación por Causa reported in 2018 at least seven thousand dead in the Strait of Gibraltar between 1988 and 2018). I look south sometime in 1970, and today, fifty years on, I remember my story from where I sit, not far from the border separating the United States from Mexico; Ben Jelloun's Azez looks north at the beginning of this century. "As if in an absurd and persistent dream" whatever I recall and whatever I think today runs through Azez's body, "split open across the chest," "open" again!, through the window views of the distant Rif one morning, through the Sonoran Desert today.

I am enrolling Genet, and Goytisolo's narrator, and ben Jelloun's character Azez in my project; they are my examples, examples for me of what I take myself to be; their view, their eyes, are mine to take and take, as if what I and they see were just what I remember, Tangier, my Tangier; as if I found it and them laid out on a bank of seaweed for me to take. And, but: Goytisolo's narrator and Azez (Azez's time, his value, his example, his South) dispossess me at the same time, in the same stroke. I, in 1970 and today, am *opened*, like Wordsworth's City: Goytisolo's narrator and Azez split open every object, every feeling, want, longing that I recall and everything I see. I'm speaking allegorically. I would like to call this "opening," this "running through," which are metaphors for principial, wild mediation that I am drawing from the cartographic imagery that my recollections favor just now, the political secret of the limit of my reason. For I cannot *reasonably, critically*, split open the syntheses wrought in and by the stories and the examples I am using: not from lack of analytic precision, but as a result of it.

The allegorical object that I draw from my thought-image, and which is its subject as well—"I"; *la Cava*; don Julian (treacherous but also vindicated); Genet; and/or Azez—expresses one way that I think. The subject-object is an allegorical thought-image but also an image *of* thought inasmuch as thought is allegorical, inasmuch as thinking settles sense and emotion on circumstance and becomes allegory. "I," *la Cava*, don Julian, Genet, and/or Azez, are tendentially both synthetic *and* critical, divisive, analytic: like Hercules, we *want* to straddle continents, and seek institution wherever our eye can reach, wherever the extractive reach of our glance touches.

But the object that we are—the concept of our thought—is perilously *open*. For Hercules is said to have stood astride the Strait with one foot in Europe and the other in Africa. (The impersonal phrase "is said" just means: Hercules is fashioned so, now and then, for a class of subjects that includes me, by an institutional interpretant or interpretants.) He is said to have set one pillar on firm ground on each side of the Strait, he is said to have broken land to create a passage from the Mediterranean to the Atlantic, and he is said just to have broadened it.

But the *grottes d'Hercule* sit across the Atlantic from Tarifa, Spain—caves, just where mountains, *pillars*, are also imagined. On one hand—on one shore—thought, installed on stone, well founded on the rock of the classic, rhyming concept; on the other, thought mined by caves, imaginary, imaged. Now I remember: the personal escutcheon of Charles I bears Hercules's old columns. The ambivalent, synthetic figure sat on the Hapsburg seal, where its gloss reads *Plus ultra*—rather than *Nec plus ultra* as it had for centuries—meaning that *only* the Spanish crown now could, would, venture in search of settlement beyond the Pillars and across that other passage, that other marine cemetery, the Atlantic.[20] Barring passage, the Pillars also extend the reach of *Mare nostrum*, the great Roman, Latin, Christian inland sea: they are the allegorical figure, the emblem, of limit and of conquest, of enclosure and expansion. I remember that Franco's escutcheon bears Hercules's columns, to link the dictator more closely to the imperial project.

This is how Juan de Horozco's *Emblemas morales* of 1589 describes the *highest emblem*, "*la máxima empresa*," of the emperor. Horozco is explaining why Charles V and I's emblem figures Hercules's pillars upon the waves, and not firm on stone or land, on African or Spanish soil:

> When Emperor Charles the Fifth, of glorious memory, extended the boundaries of Spain's dominions, he also extended those of the world, for it was commonly believed in antiquity that earth ended at the Spanish coast, at the cape called for that reason

*Figure 4.* Leoni Leone, *The Pillars of Hercules* (obverse image on coin), c. 1553/1555. National Gallery of Art, Washington, DC.

> Cape Finis Terrae, and that when Hercules reached Cádiz he planted two columns, as if to signal the very end of measured land, and to indicate that from that point on there was nothing more. But upon the discovery of another world, by means of the navigation that began [in Cádiz], it was right that these boundary markers [*términos*, also "terms" or "words"] be moved as well, and so [Charles V] changed the columns, and surrounded them with water and added the lemma, PLUS ULTRA. And considering the soul of so great a Prince, he meant thereby not only that there was more to the world, and that the earth did not end where it had been thought.[21]

Herculean, the inmixing figure of thought that my memories cast up on the shoulders of the institutions that fashion them offers exile and return, return and exile, in the same stroke. It *wants* to make the map of sense and value continuous and perspicuous, to cross the Strait in both directions and at all times, to settle, install or institute pillars, columns; to translate, to spread the word, *logos*;

to evangelize. It maps economic flow; it reminds me of the extractive circuits that brought silver eastward from America across the Atlantic, enslaved peoples west, and labor northward from Morocco across the Strait. But my figure of thought *also wants* to undermine the map of sense and value, to set the foundation of thought neither in the stone of experience nor in the pure intuition of thought, but adrift on a deadly watery bed; to divide Africa from Europe (and both from the Americas: the middle passage). Not to disclose to the other the *logos* I worship or seek to understand, but to deny the other access to its value, to its sense: to keep it secret, as the Pythagorean philosopher does the revelation that ratio discloses the limits of *logos*.

I want to found and to unfound, to free and to enclose: I want to *mourn* the object that Goytisolo's narrator calls "*una simple maqueta de cartón, a escala reducida, de un paisaje familiar*," "the mere cardboard model, in reduced scale, of a familiar landscape." At the same time, my circumstances nebulously *limit* what I want and what I think: they *modalize* desire and thought, in that they subtract every living being, every familiar *thing*, every circumstance, and every *cardinality* from the fields of thought's *image*; of its concept; from its rhythm, from its map of positions, from the purview of what I, and "I," can synthetically assume. What Azez calls "the centre of the sea . . . a green circle, a cemetery where the current catches hold of corpses" unsettles my mourning the loss of the object, and becomes—suddenly—melancholia, the melancholia of unsettlement.

Recall the story this chapter has told. I have offered one concept of thought that inmixes allegory's relation to the object with the production of publicly recognizable likeness among *individual* members of a set, which also means: with the production of a commonly graspable, hence also losable and grievable, object: the classic definition of the concept. This concept of thought I have called "mourning allegory." But I have suggested that there is another figure of thought, and another politics, that become available once the disposition to the object becomes, in Freud's terms, melancholic: ungraspable and ungrievable. This figure of thought, and of politics, establishes, enacts, and denies the principle that *individuals* have objective likenesses that make them susceptible of class representations. This concept of thought I have called "melancholic allegory": melancholia, Freud tells us, is a pathological version of grievable object loss, always trembling at the edge of experience, a permanent possibility of regression. I have told the story historically, as if the second, a melancholic concept of thought, a melancholic allegory and a melancholy politics, followed historically upon the first—as Freud follows upon Baudelaire, the age of global capital upon the age of the Renanian nation-state, the catastrophe upon the republic. This impression is incorrect, both as regards Freud's understanding of the couple "mourning" and "melancholia" *and* as regards my reconstruction of the two terms as principles of thought and political representation, one based in the Oedipal concept and one based in the logically undecidable structure of belonging *to* and setting the principle *for* a class or a concept in which objects are grouped. My last figure of thought, the synthetic image of the Herculean colossus, inmixes the two. Like Freud, I call the Herculean figure I am describing a "pathology." The norm of grievable object loss and the pathology of melancholic allegory coexist in an endless and nondialectical struggle (a rocking motion: Baudelaire with Whitman). Both are *to be affirmed*. This allegory of thought translates the loss of the object into the defective principle *on* which, *because* of our structural disanalogy, *because* of the conflict between institution and principle at the heart of the catastrophe of representative democracy *today*, you and I stand forth as distinctly grievable-ungrievable objects, and on this defective concept may found ephemeral, transparent, and formal administrative modes, agencies, instances or *Instanzen* of association—in short, weak republican institutions.

O leave me one: this little one yet save:
Of many but this only one the least of all I crave.

Ovid

For, alone of gods, Death loves not gifts; no, not by sacrifice, nor by libation, canst thou aught avail with him; he hath no altar nor hath he hymn of praise; from him, alone of gods, Persuasion stands aloof.

Aeschylus (attr.)

# *LACRIMAE RERUM*, OR, THE INSTITUTION OF GRIEF

I have before me Roberto Esposito's *Istituzione* (2021), an expansion of his important 2020 monograph *Pensiero istituente: Tre paradigmi di ontologia politica* (in English, *Instituting Thought: Three Paradigms of Political Ontology*).[1] Esposito enjoins his reader to abandon the "reactionary," "coercive interpretation" of institutions that conceives them as "simultaneously the system of rules governing a community, and the power that constrains [members of the community] to respect them"—"beginning with the State, the strongest and most consolidated [institution]."[2]

An institution is what we, a community, decide (a "system of rules") and then install and constrain ourselves to "respect." It has the solidity of a stone or a statue on display. Proof against time's passing, our inaugural decision persists. (Maybe, as on Searle's telling, having passed from stone to symbol.) *Stare decisis*, says the legal principle: a decision institutes, and should insist, remain, govern, found. That principle itself is not unshakable; doubts can arise regarding what Colin Starger calls the "doctrinal approach" to precedent, the "precedent about precedent" at work in the "dialectic of *Stare Decisis* doctrine."[3] For "What we can decide," runs the U.S. Supreme Court's ruling in *Kimble v. Marvel Entertainment*, "we can undecide. But *stare decisis* teaches that we should exercise that authority sparingly. Cf. S. Lee and S. Ditko, Amazing Fantasy No. 15: 'Spider-Man,' p. 13 (1962) ('In this world, with great power there must also come—great responsibility'). Finding many reasons for staying the *stare decisis* course and no 'special justification' for departing from it, we decline Kimble's invitation to overrule *Brulotte*."[4] An *undecision* is just another decision—sanctioned by the same institution, evidence of its double power (evidence, with Esposito, that the institution is "simultaneously the system of rules governing a community, and the power that constrains [members of the community] to respect them"), restrained and conditioned by the "great responsibility" that accompanies that power.

Accompanies it *how*, though? The dissenting opinion in *Dobbs v. Jackson Women's Health Organization* (the June 2022 decision overturning the right to abortion in the United States) places the "responsibility" for restraining the court's power to undecide—and by extension to *decide*—in the "obligation" to "faithfully and impartially apply the law" rather than in the "rule" of the "proclivities of individuals." Here is the conclusion of the dissent in *Dobbs*:

> The Court reverses course today for one reason and one reason only: because the composition of this Court has changed. *Stare decisis*, this Court has often said, "contributes to the actual and perceived integrity of the judicial process" by ensuring that decisions are "founded in the law rather than in the proclivities of individuals." Payne v. Tennessee, 501 U.S. 808, 827 (1991); Vasquez v. Hillery, 474 U.S. 254, 265 (1986). Today, the proclivities of individuals rule. The Court departs from its obligation to faithfully and impartially apply the law. We dissent.

"Impartiality" against "proclivity"; the "obligation" to ensure that "decisions are 'founded in the law'" against "the rule" of "the proclivities of individuals." Because individuals change—justices come and go—and because proclivities are inclinations, matters it seems of taste almost, the solid obligation of "impartiality" must be asserted. It alone resists the whims of taste and proclivity; it alone *takes* no part, because "the law" *has* no "part": it is *one*, and that quality attaches to the tradition of decisions made in the law's name and on its basis. It, too, is *one*, and the court's institutional standing stands on letting that *one* tradition of decisions remain one, fundamental, definitive. *Obligations* go with *rights* as "great responsibility" goes with "great power" in the universe of Marvel comics and of the ideology of the "precedent of precedent" that governed the United States Supreme Court's decisions up to *Dobbs*.

Yes, as classically imagined, institutions are phenomenological frames and formats (*Stiftungen*) that provide repeatability, recognition; schemes of inclusion and exclusion; protection; identities and analogies over time, even the time in which identity, coherence, and sufficient reason can take shape and *work*. On this description, institutions are objects that furnish objectality to other objects, including retroactively such things as the "communities" that set them in place decisively. "Furnish objectality" means: give them recognizable and agreed edges, times, ordinal as well as cardinal qualities. For Esposito—who follows Mary Douglas and, more remotely, Max Weber—these objective and objectifying phenomenological formats coerce, regulate, and enforce. They arrest the living movement of bodies so as to give them force and duration. But today, Esposito writes, "the requirement that life be instituted returns to the fore [*in primo piano*] in the double sense of bringing institutions to life and of restoring to life those instituting traits that push it beyond mere biological matter." This is achieved, he writes, by "mobilizing institutions, bringing them into movement, so they can once again find creative power." He frames the task conditionally, reflexively, and impersonally: *Se solo istitutionalizzandosi i movimenti acquistano forza e durata, solo mobilitandosi le istituzioni possono ritrovare potenza creativa* (If only by institutionalizing themselves [or "instituting themselves" or "by being instituted"] do movements gain strength and durability, only by mobilizing themselves [or "being mobilized"] can institutions regain creative power). Esposito offers a diagnosis and a path—but no clear sense of just *who* will act, or of *how* institutions "can once again find creative power": Do these phenomenological frames and formats act upon themselves (*istitutionalizzandosi . . . mobilitandosi*, instituting themselves . . . mobilizing themselves), or are they to be acted upon by impersonal forces, cold revengeful gods or unknown but beckoning political subjectivities (*istitutionalizzandosi . . . mobilitandosi*, being instituted . . . being mobilized)? For the diagnosis and path to be right; for it to be the case that current societies have moved into "a biopolitical dimension that is irreducible to the paradigm of sovereignty," thus toward the "the requirement that life be instituted" in the double sense that *Istituzione* proposes; for institutions to be mobilized and life instituted, the uncertainty whether the first and last movements are proper to the objects we call institutions, or are the marks of what is improper to them—what marks their edge, their *terminus*—must be maintained. And if institutions so (auto)mobilized cannot, then, be *one*—can the "life" they institute *be one*, one life, a conceptual object brought back to the fore, recovered, preserved, enforced? Does the stipulated right to *one life* lie behind Esposito's desire to "bring institutions to life and [to] restor[e] to life those instituting traits that push it beyond mere biological matter"? The right to *one* life and the right to the life of the *one* would then entail an institutionalism devoted, obligated to, responsible for, protecting and administering those rights. (A church, let's say, or a judiciary or police force.) Can a commitment to the right to the *one* serve to found democratic, defective institutions? And what might be entailed by an answer in the negative, or by the contrary position—that something like the not-one is the condition on which we can decide to *institute* in the first place? To *institute*, including instituting that communal "we" that acts to decide, here and now, to set in place a stone to mark a territory or commemorate a loss, or a victory?

Let's ask, then: What is *one* life? (Does *the one* possess or participate in life?) This is to ask: How do I grieve—for you *only* and immediately, when I grieve also with and for the ones who lost and lose you, when I have lost a world with you, when my words took you from me? And when I grieve, just for you, am I alone? What do I perform, for whom and with whom, under what conditions, and with what means and whose means, when I think of losing you?

I could have begun otherwise. I could have asked, How do I celebrate or how do I love—you *only*, when I celebrate also with and for the ones who love you, when I have gained a world with you?

Or I could have reflected that an institution makes a world out of another, or different ones—and asked, what world and worlds do I make with you, and how do I make a world when you are gone? What world do I install, grieving? And how?

In almost every way these are all the same question, but even if I nourish their differences, the stories I will tell flowing from these questions will echo each other, or rhyme, or become one story at times. Esposito's vitalism turns its eye, for to institute is not to assert the right to one life, to the life of the one, but to grieve lost life; to grieve, to institute. Niobe, the figure of institution, offers me three approaches.

## LEAVE ME (THE) ONE

> He himself, who always had the impression of being the last one (not of occupying the last place, but of being the last to witness things), now has the intolerable suspicion that he is the first witness of that vastness. Something like a dream (but in reverse, since it rescues no trace of memory or affinity) dictates to him that he is now occupying, on the edge of the crater, a place not only empty but also unknown, and that in all likelihood he may be the first of a series of silent visitors.[5]

I am writing these words about Niobe's grief with other loss before my eyes—as others have, no doubt. My mother died one month ago. My father, centenarian, is spinning into silence, forgetfulness, the dark. What will his life be like without my mother, I wonder? Sergio Chejfec, the author of the preceding passage, died suddenly two months ago. Sylvia, a bit later. And of course public loss is everywhere on screens and phones: COVID, war, the *Dobbs* decision, school shootings, the insults of predatory neoliberalism bring grief everywhere to us; they market it to us.

The long history of Niobe's allegories keeps me company. It doesn't offer consolation. It presses in different directions from her story's knots. Does it start with just a stone, with what Callimachus's *Aetia* calls "the tearful rock . . . the wet stone . . . set in Phrygia, a marble rock like a woman open-mouthed in some sorrowful utterance"?[6] "Who has not spoken at a funeral," Statius writes, in a poem grieving his father's death "of the Phrygian stone [*Phrigium silicem*]?"[7] I won't write that Niobe's story presses uniquely in so many ways or that it is even remarkable in starting, perhaps, just here, in stony ground before becoming the story I tell at a funeral, since I recall other etiological accounts and so many other, multiplying myths. Has any other of the West's stories, though, so tightly tied together the matters of number and grief, tied them together in such a way that the very number of retellings of the story also brings us to grief? Only perhaps—and it is a suggestive coupling—the story of Narcissus. Perhaps if literary culture had left just one story, or a single or even primary way of imagining Niobe's stories—*unam minimamque relinque*—perhaps I could find my way more easily to the question, How do I grieve for you alone? But Niobe is *procax*; her allegorizations are wanton, undisciplined. She figures *superbia* and stony insensitivity (Alciatus: "Pride is woman's vice, and it provokes the hardness of the mouth and senses, as in a stone" [*Est vitium muliebre Superbia, & arguît oris/Duritiem, ac sensus, qualis inest lapidi*]).[8] She represents a mother's ceaseless love, pride in a child, unending grief. She doubles herself: the statue of a statue, marble drawn from marble, *Statuae statua, & ductum de marmore marmor*, she is the limit of the sculptor's art (Juan de Arguijo, in a seventeenth-century sonnet echoing sources in the *Anthologia Graeca*, has her exclaim: "Powerful art restored me to all things, but not sense, feeling" (*A todo me dejó restituida,/mas no al sentido, l'arte poderosa*).[9] She offers politics, sociology: Jean Hardouin's 1716 *Apologie d'Homère* scandalizes Mme. Dacier by maintaining that in the *Iliad*, "Niobe is Greece" (*Niobé c'est la Grèce*). "Those twelve children are the Greek men and women killed by the halbardiers and hunters in the Trojan war, during the first nine years of the siege." "Nothing could be more amusing," Mme. Dacier ironizes back: "Here, certainly, we behold a stunning depth of genius," she adds, before "defending" Homer from Hardouin's "annoying" incoherences.[10] Nietzsche's Niobe arouses the "envy of the Gods," as the "too favoured mother" (*als überreich gesegnete Mutter*).[11] For Walter Benjamin, she stands as "an eternally mute bearer of guilt and as a boundary stone on the frontier between men and gods" (Jephcott's translation) or, in Julia Ng's recent translation, "an eternal, mute bearer of guilt and as a stone marking the border [*Grenze*] between human beings and gods, a life now, through the children's death, more inculpated

*Figure 5.* Anonymous, *Sculptuur van Niobe met haar dochter* (Sculpture of Niobe with her daughters), 1584. Rijksmuseum, Amsterdam.

[*verschuldeter*] than before."[12] For Judith Butler, commenting on and extending Benjamin, "it may be that Niobe's tears provide a figure that allows us to understand the transition from mythic to divine violence."[13]

What does it mean to grieve only for one? Is my question like asking whether *just one* "Niobe" organizes the long and incoherent history of her allegories? Or let me put it like this. Aulus Gellius notices the "remarkable, even ridiculous" "variation . . . to be noted in the Greek poets as to the number of Niobe's children. For Homer says that she had six sons and six daughters; Euripides, seven of each; Sappho, nine; Bacchylides and Pindar, ten; while certain other writers have said that there were only three sons and three daughters."[14]

Is my grief at losing some number, any number, greater than what I feel when I must lose just one, only one, call him Isaac or call her Iphigenia or Selia or Beatriz Viterbo? How to reckon singletons together, say six boys and six girls, or seven or nine or ten of each, or only one—this question has of course the most difficult logico-mathematical, religious, and ethical history. The answers that Niobe's stories provide are disconcerting in their diversity—the number of Niobe's allegories, like the number of her children, troubles our reckoning—but also in their structure. For they ask, in Niobe's name: What is *one* life?

In Ovid's telling of her story, desperate Niobe argues for one life on two contradictory lines. The gods attend to neither argument, but Niobe's grief is *instituted* to repeat, guard, and retain the incoherence she desperately expresses. (An institution as classically understood is a sort of *statue*; it is erected; it stands, firm, in stone, repetitive, to ward off finitude; because it stands against time, it makes my acts recognizable and legitimate over time; it stands you now within its closure, now outside; and it sets me outside at times, within at others.)

How to save *just one*, to fail, and then to learn how to grieve *just one*, the least one, one only, distinct from all the others: *et unam*, the last daughter. As the numbers still living drop the weight of the minimum increases, *de multis minimam*: the last one bears the weight of all my children; she stands for them. Leave me one, leave me the unit, so that I can count how many and how many worlds I have lost—since, without one, without the one, I will not be able to count my loss. Artemis, Apollo, Latona, cold gods—you should want me to tell my grief, to count my dead, now and forever, tear by tear, one and one and one child lost. Leave me one, so that I may number and mourn the others. Through and in her I will recall them and grieve for all of them in her. The Sanhedrin Mishnah 4:5 famously and controversially says, after warning witnesses in capital cases of the gravity of bearing false witness, of the dangers of uncertainty and ambiguity, that "anyone who saves a single soul [from Israel], he is deemed by Scripture as if he had saved a whole world."[15] (Controversially, some manuscripts and the humanistic Jewish tradition for the most part omit "from Israel." To save a single soul, one only, *any* soul, is to save a world.) Save me just one, so that I can count the worlds that I have lost, that you have taken from me.

Just for this reason I must deprecate the last. For just because the last one may count for them all, may be the one and one for each one, just because counting on her and with her she may bear the weight of all my children, she may save the world just herself, you may think that she can stand for them all, and that by taking all but her you will have left me the rest *in her*. So I must say instead: leave me with one, and I will call her nothing, the minimum, the least of them. Leave me the one closest to none, the least of them, the last one. I will call her just one because she doesn't count as one; she is just that, next to nothing, the *minimum*, the last. I don't love her most or least; she is just the one left. Indeed, I will take from her what made her mine alone, what made her my youngest, what made her my dearest: all that was her life I will take, so she will be just this last, *minimum* thing you leave me. Look: leave me just the last one, alone, *et unam*, and she will not add up to her siblings, indeed, she will add up to nothing, not even to herself. I cannot count her as *mine*: she cannot be a thing of mine that I can hold. She is the one who cannot be made to count. (Ovid uses the expression *et unam* on one other occasion in the *Metamorphoses*, at VI:525, describing Tereus's rape of Philomela. There a repeated conjunction in the phrase *et, et virginem et unam* works as an intensifier: a virgin, *and* alone; not one attribute added to another, but by their intensification both subtracted from Philomela. In Tereus's hands she is rendered *nothing*, unattributable, without a relation to father, sister, or even to the gods. In my despair, this, even this, is what I promise I will carry out upon my last child, if only the gods will spare her, just one, only one, *et unam*, alone.)

Niobe's grief holds together these two incompatible renderings of the one, the "one" that is each individual, the cardinal *one* that you will leave me so that I may count and grieve in counting them for each of the others, one and one and one like the dark beads of a rosary; but also (*and*) the "one" that cannot be made to count; the last, the ordinal *one* (although there can only ever be one *last* one, just which one is last has no importance: her lastness is all); the *one* that you will leave me just because she will never even count, not even as one, for her lone last self, and more: because I will sacrifice what makes her "one" to the ordinal quality of her lastness. She will not even be one, being just the last.

Grief pushes Niobe to fold one "one" into the other. For her, it is the way of despair, the last argument, the one she turns to when all other arguments have failed. Fruitlessly. Folding cardinal "one" into ordinal "last one" will not persuade the gods. No "one" can be saved by *adding* the just-one child to the just-last child.

(What sort of operation would it be, to try to add a cardinal "one" to an ordinal "last"? *Impartiality*, the objective shape of the *one*, and all the politics flowing from my desire to *be* one, to be objective, and not to be whimsical or to let "proclivities" drive me; my desire, as *one object*, to "faithfully and impartially apply the law," *the indivisible law*—these all are at stake. *Cardinality* is the primary feature of a number; it is what comes first in its order of attributes, the quality on which all others, the arithmetical or syntactical qualities of relation to other numbers, hinge. The technical question posed by the order of number's attributes hides at the center of Niobe's grief: Just what is finitude? What does it mean for one body to begin, and to end? The knot of Niobe's story here leads me to Ovid's great model regarding *minima* and bodies' beginnings and endings, Lucretius's *De Rerum natura*. Lucretius's poem builds what will become Ovid's allegorized questions into the description of matter itself. Here is how *De Rerum natura* approaches the paradoxes of numerical and every other finitude.

> Then again since each of those ultimate particles that are beneath the ken of our senses has an extreme point, that point is evidently without parts and is the smallest existence; it never has had and never will be able to have an independent, separate existence, since it is itself a primary and unitary part of something else. Then rank upon rank of similar parts in close formation provide the ultimate particle with its full complement of substance and, since they cannot have an independent existence, they must cling so fast to the whole atom that they cannot by any means be wrenched apart from it. The primary elements are therefore solid and simple, being formed of smallest parts packed solid in a closely cohering mass; they are not compounded as a result of the assembly of those parts, but rather derive their power from their everlasting simplicity; nature does not allow anything to be torn away or subtracted from them and so preserves the seeds of things.[16]

With Epicurus, Lucretius says: Atoms, *a-tomic* bodies, are precisely indivisible—they are *one*. But, Lucretius asks here, don't they have analogues of parts: orientation, upsideness, downsideness, and edges? For if it is finite, if it has an edge, an *apice* or even a *terminus*, then every atom has, at and as its end, a *last part*.[17] A *last* part that is also, as the editorial tradition that follows Lambinus's gloss of Lucretius quickly points out, a *first* part, though not uncontroversially. Here is John Selby Watson's 1893 note, from his important edition of *On the Nature of Things*: "'Id est, et prima atque ultima.' Lambinus. And so Evelyn: '—Since what we name / The first, or last, in bodies is the same.' The extreme point of a body is the first part of it, if you reckon from that point to the interior of the body; and the last part of it, if you reckon from the interior outwards to that point. Had it not been for the authority of Lambinus, I was inclined to render it the ultimate, and least part."[18] But how does what is *one* also possess a part that is different from its other parts (in being the *first* or *last* part)? A part that can be parted from it? The crucial verse, *alterius quoniamst ipsum pars primaque et una*, "since it is itself a primary and unitary part of something else" (Smith), is obscure. Leonard has: "Since 'tis itself still parcel of another, / A first and single part."[19] Some time ago, Furley's careful *Indivisible Magnitudes* locates "the difficulty . . . mainly in the words 'pars primaque et una.'"[20] Just here, Furley notes, Lucretius distinguishes between parts of one that *could* indeed be separated from the one and thus render it (or show it to have been) molecular rather than atomic; and *analogues to* parts of one that properly, indisseverably, and uniquely, belong to each one: the lastness of its edge, its orientation. The formulation in Lucretius is paradoxical. Discrete bodies, which are aggregates of similarly discrete atomic bodies, begin and end at last; they can be counted as one, they can be one body, just because the firstness and lastness of their edge is a "part" of them different in kind from the attributes and elements that make them up but can subsist parted from the discrete body: color; or the properties of duration and extension, which can be attributed to any discrete body.[21] What makes the discrete body *one* inasmuch as it is discrete, is the indisseverable, ordinal mark of firstness and lastness that its edges bear. But this indisseverable ordinal mark is, *as it were*, the sign that the discrete object's edge belongs to something other, *alter*: *alterius quoniamst ipsum pars primaque et una*. Furley throws up his hands: "I am unable to solve this problem, and can only say that somehow Lucretius believes it to be established that the minimum part cannot possibly exist in separation." In fact what Lucretius is maintaining is even less intuitively clear: that "the minimum part," the ordinally last part that marks out the edge of the one body, both is and is not wholly, only, an indisseverable "part" (in a different, analogic sense) *of* that body. The insult to the logic of identity is profound, and both addressed and performed in the poetical expression. Performed: between the ordinal *primus, pars prima*, and the cardinal attribute of being-one, *pars una*, Lucretius doubles his conjunctions,*—que*, *et*. The attributes of ordinal primacy and of cardinal numeration share conjuncts (*—que*, *et*) and substance (*pars*): the edge between them dissolves, as, if we follow Lambinus, does the difference between the first and the last, "*Id est, et prima atque ultima*." Lucretius draws ordinal primacy and cardinal numeration, like firstness and lastness, into one common body. At the same time this common body, the mark of the edge of the other, of the condition of finitude, cleaves that one common body from within with, to, the failure of the conjunct of ordinality and cardinality, of *pars prima* or *pars ultima* and *pars una*.)

The long and varied history of Niobe's grief doubles her figure, as if her statue were meant to hold together eternally each one child and every child that is the last, or the first, to die. *Statuae statua, & ductum de marmore marmor*: she becomes the statue of a statue. Moralized, this means: she was already, *at first*, as hard, as stony, as a statue, and the gods—good sculptors—*then* chip or shear from her, one child at a time, one edge at a time, all that was not marble about her, or all that hid her doubly marble form. She, too, has become *at last* truly *one*, one stony stone, a statue of herself alone, the statue of the stone that she was at first. Niobe's grief is the first institution, ordinally but also typologically. It is, like the altar that Henry James's Stransom erects in the forgotten chapel of "The Altar of the Dead," "the great original type, set up in a myriad temples, of the unapproachable shrine [I have] erected in [my] mind."[22] Mine? Ours? Niobe's grief, the first and universal institution, then helps me understand an intellectual tradition and a group of institutions that seek to conjoin ordinality and cardinality, *pars prima* or *ultima* and *pars una*, and do so in order to manage grief. The water that endlessly weeps from the stone is *another* matter—edgeless, it is what cannot be made *one* in either of our two senses—cardinal one, ordinal one—and marks what is left after the sculptural violence of institution has run its course. Does it count as one tradition and one group of institutions at all, I ask? I have in mind philosophical, theological, sociocultural institutions. How do Niobe's stories, the acts of instituting, and the institutions that her stories allegorize help me grieve for you, for you only?

Let's ask again, in Niobe's name: What is *one* life?

## DEATH ALONE

Is it this? Borges imagines the last Saxon, dying alone, "*casi a la sombra de la nueva iglesia de piedra*," nearly in the shadow of the new stone church.

> Antes del alba morirá y con él morirán, y no volverán, las últimas imágenes inmediatas de los ritos paganos; el mundo será un poco más pobre cuando este sajón haya muerto. . . . Una cosa, o un número infinito de cosas, muere en cada agonía . . . ¿Qué morirá conmigo cuando yo muera, qué forma patética o deleznable perderá el mundo? ¿La voz de Macedonio Fernández, la imagen de un caballo colorado en el baldío de Serrano y de Charcas, una barra de azufre en el cajón de un escritorio de caoba?[23]

Here is Andrew Hurley's translation:

> Before dawn he will be dead, and with him, the last eyewitness images of pagan rites will perish, never to be seen again. The world will be a little poorer when this Saxon man is dead. . . . One thing, or an infinite number of things, dies with every man's or

> woman's death. . . . What will die with me the day I die? What pathetic or frail image will be lost to the world? The voice of Macedonio Fernández, the image of a bay horse in a vacant lot on the corner of Serrano and Charcas, a bar of sulfur in the drawer of a mahogany desk?[24]

I imagine, with Borges, that what "dies with each man's last breath" may be a stubborn and unique collection of last *immediate* images, the ones I witnessed alone and alone recall: your touch, her voice, smells, my mother's face one day. A fragile set of perishing forms collected in my name and for me, of "one thing, or an infinite number of things," or as Norman Thomas di Giovanni's translation has it, "some thing—or an endless number of things." They are what counted for *one* life: what we *witness, that* is the one life we lead. What makes me—or anyone, or the "last Saxon"—both *one* and *unique* or *singular* is just the way one thing or event, or an infinite number of things or events, immediately relates to me (or anyone else, etc.) or bears my signature.

Borges's parable, approaching the definition from its other side, from some question asked after our eyes close on the last event we witnessed, makes sense intuitively (of course the image that I witnessed disappears when my memory of it does—the image *just is* my memory of it!). It rightly lays its stress on the signature, "Borges." It asks, what sort of thing is it that witnesses? Is it *like* the "one thing, or an infinite number of things, [that] dies with every man's or woman's death"? Is it just one of these things, one among many or one next to many things that I witnessed? Borges's parable asks: Does "immediate" self-witnessing *also* "die"? Who or what witnesses, immediately, what dies with the dying witness? If this who or what that witnesses what dies isn't a thing among things, then it is perhaps something like the mere thisness that supports a name, or holds together a thing I point at, say a stone. But this way too I find difficulty. "What is it in this stone," Duns Scotus asks—Scotus, whom Borges returns to again and again as "Erigena"—"by which as by a proximate foundation it is absolutely incompatible with the stone for it *to be divided into several parts each of which is this stone, the kind of division that is proper to a universal whole as divided into its subjective parts*?" (*Ordinatio* II, d. 3, p. 1. q. 2, n. 48).[25] The immediate thisstoneness of what I point to supports it; makes it *one*, particular. And every one thing shares with the infinite number of things the quality of possessing thisness. No thing is just one, entirely singular, for this reason: it shares, being one, in this universal. (And to this extent it can be likened to every other thing: it counts, like every other thing.) Not you, my friend, my father, and my last child, *et unam*.

This is perhaps too strong an argument; it leads to incoherence, to universal singularity. That every single thing—your one life among them—is a *haecceity* means that everything has, with every other thing, a common property, "being a haecceity." (I could also say that everything has in common with everything else the property "may possess a property.") If all things are "singular"—just one—does this not mean that no thing is absolutely one, since it is *like* all other things in this way at least? Or are we committing ourselves to a too strict definition of "singularity": surely a *single* property, just one alone, *et unam*, can be shared by things without foreclosing the romantically preferable chaotic disunity of universal singularity and of the absolutely discernible? (Something like the converse of Max Black's "twin spheres" argument is entailed.)

Borges allow us to weaken the argument in three ways, but the price may be too high. In his Spanish the qualifier "immediate" or "immediately," "*las últimas imágenes inmediatas*," bears a great deal of weight—so it is telling that both Borges's translators, Hurley ("the last eyewitness images") and di Giovanni ("the final first-hand images"), sidestep the term. It is, perhaps, too immediately philosophical a word for them; the register the translators seek is instead juridical: a "witness" at a trial, an eyewitness possessed of firsthand information, will at some point have the event or the image at hand or before his eyes, and will affirm so. I'll swear to it: there, in the lot at the corner of Serrano and Charcas, a brown horse. (Or is it a bay? The Argentine is "*colorado*," which is also "red." Am I seeing a color? Do color names designate real things, or are they a matter of perspective: my red, your brown, her bay?) Your verdict depends on it.

Juridical, of course. But "El Testigo" is *also* concerned with "*imágenes*," "*formas*," "*mediación*," and "*inmediatez*," immediacy; with "*conjetura*," "*cosa*," "*uno*," and "*infinito*," on a register that is not only juridical and not only colloquial. An "image" may "die"—phenomenologies are finite; we speak for instance of the persistence of vision, of afterimages; stone wears down with the flow of water, tears; I imagine that material supports fail, that my photographs of my mother and of Sergio fade or lose their digital coherence to new platforms; and my memories of my father's voice will be lost. But can a "form," *forma*, "die"? Not in the same way as the "image" does, not if we attend to the philosophical tenor of Borges's fable and despite the terms' apparent synonymy. Borges mentions the conjecture of "the theosophists" that the universe has a memory, but the conversation of "El Testigo" in 1960—like "Tlön, Uqbar, *Orbis Tertius*" in 1940 and like the even earlier conversation behind the speculative *History of Eternity* in 1936—is with Platonism's "conjecture" that forms do *not* perish, no matter how fragile and passing the material, empirical instances that participate in them: their "*imágenes*." Here in 1960 the synonymous "forma" and "imagen" are also, if anything, antonyms; "*forma*" and "*imagen*" cannot be, in the same way, "*patética o deleznable*." The paradox that Ovid condenses in the figure of the endlessly weeping Niobe, stone impervious to wear, expresses the fantasy of achieving a *poetical* expression both immortal *and* transient; Borges's parable expresses the fantasy of finding a *philosophical* expression that permits the "form" of an object or a life, of a life as object, and the "image" of an object or a life to be synonyms *and* antonyms.

*An* object; *a* life. But Borges isn't settled on how we are to count objects, things, or lives possessed of this poetical, philosophical paradox. Take the sentences I cite earlier. "*¿Qué morirá conmigo cuando yo muera, qué forma patética o deleznable perderá el mundo?*" "What will die with me the day I die?" For in every death, *en cada agonía*, in every *one* death, he says, "*Una cosa, o un número infinito de cosas, muere*." Hurley: "One thing, or an infinite number of things, dies with every man's or woman's death"; di Giovanni: "Some thing—or an endless number of things—dies with each man's last breath." We are invited to read Borges's *o*, his *or*, in the sense made possible, even likely, by works such as "El Aleph" or "La biblioteca de Babel": conjunctively, expressing synonymy or equivalence or internal translation: "One thing, *that is; or; id est*, an infinite number of things." A world, of course, in a grain of sand; a word, an image or a form in which all words are contained. In the *aleph* that the grieving Borges sees "in the heart of a stone" in the cellar of Beatriz Viterbo's house, "*Cada cosa . . . era infinitas cosas, porque yo claramente la veía desde todos los puntos del universo*." "Each thing . . . was infinite things, since I distinctly saw it from every angle of the universe" (di Giovanni).[26] Borges faces an impossible (*irresoluble*) central problem in trying to describe the *aleph*: "What I want to do," di Giovanni translates, "is impossible, for any listing of an endless series is doomed to be infinitesimal." Borges has in mind a more specific formulation: "[*El*] *problema central es irresoluble: la enumeración, siquiera parcial, de un conjunto infinito*." Not a series but a *set*; not "endless" but "infinite"; not a "list," but an "*enumeración*," enumeration. And no "doom" at all. When "*una cosa*" becomes syntactically synonymous (conjunctive "or") with "*un número infinito de cosas*" in "El Testigo," Borges has in mind to give a bounded "one" the extension of an infinite set (*un conjunto infinito*): every "*cosa*" that dies with me is *aleph* in precisely the sense in which the word is used, as Borges recalls with regard to "The Aleph," in "Cantor's *Mengenlehre* . . . the symbol of transfinite numbers, of which any part is as great as the whole." What I witnessed—ephemeral, unimportant: a horse in a lot, a sulfur bar—will turn out to be as great as the whole world of which it is just *one* part.

But Borges's "or" is not *only* conjunctive: it is also privative. A choice is to be made. "*En cada agonía,*" in every *one* death, "*una cosa, o un número infinito de cosas, muere.*" Not *one*, but an infinite number; not *id est* but the privative *vel.* One or the other. I think of it as a matter of attention, and maybe even of responsibility: to *this* event, or to *this* image, in itself: haecceity. *This* event or *this* image, not taken or experienced as *a part* or as a number counted alongside other numbers. There, in the lot at the corner of Serrano and Charcas, I saw a horse. An infinite number of images crowds the lot; the horse I saw is at the battle of Junín, Alexander rides it, the Cid, don Quixote . . . it is, in short, no longer *this one thing* or event that I witness (as the knots in Niobe's story will always lead me through others: through Ovid's verse and Lucretius's, through Borges's parables). How will I affirm that what I saw, one afternoon in Buenos Aires, was this and not that, that I saw it then and not at another moment? The piece's juridical register may bend translations of "The Witness" away from the work's philosophical commitment, but it cannot be discarded: justice requires my testimony; flowing from it, a verdict regarding what I witnessed. If *one thing* or one event is an infinite number of things or events, then the truth about this thing that I witnessed cannot be offered assuredly.

Synonymy *and* antinomy; conjunction *and* disjunction. I asked, with Niobe: what is *one life?* If I grieve for you, for what else and for who else do I grieve? Who also grieves where I grieve?

## BEING IN COMMON: THE MARK

"Transience," Judith Butler explains, "exceeds moral causality. As a result, it may be that Niobe's tears provide a figure that allows us to understand the transition from mythic to divine violence. . . . What would Niobe's expiation look like? Can we imagine? Would justice in this case require a conjecture, the opening up of the possibility of conjecture? We can imagine only that the rock would dissolve into water, and that her guilt would give way to endless tears." Thus Butler, explaining in *Parting Ways* the enigmatic appearance of Niobe in Walter Benjamin's essay "Critique of Violence." She has in mind these lines. "Violence," Benjamin writes, "therefore bursts upon Niobe from the uncertain, ambiguous sphere of fate. It is not actually destructive. Although it brings a cruel death to Niobe's children, it stops short of claiming the life of their mother, whom it leaves behind, more guilty than before through the death of the children, both as an eternally mute bearer of guilt and as a boundary stone on the frontier between men and gods." (248)

How does Butler understand "the transition from mythic to divine violence"? By first imagining grief "giving way," so that the tears of Niobe may dissolve this "boundary stone," so that, her grief having cleared the way for tears, she may dissolve herself *as* boundary stone—as the *Markstein*, the *terminus*, the mark of the minimum of sociality entailed in recognizing that a border can be drawn and attested, instituted, between two fields or two properties (understood extensively).

Thus far it is possible to conform Butler's position with Esposito's. But in Butler the "transition" between Benjamin's figures of violence maps onto a psychic and an ethico-political project that does not square with Esposito's. If I grieve for one, for one that I could hold and possess, could count and touch and point to, for one, one, the first or the last—then I mark my borders, I install myself, borrow or steal from the object my permanence as the grieving figure, sculpt myself into stone: *Statuae statua, & ductum de marmore marmor*. So far Esposito's institutional vitalism—or his vitalist institutionalism. Imagine this injunction, then *give way*, dispossess yourself of the object, dissolve the one statue you have become. A therapeutic injunction. Its ethico-political correlate: the dissolution of socialities and institutions based in property and recognition, and tending to reproduce them.[27] Butler's argument, I take it, departs from Esposito's by enjoining us, in *giving way*, to move through and beyond grievable life, and by enjoining us to imagine the uncountable institutions that may then come or may be established beyond *any* "biopolitical dimension," whether "irreducible to" or sustained by "the paradigm of sovereignty." Here is how this might be undertaken.

"Moral causality," I understand, restricts my guilt to what I can stand for—to those effects of my acts that follow, along a perspicuous or discoverable causal chain, from what I do. For instance, from my words comparing the number of my children to yours. It is a discoverable and fateful path, and when you take life from me, one child at a time, chipping at my heart as a sculptor chips away at rock to reveal the rock that lay below, you are moralizing me according to my last word.

"Transience" here means: what I am guilty of cannot be calculated. It is not composed of fixed and discrete, countable acts, events, or consequences; borders move and can be moved, or fade, or mingle, or dissolve; disorder garbles what was first or last; what was one counts as one *and* no longer does. My last word *may* lead back to me, but not (except accidentally) by a single path that lies ahead or behind me. Justice, Butler says, exceeds "moral causality" because it holds my responsibility to the test of transience. It holds me to account without counting forward to or back from the event. Because I give way, I face justice rather than judgment based in "moral causality." Now the path of expiation opens before me, uncertain, endless, conjectural: it is the way of endless tears.

"It may be that Niobe's tears provide a figure that allows us to understand the transition from mythic to divine violence." It is a careful, tentative formulation. Questions follow. Even the requirement that may flow from our understanding—the possible requirement of "a conjecture"—is followed by a double modification: "the opening up of the possibility of conjecture," "the possibility of conjecture" not just posited or instituted as a principle but "opened up," its inside revealed, maybe taken to bits, analyzed, its internal edges themselves subject to inquiry and understanding; and "conjecture" installed under the wing of its modality, its mere *possibility*. Then an answer—the conjecture that justice, *in this case*, conjecturing, stands on the answer to the question "Can we imagine?"

Behind Butler's questions we recognize the critical scheme, shaped here around three faculties, each finding its limit in the other two: "transience" described as above makes it impossible to establish judgment on *causal* understanding; "moral causality" and the faculty associated with disclosing "moral causality" find their limit in the limit that "transience" poses to the understanding; and finally the "imagination" is enrolled to supply, but *only* conjecturally and *only* "in this case," what we cannot otherwise understand, and what our moral faculty cannot grasp, because it lies beyond the limit that "transience" sets to both.

Linger on the imagination. For Butler, understanding the "transition from mythic to divine violence" passes through what justice now "requires": first, that "to conjecture" be synonymous with "to imagine"; second, that what we imagine can "only" be as she imagines ("We can imagine only that the rock would dissolve into water, and that her guilt would give way to endless tears"); finally, that *this* case, Niobe's case, may allow us to understand and open up, *in this case*, the necessity of conjecture.

Is Niobe's case singular, or can it serve as an example? How could the very singularity, the atrocity of Niobe's grief, set the single standard for general conjecture? If it does, then we will reckon our own grief by the unit she provides. (Ordinally, cardinally: always less, by a degree, by a number, for instance one child, one death, one friend.) But is her figure *one*, the highest or the base concept, the most extreme, the first–last point or part imaginable for human suffering? If so, she will mark the edge, the *apice*, the *terminus* where the concept, like dissolving stone, loses its at-oneness to "something else"—water slowly dropping, wearing it, say. And if not? Lucretius: "[the last point] never has had and never will be able to have an independent, separate existence, since it is itself a primary and unitary part of something else." Neither cardinal nor ordinal numbers end, of course; "first" and "last"-ness are notional; Niobe's exemplarity, if she is one, in this sense too. *King Lear*'s Edgar asks, aside: "Who is't can say 'I am at/the worst'? . . ./And worse I may be yet: the worst is not/So long as we can say 'This is the worst.'" Edgar slips from "I" to "we" so as to generalize his grief, so as to make himself exemplary. Worse will come, to him and to the state, one event after another. Yes. But human suffering is a matter also of *intensities*, time-stamped and time-dependent, flickering; of pasts recalled, futures anticipated, events and moments stretched out of measure, rambled, lost, and insusceptible of comparison, ordering, even designating. What counted as an event no longer does; *this*, suddenly, matters, and casts a shadow on *that*, and *that*, and ushers this other circumstance, trivial and unremembered, into the field of events I mark with a white or a black stone, now but not forever. Grief, firstness and lastness, best and worst, lose their at-oneness not to what I or we, or we *through* what *I* report, took to be the "worst," not to something else but to themselves.

Can these two logics, which entail also two phenomenologies, two notions of exemplarity, and two conceptions of history, be held together? On this question the boundary stone that Benjamin makes to speak for Niobe is clamorous. Imagine that the term *Markstein* marks a compromise between two orders or serves as their point of suture: the order of culture that we remark in the concept of *Mark*, a sign I make *for* someone and whose sense is established in context, which is to say by a third, an interpretant, a cultural function; and the lasting thing, *Stein*, on which the mark is made, or which constitutes the mark as material object. We have seen this composition stretched out, narratively, before: from the stone Searle describes, to the cultural proxy for the stone, the institution it becomes. But Benjamin's condensation of the two, of *Mark* and *Stein*, does other work than narratively linking one to the other, stone to institution stepwise, from the primitive scene of the physically protected village to the metropolitan stage where institutions conventionally establish and guard life in common. For the inscription, the mark, that *Markstein is* may not be (equally) legible from the different sides of the frontiers it marks. (For two reasons. First, it is *sides*, plural, and *frontiers*, plural: this stone that Niobe becomes does not stand to guard the single line between two fields alone any more than one single point can define a line; she, it, is rather like the *vertex*, the gathering point of an infinite number of lines, each of which may be said to *possess* that point, "Niobe." And in the second place, hasn't it always been the case that the stone that guards my village reads one way to you, inside, and another to me, outside? Comfort, protection, recognition, familiarity, even the family lie with you; the discomfort of the wild, exposure, alienation, the unfamiliar and the unfamilial with me, and that is what each of us reads marked into the stone.) But also: if and only if the *Markstein* does *not* dissolve or fade over time can we *give way* and give up the object; only in this way will the stone mark what is ideally at stake—its historicity. A distinction, in short, seems drawn between the interpretability of the *mark* ("legibility" is historically and positionally determined, and what is read differs also and similarly—and as the boundary stone on one reading marks the limit between two asymmetrical relations to history, a human and a divine one, the historicity of the mark and thus its senses and readings will be different on either side of the boundary), and the insistence of the substance on which it is made, of which it is made.

Benjamin, I remember, is at least once uncertain what the marks might *be* that he has set into his argument, and uncertain whether they come together into a single, a unitary, mark, even one shared—equally *possessed*—by infinite vectors, lines, histories. I have cited as the opening to a section of my introduction, without remarking on them otherwise, Benjamin's lines imagining "The Nordic Sea" in his 1930 travel journal. Let's bring them back and appose them to the reference to Niobe in the 1921 "For a Critique of Violence": "Who are they?—so unspeakably helpless and protesting—these Niobids of the Sea? Or its Maenads? For they stormed over whiter combs than those of Thrace and were beaten by wilder paws than the beasts, the retinue of Artemis—they, the galleons."

Benjamin has in mind, remotely, the famous so-called Uffizi Group of Niobids, but immediately the wooden *Statuen* installed in "a chamber with moss-green walls," the "chamber of the Galleons in the Maritime Museum in Oslo." And he has in mind not *just* the "single, or only, or singular, or unique Niobid assembly," *Eine einzige Niobidenversammlung*, as he calls it in his preparatory notes to "Statuen," but *also* something wilder and much more threatening than the image of Niobe's passive, dying children, something attuned to the violence causing their death instead, attuned to what once "stormed over whiter combs than those of Thrace and were beaten by wilder paws than the beasts, the retinue of Artemis." Here, seemingly condensed into a single mark, Benjamin offers what can hardly be called *one, singular, unique*: the collection, *Versammlung*, of Niobids, Artemis's victims, slain by her arrows and Apollo's; the victims of Artemis's "beasts"; and the wild Maenads themselves. (The association between Artemis, the nymphs devoted to her, and the Bacchic Maenads is a very old one.) And correspondingly, there is something like a dialectical edge, a tense, almost contradictory edge, to the conjunction of gathering together, *Versammlung*, and the strangely emphatic oneness, singularity, of the couplet *Eine*, indefinite article, "a" or "one," and the modifier *einzig*. *Ein*, *eine*, *ein-zig*: one or a one; one or a singular; one or a unique collection.

The lines, stones, or institutions keeping apart Niobids and Maenads have indeed failed Benjamin's imagination, broken down over time, and lost their commonly agreed functions and authority. But there is more at issue here than seepage and miscegenation among mythic referents. Benjamin closes the "Nordic Sea" cycle in August 1930, and publishes "Statuen" in the *Frankfurter Zeitung* in September 1930.[28] In the notes he takes toward the cycle ("On the back of the first sheet of the 1930 travel notes," writes the editor) as in the published "Statuen," Niobe's children are before him, but not alone, not only. The note asks the same questions as "Statuen" but goes farther: the Niobid assembly comes to be replaced entirely with the Maenads:

> Who are they—so unspeakably helpless and rebellious—these niobids of the sea?
>
> These images—once they moved more bacchanally than the incarnate [break]
>
> Or rather maenads? Ancient? These images that once moved more bacchanally than the maenads in the flesh. Ancient? This splintered, split wood? Ancient? These pieces . . .

Where does this detour through Benjamin's notebooks and short journal entries, composed and published a decade after the "Critique of Violence," take us?[29] Back to the complex, incomplete suturing function of the *Markstein* "Niobe" in the earlier essay. Back to the questions, what is *one life*, what sort of life does the *one* possess? Back to the question, What is entailed by affirming that something like the not-one is the condition on which we can decide to *institute* in the first place? To institute, including instituting that communal "we" that acts to decide, here and now, to set in place a stone to mark a territory or commemorate a loss, or a victory? How do those acts of institution persist, *stare decisis* again, if not set or engraved in stone?

Tremulously, the name "Niobe" reaches forward across the decade to designate a group or collection of statues that Benjamin imagines as the Niobids *and* the Maenads: the dying, suffering children, the wild, destructive votaries of Dionysus (and of Artemis, whose arrows pierce the Niobids). We will want to say: the oneness of the referent, the stubborn thing, the object before it is collected, before it becomes part of the collection of objects, makes possible the twoness of the competing, even mutually destructive names, Niobids and Maenads. The *one* lives, possesses "life," in these stone or wood objects; then, subsequently, gathered in the imagination, where the stone or wooden objects become statues and gather names, *there* the *Einzig may* fall apart, into parts, *may* become partisan: from *Stein* to *Mark*, object to culture, things *may* fall apart.

But this is not right either, because the *gathering* of the object and its setting before the imagination, its acculturation, has already taken place in and depends upon an institution—for instance, it is a *Phrygian* stone, or it lies in the Uffizi (already *part* of the Niobid group), or the Louvre (a mark upon the Niobid krater), or in the "chamber of the Galleons in the Maritime Museum in Oslo," and everywhere the objects gather on ground tilled by Callimachus and Ovid and countless others. They gather, they are gathered, *versammelt*—settled cultural debris *already* bearing the violent marks of collection, extraction, curation, ordering, and presentation. "Who has not spoken at a funeral," Statius writes, "of the Phrygian stone [*Phrygium silicem*]?" Statius means by "Who has not spoken," *quis non in funere cunctos / Heliadum ramos lacrimosaque germina dixit / et Phrygium silicem*, that the weeping stone, "Niobe," the Phrygian stone, like all the tropes of grief he lists, is already a cliché; already worn from telling, already acculturated, inadequate, for its very recognizability, to the singular grief he feels. So a different story and different names will have to be supplied to grieve just one, since always and already, even before losing their mute insistence to the divided clamor of their symbolic proxies, things, stories, or stones, have been acculturated into, in, by antecedent institutions: collective grief (the funeral), the market, a geopolitics (Phrygia), colonial extraction, the culture industry.

Who has not spoken in grief and found herself speaking names that others already know, for comparison, for orientation? When I seek to take account of my grief at losing you, just you, just one, you are already more than one; more faces and other names than just yours come to me, wood or stone, gathered together. So I imagine life beyond what I count as one life, more than one life. I find that life that is not-, other-than, and more-than-one stands on and marks mute historicity, as the *Markstein* "Niobe" does in Benjamin, but also on *Phrygian* stone, on the divided, incongruous ground of antecedent proxies, decision and undecision, institution and abolition. "But also" means: your death abolishes the life of the one, the one of the law and also my one life, *but also* stays with me, as me, as the no-one, not-one, more-than-one, that I and we must be to *institute* being in common, which is to say, to abolish, *by any means necessary*, the claim to life of the one.

# 5
# ALL COPS ARE BASTARDS

The problem . . . "Who is the legislator?" in a country—can be posed again by defining other questions in a "real, " not "scholastic" way. For example, "What is the police ?" . . . What is the police? It certainly is not just that particular official organization which is juridically recognized and empowered to carry out the public function of public safety, as it is normally understood. This organism is the central and formally responsible nucleus of the "police," which is a much larger organization in which a large part of a state's population participates directly or indirectly through links that are more or less precise and limited, permanent or occasional, etc. The analysis of these relations, much more than many philosophical juridical dissertations help one understand what the "state" is.

Antonio Gramsci

Without the police and the police organizations, with all their many defects, anarchy would be rife in this country, and the civilization now existing on this hemisphere would perish.

August Vollmer

About the police, August Vollmer concedes their *defects*, "all their many defects."[1] Here "defects" means what the figure "a few bad apples" does today and did on May 31, 2020, when Robert O'Brien, Donald Trump's fourth National Security adviser, remarked, "No, I don't think there's systemic racism. There's a few bad apples that are giving law enforcement a terrible name." George Floyd had been murdered five days earlier.[2] "A few," that diminished kin of "some." "A few" weighed against what might be "systemic," or institutional; "a few" marshaled against the *all*.

For *all* institutions have their police forces, their gendarmeries, their bobbies, coppers, repressive apparatuses, their corps of coercion. We may not recognize them exactly as such, but they and the institutions they serve provide us—both as we belong to these institutions and when we identify them *as* institutions to which we may or may not belong—with acceptable ways of recognizing, identifying, sorting, emplacing, judging, responding, desiring, working, dying, living. This is trivially true, whether the institution at issue is the police itself, or the state, the army, the school, "race," the university, or the family. We need just understand "police force" elastically—it will stretch from *authority* to the force of law and the censorious gaze, from the letter of the law to its metaphorical content.[3] Recall Seumas Miller: "Social institutions are constituted and animated by human beings, and human beings are intrinsically moral agents." That "It does not follow from this that *all* human beings are moral agents" just means that although "some may not be [moral agents], but, if so, then they would be defective *qua* human beings," my emphasis on Miller's *all*.[4] There is, then, a policing mechanism to determine just what is a "moral agent," and to enforce the rule that if a "human being" is not an "intrinsically moral agent," then that being is "defective *qua* human being." Just what future is reserved for defective human beings, from schooling to institutionalization to extermination, is the matter of "human" history. And it will not be just "some" cops, "a *few* bad apples," who will sort out what is a "moral agent" from what is not, who will enforce the rule that equates a lack of "intrinsic morality" with defective humanity, but *all* cops: not "some," not the "few," not defective ones, not a "few bad apples," but *all* cops inasmuch as they are cops. It is baked into the structure of the classic institution: *all* institutions, as such, inasmuch as we can say about them that they are institutions, have their police forces. We can think of these as minimal forces first. Once an institution's domain and functions are set these police guard its authority and its borders, external as well as internal, and tend to its time and to its permanence. *All* such police are a dispositive that serves to administer how terms like "all," "some," and "no" are used: how they are understood, to whom they are applied, by whom, and to what ends. Before a state, the army, a school, the concept of "race," or the university, has a physical police force working among other things, as Althusser's nearly infamous piece of theater has it, to "interpellate individuals as subjects," it has just this conceptual support—necessarily. If the police and the institutions they serve install and protect the "civilization now existing on this hemisphere," as August Vollmer puts it, it is because all institutions and their police corps are correlative.

All this is true, I said, trivially, even definitionally. Is there a way of imagining institutions (the police, the university, the family, and so on—though the question is open, should the same names be reserved for them? On whose authority would the names be changed, how would the changes be enforced?) that do not only or tendentially serve the sovereign claim, that is, that are not only or tendentially dispositive, technical "devices," and do not only or tendentially produce and police hegemony? Can we imagine institutions that, rather than *tend toward* that producing-policing function, *tend away from* the brutal dialectic of the one, the *all,* and the *few*? Institutions that also produce, guard and administer nonhegemonizing, noncommon, disputable experiences?

Not easily, for it isn't quite right or completely right either to understand "police" elastically or to grant the abstract observation that all institutions and their police corps are correlative—and this for at least four sorts of reasons. In the first place, obviously and urgently, for practical reasons: for there are all around us physical, quite concrete police forces we can point out, of different degrees of brutality, serving different sorts of institutions. Just *who* can point them out; just *who* can seek to obscure their brutality under the shield of the *few*, the "few bad apples"; just *who* can make claims about the police, including the claim to define what the police are and whether they wield physical or conceptual batons. These are hardly abstract questions. They are governed by specific conditions. Who speaks; when; where; to whom; in what language and medium; how loud: these are the conditions on which statements about the police depend, not just to be true or to be forceful, but to be recognized as statements in the first place. Thus all claims about the police—that seemingly elastic, abstract term—are radically and peculiarly, even uniquely, *indexical*—and a statement like "All institutions and their police corps are correlative" runs aground on just this unique indexicality. (Even Vollmer, the criminologist and police reformer credited both with laying the foundations for the militarization of police forces in the United States, *and* with arguing "that policing should be professionalized and focused on improving society," specifies: without police, "the civilization *now* existing on *this* hemisphere would perish."[5] Other times, other hemispheres, would be the occasion for other sorts of claims, other all's, other no's.) And so how does the philosophy of institution today take account of the *indexicality*, the *who says when what whyness*, of the institution and policing of *race* to which "the civilization *now* existing on *this* hemisphere" seems bound? An advisor to the U.S. president, a National Security advisor, says, on May 31, 2020, that "a few bad apples" and not institutional systemic racism explains George Floyd's murder five days before: *who says when what why*.

In the second place, there is this sort of question. For Althusser, the relation between the police and subjectification *always* runs through a demand and expresses the bad conscience, even the guilt, of a subjectivity always already dependent on antecedent authority. Is there then, as I am also claiming, a *general* relation between the demand of the police and *quantification*? If not—but also if so—what is the work done in sentences and on the streets by the operator "all" and the operator "no": either "No cops are bastards" or "No cops are not bastards"? Would abolishing the police entail abolishing the "all," and the "no" as well? Would the destitution of the "all" and the "no" just leave us in the gray world of the "some" and the "few"? Would it entail restricting the purview of quantification? What and how do they—the police, the quantifiers I have listed—make demands, and when, and under what sorts of circumstances? The structural description of the subject to be formed in the demand, who is primitively "always already" guilty, will not allow us to bypass the following historical objections: something like the *modern* institution of the police emerges in Western societies roughly in the first quarter of the nineteenth century; but *quantification*, whether in the shape of statements like "All cops are bastards," "All men are mortal" or, as in Aristotle, "All men by nature desire to know," *pantes anthrōpoi tou eidenai oregontai physei* (*Metaphysics* 1:980A), has been around much longer. ("All" in Aristotle, *pantes*, the plural form of *pas*, can be substantivized: *the all, totality*.) Now attend on this level to the questions who, when, under what conditions, gets to make statements *about* institutions, or has the *authority* to ask questions about them, for instance (but it's not just any example) about the police: Can we say that "all" white people, and "no" Black people, or only at most "some," maybe just a "few," get to, today, in the United States? If, as it seems, universal quantification—*all*-ness, *no*-ness, *some*-ness, *a few*-ness—is closely tied to racialization, indeed if the two are inseparable (today—but were they always? On what concept of "inseparability?)—then *that* history will be different from the history linking *all*-ness to the police.[6] Just how will the police, racialization, and *all*- and *no*-, *few*-, and *some*-ness, fall into line?

In the third place, there are conceptual as well as historical reasons to avoid granting that all institutions and their police corps are correlative. Just what *is* the relation between the police, however elastically we understand it, and *authority*? On one description—Hannah Arendt's, to which I will return—the coercive quality of the police runs contrary to their bearing authority, classically conceived. So where does this leave my claim that *all* institutions have their police forces, their gendarmeries, and so forth? Won't this mean that the coercive dimension of institutions—the work they do, as institutions, to separate, include or exclude, order, produce and regulate subjectivities and objectalities—excludes their being *authoritative*?

And in the fourth place—and closely tied to the question of the authority that institutions may claim—I've exclaimed, with you, with others on the street today or yesterday, "All cops are bastards!" I've just wondered at my use of "all." Now I remember one famous literary defense of bastardry and I think, does disqualifying the police as "bastards" not entail affirming a normative familial order? The *connubium*? Legitimacy itself? *Lear*'s Edmund says: "Why 'bastard'? Wherefore 'base,' / When my dimensions are as well compact, / My mind as generous and my shape as true / As honest madam's issue?" He continues famously:

> Our father's love is to the bastard Edmund
> As to th' legitimate. Fine word, "legitimate."
> Well, my legitimate, if this letter speed
> And my invention thrive, Edmund the base
> Shall top th' legitimate. I grow, I prosper.
> Now, gods, stand up for bastards! (I.2.6–9, 18–23)

"Fine word, 'legitimate.'" Am I not leaning, with you, here on the street, on some such "fine word," when we say together, "All cops are bastards"? Does not the ghost of legitimacy, or a nostalgic attachment to a legitimacy beyond and more fundamental than mere policing, inspire and condition my desire to abolish the police? "Bastard" is a name for the ex-terminal, a name that an established order gives to what issues outside the conventional family, the agreed family, the institutional family, the circle of legitimate kin relations. How do I take a stand against police without leaning on the "fine words" offered by antecedent and foundational institutions? But also: How do I take a stand against the metaphysics of "legitimacy," and how do we "stand up for bastards," without standing up for the police?

Let me see what it would mean, as a philosophical matter, to abolish the police.

All my life I have detested statements predicated on quantifiers, and especially on the universal quantifier—the indefinite pronoun, if you will—"All." It has been almost a point of honor to shoot back an exception: "Well, not all, I know at least one X that is not Y." There is a commendable moral itch being scratched here—after all, all generalizations are odious—but it makes for bad conversations. Worse, I suspect that at bottom when I object, "No, not *all* X are Y, I know at least *one* X that is not Y," I am protecting something.

I would like to think that I am protecting what *all* humans, as humans, guard themselves against, at least on one standard account. Freud wrote in 1919, "It is true that the proposition 'All men are mortal' is paraded in text-books of logic as an example of a generalization, but no human being really grasps it, and our unconscious has as little use now as ever for the idea of its own mortality."[7] He is perhaps remembering Tolstoy's "Death of Ivan Ilyich." Ilyich, near the end, remembers "The example of a syllogism he had studied in Kiesewetter's logic." The syllogism this time runs:

> Caius is a man, men are mortal, therefore Caius is mortal. . . . [It] had seemed to him all his life to be correct only in relation to Caius, but by no means to himself. . . . And Caius is indeed mortal, and it's right that he die, but for me, Vanya, Ivan Ilyich, with all my feelings and thoughts—for me it's another matter. And it cannot be that I should die. It would be too terrible.
>
> So it felt to him.[8]

I would *like* to think that when I balk at alls I am in Ilyich and Freud's company, that I step away out of fear of the dire wolf, fear of the general mortal condition: every "all" is not only a local universal quantifier, you might say, it is also the general mark of necessity, of what pertains to this or that *as* this or that, by definition; it is what pertains to *all* humans *qua* humans; to *all* institutions as such; to *all* cops inasmuch as they are cops; and so on. In other words, what is repulsive about "all" is that it stamps *this* human life, *this* particular institution, *this* cop, with the limit of its concept. (*All* this, and nothing more.) I hear you say, "All bachelors are unmarried men," or I hear you sing Beethoven's rendition of the lovely Schiller line, "*Alle Menschen werden Brüder, / Wo dein sanfter Flügel weilt*," All men become brothers / Under the sway of [Joy's] gentle wings, and something grates, and I remember the "Pirate Jenny" song from Brecht's *Threepenny Opera* (on which I will set the schema of abolition in the chapters that follow): "*Wenn man fragt, wer wohl sterben muss / Und dann werden Sie mich sagen hören 'Alle!'*" (When one asks, Which will have to die?, you'll hear me say: "*All* of them.").[9] I hear you—someone—say "All," and I want to raise a hand against the analytic proposition out of fear of the finitude to which it consigns *all* subjects, but me in particular: you say "all," and I hear, not "all men are mortal" or "all men are or will be brothers," but "you, Jacques, will die."

That's what I would like to think that I am defending against, when I say that "all" always repels me, and maybe that's it in part, though I fear it is a more specific cowardice; that I want to protect something that bears my name properly (that bears what Ivan Ilych calls "all my feelings and thoughts," my history, my memories). Phrases in Castilian Spanish tend to leave out the pronouns in the subject position in first-person expressions ("*Como pan*" rather than "*Yo como pan*"), and also indefinite pronouns modifying plural subjects: "*Los hombres comen pan*" instead of "*Todos los hombres comen pan.*" English will sometimes allow itself the latter, seldom the former. In my house I heard from my father, speaking in the clear tones of his generation's racism, "*Los moros son . . .*" or "*los gitanos quieren . . .*" (Arabs are . . . , gypsies want . . .). On the streets of Madrid and Caracas, growing up, I heard "*Los judíos son . . .*" (Jews are . . .). Behind the casual phrases beat two alls, two *todos*: the *all* we all share, we who listen, we who understand his language and assent to it, here and now, as it institutes the here and now, the inside and the out, of our household or our family or our community; and the *all* of the object, *todo moro*, *todo gitano*, *todo judío*.

I am protecting, shying away from, trying to forget something when I balk at your or anybody's "All." Those scenes—Madrid, my father's voice, Caracas, others'. Let me not speak my father's language, or think his thoughts, or follow him, or understand him when he says "All." Let there be, if not a "few," then at least "one" who falls outside his "all" and your "all." Let me say, on the streets in Madrid or in Caracas, "Not *all.*" "*Todos, no; este judío que te está hablando, por ejemplo . . .*"

But I am not one, or not alone. Here is what I remember when you say "*todo judío*" or when my father says "*los moros*," and I say or want to say "*Todos, no.*" My great uncle, the Communist, anti-Zionist dissident Abraham Serfaty, who, arrested by the state police and consigned to nearly two decades of jail and torture in Morocco, would refer to himself as "*arabe juif*" and "*juif arabe.*" Mizrahi. During the summers that we spent in Tangier while Hassan II still lived, my sisters and I were warned by my father and my grandparents never to mention Serfaty's name: everybody and anybody, *all* and *any*, *todos*, *cualquiera*, might hear and point us out. Let there be *one*; let me be *one*, just *one*. Let me speak Abraham Serfaty's name; let me hear, speak, and be "*juif arabe*" and "*arabe juif.*" Let me speak my grandmother's name and my full name—though this will put me outside my father's language, outside the "all" of his unthinking institution. Let me speak without fear of the police. But "let me"? Just what other am I, is one, addressing, if not them?

## THE DISAPPEARANCE OF *KIND*

> This progress of similarity standards, in the course of each individual's maturing years, is a sort of recapitulation in the individual of the race's progress from muddy savagery. . . . In general we can take it as a very special mark of the maturity of a branch of science that it no longer needs an irreducible notion of similarity and kind. It is that final stage where the animal vestige is wholly absorbed into the theory. In this career of the similarity notion, starting in its innate phase, developing over the years in the light of accumulated experience, passing then from the intuitive phase into theoretical similarity, and finally disappearing altogether, we have a paradigm of the evolution of unreason into science.[10]

Let me start over. I am writing these words in October 2021. I am trying to understand how racialization, *all-* and *no-*ness (and *some-*ness, and its kin *few-*ness), and the police fall into line today. Of course I wonder who "all" refers to today, and how—*who* it refers to, and how exactly or how nearly it refers. I wonder who "we" are, as I write this, here in Los Angeles, to you. What is "ours," I wonder, and who are "we." I wonder what it means for a pronoun to be *indefinite* today; where the quantifier "all" ends and where the pronouns' edges are; who or what gets to rest in their shade; who guards their borders; with what force and at what cost that rest is purchased. Who is forced into it, who excluded? *I* wonder, who have just one white man's experience. Further differentiations, barely pertinent, it seems. *I* wonder, white (as you might say), but Spanish, Sephardic, also straight, an academic, also writing *today* rather than *then*, "in this hemisphere" rather than another; and so forth. It is a split question that I, and perhaps nearly all of us, here generalizing the pronoun, *all* of us *should* ask: it's 2021; the Black Lives Matter movement on the one hand and the sinister international consolidation of ethnonationalism on the other demand it. (Other demands follow: reparative, retributive, distributive. But this one is primary.)

There is a primary demand that the unmarkedness of "all" be marked. Of whom and by whom is this demand made? How and on what grounds is that demand authorized? *When* is it made? The demand is ethico-political; the questions, the who, how, when, and why questions, are epistemological. In 1966 James Baldwin's "A Report from Occupied Territory" will famously answer one way: he calls for *recognition*, hinging the settlement of the two questions, the primary ethico-political demand that the unmarkedness of "all" be marked, and the primary epistemic question on what grounds that demand is authorized, on "the recognition of our common humanity."[11] He makes explicit what Truman Nelson's *The Torture of Mothers*, on which Baldwin draws for his "Report," marks as a rhetorical gesture: "Perhaps," Nelson writes, "I could get you in that region where *all* humanity can merge in a common sadness over human hurt," perhaps then, perhaps, *you would believe* what happened in Harlem in the spring and summer of 1964.[12] For "without this recognition," Baldwin concludes his "Report," "our common humanity will be proved in unutterable ways."

It's July 11, 1966. Baldwin's "Report from Occupied Territory" comments, as I said, on the events of the last two weeks of April 1964—"based, in part," as Baldwin puts it, "on Truman Nelson's *The Torture of Mothers* [1965] . . . a detailed account of the case which is now known as the case of The Harlem Six," later behind Steve Reich's tape piece *Come Out* (1966) and later still (1980) a film directed by Woodie King, *The Torture of Mothers*: the "Harlem Fruit Stand Riot," the police beating of Frank Stafford, and the arrest and convictions of the Harlem Six.[13] Baldwin remembers Stafford:

> "The cop turn around and smash him a couple of times in the head." And one of the youngsters said, "He get that just for a question. No reason at *all*, just for a question." . . . The salesman is on the streets again, with his attaché case, trying to feed his family. He is more visible now because he wears an eye patch; and because he questioned the right of two policemen to beat up one child, he is known as a "cop hater." Therefore, "I have quite a few police look at me now pretty hard. My lawyer he axe (asked) me to keep somebody with me at *all* times 'cause the police may try to mess with me again." . . . The salesman's name is Frank Stafford. At the time *all* this happened, he was 31 years old. And *all* of this happened, *all* of this and a great deal more, just before the "long, hot summer" of 1964 which, to the astonishment of nearly *all* New Yorkers and nearly *all* Americans, to the extremely verbal anguish of *The New York Times*, and to the bewilderment of the rest of the world, eventually erupted into a race riot. It was the killing of a 15-year-old Negro boy by a white policeman which overflowed the unimaginably bitter cup. . . . These things happen, in *all* our Harlems, every single day.[14]

*All*. I've emphasized the indefinite pronoun. Nelson's *The Torture of Mothers* had opened wondering, "How can I make you believe this?" Nelson continues, in full now:

> Perhaps if I said the victims were guilty, in some small way, I could get you to suspend your disbelief. Perhaps I could get you in that region where *all* humanity can merge in

> a common sadness over human hurt . . . there beyond *all* the rules of innocence and guilt that man has made. Very well, three boys, *all* black, and two men, one black and one white, did interfere, or did interpose, in a questioning or resistant way between the police and some supposed wrong-doers.

Everything about the scene, Baldwin's and Nelson's scene, bears on *all*. Nelson: "*All* humanity can merge." "Beyond *all* the rules of innocence and guilt." "*All* Black." Baldwin: *all*, or "nearly all." Worlds hang on the sense and scope of the quantifier. Yes, all institutions produce and regulate what is *all* for them: they are means of quantification. In Nelson we have three domains: "humanity," a general ontology; "*All* Black," a political ontology; "*all* the rules of innocence and guilt," a normative ethics. Nelson is being unsystematic about sense and scope here; his possibilism carries him too far, perhaps. Baldwin is devastating and devastatingly systematic, but he too will be carried on by, and to, the transcendental spot where *all* gathers together all humanity, all rules, and all cities.

But this is not obvious at first in Baldwin's "Report." "To the astonishment of nearly *all* New Yorkers and nearly *all* Americans." Baldwin means, exactly, *not* all New Yorkers and not *all* Americans—only those who make up the world that matters to the *New York Times* in 1966, the unmarked "all" for whom "*all* this . . . and *all* of this [that] happened, *all* of this and a great deal more," does *not* happen. Baldwin means *bien pensant* Americans, nearly all white, for whom Harlem is just *one* and in any case never, as Baldwin puts it, "ours" ("These things happen, in *all our* Harlems"). The general plea—the plea for *all—also* has a specific foundation, a signature:

> My report is *also* based on what I myself know, for I was born in Harlem and raised there. Neither I, nor my family, can be said ever really to have left; we are—*perhaps*—no longer as totally at the mercy of the cops and the landlords as once we were. In any case, our roots, our friends, our deepest associations are there, and "there" is only about fifteen blocks away. This means that I also know, in my own flesh, and know, which is worse, in the scars borne by many of those dearest to me, the thunder and fire of the billy club, the paralyzing shock of spittle in the face, and I know what it is to find oneself blinded, on one's hands and knees, at the bottom of the flight of steps down which one has just been hurled [my emphasis].

Baldwin's report, then, pleads on two grounds and appeals to two authorities—the general, what is "common" to *all*; and also the particular, the "there," what can be indexically grasped ("our deepest associations are there, and 'there' is only about fifteen blocks away"): what pertains to *all*, set alongside "What I myself know." Baldwin wants to provoke, in nearly all his readers, an identification like the one he feels then, when he is writing, with the "there" of Harlem. The strategy is sanctioned: induction; testimony; the report. These ways of speaking and writing blaze and guard the path between first-person statements concerning what "I know in my own flesh" and statements concerning "all our Harlems."

That was 1966. Baldwin is appealing for "recognition" on double grounds, to different readers, to diverse effects. He is using the term to mark distances—by means of the *indexical*, first-person, signed side of his argument, from the language of "human recognition" in liberal, integrationist writers like Penn Warren (who organized the landmark 1964 collection of interviews and reflections *Who Speaks for the Negro?* around the proposition, unquestioned by nearly all his interlocutors, that "human recognition" exists and can have a normative value: "Integration itself is," writes Penn Warren, "ideally considered, the state of mind, the condition of the soul, in which human recognition and appreciation would be mutually possible for us all, black and white").[15] Also—by means of the *universal*, *all*-bearing side of his argument, from what in December 1964 the sociologist Calvin Hernton had called the "*Institutionalization* of the Negro struggle"—an "institutionalization" amounting to the capture, commercialization, and eroticization of "the Negro struggle" by mainstream white society.

But now it's 2020, and Frank Wilderson's book *Afropessimism* tells a different story from Baldwin's.[16] What has been proved in those fifty-odd years?

Wilderson's 2020 story goes back twenty years, to 2001, when the organizers of the "Race Rave" conference in Santa Cruz, California, demand that the conference participants split into different "color rooms" according to how they are seen by the police. It's 2001 in Wilderson's story. There's debate; the biracial group at the conference protest. They require, and get, their own room. The conference then split into assigned rooms; each group, Red, White, Black, Brown, Biracial, holds a discussion that they're eventually meant to report to their "allies." The Black group, Wilderson says, tears up the sheet of instructions and "liberated ourselves from the constraints of having to make our suffering analogous to the suffering of the people of color" (205). When the groups reconvene, he writes, the White group's discussion turns out to have splintered so that "My wife, Alice . . . exploded. 'This doesn't have a damn thing to do with our relationship to the institution of policing! Let's get back on track.'" Wilderson continues:

> But no one was willing to get back on track. The interesting thing about the trajectory of the conversation in the White room was the way it uncannily mirrored the absolute refusal of the exercise that was going on in the Black room—albeit for different reasons. Alice was shut down because the exercise threatened the most constitutive

> element of Whiteness: White people are the police. This includes those White people who, like Alice, at the level of consciousness, do not want this birthright deputation. At a deep unconscious level they all intuited the fact that the police were not out there but in here, that policing was woven into the fabric of their subjectivity. (208)

Here, then, are contrasting dispositions, Baldwin's and Wilderson's. The latter's "pessimism," from Wilderson's title, is one way of marking the difference between them. The story of the contrasting dispositions will go like this. Everything about us makes clear that Baldwin's 1966 plea for recognition went unheard in the United States. (Or rather—that, heard or unheard, it failed to produce equality and to reduce violence against Black people.) The Civil Rights Act of 1964 could not desegregate so radically and violently segregated a society; the police would not shed an identity forged in slave patrols and later confirmed in training protocols.[17] "Proving" the "common humanity" of the children of former slaves and former slave owners required something else, one more effort, another institution, much more time; it required uttering another word. But Baldwin's disposition in 1966 is not *yet* pessimistic. *After the next time*, *after the next fire*, it seems, there *may* be something like an "Aha!" moment: "Oh, now *we* see," the impervious, *bien pensant* liberal class says, "it was *that* Harlem all along, *our* Harlem, *my* Harlem!" The language of the 1966 "Report" is a description, a warning, and an exhortation—and to this degree it envisions an open future. Its modality is possibility; like Nelson, it offers "Perhaps." So imagine a politics of modality: Baldwin places the figure of necessity, the gendarmerie composed of my old friends "All" and "some" and "no," under the sovereign hand of the figure of *possibility*, of *perhaps*. "Without this recognition," Baldwin concludes his "Report," "our common humanity will be proved in unutterable ways." Here, the word "without" means that it's at least *possible* that "this recognition" will occur, that it may occur in part because by reading Baldwin's "Report" the *bien pensant* New Yorkers will recognize that all is not right with *all*, and then "all" may open wide its arms, and common humanity may at last embrace *all* its children, and then—and only then—*all* the police may wither away. *Without* this possibility, without this chain of perhapses, and maybes, and contingencies, then "our common humanity" will necessarily be proved in unutterable ways. But the *necessity* of that "proof," its holding for *all* our Harlems and for *all* the New Yorks that we can imagine here and to come necessarily—that *necessity*, Baldwin's "Report" wants to say, is still only a *possible* outcome in 1966.

Wilderson's "pessimism" stands on a different story and on a different way of imagining how his own "reports" work. As regards the latter: the path between the first-person report and the "common" experience has lost its protection for Wilderson. It is no longer secure (and is, indeed, revealed to have been false at times, when most secure): the authority of induction, testimony, and report may not translate into language we hold in common. A shadow, many shadows, fall between "I" and "all." Decisively, today the humanist avenues of identification, analogy, and especially "recognition" are foreclosed. Saidiya Hartman has in mind the experience of enslavement of Tom Windham and Charlie Moses. She might have been writing about Penn Warren, Nelson, even Baldwin and Hernton, and about contemporary philosophers of recognition like Axel Honneth: recognition flows from kind, kind is confirmed by recognition.[18] "The selective recognition of humanity that undergirded the relations of chattel slavery had not considered them men deserving of rights or freedom. Thus in taking up the language of humanism, they seized upon that which had been used against and denied them."[19]

To say that the humanist avenue of recognition is foreclosed (along the lines opened up by Fanon, Hartman, and Wilderson) is not to say that *some* will not "recognize" and identify with Baldwin's account: "nearly all" people who have "roots . . . friends . . . deep . . . associations" with the experiences and the places that Baldwin describes may well. *Similarity*, *recognition*, and the production of *kind* are ungovernable, wild; they are "animal"; they are (*pace* Quine) irreducible; they are "muddy savagery," and they exclaim savagely against the idea that as "science" *matures* "the animal vestige is wholly absorbed into the theory."

To say that the humanist avenue of recognition is foreclosed today is to say that *similarity*, *recognition*, and the production of *kind* fall outside of what we theoretically call "human." This means—as regards Baldwin, now—two things. In the first place, that none of Baldwin's English words for the "common" works, recognizably, for *all*, as a kind-term or as a means to producing kind-terms: not "humanity," not "common," not "recognition." Or rather—since they never *did* work in this way for *all*, even for *all* speakers of English (though just who *those* are is not given, not when Baldwin is writing and not today)—I mean, following Hartman, Wilderson, Jackson and others, that the terms fail today for different reasons than Baldwin might have imagined: "humanity," "commonality," and "recognition" fail in terms "unutterable" to Baldwin. What are those terms?

But first, a second way into the foreclosure of humanist "recognition" today. Recognition, similarity, analogy, "our common humanity": whether we set them in the lifetimes of Tom Windham and Charlie Moses; or in 1966 (Baldwin's "Report"); or at the time that Quine is drafting "Natural Kinds," in early 1967; or in 2001, or in 2020, or in 2021; or in a notional time to come—they all answer to the demands of kind: "what *is* this?" means "what is *like* this?" And wherever there is a *demand* necessity conditions possibility; there is discipline; a force; a police—to make sure that you and I, and *all* to whom the demands of kind are addressed, answer to this demand. Someone asks me, "Who are you?" or someone calls out on the street (we have heard this story before; I'll come back to it): someone means, "What are you like, what things that I recognize do you resemble or claim to resemble?" Perhaps someone who is endowed with an authority I recognize, someone acting for an institution, in the name of a university or a school, say, will tell me that I am not speaking English, not properly, not to standard: she will demand that I speak or write it as others do. Or he will say that I am not acting in such and such a way; or not conforming to this or that norm; the usual. We will always, still, find someone speaking *with authority*; he or she will be telling us that "humanity," being the property of the kind of animals that we are, demands this or that of us.

Follow Baldwin and Nelson for a moment. My ghostly "someones," endowed with institutional authority and supported invisibly or visibly by the coercive power of the police, are figures of exclusion and inclusion. Agents of property, they confirm, positively and negatively, that I, and we, possess at least one property in common, a property that belongs to "all." They ensure that I and we, and I inasmuch as I belong to we, are kind, since we *all alike* belong to the property that is our common property, predicable of us, each alone and all together. On my "someone's" authority, on her demand, we *recognize* that common property in each other. A circle, in short, is drawn here—brilliant, blue-shining, encompassing Penn Warren, Nelson, even Baldwin and Hernton, and on to contemporary philosophers of recognition like Honneth: recognition flows from kind, kind is confirmed by recognition.

From just outside this circle, though, someone or something reports. I have just cited Saidiya Hartman on the enslaved person's appropriation of humanist universalism. But her *Scenes of Subjection* goes a step further.[20] "Suppose," she continues,

> that the recognition of humanity held out the promise not of liberating the flesh or redeeming one's suffering but rather of intensifying it? Or what if this acknowledgment was little more than a pretext for punishment, dissimulation of the violence of chattel slavery and the sanction given it by the law and the state, and an instantiation of racial hierarchy? What if the presumed endowments of man—conscience, sentiment, and reason—rather than assuring liberty or negating slavery acted to yoke slavery and freedom? Or what if the heart, the soul, and the mind were simply the inroads of discipline rather than that which confirmed the crime of slavery and proved that blacks were men and brothers? (5)

Hartman argues—in the form, here, of a chain of suppositions, hypotheses, to be tested in the balance of *Scenes of Subjection*—that the circle formed when recognition flows from kind and kind is confirmed by recognition "rather than assuring liberty or negating slavery acted to yoke slavery and freedom." She is writing about the nineteenth century and about the United States, but the argument travels. Terms like "humanity" are *not* held in common, since holding in common is not predicable, in the same way if at all, for those who descend from others' property and for those who hold or held such property; for African Americans and for European Americans.[21] Or rather, if holding humanity in common *is* predicable of *all*, it is only to the extent that within that "*all*" individuals and groups subsist that hold holding in common so differently that they will only ever approach each other *nearly*, and never closely enough to recognize, in each other and in the same way, the common right to property (and properties). It's not just that the property of "whiteness," as Hartman's analysis of the Plessy case shows, could be assigned aspirationally the sense of "what humans desire to hold in common," but that the base concepts of the phrase, not just the concept "human" but also "desire," "holding in common," "holding," and the concept of *property* that draws together political economy and logic, are not recognized as common property. The expression "the animals we are" will mean different things to those on one side and the other of the blue line. The authoritative circle formed by "kind" and "recognition," wrought and protected by loose institutional meshes, reciprocally endowing those institutions with the authority to include and exclude, to recognize, identify, sort, emplace, respond; to sanction or prohibit desire; to regulate work; to judge who will die (Jenny: "*Alle!*") and who will live, what "living" and "dying" mean—a circle instituted upon a circle—both fall open.

## "UNUTTERABLE WAYS": INSTANCE OF THE POLICE, END OF HEGEMONY

In 1968, Hannah Arendt opened "What Is Authority?," an essay that she would later republish in the volume *Between Past and Future*, with a remark about her title. This is Arendt:

> In order to avoid misunderstanding, it might have been wiser to ask in the title: What was and not what is authority? For it is my contention that we are tempted and entitled to raise this question because authority has vanished from the modern world. Since we can no longer fall back upon authentic and undisputable experiences common to all,

> the very term has become clouded by controversy and confusion. Little about its nature appears self-evident or even comprehensible to everybody, except that the political scientist may still remember that this concept was once fundamental to political theory, or that most will agree that a constant, ever-widening and deepening crisis of authority has accompanied the development of the modern world in our century.[22]

I have described the critique we might raise against the authoritative double circle of *recognition*. What, *now*, *today*, after *recognition*, gives institutions sovereign authority over political subjects? Arendt makes the question depend on historical considerations, and so should we, initially. Let's say that today, where sovereignty and authority enter into dispute, the police insists: a symptom, a means of mapping the relation between contemporary sovereignty and contemporary authority, but also the point from which the *necessity* of that relation can be brought into question. Can we imagine institutional sovereignty—without investing institutions with authority? Institutional authority—without sovereign power? What sort of thing hangs between my two "withouts"?

Guided by the sense that the *relation* between "sovereignty" and "authority" is not "self-evident or even comprehensible to everybody" we may feel entitled to ask not just "What is sovereignty?" but "What *was* sovereignty?" We are moved, though, by reasons different from those that Arendt offers in 1954 for asking the questions concerning "authority." Indeed, there is something about Arendt's entitlement to pass from the present tense to the past, from "What is authority?" to "What was authority?," that seems on its face off with regard to the term "sovereignty"—and perhaps this sense that we are not in the same way, if at all, entitled to consign "sovereignty" to a historical past may help us understand just what the term can mean, today. For although the sense of the term "sovereignty" too has "become clouded by controversy and confusion," it is not because whatever "sovereignty" designated or designates has vanished from the modern world.[23] I cast my eyes around and see that everywhere sovereign power and sovereign right are claimed and asserted; everywhere there is a figure that will assert the right to govern a territory, or to define and police the uses of a concept or the rules governing a market. The classic, Westphalian forms of sovereignty persist distributed, sometimes conflictingly, among states, nations, and individuals. They persist alongside emergent forms of sovereignty, and emergent ways of *claiming* sovereignty. Indeed, something like a generalized, if unequal and discontinuous, distribution of the right to claim sovereignty seems at work—ranging from the judicial doctrine of the strong unitary executive propounded by conservative legal theory in the United States; to claims that First Nations make to land and culture against and within "modern," colonial states; to the forms of sovereignty arrogated to metanational institutions (the ICJ at the Hague, of course, the WTO, IMF, and so on); to claims offered by nonstate organizations, from "terrorist" networks (Al-Qaeda notoriously) to corporations (including universities) invested with powers of legislation, value-determination, legitimation, and coercion throughout the late-capitalist world. Duplicate, doubled formulations, once safely remitting to an authoritative, consensual understanding, now fall apart: how is *the* right to rights claimed? How is the act of claiming mimicked, *performed*? The singularity of the concept of "right" has lost authority. Yes, whatever "sovereignty" is *today*, it is not what it *was* in the line that leads from Hobbes to Schmitt and Kantorowicz. That this distributed sovereignty *is* other than it *was* in no way diminishes the force of its claims. Neither does the difference between that "sovereignty" *was* and what it *is* authorize us to assign our claims *about* sovereignty today any greater or lesser value than they once had, explanatory or descriptive or normative. (This is not to say that our claims in this regard have no force, just that their force cannot be founded on that difference.)

In 1954 Arendt takes the dispersal and confusion of senses of the term "authority" as evidence of the effective absence of authority itself: absent "authentic and undisputable experiences common to all," the authority of the term "authority" is shaken. Some four years later she delivers a lecture on "Freedom and Politics" in which she strikingly argues, "Under human conditions, which are determined by the fact that not man but men live on the earth, freedom and sovereignty are so little identical that they cannot even exist simultaneously."[24] The lecture, revised and supplemented, makes its way into *Between Past and Future*, where it follows the chapter "What is Authority?" Arendt does not alter her claim in revision. In both the "Lecture" and in the chapter called "What is Freedom?" she continues: "Where men wish to be sovereign, as individuals or as organized groups, they must submit to the oppression of the will, be this the individual will with which I force myself, or the 'general will' of an organized group. If men wish to be free, it is precisely sovereignty they must renounce."[25]

"Sovereignty" is then a different matter from "authority," and it has not, in 1954, not in 1960 or 1961, and not *today*, "vanished" as authority has, or been "renounced" in favor of "freedom." In the question, "What, *now*, gives institutions sovereign authority over political subjects?" the couplet "sovereign authority" designates simultaneously a tautology—what "authority" is not "sovereign"?—and an impasse. For my sense of things differs from Arendt's in two ways. I am not confident that the same frame can be used where "the individual will with which I force myself" is concerned and where "the 'general will' of an organized group" is concerned. "Sovereignty" is not the same in one and the other domain, and the analogy, even the synonymy, with which Arendt treats the two wills, although it expresses something of the critical view of an age in which the psychoanalysis of culture was on the ascendant, is fragile. Then too I am not certain that "sovereignty"—perhaps unlike "authority"—is the sort of thing that "vanishes" or can be *renounced*.

We will find hints of these positions—that "sovereignty" only muddily and ephemerally covers the oppression of both the individual and the general will; that "sovereignty" does not vanish historically; and that "sovereignty" is unlike "authority" in not being the sort of thing that "men" can "renounce," as a monarch would "renounce" her or his crown—in Arendt's own formula, "If men wish to be free, it is precisely sovereignty they must renounce." Am I free to "renounce" "sovereignty"? On what authority will I stand, to what authority will I appeal, in order to "renounce" sovereignty effectively? What sort of act of will is "renouncing"? And perhaps most consequentially: can I "renounce" the sovereignty offered me by this institution (including self-sovereignty: my command of myself, of my decisions), without undermining, if not abolishing, the sovereignty *of* that institution? And reciprocally—does the abolition of that institution hang on my renouncing the sovereignty it arrogates to me, my self-sovereignty, my self-possession? Does it hang on my sovereign decision to renounce its sovereignty?

"Men" in Arendt's phrase "If men wish to be free" must mean singular "men," specific "men," this or that "man"—and not "all men," not "man," generic man, "the collective species," as the alternate translation of Arendt's "Lecture" published in 1961 has it. But Arendt's "must" expresses more than the desire that this or that man should "renounce" sovereignty (his crown, his position and power): it submits the general term, "*all* men," to the command: "you *must* renounce, if you will be free!" Am I, this-or-that man, then "free" *not* to renounce sovereignty? Am I free *not* to be addressed or interpellated by Arendt's normative call? Not if I am to belong to the class of "men" of whom "freedom" is the definitive political foundation. What is perhaps the most famous renunciation scene in literature, Richard II's self-deposition in Shakespeare's play, hangs its discomfort on the question, *can* I renounce what "I" is, or am? What sort of performative act, felicitously grounded in what sovereign authority, am I carrying out when I undo myself, and when I say, with Richard, "I resign to thee . . . I will undo myself; / I give this heavy weight from off my head / And this unwieldy sceptre from my hand"? To *whom* or to *what* do I resign sovereignty? Deposing myself, I pose myself as a naked, immediate subject—in both senses of the term "subject."

Even this is wrong, though: nothing about my experience of subjection is immediate. Here, as you read my words, you remark that I am operating by analogy, if not by synonymy: Richard's experience is sufficiently like my own, and sufficiently like a general experience of sovereign "resignation," that I recognize myself in it and that it can stand in for mine and that of others. On these grounds, on grounds of recognition, analogy, even synonymy, I have invested my argument with the authority of the culturally sanctioned citation; you see me bathing my speech in light that's useful to me, plunging *ad fontes, ab auctoritate*, because Shakespeare—that sovereign value, that figure whose work offers "authentic and undisputable experience" that *should* be "common to all" inasmuch as it has been used, by classes invested in the designation, to name what is indeed culturally common to "all" men—because Shakespeare offers "perhaps the most famous" index in elite Western European culture *of* renunciation and deposition. "To renounce" is to abdicate sovereignty *to* someone, on the foundation of an authority outside me, at another's command: *you must*, whether it's uttered by Henry Bolingbroke or Hannah Arendt. I am offering you as mine King Richard's words in Shakespeare's lines, renouncing my claim to my words and to my argument, but also taking for my purposes from Shakespeare, the figure to whom I have abdicated, his cultural authority. In this I follow Richard himself, who dons Christ's figure momentarily. Richard's analogy—sanctioned by the long tradition asserting the divine right of kings, the synonymy between the sovereign and God:

> I well remember
> The favours of these men: were they not mine?
> Did they not sometime cry, 'all hail!' to me?
> So Judas did to Christ: but he, in twelve,
> Found truth in all but one: I, in twelve thousand, none.

My abjection; my subjection; my sublime subjectivity. To imagine that I can "renounce" sovereignty is to imagine that I can freely, authoritatively, by means of a sovereign act of decision, refuse the address, the interpellation, of Arendt's commanding "must," and that I can address you shorn of analogy and synonymy, shorn of another's cultural authority. It is to imagine that my abjection becomes, by wandering and slow steps, subjection, then subjectivity. It is to imagine that I can *first* cut myself off from analogies, or synonymies, which may supervene even when I don't command them, when they're not at my hand and at my command; *and then*, patient, suffer them to invest me with the sovereign freedom to act. To imagine this is to seek a model of invulnerable, pristine, and deciding political subjectivity, self-deposing and self-founding as Richard is both self-deposing and self-founding when he hyperbolically claims for himself suffering even beyond Christ's ("but he, in twelve, / Found truth in all but one: I, in twelve thousand, none"). To imagine that I can "renounce" sovereignty entails believing one can claim it in the first place, or possess it. To imagine renouncing it means imagining, and seeking to found, in the abject gesture of self-undoing, a subjectivity untouched by the constraints of disciplines, institutions, and other worlds. Untouched, unthreatened—but also rendered useless or unintelligible inasmuch as it is unmoored from the felicity conditions produced by constraining disciplines, institutions, and worlds of speech. Neither the authority on which I stand in order to depose myself, nor the other to whom I deliver my sovereignty in order to receive, in return, my naked subjectivity and subjection, is given, or in my hand, or present to me, or even intelligible to me.

To understand the abject and self-abolishing gesture of unmooring and mooring myself to what is like; to understand this unfounding foundation, we will want to know what follows from insisting on the irreducibility of "sovereignty" and on its structural, if aporetic, complicity—*pace* Arendt—with authority. We will wonder at the specifically *masochistic* disposition on offer. (Richard's masochism has been remarked on more than once.[26]) We will wish to know whether it is true that constraint, even the *police*, provides felicity conditions for my speech; whether my subjection is indeed the condition of my subjectivity, the condition on which I can arrogate to myself the subject's sovereign power to answer to a demand, even the demand to "undo" himself. I will want to ask in what order of speech or description, at what level of analysis, this "irreducibility" operates. Am I (who, I? And who is this "we" who's been following my steps?) not catching myself in Arendt's trap—doesn't sovereignty so designated lead, in her words, "either to a denial of human freedom namely, if it is realized that whatever men may be, they are never sovereign or to the insight that the freedom of one man, or a group, or a body politic can be purchased only at the price of the freedom, i.e., the sovereignty, of all others"? (164).

I take it that for Arendt the path into this dilemma cannot be avoided, whenever "freedom" and "sovereignty" are made synonymous and, together, foundational for political subjectivity, as in the Rousseauvian tradition that she analyzes.

But this is not the *only* conception of sovereignty, authority, and political subjectivity at hand. We find others precisely where the assertion of analogy or synonymy, that is, where the mooring of different terms to the same substance or concept, becomes explicitly a political value.

Let me underscore four differences between sovereignty or sovereign power, and the concept of "authority" (and claims that rest upon it). I am listing them in increasing order of controversiality.

"Authority" cannot stand upon persuasion or coercion, Arendt points out; but "sovereignty" and its claims are indissociable from coercion.

That authority is founded in "authentic and undisputable experiences common to all" "entitles" Arendt and her readers to ask after its absence. The *authority* of such experiences is the title on which the question of "authority" is posed; that these experiences persist or can be revived or evoked, and that their authenticity remain unchallenged, simply *is* "authority" for Arendt. Claims to sovereignty or sovereign power, however, are not, and were never, *founded* in this way. This is not a historical, but a structural and conceptual matter: authority and sovereignty have different, incompatible relations to *foundation*. A figure—a monarch, the Church, an institution like the connubial family or the university—may possess or have possessed authority founded in "authentic and undisputable experiences common to all," but it is or was sovereign because it produces and polices the quality of common-to-allness that makes it possible to assert that this is like that in respect to a third term. That my argument is *like* the lines that Shakespeare gives to Richard in this or that way; that Richard's experience is like Christ's; and so on.

Sovereignty not only is not founded in the recollection or the assertion of a moment in which there were "authentic and undisputable experiences common to all"—it is not *founded* in experiences at all. The sovereign claim *founds* experience, including the experience that "authority" *was*, and *is* no longer.

Finally, note that a great deal of what I am proposing hangs on how we understand the power to produce and to police consensus, or what is "indisputably" "common to all"—what Gramsci and others in his wake have called *hegemony*. I will return to the difficult quantifier "all" in brief. For now, we might agree that for Arendt, experiences "common to all" are indisputable, because disputing them places one outside *what* is and *who* is "common." If I dispute the common understanding of these experiences I am no longer one of many "men," a man in relation to other men, part of "the collective species." Hence the *police*—the institution that the modern state charges, whether explicitly or implicitly, with regulating consensus and with rendering its sovereignty indisputable; hence the efforts modern states make to

> invest the police with *authority*; to make of them an institution *commonly understood* to be founded in what is "common to all"; *commonly understood* to be founded in a normative, presocial idea of the "common" good or common weal. The police is *authoritative* and *authorized*, when it is not understood as an institution-device compounded of devices for producing, normalizing, and administering the *experience* of commonality, and of determining not just what may or may not, but what can and what cannot be experienced *as* common. The devices at hand for this institution-device we call the police: all the technology that comprises the surveillance apparatus; the palette of coercive instruments ranging from the hand or the knee, as in Eric Garner and George Floyd's cases in the United States; to the club, the Taser, and the gun. The police is *authoritative* and *authorized*, when and because it is invested with what jurisprudence in the United States has called "qualified immunity" from prosecution. The explicit legal formulation of such immunity—for instance, in cases built on the precedent of the 1967 *Pierson v. Ray* decision—is secondary to the implicit formula of immunity, to the implicit immunization, that the sovereign always employs when authorizing device-institutions to produce and police, as "common," the experience of its foundation.[27] The police is *authoritative* and *authorized*, when that other set of institutions, the school and the culture industry, have erased from view its function as the instrument-device for producing and regulating consensus.

This is all clear enough today. Is there an alternative?

Let's work our way back to the classic definition of the police in the modern state: it is the institution by means of which the state retains and administers, with regard to the subjects comprising it, a monopoly of violence.[28] I am lifting this standard definition from Weber's essay "Politics as Vocation," which I will consider in brief. In this definition the phrase "with regard to the subjects comprising it" does this work: it draws a distinction between the military and the police, as between institutions with different objects, one external as it were, the other internal. Of course today, in the United States and increasingly in other countries, the line between the police and the military is crossed and blurred by the flow of arms and personnel and by the migration of techniques, language, and goals between the two institutions.[29] (Remark what this crossing and blurring of bounds between the institutions also obscures: what and who lies *within* or *without* the State, or just who and what will be subject to its purchase, laws, and violence. And remark as well that this obscuring, crossing and blurring, occurring on what appears a *political* level, enables and is enabled by globalizing capital's various effacements or transvaluations, on the *economic* level, of spatial distinctions broadly, as these concern the circuits of extraction, manufacture, distribution and consumption.) The police *classically understood* would be the means or device, the *dispositive*, the legitimate means by which the state enforces its monopoly of violence.

It is something more still. Let's set next to Weber's this summary found in August Vollmer's 1936 book *The Police and Modern Society*. Vollmer, who serves in the literature on the history and sociology of policing as the imaginary founder of modern policing in the United States, represents *The Police and Modern Society* as "the fruit of an earnest desire to understand the human spirit in its waywardness and of a lifelong study of certain problems of human behavior." His goal is to correct "the overwhelmingly indifferent, negative, attitude of the public, punctuated by spasms of short-lived, ineffectual indignation, that in no small degree nullify the effectiveness of police and other restrictive governmental authority." For, Vollmer says, "Public opinion in this country, with respect to the police and to the fundamental, indispensable quality of their functions in any state of society that hopes to endure, is almost disastrously ignorant." He concludes:

> Friction between classes and between races, and between those of differing political, social, or religious beliefs seems to be a universal law. As long as this is true, there will be need for police to preserve order, protect lives and property, and finally, to preserve the integrity of the state and nation. Whatever else may be said of the American police, this fact should be more widely known; namely, that without the police and the police organizations, with all their many defects, anarchy would be rife in this country, and the civilization now existing on this hemisphere would perish. The American police are justified, if for no other reason than because in their hands rests in large measure the preservation of the nation. (185)

*Uniquely*, then, the existence of the police raises the question that Vollmer deems settled ("without the police and the police organizations . . . anarchy would be rife in this country. . . . The American police are justified, if for no other reason than because in their hands rests in large measure the preservation of the nation") but which Weber explicitly poses in "Politics as Vocation": is the state to exist? These are Weber's famous questions: "Like the political institutions historically preceding it, the state is a relation of men dominating men, a relation supported by means of legitimate (i.e. considered to be legitimate) violence. If the state is to exist, the dominated must obey the authority claimed by the powers that be. When and why do men obey? Upon what inner justifications and upon what external means does this domination rest?" We may want to weaken or modify the question that is posed by the existence of the police a bit and ask instead whether when the state is understood to be a relation of humans dominating humans, when it's understood to be a relation supported by means of legitimate, that is, "considered to be legitimate," violence—whether such a state is to exist. The existence of the police opens the question of the necessity of the existence of the state. When and why do men, *Menschen*, obey the police?

Weber in one key and in another Vollmer offer a circle: the police borrows its institutional authority from the authority of the sovereign state, and the state uses the police as a means of self-authorization for the legitimation of its monopoly on violence. The circle formed by this "borrowing" and "using" is definitive of the modern conception of both state sovereignty and police authority. (A third circle! And this one standing, too, upon my first two.)

Let's call the closure of this circle the *instance* of the police. Let's say it is this closure that we desire: we desire it inasmuch as it opens the wandering path from our abjection to our sovereign subjectivity. (Just who "we" is—where the encompassing pronoun's edges are, who or what guards them, with what force and at what cost, I will get to.) To take the instance of the police as our object means addressing the procedures of legitimation by means of which the police acquires, for *some*, legitimacy as *agents of the law* or means of realization of the state, and the state acquires, for *all* its subjects as such, legitimacy as the bearer of the monopoly of violence. These procedures of correlative legitimation involve independent institutions (the school, the university, family, church, the usual lot), the devices for creating consensus in the society, and specifically for the collectivization and regulation of memory and of aspiration, that is, the collectivization and regulation of temporality in the schools, in jurisprudence, the creation of consensus that this or that has always been so and thus, inasmuch as it represents collective wisdom and collective history, and thus that it deserves obedience and has legitimacy—that it is *authoritative*; and that this or that is to be aspired to because it will be the enactment of that collective wisdom and collective history.

The *instance* of the police, then, has the singular function of creating hegemony, that is, of setting the borders for what is "indisputably" "common to all," in Arendt's words. It serves to regulate—to police—analogy and synonymy. It regulates memory and aspiration. It founds what is to count *as* a concept, and as an institution, in sovereign states.

What do I mean when I assert that the instance of the police is *necessary*? I am trying to bypass the dilemma of "fine words" that we encountered when noting that "bastardy," used as a term of exclusion or abolition, implies the "fine word," *legitimacy.* I am not asserting that the institution of the police or of the connubial family is necessary—quite the contrary. Set aside providential or logical-discursive necessity (analytic necessity, or strict implicature, or entailement, or correlation: *necessity* will be the subject of chapter 7), and imagine that the modern state develops as an accident of historical events that could have eventuated otherwise: now the instance of the police is other and more than the means by which the state maintains and has maintained its monopoly over violence. The instance of the police represents the irreducibility of *necessity* in the field of politics or of the necessity of necessity in the field of politics.

In Weber, the second-order function of the police—what I have been calling "the instance of the police"—is at work when what is "legitimate" is made necessarily synonymous with "what is considered to be legitimate." *At work*, like a crossing guard or a doorman, regulating the transition or the story, the time, leading from "what is" to what is *als legitim angesehenen*, that is, *das heist*, from "what is" to "what is considered to be," to what is "commonly" and indeed indubitably *viewed as* legitimate. Under the watchful eye of the instance of the police, what is "legitimate" is not just *like* or analogous to what is seen to be legitimate: it *can become* the same.

The rendering as the same of the legitimacy and perception of legitimacy of the object, state sovereignty, is the function of the instance of police. It remains to ask what sort of political *subjectivity* the instance of the police, the figure representing the necessity of necessity in the field of politics, makes available—to whom, and just why it might be that it is meant to be recognized, desired, and obeyed *by all.*

## DRAMATIS PERSONAE

> Brown, the Chief of Police, is a very modern phenomenon. He conceals within himself two persons—the private individual being entirely different from the official. And this is not a dichotomy *in spite* of which he lives, but one *because* of which he lives. And besides him, the whole society lives through this dichotomy of his. As a private individual he would never lend himself to what he considers to be his duty as an official. As a private individual he could not (and must not) hurt a fly. . . . So his affection for Macheath is thoroughly genuine; certain commercial advantages which spring from it cannot cast a slur on his affection. It is Life that soils everything.[30]

Back to recognition. I have in mind a bit of theater: the moment when the individual on the street is hailed and, feeling herself or himself interpellated, turns around *for some reason.* The scene, as is well known, as is commonly understood, is to be found in Althusser's 1970 essay "Ideology and Ideological State Apparatuses." "Ideology," says Althusser, in Brewster's translation, "'transforms' the individuals into subjects (it transforms them all) by that very precise operation, which I have called *interpellation* or hailing, and which can be imagined along the lines of the most commonplace everyday police (or other) hailing, 'Hey, you there . . .'"[31] *For some reason*: "Why does this subject turn toward the voice of the law," Judith Butler asks, "and what is the effect of such a turn in inaugurating a social subject? Is this a guilty subject and, if so, how did it become guilty? Might the theory of interpellation require a theory of conscience?"[32]

It does, on Butler's account. It requires, too, an account of its historicity. What it means to be or become guilty (or innocent), to hail and to be hailed have different values today than in 1970; the sense of the call, the *experience* it entails, the world it sets in place—all these depend on factors too often viewed as incidental, like the location of our little scene; the race of its actors; their class; and so on. The scene was never innocent and certainly not so when and where Althusser is writing. In the United States today it is the sign of the worst. Hailed, today, many will run, not turn; in 1970 no less so. (Pontecorvo's film *The Battle of Algiers*, released in 1966, rehearses every response to interpellation, at every level—the film's characters turn around to face a call, as Althusser's theatrical characters will do; they run from the police; they fight; they ignore the call; they take the police officer's voice for their own and turn it into a call to arms. Modes of popular resistance, weapons of the weak: spontaneous, like the fantastically resurrected rebellion with which the film closes, where it is as if the inhabitants of the Casbah *call back* in the face of the French colonial police.) And this is how Fred Moten has rewritten it, by means of an analysis of a scene from Pras and kris Ex's 1999 novel *Ghetto supastar*: "Diamond," Pras and Ex's character,

> comes upon the policeman and his gaze rather than being surprised by it from behind in the now-classic Althusserian scene; so we're working in the impossibility of a certain kind of surprise that comes on line when such scenes are transposed into a different venue and recast with different prospective subjects. It takes a special kind of subject-in-waiting to be surprised by the presence of the police or, more problematically, to respond to that surprising hail in a way that betrays the uncut version of what Butler calls a "passionate attachment" to the law. Happily, this special kind of subject-in-waiting is not the universal model. Instead, we've got Diamond, the sentient, sounding object of a powerful gaze. His resistance to that power predates it, indeed is the condition of possibility not only for that power but for a response to that power that is knowing, strategic, appositional. Nixon's interpellative call has practically every institutional apparatus behind it: school; the seductive, mystico-economic power of civil service and civil surveillance in the form of "the force"; even the vulgar parody of

> a kind of filial concern. And even if his insidious demand for recognition works in tandem with Diamond's multiply sourced feelings of guilt, the object resists here and in so doing rearticulates the condition of possibility of the liberatory. Nixon's attempt to reinitialize the "scene of subjection," to replicate the scene of his own subjection, is cut by another mode of organization, the (necessarily musical) theater of objection, black performance as the resistance of the object.[33]

The version of the "Ideology and Ideological State Apparatuses" essay known most commonly in English (and commonly known as the ISAs essay) is the one published in *Lenin and Philosophy*. A longer treatment is to be found in the set of essays published in 1995 as *Sur la reproduction*, which includes—just after the passage I cite above in Ben Brewster's translation—a brief set of remarks that merit attention, in part because they confirm aspects of Moten and Butler's rereadings of Althusser's "theoretical theater," in part because of what they say concerning the reasons the sovereign instance of the police is *desired*. Here is the section omitted from the essay's first publications (in *La Pensée* in 1970 and in *Positions (1964–1975)*, in 1976), and from the version in *Lenin and Philosophy*.[34] Althusser has just posed that matter of interpellation I raised earlier. "The hailed individual, nine times out of ten the right one, turns around, one hundred and eighty degrees: becomes a subject." "Nine times out of ten the right one." The manuscript of *Sur la réproduction* retains a clause that works as a kind of retraction, a switch in direction, a *volte face*, almost a *palinode* in the long Platonic tradition. Here is the passage in full, then Goshgarian's recent translation:

> L'individu interpellé se retourne. Par cette simple conversion physique de 180 degrés, il devient sujet. Pourquoi ? Parce qu'il a reconnu que l'interprétation s'adressait "bien" à lui, et que "c'était bien lui qui était interpellé" (et pas un autre). L'expérience montre que les télécommunications pratiques de l'interpellation sont telles, que l'interpellation ne rate pratiquement jamais son homme: appel verbal, ou coup de sifflet, l'interpellé reconnaît toujours que c'était bien lui qu'on interpellait. C'est tout de même un phénomène étrange, et qui ne s'explique pas seulement, malgré le grand nombre de ceux qui "ont quelque chose à se reprocher", par le sentiment de culpabilité—à moins que tout le monde ait effectivement quelque chose à se reprocher sans arrêt, donc que tout le monde ressente confusément qu'il a au moins, et à tout instant, des comptes à rendre, c'est-à-dire des devoirs à respecter, ne fût-ce que celui de répondre à toute interpellation? Étrange.

Now Goshgarian's translation:

> With this simple 180-degree physical conversion, he becomes a subject. Why? Because he has recognized that the hail "really" was addressed to him and that "it really was

> he who was hailed" (not someone else). Experience shows that the practical telecommunications of hailing are such that hailing hardly ever misses its mark: verbal call or whistle, the one hailed always recognizes that he really was the one hailed. This is a strange phenomenon, after all, one that cannot be explained by "guilt feelings" alone, despite the large numbers of people with 'something on their consciences.' Or is it that everyone always has something on his conscience and that everyone confusedly feels, at least, that he always has accounts to render or obligations to respect—if only the obligation to respond to every hailing? Strange.

Goshgarian's translation allows the strangest points of Althusser's phrase to slip by. He elides a hesitation or reduplication surrounding just what it is that the interpellated subject "confusedly" *feels*. Goshgarian's translation goes, "This is a strange phenomenon, after all, one that cannot be explained by 'guilt feelings' alone, despite the large numbers of people with 'something on their consciences'. Or is it that everyone always has something on his conscience and that everyone confusedly feels, at least, that he always has accounts to render or obligations to respect—if only the obligation to respond to every hailing? Strange." A more literal translation of the last sentence runs like this:

> Unless, that is, everyone has, in fact, something to blame him or herself for incessantly [*sans arrêt*, without arrest, without warrant, without a sentence, as in Blanchot's *L'arrêt de mort*] and thus that everyone feels confusedly that at the very least, and in every instance, she has an account to give, that is [*c'est-à-dire*], duties to respect, even if only the duty to answer to every interpellation. Strange.

Why would Althusser have cut these sentences? Why does Goshgarian get them wrong? The answers to these questions may not be the same, of course. Yes, the dropped lines are more discursive, more informal, than much of the balance of the essay. Still, it seems possible that Althusser cuts them and Goshgarian mistranslates them, not for stylistic reasons, but because they represent something like a 180-degree turn in Althusser's argument, the response to a call or a demand from elsewhere. Judith Butler describes the "tropological quandary" of subjectification in general. Althusser and his translators face it here, at the moment when the subject's formation is thematized, on offer *both* argumentatively (the scene of interpellation is the scene of subjectification) *and* rhetorically. (Althusser's "à moins que," his *unless*, marked with the double use of "strange," *étrange*, signals a strange, simultaneous broadening and weakening of the scene of interpellation: if *all* individuals as such, as individuals, have "an account to give, that is [*c'est-à-dire*], duties to respect," then ideological interpellation, the acting, meta-*subject* of subjectification, works without working on or through particular *objects*: and we must either lose the link between subjectification and specific material institutions like the family, the church, and especially the school, or make that link axiomatic, external to the scene of interpellation, transcendental.) St. Paul's conversion thus lies behind this scene of turning and conversion, of course, as is indicated by the reference to Paul some pages above. Saul, prepared to walk on to Tarsus, *à moins que* . . . And this is how Judith Butler frames the matter:

> Power that at first appears as external, pressed upon the subject, pressing the subject into subordination, assumes a psychic form that constitutes the subject's self-identity. The form this power takes is relentlessly marked by a figure of turning, a turning back upon oneself or even a turning on oneself. This figure operates as part of the explanation of how a subject is produced, and so there is no subject, strictly speaking, who makes this turn. On the contrary, the turn appears to function as a tropological inauguration of the subject, a founding moment whose ontological status remains permanently uncertain.[35]

The primal scene of subjectification, the "tropological inauguration of the subject," is the scene of the interiorization of this turning. It is also, we understand, the primal scene of philosophy, the discipline, the practice: whether in the shape (Butler) of "conscience" or "consciousness," or in the archaic, Greek shape of philosophical self-disciplining. Socrates is he who turns back; Socrates, who, obeying the sound or the sign of the *daimonion*, the policing figure that says *no* to quitting Athens on peril of life; *no*, or *unless*, or *but*, or *à moins que* to the false argument. Socrates, and Althusser millennia after him, turns back midstream (as in the *Phaedrus*, as in "Sur la Réproduction") to recant and retell his story. What does the scene of interpellation *get wrong*? Why turn back just here?

The police scene, it happens, turns on an unresolved philosophical matter that complicates the exposition excessively and opens a particularly dangerous way into the question of the irreducibility of the necessity of necessity in the field of politics. I touched on it in my description of Niobe's grief, of her efforts to persuade the gods by holding together two incompatible renderings of the one: the "one" that is each individual, the cardinal *one*; but also the "one" that can't be made to count; the last, the ordinal *one*, the *one* she prays the gods leave her just because she will never even count, not even as one, for her lone last self. Grief pushes Niobe to fold one "one" into the other. Fruitlessly, we saw. It is the way of despair, the last argument, the one Niobe turns to when all other arguments have failed to persuade. It is also a point of suture offered, imaginarily, in and by means of institution—the suture, synonymization, or folding in of cardinal *one* and ordinal *one*, and, as staged in Althusser's scene, of different and contrasting subjectivities.

Take, on one side, the feeling of guilt that provokes one (again: a radically differentiated "one," along the lines I have mentioned) to answer or to turn around or to call back: "So, are you talking to me?" when one is hailed, the uncomfortable feeling that one has an account to give. Take, on the other, the feeling or the sense that the interpellation might evoke, that one has "duties to respect, even if only the duty to answer to every interpellation." Are they the same? Here the expression for synonymy is the figure of internal translation, Althusser's "*C'est à dire*," Weber's *das heisst*, that is to say, "that is to say." "*C'est à dire*" does the work of rendering synonymous a subjectivity understood to mean that which can render account of itself and its actions (I say, "I am the one who did this or that . . ."), and a subjectivity understood to mean what is nakedly responsible to a duty (I say: "I am what obeys, even if only . . .").

The two positions that Althusser's elided phrases render synonymous line up with two different, classical models of subject formation. On one side, the subject is understood as the aggregate of experiences for which an account can be given, experiences which one can designate and more or less count. On this hand lies an empirical, even empiricist account of subject-formation. On this side, I am what recalls events for which I stand to account—incidents in my life; moments; specific engagements. On the other side stands the empty, formal constitution of the ethical subject: empty, that is, possessed of no specific historical or empirical content. On this other side, my subjectivity is the empty event of my response to an interpellation, to the demand: Obey!, to what Levinas would call an ante-predicative response to the interpellation by the Other.

Every event in my life, inasmuch as I can designate it *as* an event in my life, must under this double description, under the regime of synonymy, be recognized as also an event for which I can be responsible, formally and abstractly and emptily. *Sur la réproduction*—and, vestigially, undercover (for the police also operate undercover: they are not just the *visible* force, "the central and formally responsible nucleus of the 'police,'" as Gramsci said, but "a much larger organization in which a large part of a state's population participates directly or indirectly [I add: wittingly and not] through links that are more or less precise and limited, permanent or occasional, etc.")—the shorn ISAs essay, tell this story: the police interpellate me and I turn around, not only because I feel myself concretely being called to, called to with respect to an event or an incident that I recall or to an obligation I assume as the object of the call, nakedly: but *because* by turning around I institute my subjectivity as the point of suture between these two subjectivizations. Every cardinal event in my life is henceforth part of a list, not just ordinally, but also indexically: it is an event with a proper name for and to which I am responsible. Now, that conjunction, that suture-term, that synonymy that Althusser offers in this excised section of *Sur la réproduction* expresses what the instance of the police *does*, as it expresses the necessity of necessity in the field of politics. The instance of the police, philosophical self-discipline, calls on me to turn towards myself. It installs and protects the regime of synonymy, and moors me to what it institutes as *like* me; it sutures the subject in two synonymized aspects, as empirically constituted by denumerable experiences and as formally, transcendentally responsible for every experience in the abstract; it allows me to recognize myself; to become conscious of myself as *like*.

Theater, I think: institutions are like the theater, standing on the coupling, the *doublet*, of the actor's body in her role, the *doublet* of theatrical presentation and the ideologies it represents, for an audience's *recognition*.[36] The regime of synonymy is what is wanted in the *classic* theater-house: it is the regime of the familiar, of the *family*. Here are Althusser's famous lines regarding the classic theater. He is writing just a few years before drafting the essays that make up *Sur la réproduction*:

> The material, or the themes, of the classical theatre (politics, morality, religion, honour, "glory," "passion," etc.) are precisely ideological themes, and they remain so, without their ideological nature ever being questioned, that is, criticized ("passion" itself, opposed to "duty" or "glory" is no more than an ideological counterpoint—never the effective dissolution of the ideology). But what, concretely, is this uncriticized ideology if not simply the "familiar," "well-known," transparent myths in which a society or an age can recognize itself (but not know itself), the mirror it looks into for self-recognition, precisely the mirror it must break if it is to know itself?[37]

Brecht and Artaud and their followers seek not *recognition*—opposed here as in *Reading "Capital"* to *cognition*, *connaissance*—but estrangement: theirs is theatrical modernism, defamiliarization, cruelty. Works like Brecht's *Galileo* or *Threepenny Opera*, or Artaud's projected performance, "Disregarding the Text," of "The story of Blue Beard, reconstructed from historical records, containing a new concept of cruelty and eroticism" set out to break the mirror, to crack the *doublet* of subjectivization that offers recognition on condition that we recognize the authority of the stage that calls us—the audience—into similitude with the ideological forms that play upon it.[38]

But the Althusserian scene of suture that I have been evoking is not yet as cruel and unfamiliar as its Brechtian and Artauldian kin (or rather, it only becomes unfamiliar if its *palinode* is restored: if we return Althusser's "strange" gesture of broadening and weakening the claims of subjectivation to the scene of interpellation). It can become still more familiar, philosophically; portentous, even; if we give the subjective positions that Althusser's bit of theoretical theater sutures together, and the procedure of suturing or synonymizing that the scene performs, the names current for them when Althusser is writing.

In 1965–1966 Michel Foucault published *Les mots et les choses*—to considerable controversy.[39] Two years earlier his translation of Kant's *Anthropologie du point de vue pragmatique* had appeared, with a brief introduction announcing the longer work. Foucault closes *Les mots et les choses* diagnostically, referring notoriously to the *doublet empirico-transcendental* that "man" becomes "by the constitution of an empirico-transcendental doublet which was called man." (347) "Man," Foucault writes, "in the analytic of finitude, is a strange empirico-transcendental doublet, since he is a being such that knowledge will be attained in him of what renders all knowledge possible."[40] Just *what* the "doublet" between the empirical and the transcendental is has been a matter of debate since the publication of *Les mots et les choses*. Diverse answers crop up on different levels of analysis. The "empirical" will mean *empirical judgments*, that is, judgments I make regarding concrete subjective experience, historical situatedness, this or that state of affairs. The "empirical" will *also* be synonymous with all that my "empirical judgments" concern (it is a semantic operator too). The "empirical" will stand in for the material substance of the Cartesian *res cogitans*; and for what is accidental, contingent. On the other hand, the "transcendent" will mean *transcendental judgments*, that is, analytic judgments that regard concepts and abstract universals. The "transcendental" is *also* synonymous with just those concerns (abstract universals, empirical concepts, pure concepts). It stands in for the thinking instance in Descartes; in the doublet *ego sum, ego existo*, the "transcendental" is the common subject of which existence (*sum* or *existo*: again, synonyms) is predicated on the basis of the intuition that it is thinking (*sum res cogitans*, accent on the imperfective tense). The transcendental stands in for what is analytically necessary.[41] Calling the coupling of "empirical" and "transcendental" a *doublet* then reorganizes how judgments are to be imagined and how their objects are as well.

So let's call the two subjectivities rendered synonymous, instituted, in the theater of Althusser's *Sur la réproduction* by these names, "empirical" and "transcendental," and link what I have called the regime of synonymy, the suturing accomplished by the instance of the police, to Foucault's expression: "Man, in the analytic of finitude, is a strange empirico-transcendental doublet." Now, just what a "doublet" *is* seems just as unsettled as the suturing or synonymizing of subjectivities delivered by Althusser's "strange" scene—perhaps because Foucault uses the term *doublet* both in a rather loose and in a more strictly philological sense in *Les mots et les choses*. The former, looser usage crops up when he is discussing Velázquez's *Las Meninas*. Here Foucault's prose arranges matters spatially, as we would expect of the description of a painting; the *doublet* is a visual doubling, a correspondence:

> Two other groups made up of two figures each: one of these groups is further away; the other, made up of the two dwarfs, is right in the foreground. One character in each of these pairs is looking straight out, the other to the left or the right. Because of their positions and their size, these two groups correspond and themselves form a pair: behind, the courtiers (the woman, to the left, looks to the right); in front, the dwarfs (the boy, who is at the extreme right, looks in towards the centre of the picture). (12)

"Former doublet" becomes, translated, to "form a pair." Certainly, and the characters depicted in *Las Meninas* are indeed organized roughly in paired form. If pressed, we'd then say that here in *Les mots et les choses* the *doublet* is conceived empirically. The experience of viewing the canvas is primary; *someone*'s solitary, sovereign experience, indeterminate "someone," then famously leads, according to the order of exposition, to the emptying out of that viewer's position, filled thereupon by the ghostly figure of absent sovereignty. First the description of a subject's *empirical* experience of a concrete spatial organization, then the extension of that experience to a *transcendental* disposition: the order of exposition mimics and supports that of experience. First one, then the other; one "I," then another. But the sense of *doublet* is stronger and different in the better-known expression *doublet empirico-transcendental*, which I am suggesting we use to translate Althusser's suturing of subjectivities in the theater of his essay. In the later use of the term in *Les mots et les choses*, empirical and transcendental judgments are not paired spatially; or told sequentially; or twinned formally so that they capture someone's, our, attention for their similarity; or made to rhyme or echo; or made to follow an order of experience coupled or joined to an order of exposition—phenomenal qualities that will strike the eye and ear. In English linguistics, *doublets* are also called "etymological twins" or "twinlings." (A family; common ancestry; derivations; inherited likenesses: all the baggage of the nineteenth century's biological linguistics is with us, including its kin, racialism.) So too in French. *Doublet*, as applied to the relation between concepts that becomes "man," between the *empirical* and the transcendental, is a term for a marked synonymy—an expression for a linguistic repetition with an accidental difference artificially ascribed. Here is Littré's definition: "Name given to words which, being fundamentally the same and differing only in some quality of orthography or pronunciation, have been given special senses by their usage, for instance 'attack' and 'attach' . . ." What I was describing as Althusser's suturing of subjective positions would, in this Foucauldian translation, remit the relation of the two positions to neither the empirical side of the "doublet," nor to the transcendental one, but to a fundamental and sovereign synonymy between the two, even to a common (linguistic!) ancestry: *c'est à dire*. But also—note—to an artisanal, even a *theatrical* scene. (Artisanal: something *sutured* is perhaps repaired; the stitches show its history; scars; traces of violent difference.) On the *doublet*'s artisanal stage, theatricality, deception, even a cosmetic meretriciousness are at work. For a *doublet* is not only a formal couplet, a doubling, a twinning, or a pair of synonyms to which a history of usages has superadded an orthographic difference. A third is always at work, hidden or overt, to add recognizable value (to add the surplus-value of recognition) to the *doublet*. Yes, the empirical "I" and the transcendental "I" answer at once when hailed in Althusser's scene: they are like crystals sutured together and meretriciously dyed to resemble a single and precious stone. Littré: *doublet*, "*Faux brillant formé de deux morceaux de cristal qui, joints ensemble, ont entre eux une feuille colorée*" (a false gem made up of two pieces of glass which, joined together, have between them a thin colored sheet, film, membrane, surface, *lamina*). Littré gives as an example this phrase from Bernard Palissy: "*Considère un doublet, tu trouveras aucuns lapidaires qui font de fort belle couleur de ruby et de grenad, de quelque sang de dragon ou autre matiere, et, ayant taillé deux pieces de cristal, ils en teindront une de cette couleur rouge, et puis mastiqueront l'autre dessus icelle*" (Consider a doublet. You will find some lapidaries who make a very fine color of ruby and garnet, of some dragon's blood or other matter, and, having cut two pieces of crystal, they will dye one of them of this red color, and then putty [*mastiquer*, glue, putty] the other on top of it). A doublet is a bastard.

## "DRAGON'S BLOOD OR OTHER MATTER"

I opened this chapter asking four questions. I have offered my answers to them lopsidedly. Here they are again:

> How does the philosophy of institution today take account of the *indexicality*, the *who says when what where whyness*, of the institution and policing of *race* to which "the civilization *now* existing on *this* hemisphere" seems bound?

Is there a *general* relation between the police's demand and *quantification*?
Just what *is* the relation between the police and *authority*?
How do I take a stand against police without leaning on the "fine words" offered by antecedent and foundational institutions? But also: how do I take a stand against the metaphysics of "legitimacy," and how do we "stand up for bastards," without standing up for the police?

What does this last detour from Althusser's theoretical scene of subjectification through the workshop or the backstage of Foucault's lapidary get us? The authority of *all* institutions tends to *hegemony*, inasmuch as *all* institutions dispose of devices for sorting out what (and who) is "necessary" from what is not; for affirming what is "all"; what "belongs"; what counts or can be made to count as *one*, a *doublet*-one, as one element that "belongs"; for stipulating how the elements that belong relate to one another (their ordinality, for instance: whether *one* comes *the first* or *the last*); how those relations are formalized and invigilated. We called these devices the police, the instance of the police; call them also, turning to a mythical register now, the lapidary's dragon's blood, or the *mastique* holding together two worthless bits of glass; or the dramatis personae gathered together for the purposes of telling a recognizable story. *All* institutions so conceived dispose of second-order devices for affirming, for naturalizing, and for interiorizing (as *conscience*, as *identity*) these devices. Recall, however, Moten's analysis of the scene of police interpellation. He is describing the character "Diamond, the sentient, sounding object of a powerful gaze" who responds to the "policeman's" gaze differently from both the guilty subject-in-waiting of the famous Althusserian scene; the "special kind of subject-in-waiting . . . surprised by the presence of the police"; and, "more problematically," the "subject-in-waiting [who] respond to that surprising hail in a way that betrays the uncut version of what Butler calls a 'passionate attachment' to the law." Moten concludes, as we have seen:

> And even if [the policeman and his gaze's] insidious demand for recognition works in tandem with Diamond's multiply sourced feelings of guilt, the object resists here and in so doing rearticulates the condition of possibility of the liberatory. Nixon's attempt to reinitialize the 'scene of subjection,' to replicate the scene of his own subjection, is cut by another mode of organization, the (necessarily musical) theater of objection, black performance as the resistance of the object.

Moten has been describing just *one* work that concerns him, but it is exemplary, and he moves from the *index*, from the local work, from what is indicated by his "here" ("The object resists *here* and in so doing rearticulates the condition of possibility of *the liberatory*"), to the most general level, the level at which modifiers bear the dignity of substance and concept ("the liberatory"), with entailed *conditions of possibility*. Other "liberatory" models of political subjectivity, objectivity and objectality, and other models of institution—if we can still call them by their names, "subjectivity," "objectality," and "institution"—can be rearticulated where the synonymies that the (mythic) instance of the police installs fail. These subjectivities and the objectalities that perform them unmoor and unfound; they disjoin my experience from my formal responsibility for its event. They make possible, it seems, paradoxical, noncoercive universal quantification: disjoining empirical and transcendental subjectivities, "black performance," "(necessarily musical) theatre," the performance of "the sentient, sounding object of a powerful gaze" steps from *here* and from *one*, one performance, one example, one sounding, to *all*.

From *this here*, then, to *all*. It's a good, old philosophical story that has been keeping us company all along. I told it first as my story, the story of my old revulsion at moving from *here* and *one* to universal quantification—and of the fears that may underlie that revulsion, mine and maybe others'. I resist *all*-ness; I invite you to recognize in yourself ("All men are mortal") the source of this resistance; but just how does the object, this one *here*, in Moten's argument, *resist*? How does *one object* call out? Can we call it the antitype of the policing philosophical voice that calls to Socrates "*No*," or "*unless*," or "*but*," or "*à moins que*," and calls him back from flight to the city, demanding that he turn back midstream; recant; assume a properly philosophical subjectivity; and retell his story? Or is the "sentient, sounding object's" resistance like the antitype of the logical, moral, even political transitivity demand that what's true *definitionally* of *one* case be true for *all* its synonyms, for all other individuals who fall under that same concept: *all cops*? (Again: "All men are mortal.") For Moten, the object's resistance "cuts through" the institution of unitary subjectivities, transcendental and empirical doublets, synonymized actors, definitionally transitive quantifications, elements allowed to count as one, lost or loved *as one*, and through "the uncut version of what Butler calls a 'passionate attachment' to the law" (as Moten puts it). *This* "sentient, sounding object" in particular, this one *here*, "cuts" inasmuch as it *is* "black performance."

So it's not quite right to say "the object's resistance" and have in mind something that I could generalize philosophically ("I fear 'all'-ness because it brings me before my finitude in the form of my concept: I am a man," or "the object's resistance is the insistence of singularity where the claim of *all*-ness is made") or metaphilosophically, as when I'd want to claim that "the object's resistance" is like a tool of thought, *one* tool, critical-analytic, serving to interrupt stories and transitions or to "cut" apart *doublets*, or to "cut" apart the police's call to suture subjectivities, or to "cut" apart the institutions that promise or seek to guard their suture and synonymy. Moten's description—almost a definition—of that "sentient, sounding object" is specific. It is offered at a moment, and it is engaged with a particular way of posing the relation between "race" and quantification, *one-ness*, *all-ness*. The indexicality of his claim, its "here"-ness, has just to do with *black performance*, with "sounding," with live (necessarily musical) theatre, with the experience of *this or that* set of events under *those or other particular* conditions. Not just *any* object "resists": the "sentient, sounding" object inasmuch as it is black deforms the political scene by offering "another mode of organization, the (necessarily musical) theater of objection, black performance as the resistance of the object." The "(necessarily musical) theatre of objection" *is* "black performance *as* the resistance of the object." The *object objects*; *sound sounds*; and it thus seems that concept, noun, and substance ("object," "sound") *become* verb, event, performance (an "objection," the staging of an act, "to object" or "to sound"). The *eventing* of the substance-object draws it toward becoming a moment of performance, enunciation, toward this or that location, circumstance.

"Become" is wrong, though. ("Become," when? How? For whom? Under what pressures?) Where the Althusserian theater had ideology call individuals into subjectivity, Moten's *musical theater* works to stage the black individual as object's objection—to being called, to being quantified, to remaining just "here." We are no longer in the arc connecting Baldwin's call for recognition to Wilderson's pessimism regarding the concept. Here, in the "theatre of objection," the police scene of recognition becomes (is made into) the scene of abolition. Of recognition itself, but also of institutions built upon it, of authorities that stand on recognition, of old stories, old forms of storytelling, and old logics, among others. The objection of a "sentient, sounding object" is and is not "one" (it is a substance, an event, an eventing) and does not intrinsically, without force, without some policing, become or even bear sense for "all." It is not *performance* in general, unmarked, but *black* performance that "rearticulates the condition of possibility of the liberatory." (Abolition, then, of the principles of identity, noncontradiction, and transitivity.)

If the "(necessarily musical) theatre of objection" is the stage where *abolition* is performed we want to know just *how* abolition is accomplished; just what is "black" about this performance (abolition is never, then, a *universal* result of "objection"); where that theater stands; who has access to it; why; when: its schema. Just what is *necessary* about the *musicality*, the "sounding" that Moten associates with "black performance"?

We have called the *police*, allegorically, the figure for the necessity of necessity in the field of politics—and will submit that figure to the scheme of abolition. We are calling the *family*, allegorically, the figure for the necessity of necessity in the biopolitical imagination of *relation*. We will submit it, too, to the scheme of abolition.

Let's divide the questions and close *Defective Institutions* addressing each in turn.

# 6

# THE SCHEMA OF ABOLITION

And what does it take to make the slave weep?

Simone Weil

Even the blossoming tree lies the moment its bloom is seen without the shadow of terror; even the innocent "How lovely!" becomes an excuse for an existence outrageously unlovely, and there is no longer beauty or consolation except in the gaze falling on horror, withstanding it, and in unalleviated consciousness of negativity holding fast to the possibility of what is better.

Theodor Adorno

How do we memorialize an event that is still ongoing? Might we instead understand the absence of a National Slavery Museum in the United States as recognition of the ongoingness of the conditions of capture? Because how does one memorialize the everyday? How does one, in the words so often used by such institutions, "come to terms with" (which usually means move past) ongoing and quotidian atrocity?

Christina Sharpe

The "(necessarily musical) theatre of objection" about which Fred Moten has written, as we saw in the preceding chapter, is the stage where *abolition* is performed. But just *how*? Just what is "Black" about this performance? Where does that theater stand, where *abolition* is performed? Who has access to it? Why? When? What is its schema? Just what is *necessary* about the *musicality*, the "sounding" that Moten associates with Black performance?[1]

I have been stressing "performance," but Moten's argument is stronger, for a "performance" may be captured and limited by the stage on which it is performed, by the classic institution that makes it legitimate. It may be *just* a performance—but "resistance" as he understands it, even more than the "*recognition* of the ongoingness of the conditions of capture" (to use Christina Sharpe's words, with my emphasis on "recognition"), seeks to provoke the *abolition* of those capturing-legitimating institutional conditions.

A performance moves me (I have been to see a performance of *The Eumenides*, for instance), or something I see, or something my body feels. (But how?) Like Baldwin, I feel outrage; I take steps, take action—for example, I *report* or I *object*: abolition (say) follows, reparation perhaps as well. This is the classic phenomenology of aesthetico-political experience, its storyline, its fantasy. You might say: first the reality of the stony fact, then its performance, then in the domain of the symbolic a *report*, then perhaps collective action, or individual: an objection. We aren't far from Searle's primitivist allegory, after all. The story I am telling has been the subject of controversy since Aristotle; it comes into sharp focus and renewed question, academically, with the Brecht-Lukács-Bloch debates regarding modernist aesthetics. Outside the university, more proximately, on screens everywhere, the world of hypermediatization, false news, and technological overrepresentation shifts and distresses the story, the fantasy, and the phenomenology.

Something else is at play. Say we follow Moten and Stefano Harney again (who are remotely echoing Du Bois and Carter on "abolition democracy"): "What is, so to speak, the object of abolition? Not so much the abolition of prisons but the abolition of a society that could have prisons, that could have slavery, that could have the wage, and therefore not abolition as the elimination of anything but abolition as the founding of a new society."[2] "So to speak" here marks a play between the "object" of abolition, which is something like an "object" that can indeed be eliminated—a society composed of institutions like prisons, the wage, or slavery (Moten and Harney's examples; let's add to these the family); the "object," that is, the *goal* or the "objective" of abolition: "the founding of a new society"; and the *means of achieving* that second "object": "objection."

Abolition as Moten and Harney imagine it involves, so to speak, the abolition of "eliminative" abolition (which takes aim at specific institutional objects, including meta-institutions like the Rawlsian "social union of social unions" that is a "society that could have" or be made up of slavery, the wage, etc.), and its replacement by "foundational" abolition, by means of "objection." I take it that the first, eliminative abolition is simply not sufficient, not adequate to the object of the second—not that it is unnecessary, but that it is not enough. And certainly, the formal abolition of *slavery* in most Western societies, of the *wage* in command economies that took that step, of prisons (if, when, that happens), of the family—none of these has meant or will mean the "foundation" or institution of a society in which such institutions are not *possible*. Quite the contrary: these persist and will persist under other names and with slightly altered attributes, rearranged, recombined. Recall Maurice Hauriou's description, in "La théorie de l'institution et de la foundation" of 1925, of the "subconscious ideas" that give rise to "juridical situations," then to institutions:

> If we go to the heart of the matter, we see that the juridical situations that seem self-sustaining are in reality bound to ideas that remain subconsciously in the minds of an undetermined number of individuals. Subconscious ideas are those that live in our memories without at the moment being consciously willed. They are ideas that we have perceived, stored away, and then lost sight of. They live in us without our realizing it, and even influence our judgments and our acts, just as the presence of familiar objects reacts upon us. Subconscious ideas are objects that live within us.[3]

Wage slavery; domestic labor, including gestational labor; carceral states: so much familiar, familial furniture acting in, behind, what we will. A general biopolitics emerges and takes shape. It embeds institutionalism, as we saw in Esposito's *Istituzione* and already in Hauriou's adaptation of Bergson, *élan vitale* become *élan sociale* (though in both Esposito and Hauriou in the key of life and liberation), in the molecular life of organisms. Deleuze, an exceptionally close reader of Bergson and Hauriou, stresses the distinction between "instinct" and "institution."[4] When institutional biopolitics emerges, hand in hand with the new nonstate sovereignties of global capital that it enables and expresses, Deleuze's distinction has been *abolished*.

How then do we abolish these objects we have stored away (*emmagasiné*), that inhabit us and act on us like the sense, the ambiance, offered by familiar, familial, forgotten things? That have become, today, the shape of instinct? How to pass from "eliminative" to "foundational" abolitionism—that is the question to which the schema of abolition answers today.

It is notoriously difficult to eliminate objects—instincts, things, intentions—forgotten, warehoused, still active. First, it seems, they are to be unforgotten; they have to be *objected*; first, the old distinction between instinct and institution must be reestablished or at least *recalled*. But this is perilous, since I may be reestablishing, willy-nilly, an old distinction between nature ("instinct") and society ("institution") unthinkable outside the very history of colonial, racial, and civilizational uses that I am also seeking to abolish. Objecting, I may be reinstalling a regime in which bodies, objectified, can be used the way stones or instruments are used. The schema of abolition, then, suffers from paradox and courts danger. Abolition, I remember, is the institutional means that European legislators and sovereigns employed to "manage forgetting and abolish the past," as the historian Claude Govard puts it.[5] It is not a pardon; it is not remission—although, like both, abolition is an expression, rather than a limit, of institutional power—perhaps the most radical expression of that power, since it casts its hand over what has *already been*, erasing, defacing, unmaking it. The policing power of the institution as such, which has walked alongside us over these last chapters, is brought to bear, under abolition's name, upon the past itself, in the name always (of course) of the perdurance of the abolishing institution. *This*, and not *that*, is made part of the legal, juridical, factual history composing it. The inclusion or exclusion of one or another event in a history lay always within the purview of different institutions, which make themselves by telling allegories of their emergence and endowing them with retrospective necessity and coherence. Now, a specific object or an institution I can point to, something settled, a decided part of history—*stare decisis*—can be eliminated, erased, abolished.

Only, though, if what was settled, what is counted as a decided part of history, is *one*; if it is indeed decided, accomplished, and sustained by an institution, itself ongoing; and not, with Sharpe again, if the *object itself*, the event, what is counted as a decided part of history, is "ongoing," that is, *not* one, not now one, perhaps never one. "How does one," she asks, "in the words so often used by such institutions, 'come to terms with' (which usually means move past) ongoing and quotidian atrocity?"

Here is a different way to tell the story. (Yes, I am comparing small things to great: what protocols, what rules of decorum and measure, permit such comparisons?) My mother, a gentile from the United States, married a Moroccan Jew. Before I was born she converted to Judaism according to the usual rites and with the agreement of the Comunidad Israelita de Madrid, the small Sephardic community in Madrid. So small was it that the Comunidad fell, administratively, under the governance of the London rabbinate, which approved my mother's conversion. Years later, all of us having made our way in Spain and elsewhere as Jews, practicing occasionally, temple and camp and feast and funeral, my sister approaches the rabbi in Madrid about her daughter's Bat Mitzvah. Naturally! But when the records are unsealed a different institutional eye looks over them from the one that had thirty-five years before. Administratively, Madrid now falls under the governance of the Orthodox rabbinate of Jerusalem, which does not recognize Conservative conversions and disallows my mother's, and in consequence un-Jews me and my sisters and our children: abolition, if you will, of a petty sort, with consequences stretching past and future, unfinishing what had seemed settled, asserting an institutional power on the ruin of another and of the identities it had established.

Where small matters and great are concerned, the little business of one particular Spanish-Moroccan-American Jewish-not-Jewish family or the great historic catastrophe of transatlantic slavery and its sequels, we are looking for abolition that is not sustained by an institution, itself ongoing; that does not rest, for its legitimacy and performative efficacy, upon the integrity either of an institution (a classic institution, autopoetic, envisaging itself to be perpetual, the guarantee of identities, of signatures, well policed) or of the events that make up the allegory of that institution. We are looking for a perilous, *suspended* unforgetting; a *suspended* objection. For otherwise no institution, not slavery, not the family, not the police, can be abolished without ushering onstage another familiar, forgotten object ("nature," "culture"): without, indeed, confirming its antecedent sovereignty.

With Moten, I am looking for *this* abolition in the "(necessarily musical) theatre of objection." How will that theater tell abolition's story, whose sense, events, and value are not one, whose time is ongoing, whose responsibilities are revisable?

## AESTHETICS: "COUNTING YOUR HEADS / AS I'M MAKING THE BEDS"

> Scent of magnolias, sweet and fresh . . .
>
> Meeropol, "Bitter Fruit"

I take my head-counting from Nina Simone's famous 1964 cover of the Blitzstein translation of the Weill-Brecht ballad "Seeräuber Jenny," from *Threepenny Opera*. The "piracy" I am interested in calling up immediately covers the usual registers—the *Seeräuber*, the sea-thief, the unlicensed borrower of valued objects and protected materials. A figure, in short, like *Threepenny*'s Macheath himself, but a figure also intended to describe the remarkable—I won't say unique—fate of John Gay's 1728 *Beggar's Opera* in Brecht-Weill's version of the work. That version differs from the many appropriations and adaptations—the many *piratings*—of Gay's work by hinging Gay's interest in the marginal culture of begging with the 1920s and 1930s vernacular Marxist critique of *appropriation*, *circulation*, and *commodification*—terms organized, ever since sea-thieves were imagined as *hostis humani gentis*, about the notion of the pirate.[6] This folding back of the work's subject matter upon the rough history of its pirating, uses, and reuses in the course of the twentieth and twenty-first centuries finds its way rather wonderfully *back* into the matter of the work—for instance, when Louis Armstrong namechecks and inserts, metalyrically, Lotte Lenya's name into the list of Macheath's lovers in Armstrong's cover of the *Moritüt* (later incorporated in the 1959 Bobby Darin/Richard Wess hit version). This opens or continues a tradition followed by Darin: there is, for instance, Ella Fitzgerald ("Oh Bobby Darin and Louis Armstrong/They made a record, oh but they did/And now Ella, Ella, and her fellas/We're making a wreck, what a wreck of Mack the Knife"). And (among many others), there is Sinatra:

> Ah, old Satchmo, Louis Armstrong, Bobby Darin
> They did this song nice, Lady Ella too
> They all sang it, with so much feeling
> That Old Blue Eyes, he ain't gonna add nothing new
> But with Quincy's big band, right behind me
> Swinging hard, Jack, I know I can't lose
> When I tell you, all about Mack the Knife babe
> It's an offer, you can never refuse.[7]

Taken together, the counting figure and the strange, self-reflexive, self-commodifying figure of pirating in *Threepenny Opera* and in "Seeräuber Jenny" above all crop up at different moments, adding something new at each, causing and expressing differently at each moment what we might safely call *aesthetic outrage*—on two levels. First, as regards the *moment*, the signature, the circumstance in which (say) murder or slaughter, or piracy (extensively), is contemplated or takes place: outrage at the wild economic inequality that marked the jazz age in Europe's bourgeois capitals and in the United States (the opera's concern with counting, accounts, and with those in society who *don't count* re-revalues Armstrong's rendition of the namecheck in "Mac the Knife" at a third order, incorporating into the account of Macheath's lovers not just the names of the song and the opera's previous performer, Lotte Lenya, but also the bread lines from the Depression setting: "oh the line starts at the corner," the line of performers, beggars, and lovers). Outrage too at the political and social closure of Cold War society in the United States; outrage, in the 1960s and later, as in Nina Simone's extraordinary 1963 and 1964 rendition of "Pirate Jenny," at racial violence and segregation; outrage expressed as "so much feeling" about one or another historical circumstance, well understood, differently understood, when sung by Lenya, by Simone, or about them.

But second, outrage with respect to an aesthetic mode entwining metalyrical self-commodification with the performance of the lyrical *critique* of commodity culture: so we can only refuse both, never only one, when, as here, they are on offer.

And a third, linked, source of outrage: we cannot, I say, reject either the aesthetic mode or the mode's self-commodification without rejecting the other. Neither can we subtract our own heads from the long line the operetta counts too: the implied *audiences* herded in on the heels of every Lotte, Louis, Bobby, Ella . . . The *Morität*, "Pirate Jenny," and all of *Threepenny Opera* enroll us by preterition, every one: the work captures, judges, and condemns universally and without mercy. (That we may *enjoy Threepenny Opera* intensifies its coercive, universal grasp: you, and you, and I, and we, are on the block, seduced by Macheath, judged and condemned by Jenny.) Like it or not, the line we're in starts at the corner. *Threepenny Opera* makes an offer we can never refuse.

"Aesthetic outrage," then. Linked, inseparably, *both* to historical outrage *and* to the outrage the spectator cannot refuse at the added value, the added commodity value, of the history of uses the work makes patent when it counts the events of its previous performances, and the names of its performers, among the heads or the bodies on display *within* it. But *is* the counting song, the song that Ernst Bloch marvelously refers to as "the little song of Pirate Jenny, delivered by Polly on her wedding day. An innocent joke, which always helps the mood at festivities of this kind, where one takes the good intention for the deed," is "Pirate Jenny," in any of its iterations, and especially just here, at the extraordinary moment when Jenny switches from *allegretto* to what Weill's score calls *meno mosso (wie ein langsamer Marsch)*, like a slow march, is "Pirate Jenny" an example of "aesthetic outrage"?[8] Is "aesthetic outrage" what we feel today, when this bit of shocking news or that snippet of ghastly comment by a politician crawls across our feed? Surely not, or not easily: it's not what we can say, in good conscience, or think that we're feeling.

I will switch to the first person: here is *my* signature. Small things and large again. "Outrage," as well as contempt and disgust, anger too, betrayal, even guilt, are what I felt in June 2017 on hearing the results of the Modern Language Association vote on Boycott, Divestment, and Sanctions (BDS) in 2017—the second of two votes, by the Delegate Assembly and then by part of the membership, to "refrain from endorsing the boycott" of Israeli academic institutions. "Outrage" and the attendant emotions—but would I have called it "aesthetic" outrage? Will I call it that now? "Moral," yes, or I suppose "ethical," and of course "political" outrage, yes. What sort of qualifier is "aesthetic," exactly? We would resist agreeing that "outrage" can be unproblematically "aesthetic," I think, out of a sense that whatever it is we feel when we are outraged isn't *merely* of the order of the aesthetic, not merely a question (on a very impoverished definition of the aesthetic) of a lapse in style, a vulgarity, a tasteless crack. In fact we will feel more than a qualm, more than resistance when "outrage" sails into the domain of the "aesthetic": we may be outraged at the suggestion that our immediate, spontaneous outrage at the radical mendacity and depredations on display, for instance by the Trump administration and its fellow travelers and enablers in the media, judicial system, or the Democratic Party, or by supporters of the racist policies of the Israeli government, could be judged to be an aesthetic matter, again a "merely" aesthetic matter. But the seeming alternative to the aestheticization of outrage taken in this weak, gastronomic, and immediate sense gives us pause as well: on the other side, we are rendering the aesthetic outrageous. The work of art, on this other side, is changed into a matter of technique and becomes a tool with which we are charged to change the world, even to make the world. The rhetoricization of aesthetic experience. On either side worlds are lost, outrageously. Is this the condition we inhabit, then—the twenty-first century's version of the Scholastic donkey, Buridan's ass? Balanced between lost worlds, lacking grounds for grieving one more deeply than the other, we are no longer able to express outrage at outrage's complicity in the loss of our worlds; we can no longer even say, with Brecht's characters, "*Die Welt ist arm, der Mensch ist schlecht*," or in Blitzstein's translation "The world is mean, and man uncouth," and in Ralph Manheim and John Willett's "the world is poor, and man's a shit."[9] The naked imperative, "resist," steps in just here, as the strange noun-verb "hope" did in Obama's campaign—objectless and subjectless expressions, generalized, too rich in "world," too rich in the idea of world, overflowing in counterfacticity, but poor in program.

We should not agree to this primitive, pre-Brechtian construction of the alternative. Or rather, *a certain* "we" should, can and does agree, a modern, even modernist "we"—a strange, denudedly objective, even neutral "we" can, the "we" that includes oneself and the vague "the others" or *das Man*, the "they," as Heidegger has it in paragraph 27 of *Being and Time*.[10] An "everyday" "we" "at the disposal of the whims of the others." But perhaps *we*, another *we*, should not. Will a mandarin contempt for *the* "neutral" *they*, for the antimodernist others who count themselves into a collective world and into a collective pronoun prematurely, form "our" *we*, then? *They* are consigned to the line that start at the corner; but *I* stand apart; *I* enter by a different door or refuse to enter. *I* can hear without being seduced, see without being caught, act without judgment or punishment, live without dying. Like wily Odysseus, like every aristocrat, *I* tie myself to the mast of my ship, enjoy the songs, and sail past the operetta's dangers, past aesthetics' coercion, its outrage. Is there a way of approaching the aesthetics of outrage that will yield a different outcome? A way that doesn't secretly or overtly install an aristocracy, a priority of the counterfactual over the factual (or the reverse), of the mediate experience of the aesthetic over the brutal, *lumpen* experience of the facts of the world (or the reverse)? A path that doesn't end in impasse, in symmetry, or in a generalized principle of translation? (It may well begin there.) That doesn't lead to the choice between a populist, antimodernist collective subjectivity on one side, and a reactionary aesthetic subjectivity on the other?

I think so. I have been calling it the way of "abolition."

What is the schema of abolition? Constructing it requires at least two things. First, it requires doing violence, grave violence, now rather than later, to "the world" understood as an aesthetic object, as an object for show, for use, or for enjoyment, for instance for show to the Homeric gods, to the human animal, or to the intellectual or the pundit; an object for the use and pleasure of the consumer. Second, to construct, address, and install the schema of abolition requires that poverty-of-world, Heidegger's notorious characterization of being without a world language, of merely animal being, be wrenchingly reappropriated. These two violent gestures have an old name: piracy. Piracy in the complex sense in which Simone, Weill, Brecht, and others in the materialist tradition understand it is the contemporary path that binds aesthetic outrage to abolition.

Let's rephrase the question. To get at what still, even after Brecht, might make us uneasy about the expression "aesthetic outrage," it is useful to give it a different shape. To do so allows us—here "us" remains still indistinct: both collective subjectivities, as before, are interpellated, all heads are counted, though not equally—to imagine how to be outraged and what to do with outrage at a moment when the disaggregated beginning of political organization seems on offer

(Black Lives Matter, *Me too,* the constituent processes in Chile, *alter-mondialist* movements across the "developed" and "developing worlds," and a long et cetera: my own preterition . . .). A rather hazy sense of "resistance" infuses (and is captured by) the moment's art and media forms (TikTok, the meme); quiet and loud experiments in productive violence are not infrequently its means (Chile's "*revuelta*" again, but also the creation of autonomous zones in Western cities, syndicalism as a form of resistance to the poieticide promised by AI.)

"'*Fiat ars-pereat mundus*,' says fascism, expecting from war . . . the artistic gratification of a sense perception altered by technology."[11] Thus Walter Benjamin in late 1935 or early 1936. "This is evidently the consummation of *l'art pour l'art*," he famously continues. "Humankind, which once, in Homer, was an object of contemplation [*Schauobjekt*] for the Olympian gods, has now become one for itself. Its self-alienation has reached the point where it can experience its own annihilation as a supreme aesthetic pleasure. Such is the aestheticizing of politics, as practiced by fascism. Communism replies [*antwortet ihm*] by politicizing art," he concludes. Communism answers to the nihilism of fascist aestheticization presumably by world-making rather than by destroying worlds. *Pereat ars*: the *merely* aesthetic, the *merely self-contemplative*, all mere gastronomy, all showing itself, art for the sake of art alone, this all is to perish. Then—*Fiat mundus*, a new world. Benjamin's closing sentences lend to *one* historical-political formation, to his day's fascism, the languages of the *imperium* as well as of the dandy and the aesthete—the Latin of *Fiat ars-pereat mundus* and the French of *l'art pour l'art*. Marinetti's Italian lurks somewhere in the wings as well; the Greek philosophical lexicon hangs over the scene, moving pieces onstage as the Homeric gods who contemplate the show thing of human history intrude at times in it. And then, having lent fascism its languages, Benjamin translates them into workaday communism's German answer: "*Der Kommunismus antwortet ihm mit der Politisierung der Kunst*" (communism answers by politicizing art). An outrageous confidence in our hard-gained capacity to separate an art that is self-contemplating from one that is not seems implied. A symmetrical, facing personification of the two tendencies, fascism and communism, the aesthetic destruction of the world and the worldly destruction of aesthetics, *seems* implied. Mutual translation; a proposal, made in the Latin of general humanist speech, correctly interpreted *because* of its humanist universality, because of the legitimacy granted the proposal by its articulation in the language of classical authority, and answered. (Though not, and this is definitive, *in* that language: not answered in Latin but in workaday, Communist German, the new International, the new language of the newly human universal class. Where we remembered the city and the community in Greek, the *polis*, now we hear and see it reworked, like raw matter in the hands of laborers, Germanized: *Politisierung*.)

If *that way*, in the direction of spontaneous outrage, lay the Scylla of unthinking, natural, reflexive emotion, then *this way*, the way of self-contemplating art, and the way of the enjoyment *of* self-contemplating art as such, *this way*, disguised as the critique of mere aestheticism, lies the Charybdis of the most hieratic of modernisms, the most aristocratic. *That way*, a *lumpen*-aesthetics, and *aisthesis* defined as the body's dumb and passive reception of the senses' impressions. The physical world of hands and bodies lies *that* way. *This way*, a new class is announced, composed of those who experience with supreme pleasure their reflection upon their own birth as the class of producers of the world; *aisthesis* defined as pleasure in reflection; a blood aristocracy of the aesthetic, drawing sustenance and making its world from the reflexive surplus enjoyment of the world of hands and bodies. *This* way, the world of the aesthete; of cultivation in its secondary, class-marked sense rather than its primary, earthbound sense; of thought rather than outrage.

I can now rephrase my opening provocation, unfolding how abolition's scheme leans on "aesthetic outrage" in three directions.

First, stress on the first term: aesthetic rather than, for instance, moral outrage, or political or personal outrage, or whatever other modifier we might choose. We imagine a cluster of sorts of outrage, and our focus today would be in the subclass of "outrage," for instance the outrage that a bourgeois or a liberal electorate or audience might feel at what Hannah Arendt describes, in a passage I will shortly return to, as "cruelty, disregard of human values, and general amorality," the hallmarks not just of 1920s Germany but also of the neoliberal, predatory, and racialized capitalism we witness in the United States today; or outrage at unfairness, at economic inequality, at insult, that is expressed in any of the domains that configure the field that since Baumgarten we call aesthetics. Here we run the classic danger of trading, in place of what we would like to believe is a spontaneous and common feeling, perhaps not yet articulated, perhaps not yet available formally, the formal arsenal developed for the field of aesthetics—the generic and other devices used to express what came before, that genuine sense of outrage. Aesthetic outrage—outrage aestheticized, recognized as such in the lexicon or lexicons given us. Think *Guernica*, always the secondary expression of the shock that the newspapers the painting seems to catch and distress and materialize, would offer.

Second, stress on the noun. Aesthetic outrage: whatever object, or work, in that domain, causes outrage. It's an outrage, this work: it causes that sensation, if that's what it is, a sensation. The object, or the work, works some sort of violence upon the form of expression, its conventions, history, genealogy. This may be in the service of a political or moral outrage, or not.

Finally, a matter hovering between the adjective and the noun: Just what is outrage? On the moving map of affects and affections, will it fall closer to the reputable neighborhoods of the feelings of the beautiful and the sublime? Is outrage closer to disgust, that famously resistant term? Has it always been in the same location on this map, or does outrage travel with other affective, philosophical, and psychological forms?

Each of these directions to our expression will have a historic determination, or any number of them: *aesthetic* outrage, aesthetic *outrage*. A general relativism is in play; at some point, say now, or in 1964, or just after news of the extermination camps became current in Europe and in the United States, or in 1933, or in 1928–29, at some point the experience has one shape, at another the objects that will elicit, for this or that group of people, an experience—changes. "Aesthetic outrage" for our time, in our time, in our world, is at work where the call-and-response that Benjamin seems to offer is interrupted, wrenched from its reflexive, symmetrical circuits: where it is *pirated*, where fascism's proposition *Fiat ars-pereat mundus* doesn't translate into the answering communist alternative, *Pereat ars-fiat mundus*, or vice versa.

Let me show you what I mean. You saw me use, improbably and colorfully, two words. One was the word "pirate," in its verbalized form, "pirating," to describe the interruption of the aesthetic circuit joining the aestheticization of politics and the politicization of art into a call-and-response mirror shape. The other was the word "translation" to define or characterize that circuit. My claim was that this mirroring form, this generalized translation, is interrupted at the point where "aesthetic outrage" enters the game. This becoming-popular of the high modernist critique of merely outrageous, that is to say, merely spontaneous "art" (which reflects ideology and provides no critical, Homeric vantage outside it, no godlike place for self-consciousness to fail at coinciding with itself) becomes, for instance in the view of antimodernist critics from Arendt to Russell Berman, an index of "the obsolescence of the categories of the historical avant-garde," which is also, for the same line of critics, the obsolescence of the categories of vanguardist Marxism. I was thinking about Nina Simone's cover—her *pirating*—of "Pirate Jenny." About Berman's claim that Simone intends "not to hone rational criticism but rather to appeal to emotion, to the terror and pity that characterize the Aristotelian poetics for which Brecht reserved only contempt . . . Wagnerian sentimentalism . . . sentiment . . . sentiment alone" not much needs to be said.[12] More interesting is Arendt's notorious dislike of the *Threepenny Opera*, tellingly expressed in symmetries that evoke Benjamin's, without the edge to his critique. "Particularly significant in this respect," in signaling a misunderstanding of how the aesthetic presentation of outrage would produce pleasure at or resignation to the outrageous in all audiences rather than produce ironic externalization and critique, "particularly significant," Arendt writes,

> was the reception given Brecht's *Dreigroschenoper* in pre-Hitler Germany. The play presented gangsters as respectable businessmen and respectable businessmen as gangsters. The irony was somewhat lost when respectable businessmen in the audience considered this a deep insight into the ways of the world and when the mob welcomed it as an artistic sanction of gangsterism. The theme song in the play, "Erst kommt das Fressen, dann kommt die Moral," was greeted with frantic applause by exactly everybody, though for different reasons. The mob applauded because it took the statement literally; the bourgeoisie applauded because it had been fooled by its own hypocrisy for so long that it had grown tired of the tension and found deep wisdom in the expression of the banality by which it lived; the elite applauded because the unveiling of hypocrisy was such superior and wonderful fun. The effect of the work was exactly the opposite of what Brecht had sought by it. The bourgeoisie could no longer be shocked; it welcomed the exposure of its hidden philosophy, whose popularity proved they had been right all along, so that the only political result of Brecht's "revolution" was to encourage everyone to discard the uncomfortable mask of hypocrisy and to accept openly the standards of the mob.[13]

The pirate—"*die Figur des Piraten*," Carl Schmitt would call it, though he also refers to "*Seeräuber*," sea-thieves—did not, at the time that Brecht was writing his adaptation of the Gay opera, have quite the standing in international law that it would come to have in the wake of the 1937 so-called Conference of Nyon on international piracy. Nor did it have as commonly the specific sense we hear today, the taking over of intellectual property. (Simone, the greatest cover artist, uses the word constantly in interviews.) When Jenny sang "Seeräuber Jenny" in 1927–28, the figure of the "*Seeräuber*" would more likely have called up Schiller's Karl Moor, in *Die Räuber*, to a Berlin audience than the arcana of international jurisprudence. The song had been written for Polly Peachum, but Weill rearranged it and gave it to Jenny, as he did with a number of songs in the course of production. But this one is of particular importance: the ballad could have been sung, in fact, by *any* of the characters. It represents strikingly the relation between the domains of the play's setting—the bleak landscapes of SoHo, the circumstances of Berlin—and the aspirational role played by the character as a pirate queen, unrecognized by all, *always* unrecognized by all, who, in Marc Blitzstein's translation, will "never know to who you're talking," not now when I, Jenny, scrub the floors for you, not tonight, when I pronounce your death sentence, and never after, when your heads roll and you're nothing but counters. "Whoever is alert can sniff out what's always cooking, because it was never yet done cooking," writes Bloch about this moment in the song. "In this Weillian 'Prayer of a Virgin,' the motives for flight are not just sentimental, and the "piety" is not romantic. One discerns the shifting background of the time. . . . This too: the line 'they haven't the least idea who I may be' would not have its sweet and dangerous overtones, if there was no revolutionary condition in the world and if oppressed humanity was not rising up to fully realize itself."[14]

The complication in Brecht is characteristic: the "sweet and dangerous overtones" of the Pirate song flow not from the song's violent content, but rather with the string of indecisions and undecidable functions it sets before the outraged audience—both the ignorant audience Jenny is serving in the cheap Southern hotel, "*dies lumpige Hotel*," and the audience—Arendt!—outraged at the *Threepenny Opera*'s seemingly cheerful nihilism. Recall the moment I opened with—when Jenny's song, leaping in Weill's score a perfect sixth into seemingly lyrical heavens, into fantasy and counterfacticity, leaping out of the physical world of the Southern cheap hotel, of "*meine lumpen und dies lumpige Hotel*," and into the consoling dream of the kitchen maid, leaping into the genre of the revenge song, the *Rache-lied*, leaping into the world of fantasy, may fall into one construction of aesthetics, into *mere* aesthetics. Is what is being staged in the Kitchen-maid's dream song, as Brecht would call it in his *Threepenny Novel*, is the dream-vision supposed to function as an idea planted in the audience's mind, the possibility of a revolutionary change, the abolition of the sorts of classes that maintain the *Lumpenproletariat* in subjection? (Remember Bloch: "The line 'they haven't the least idea who I may be' would not have its sweet and dangerous overtones, if there was no revolutionary condition in the world and if oppressed humanity was not rising up to fully realize itself.") Then anyone, unbeknownst to the exploiting class, could be the bearer of their last word, the unacknowledged sovereign, the figure of the pirate at home in their bosom. Or is the role of Jenny's fantasy to maintain the relations just as they are—that is, to make it possible for her to have a counterfactual experience, to cultivate a private smile and an interior fantasy life that keeps her at work in the subjunctive mode—you may *think* I'm just scrubbing the floors, but mark my words, the day will come, the lonely hour of that promised moment, and then my sovereign right to dispose of you and abolish this regime will shine through, and the heads I count silently now, under my breath, will roll, and my robbers and I will command. The revolution, in short, will someday arrive, like a ship sailing into the harbor, and *then*, but only *then*, will my band of robbers, *die Räuber*, cash in the heads I'm counting now, silently, to myself. (The extraordinary version of "Pirate Jenny" that Bernard Nicolas's 1977 short "Daydream Therapy" offers stages the seeming decision between these alternatives, a generalized insurrectional subjectivity and a counterfactual, deferred, *therapeutic*, dream scenario; subjection or dream, rather than revolt; either Simone's counting song or Archie Shepp's "Things Have Got to Change.")[15] Or more disturbing, more outrageous still—yet another construction of aesthetics: Jenny *takes pleasure* in the world from which her revenge song threatens, or seems, to release her; sacrificially or selfishly, she takes pleasure *in abjection*, in what Chico Buarque's "Geni e o zepelim," the great Brazilian rewriting of "Seeräuber Jenny," calls the abject, deep, even Christlike "goodness" that Geni manifests in giving herself to anyone, and in secretly preferring the love of "*bichos*," a wonderful portmanteau word for the vagrant, the beggar, the lost, the animal, the ugly, the angry; for a bug, for a work—in short, for whatever it is that has no value, for what one finds, indeed, in a *Threepenny Opera*, in "dies lumpige Hotel" and in the *Lumpenwelt* generally. (Geni/Genet.)

| | |
|---|---|
| De tudo que é nego torto | Of all things bent and twisted, |
| Do mangue e do cais do porto | From mangrove to the port's back alleys |
| Ela já foi namorada | She was the lover |
| O seu corpo é dos errantes | Her body belongs to the wanderers |
| Dos cegos, dos retirantes | Blind men, vagabonds, homeless |
| É de quem não tem mais nada | Whoever is destitute |
| Dá-se assim desde menina | She gives herself to them since a child |
| Na garagem, na cantina | In the parking lot, in the tavern, |
| Atrás do tanque, no mato | Behind the pond, on the hill, |
| É a rainha dos detentos | She's the queen of jailbait, |
| Das loucas, dos lazarentos | Crackheads, beggars, |
| Dos moleques do internato | Vagrants from asylums[16] |

The entire opera presents itself under the sign of this dilemma or trilemma—as if the "Pirate song" were the figure of the play and reigned sovereign over it. Any of the characters in the *Threepenny Opera*, and not just Polly Peachum or Jenny, could have sung "Pirate Jenny," because the opera generalizes the condition the ballad describes and makes it the opera's *subject*: abjection its secret pleasure. Aesthetic outrage may be enjoyed, drawn out, like a note sung high and long a perfect sixth above the humdrum march or the mechanical dance of our melodic, impoverished lives; or *any* note, like any event and any one of us, installs the axiom of abolition and carries the seed of that alternative, revolutionary, perfecting and harmonizing lyrical resolution or institution, which we reach for one night, when the ship, the black freighter, lies at dock at last.

But this construction of our sovereign and common dilemma or trilemma is wrong in two important ways. What happens if, and when, we cannot decide whether this object at hand, the ballad "Pirate Jenny," works to aestheticize outrage in that other object of which it is a part, the aesthetic object we call *Threepenny Opera*? Jenny's ballad-object, I said, could have been sung by any of the characters, inasmuch as it provides the shape of the critique of aesthetic sublimation that is the opera's structuring political concern. But is this true—for whom, under what conditions? As true for those standing in line, unable to resist, as for the *aristoi*? Is Jenny's ballad-object then equivalent to every other part of the operetta, or does it stand out of line, an exception, sovereign? What happens if and when we cannot decide whether "Pirate Jenny" works to reproduce, or to announce the end of, or to abolish, the regimes of exploitation that Brecht and Weill, and Nina Simone and Chico Buarque after them, depict and obviously deplore? What can we expect if we thus can't decide whether the figure of the sovereign pirate, offered ostensibly as the heroic leader of the vanguard is also, not implausibly, the taskmaster who has armored herself sadistically in the leader's cloak, the better to maintain, or even worse, to naturalize, the outrageous conditions the opera deplores? What happens when we find, with Jenny/Geni/Genet, that we love the abject, *os bichos*, the beggars as such, love them as we love ourselves?

Well then: if in short the ballad is undecided as to its understanding of the sovereign function of the aesthetic image, then how will we decide whether it, the ballad, has or has not reigned sovereign, always and already, over the opera's understanding of itself? It cannot be decided, on the model (if it is a model) that is offered by "Pirate Jenny," whether "Pirate Jenny" is or is not the hieratic figure into which the balance of the *Threepenny Opera* can be translated. Its sovereignty over the work—that is, the sovereignty of the ballad, *this* ballad, over the formal and ideological claims of the opera—is subject to the same undecidability as its content, Jenny's vision of herself as sovereign over the pirates. And notice then two things, from a conceptual point of view even more intriguing, even more outrageous. The ballad's sovereign capacity to provide a principle that makes the work cohere, what we might call an immanent principle that furnishes the objectality of the work, that sings it, that translates it into the aesthetic register—surely this, too, will now vanish. And then we will conclude that what makes a work like *Threepenny Opera* useful, what turns it into a means or a tool for abolition and for conveying the aestheticization of outrage at historical moments other than those marked in its deictic, historicizing gestures—what makes *Threepenny Opera* translatable—lies just here, where it does not offer itself as an organized, countable historical object, which is to say, just where it performs the undoing of its objectality.

Brecht, Weill, Hauptmann, Blitzstein, Simone, and Buarque's undoing of the aesthetic object makes it untranslatable too—and here perhaps lies the moment of greatest violence in the opera. The general condition that is meant to characterize every character, every way of being in the *Lumpenmwelt*, is also not translatable from one situation, one character's experience, one language to another, not from Brecht's verse to Weill's score or back, and not from German to English or Brazilian Portuguese. At the moment when "Pirate Jenny" suddenly shifts tempo, from the *allegretto* to a *langsam* march, the German says: "*Und ein Schiff, mit acht Segeln, wird liegen am Kai.*" Weill/Brecht's *wird-* construction is particularly striking, and typical of Brecht, of this opera, and of Weill and Brecht's collaborations at this time—this construction of *wird-* as both a future condition, an active, and a descriptive verb. (For instance, in "Surabaya Johnny.") When it comes to translating the expression, Mannheim and Willett have [the ship] "Has tied up the quay" for *Wird liegen am Kai*; Blitzstein translates the verse in full, with a violent colloquialism, as "There's a ship / The black freighter / With a skull on its masthead, / will be coming in." Neither translation quite captures the conceptual oddity of the expression, though Blitzstein's does some of the German originals' work by jamming up the present tense "There's a ship" with the unusual future progressive, "Will be coming in." Brecht's German makes a historical event, abolition, the arrival of the revolutionary ship, of the revolution; the conversion of oppression into sovereignty; the translation of outrage into aesthetic form; the conversion of the aesthetic form into a revolutionary, physical reality with the application of revolutionary force—Brecht's verse makes this event into something that *will lie* in the world. One day, it will be disclosed always to have been lying there already, this ship, this event. The possibility of revolutionary sovereignty enters the scene suddenly, one night, with shrieks and violence, a cut, a distinct historical event, something we could count as we count heads; but it *also* lay there already, always and already. Weill's score seeks to translate this philosophical-grammatical proposition by showing that *any* melodic line and *any* tempo can be interrupted or completed, perfected, through transposition or through modulation. In the very last verse of Nina Simone's version the danger of this modulation is apparent: the note to which she leaps threatens not to end; her breath, infinitely drawn out, arrests the event; the word loses its sense. The love and pleasure of the abject hanging note empties the opera of philosophical, historical, political content; like heads just rolling, the note rolls on and on. (A *hanging* note. Simone covered "Strange Fruit," that most terrible of songs about *breath* and *hanging*, in 1965. She hangs the B♭ on "leaves," in "for the leaves to drop," for an unendurable nine seconds, dropping first one and then a second half-note. Billie Holiday had tended to sing the equivalent "tree" briefly, in "for a tree to drop," and to hang on "to drop," then again on the closing, rhyming "crop"—but just a beat or two, devastatingly, with a full articulation, losing no sense, dropping to the scored note from a half-note above it. Notice the translation from the figure of the tree dropping its fruit in Holiday to the much stranger, even improper "for the leaves to drop" in Simone's version: Do leaves drop "strange fruit"? Or don't they rather themselves *drop*, like fruit, from the branches of trees? Why this strange and estranging enjambment in Simone's cover? The phrase "for the leaves to drop" must also mean that the hanging bodies, the "strange fruit," cause the tree's leaves to drop: that is part of what they are "for," part of their effect. No longer *just* objects, they act, they estrange, they unfinish the scene.)

The unfinishing of the aesthetic object, of the aesthetic image, is accomplished in Brecht and Weill's score and lyrics temporally, and it cannot rightly make its way from German into English. This violent untranslatability is just what makes possible the ballad's uncomfortable drift into other moments and other times. Never just an instrument, never just self-referring, never having a determinate or indeed determinable effect, never just sovereign, never easily *like* one thing, "Seeräuber Jenny" drifts from voice to voice, from Lotte Lenya to Judy Collins to Nina Simone to Chico Buarque and others; from the signature of the crises of capital in the European metropolis to the cheap racism of the Southern hotel, the hypocrisy of bourgeois mores in the emergent capitalist economy of the Brazilian city. "Drifting" here should appear a violently paradoxical term, since it is on the principle of the work's staging and enjoyment of sovereign *untranslatability* that I am saying that it "drifts," or moves, modulates, transposes, even *translates* across times, locations, and characters.

I would be happy to end on that note, on the claim that the pirate aesthetics that Weill and Brecht together diagnose for the crisis of capitalist societies is indeed violent, paradoxical, mobile, singular, modal, abject. Like Jenny, or Polly's, revenge song, one day it lies there, and the worst will be abolished, and the world will change.

Ending there leaves open, though, the question, for whom, to whom. It leaves open the matter of address, of political subjectivity. I am now asking how and whether a work, *Threepenny Opera* or Nina Simone's counting song "Pirate Jenny," can serve to bring about "not so much the abolition of prisons," Moten and Harney said, "but the abolition of a society that could have prisons, that could have slavery, that could have the wage, and therefore [bring about] not abolition as the elimination of anything but abolition as the founding of a new society" (114). Can a work of piratical abolition like *Threepenny Opera* or Simone's "Pirate Jenny" serve to found, to institute, or to build (or, more weakly, to abolish *and* build) something like a collective subjectivity? If so, we will no longer call this "we" built/produced upon the suspended, hanging note of abolition *either* popular and antimodernist *or* aesthetic-modernist; *lumpen*, or *aristocratic*. *This* subjectivity instituted-addressed, addressed-instituted might not be content to wait for the appearance, one day, of the always-already-present event of the arrival of revolutionary subjectivity. *This* subjectivity might work *from* constructing the defective, piratical schema of abolition, *toward* its production, *toward* its indecisive, unnecessary translation, *toward* radicalizing its drift, *toward* making Simone's leap to the hanging note, for a moment, permanent. *Toward* "the founding of a new society." The ship, brought to harbor; the crisis, for a moment, made permanent. A revolutionary subject, in short; our outrage, drawn out all the length of our breath: *Meno mosso (wie ein langsamer Marsch)*.

# 7

# ABOLISH THE FAMILY!

. . . to recall each time another end of the world, the same end, another, and each time it is nothing less than an origin of the world, each time the sole world, the unique world, which, in its end, appears to us as it was at the origin—sole and unique—and shows us what it owes to the origin, that is to say, what it will have been, beyond every future anterior.

Jacques Derrida

Life becomes impoverished and loses its interest when life itself, the highest stake in the game of living, must not be risked. It becomes hollow and empty as an American flirtation in which it is understood from the beginning that nothing is to happen, in contrast to a continental love affair in which both partners must always bear in mind the serious consequences.

Sigmund Freud

I must admit to finding some satisfaction in the thought that the three main areas of human thought—metaphysics, science and ethics—should each give rise to their own form of necessity. There has been a tendency in recent discussions of modality to focus on the notion of metaphysical necessity just as earlier there had been a tendency to focus on the narrow notion of logical necessity. But it needs to be remembered that there are other forms of necessity, not intelligible in terms of these, that are equally important for philosophy and equally worthy of study. Philosophers like to think of themselves as having found the key to the universe. But where there are many locks, it should be recognized that we may have need of many keys.

Kit Fine

A methodological anxiety.[1] I'm arguing *normatively*: "the institution of the police must be abolished," "the institution of the connubial family must be abolished" (and replaced by the *contubernium*, the low alliance). The schema of abolition must be constructed and instituted so that the contemporary crisis can be rendered, momentarily, permanent and something like collective subjectivities can emerge. Now, normative arguments stand on ground-norms; solid or relatively solid rocky foundations (recall the schema of foundation on which I opened); they entail policing devices; mechanisms of recognition; and so on. Am I not treading perilously close to Graeber's gamification of play? Where does the normative claim of my argument stand? I have associated the schema of institution with universal quantification; with foundationalism; and the (instance of the) police with the necessity of necessity in the field of politics. Don't my "musts" entail "alls" and necessities? Don't they stand on the broad shoulders of antecedent and settled agreements?

Since the term "necessity" does double duty, working on both sides of my scheme, not just where classic institutions are concerned but also on the side of defective institutions—in other words, since I am arguing that both classic and defective institutions are in some sense *necessary*—it is best to tackle "necessity" straight off. I will ask: how is "necessity" to be understood when characterizing the classic institution as well as the defective one; how can "necessity" in the field of politics be reconciled with *disobedience*, and with the schema of abolition. I have also left pending the questions whether, and how, that most basic, that most *necessary*, of institutions, the connubial family, should be subject to abolition. In this concluding chapter I bring these pending questions together.

## *UN*-HAPPINESS?

"All happy families resemble one another; each unhappy family is unhappy in its own way," reads a recent translation of the opening line of Tolstoy's *Anna Karenina*.[2] Now in German: "Alle glücklichen Familien sind einander ähnlich, jede unglückliche Familie ist unglücklich auf ihre Weise."[3] The 1910 French translation unusually dispenses with the family and substantivizes what English and German render as a modifier, the Russian *schastlivyy*, *schast'ye*, "happy, happiness"; more gravely, it hides what both the English and the German retain, found in Tolstoy's Russian: the old sense of "happiness" involving just what *happens*, what occurs by *hap*, luck or fortune, *Glück*.[4] Hides it, by dividing what was *one*: the compounded sense of *schast'ye*, "happiness," that shapes the modifier "happy." "*Tous les bonheurs*," runs the French translation, "*se ressemblent, mais chaque infortune a sa physionomie particulière*" (All happinesses look alike, but every misfortune has its special physiognomy).[5] *All* "happy families," "all happinesses"; *every*, *each*, *jede*, *tous*, *toute*, "unhappy, *unglückliche*, *infortunée*," family. What are they, these "happy" and "unhappy" or "unfortunate," *unglücklich*, families?

*All*-ness, universal quantification across a domain ("all humans," "all cops," "all decisions handed down by the U.S. Supreme Court"), is *always* a family matter, a matter of the happiness of families, "domains" entailing principles of inclusion and exclusion, internal and external relations, policing, foundations, a politics of the one. The conceptual work that the classic institution does, the police and family work of making *properly* its own the cases, behaviors, events, subjects, and objects that it covers, can be described, exactly, as the work of making what is accidental or contingent about its domain, what is "happy" in the sense that *it just occurs*, into something "happy" or felicitous in the second, more usual sense: making *fortune* into *bonheur*, or, strangely, making the "happiness" of occurrence "*un*-happy." *This* is like *that*, in a sense; and this similitude, *this* family resemblance I am disclosing, depends on making all families "un-happy" in *that* specific sense. Will this mean that the family, correspondingly, is a matter of *all*-ness? That *all* families necessarily follow from, and are organized by (in the way that I said that all families are organized around terms like *contubernio*), a statement that "All" its members are *this* or *that*, or have *this* or *that* quality? Here our guide might well be the long debate following Wittgenstein's proposal that there is a "family resemblance," rather than a relation of strictly sharing properties, among elements constituting a concept, and that because "family resemblance" cannot be restricted *to* those elements but includes resemblances to things, elements, objects, relations, and the like falling outside the concept, there results conceptual indeterminacy.[6]

I am guided by Wittgenstein's proposal, though an indeterminate concept is not yet and may never become naturally on its own, the stronger thing that I have been calling a "defective" concept. The *Philosophical Investigations* asks its readers to imagine how to provide the concept that answer the question, "What is a game?" Wittgenstein suggests that the elements we group as "games" do not share a *single* property but should instead be seen to conform "a complicated network of similarities overlapping and crisscrossing: sometimes overall similarities, sometimes similarities of detail."

When I approach, so as to estrange and defamiliarize it, the work of familiarization that the concept of "family" carries out, I will first be imagining "family" as "a complicated network of similarities overlapping and crisscrossing." *Networks*, though, like landscapes or cityscapes over which one passes one's eye scanning for similarities here and there, are temporally flat surfaces composed of perduring, self-identical objects—things I can point to, and which could be translated, for instance from this spot to a similar one in a different flat space, according to a formula.[7] Indeed, temporal flatness and self-identity are what makes it possible for me to establish either, and both, that *this* is indeed similar to *that* (offering the sort of description of the organization of concepts that Wittgenstein will criticize); *or*, *and*, that *this* and *that* are related criss-crosswise, overlappingly, and thus form part of an *indeterminate* concept. Here, the similarity between *this* and *that* overlaps with the similarity of one element to a third to which the second element bears no resemblance whatsoever in itself. (We are restricting transitivity radically.)

When I frame the question of the family—a concept that, though permanently in crisis, today takes shape "between neoliberalism and the new social conservatism," in the wake of the crisis of the Fordist family, as Melinda Cooper has beautifully shown—I immediately run into the same sorts of historical problems that we saw when I brought the concept of "institution" and the matter of *All*-ness up against each other in chapter 5, asking after "All cops" and "All humans."[8] The family—if the term can even be given the definite article—has a different history from *All*-ness, and has even a different historicity.

So let's say that the history of the family-institution does not interest me, or not as much as its concept, and this, I find with Wittgenstein, is indeterminate. But *indeterminacy* is not *defectiveness*. Now I imagine an even *lower* sort of association (a *contubernial* logic of association). Here, the component elements of games and families are not only indeterminate, but their *elements* do not possess or even "share" properties in the same way or at, even *in*, the same time. Even the properties that the elements of "games" and "families" seem to share irreducibly, atomically, necessarily, *as* naked elements—the properties of self-identity and continuity, the property "is an element of . . ."—they share only when it is established they do by a third, an interpretant (with the consequences for self-possession and self-identity that we have seen). This way, *defectiveness* lies. It is the way of Oedipus, where the "natural virtues of kinship obligations" (Cooper's spot-on characterization of postwar neoliberals' position regarding the positive effects of the market, which will "automatically" restore these virtues if left unfettered) are denaturalized, as a consequence of the occurrent, *happy*, overdetermination of "kinship" relations; and it augurs the end of the city.[9] What would it take, and what would it look like, to form (part of) such a contubernial, low family?

It would take abolishing the classic family and formalizing what this thing I have called "low alliance" means. How can *contubernial*, low alliance replace the genital, blood, and contractual bases of the connubial family? What is meant by "replacing" here? Surely we don't mean the sort of "replacing" we do when we use a synonym in place of a given word (the aesthetic principle of "elegant variation"), or when we use the English word "bread" instead of the word "*pan*" in Spanish and imagine ourselves to have translated one with the other and adduced all the opportune safeguards regarding the different connotations, and even denotations, of each word. How does "low alliance" help with seeming biological and sociological necessities—with irreducible species-needs, like the need to care for children?

Let's return to the "natural virtues of kinship obligations." Cooper understands that neoliberalism wishes to restore these "virtues" by allowing the market to do its work. Neoconservatives, in contrast, understand "the ideal family" as an "institution that in some sense opposes the market and lies outside it. Its fundamental values must be actively protected by the state." A difference of means not ends seems entailed: "kinship obligations," which both neoliberals and neoconservatives cherish and take to be "natural," express themselves naturally as "virtues." To see why this might be—and the matter is complicated, since when both "nature" and "virtue" are at work we are moving happily and unhappily in muddy water between anthropology, sociobiology, and moral philosophy—let's turn to the portion of *A Theory of Justice* that John Rawls devotes to framing "the course of moral development as it might occur in a well-ordered society realizing the principles of justice as fairness" (404). His scheme, much indebted to Weber and ultimately to Kant, transits from "the morality of authority" ("childish," "primitive") through the "morality of association," to the "morality of principles."[10] It is a stepwise, ascendant "process" from "primitive" and childlike, imitative behavior, to behavior arising from autonomy, when "a person becomes attached to these highest-order principles" and acts in step with the "morality of principles" and out of a desire to be a "just man" (always gendered male in Rawls) (414). Stepwise and developmental, and thus, it seems, continuous—so long as the necessary conditions are met. For the first, "primitive" stage, "The child's having a morality of authority," Rawls writes,

> consists in his being disposed without the prospect of reward or punishment to follow certain precepts that not only may appear to him largely arbitrary but which in no way appeal to his original inclinations. If he acquires the desire to abide by these prohibitions, it is because he sees them as addressed to him by powerful persons who have his love and trust, and who also act in conformity with them. He then concludes that they express forms of action that characterize the sort of person he should want to be. In the absence of affection, example, and guidance, none of these processes can take

> place, and certainly not in loveless relationships maintained by coercive threats and reprisals. (408)

The ecology furnishing love and trust is "the family in some form," meaning "therefore that children are at first subject to the legitimate authority of their parents." Rawls grants that other-than-family structures may take the place of the family classically conceived, but they are in the definitive respect *synonymous* with it, with just some adjustment: "In a broader inquiry," he says, "the institution of the family might be questioned, and other arrangements might indeed prove to be preferable. But presumably the account of the morality of authority could, if necessary, be adjusted to fit these different schemes." (405)

*Ad-justment*: Rawls is playing with the notion of bringing other-than-family structures into a just alignment with the family, which is the natural relation furnishing the just model to which other structures must be adjusted. He has acknowledged as much: "The account of moral development is tied throughout to the conception of justice which is to be learned, and therefore presupposes the plausibility if not the correctness of this theory." *Ad-justment* means bringing to justice; it means a police force, or a conscience, its psychological shape. The *connubial* principle, to which other-than-family structures are to be "adjusted," entails bringing something divergent, wild, queer, antinormative or nonnormative, into adjustment to a primitive and presupposed form: to the family, when we consider other-than-family structures; to natural, staged development in animal life, when we consider the course of moral development. There is barely any need of adjustment: the scheme of transit from child to adolescent to the fully mature, autonomous adult offers us the scheme of transit from the "primitive" authority of morality to the morality of association ("we should note that the morality of association quite naturally leads up to a knowledge of the standards of justice" [414]) and on to the morality of principles. In Kant, the ontogenetic scheme is historical as well, and the Enlightenment occupies the place of the adult and of the "morality of principles."

The connubial principle, the policing principle of adjustment, the naturalized schemata of transit and development, the history and histories that rest upon them: it is *these* that stand to be abolished.

The strongest contemporary arguments for family abolition have slightly different briefs. They—and I—take as demonstrated the imbrication of the contemporary family with the economic logic of industrial, reproductive, and information capitalism. (Cooper's historical work, drawing on a great theoretical, political, and historical archive, seems to me definitive.) I thus follow Sophie

Lewis and M. E. O'Brien in imagining family abolition and what O'Brien calls "communist gender freedom" to entail "the (necessarily postcapitalist) end of the double-edged coercion whereby the babies we gestate are ours and ours alone, to guard, invest in, and prioritize" (Lewis) and "the simultaneous abolition of wage labor and the state" (O'Brien).[11] Without a positive account of the abolition of the connubial principle, however, the policing principle of adjustment, the naturalized schemata of transit and development, and the allegorical history and histories that support and make these widely known will be reinstalled. Here's how that happens in M. E. O'Brien's *To Abolish the Family*. "Communist gender freedom," O'Brien concludes,

> necessitates the simultaneous abolition of wage labor and the state. . . . The positive supersession of the family is the preservation and emancipation of the genuine love and care proletarian people have found with each other in the midst of hardship: the fun and joy of eroticism; the intimacy of parenting and romance. This love and care, transformed and generalized, is what is to be preserved in the abolition of familial domination. Loosened from the rigid social roles of heteronormative gender and sexual identity, the material constraints of capitalism, and remade in the intensity of revolutionary struggle, the potential of love and care can be finally freed onto the world. The abolition of the family must be the positive creation of a society of generalized human care and queer love.[12]

O'Brien's "positive supersession" translates the word Marx and Engels use throughout the *Communist Manifesto* when addressing abolition—wage abolition, the abolition of the classed society, the abolition of the family: the word *Aufhebung*, cancellation, elevation, sublation. Nowhere in Marx—or in Hegel, from whom the term is of course borrowed—is the term free of violence. That it is "positive" here means that the violence of supersession is correctly directed (Rawls: "adjusted"), and has the effect first of preserving, then loosening, remaking, transforming, emancipating, and generalizing what was proper to the proletariat under conditions of exploitation. By what means is this accomplished? Is the abolished family—or some version of the family—the means or the end of this preservation-transformation? O'Brien is not clear. The exhortation closes an argument that wants to maintain the ambiguity the last line forcefully captures: "The abolition of the family must be the positive creation of a society of generalized human care and queer love." Does "must be" mean that the abolition of the family will have been made possible by "a society of generalized human care and queer love"? Here we mean "must be" as when we say, "A proletarian state must be the creation of a revolutionary class," and mean that the revolutionary class creates the proletarian state. Or does the abolition of the family entail "the positive creation" of that "society"? Here we mean "creation" as when we say that "The organic intellectual must be the positive creation of the revolutionary class," and mean that the class creates the intellectual.

The ambiguity, even amphibology, of O'Brien's line is not a mark of confused argumentation but a *necessary* aspect of the argument. For the violence of supersession to be correctly directed, and for what was proper to the proletariat under conditions of exploitation (not *everything* that was proper to the proletariat under those conditions, just all the positive affective relationships privative to the proletariat as such) to be preserved, then loosened, remade, transformed, emancipated, and generalized, it is necessary to maintain the uncertainty whether abolition is something *done by* an existing class or institution which, acting, preserves and expresses itself (the proletariat, acting to preserve and transform its joy, etc.: a kind of *conatus*); or *done to* an existing institution or class, in order to preserve, transform, generalize, etc. qualities first proper to it. *Necessary*, because this uncertainty allows O'Brien both to retain the scheme of the proletarian family (as the just form demanding later adjustment: positive supersession) and to abolish it along with *all* families (cancellation, *Aufhebung*, sublation). The proletariat, O'Brien tells us, "have found" "genuine love and care . . . with each other," found intimacy, joy, love. The "society of generalized human care and queer love" to come adjusts the present and future to that "found" past, and takes from it value, promise, and a way of measuring whether the "society" to come, the society to follow abolition, has indeed reached what proletarian affective life found and preserves.

It may be very difficult, today, *not* to install and preserve an imaginary form of the antecedent institution that we are setting out to abolish, and *not* to adjust to it our desires and the shape of institutions to come (families, classes, judiciaries). We have seen that the schema of abolition, juridically, requires the production and imaginary preservation of a supplementary institution that guarantees the felicity of acts and practices of abolition. (The "musical" suspension-destruction-abolition of this supplementary institution was the subject of chapter 6.) For the ghostly "preservation" of some antecedent from which value is then derived, loosened, remade, transformed, emancipated, and generalized, is the logic of commodity-value that shapes our ecology. O'Brien, for instance, leans on that logic heavily when arguing for the three-way, simultaneous abolition of wage labor, the state, and the family: "found" intimate moments then "loosened" from the conditions of exploitation in which they occur, but preserving the intimacy, the face-to-faceness, that is fundamental to them. The scene so preserved, to which the future will be adjusted, itself remotely preserves, echoes, and draws conceptual value from the intimate, immediate story of value-production as told by classical economists. *First* use-value, the value to me of this thing I fashion as a tool with a purpose, and keep ready to hand; *first*, intimacy, joy, eroticism, communalism, which I experience myself when I stand before you, or when I am fashioning something for my use. *Then* exchange-value, the value to you and me, and most important to you and me as members of a class, the proletariat in O'Brien's story, that this thing has inasmuch as it can stand for other things that you or I need (the complex procedures of value-indexing, of Aristotelian chrematistics, of *translation*, intrude here). *First*, the phenomenology of individual perception and the intimacy, the immediacy, of the tool's *end* to its *use*; *then*, loosened, generalized, the value this thing has to a class *and* as a token for other, mediate, distant uses. *First*, the word-tool "family," used to name kin and blood relation; *then* the figure "family" loosened from its seemingly literal domain, used to name a collection of things that resemble one another in different ways. *First*, stipulatively, immediately, intimately, Marx and (especially) Engels's reflections on "this infamous proposal of the Communists" (as Marx and Engels put it in the *Manifesto*), the abolition of the family; and *then*, and *now*, loosening and generalizing their arguments but borrowing the prestige and the framework of the *Manifesto* and of Engels's *Origins of the Family, Private Property, and the State*, O'Brien's "To Abolish the Family: The Working-Class Family Liberation in Capitalist Development."

When Sophie Lewis advocates for *Full Surrogacy Now*, her project deliberately sets about to dismantle this *first . . . then* scheme, the connubial principle, the policing principle of adjustment, the naturalized schemata of transit and development, the history and histories that rest upon them. Gestational freedom and full surrogacy, anti-work matters, "challenge . . . the logic of hierarchical 'assistance' and [offer] a premonition of genuine mutuality." Economically, sociopolitically, the challenge flows from rendering gestational labor not just value-neutral but *unprofitable*. (Just how this is to happen, beyond the "universalization" of gestational practice, remains unclear.) Conceptually, it flows from Lewis's subtle replacement of the genetic, biological scheme we find still in O'Brien (and in classic abolitionism), the scheme of "positive supersession" and *ad*-justment, with the scheme of surrogacy, a specifically abiogenetic scheme that interrupts, suspends, the *necessary* preservation of the "first" in what follows from it, "then" and "now." This is how *Full Surrogacy Now* concludes. We are no longer in the world of "positive supersession," but O'Brien's Utopian tone still sounds:

> There's a world worth living in, unfurling liquidly through the love and rage of—among other things—contract gestators' refusal to be temporary. Surrogates' struggle is a challenge to the logic of hierarchical "assistance" and a premonition of genuine mutuality; it is an invading mode of life based on mutual aid. For if babies were universally thought of as anybody and everybody's responsibility, "belonging" to nobody, surrogacy would generate no profits. Would it even be "surrogacy" at this point? Wouldn't the question then simply be: how can babymaking best be distributed and made to realize collective needs and desires? Formal gestational workers' self-interest, like that of their unpaid counterparts, is an anti-work matter, and anti-work in the domain of care production is admittedly sometimes bloody. Their tacit threat to reproductive capitalism, whose knowledges and machinery they embody, takes the world a few steps toward queer polymaternalism. Terrifyingly and thrillingly it whispers the promise of the reproductive commune.[13]

Just how are "collective needs and desires" made and recognized? The semantic landscape is terrifying and thrilling; threatening; it is bloody; something—queer polymaternalism?—whispers; something invades. (Something prowls? Recall Lyotard on vengeance.) The operations: *distribution* in the interest of *realization*. The genre: *Gothic*. What is it that whispers or prowls—formally, conceptually—in the normative call for full surrogacy?

Full surrogacy *promises*, among other things, the abolition of family and of the institutions charged with reproduction in all senses—from "babymaking" to the reproduction of class identity. And surrogacy is *full*—here I am walking a road that Lewis does not step on, but which *Full Surrogacy* opens and partially illuminates—when it not only interrupts the reproductive logic of capitalism but also suspends the ghostly logic of commodity-value, the logic of adjustment, of necessary antecedence and "preservation" that shapes our ecology.

We have seen how a certain sort of musicality—musical theater, in the unfinishing mode of Simone, Weill, Moten, and others who have kept us company throughout *Defective Institutions*—can suspend or abolish the figure of institution. Of what defective concept is this musicality a figure, an allegory? What is the Gothic family story it sings?

## DISOBEDIENCE

> *Ariane*: First, disobedience (*D'abord il faut désobéir*), that's the first duty when the order given one is threatening and inexplicable.[14]

Here are scenes from a well-known tale. The women in my story are alike in some ways—in having married a murderer, in being victims of a crime, in being possessed of the quality of *curiosity*, in leaving one family, joining another (and another *sort* of family), and then returning to the first, having destroyed or helped destroy the second. I am thinking of the Blue Beard tale—in Charles Perrault's "La Barbe bleuë" and in Angela Carter's retelling, "The Bloody Chamber."[15] Both—though with evident differences, due to historical and other circumstances—bear on the necessity and limits of the family. I am leaning on this old story to offer an allegory. The Gothic world of Blue Beard's castle is *like* the world of the classic institution but also like the family forms that Blue Beard's last wife leaves and then returns to: the story of Blue Beard is an allegory of institutional closure, of disobedience to such closure, and of its eventual abolition. For the castle-world-family offers closure, protection, imprisonment; it creates and defines *necessities*; it sets rules for sorting needs; offers doors and keys to them, each to each; a unitary sovereignty and docile subjectivities; secrets possessed by the former and unavailable to the latter. And as the old allegory shows, the Gothic family-castle-institution proves sinister, haunted, and—*necessarily*—internally vulnerable. Blue Beard himself exacerbates, to the point of crisis, the family. Let's let his last wife, the last of the series, stand for that crisis. She is its mechanical cause, as any other *last* wife would have been. We have seen how the ordinal properties of "lastness" and "firstness" interfere with the oneness of every denumerable element in a series, and how we mourn what counts as one resultingly. When Blue Beard chooses his wife her "lastness"—we might say" her possession of the quality of "lastness"—is still only a possibility, but she is ushered into a world of necessities as soon as she steps into the castle.

Here is Carter:

> Then, slowly yet teasingly, as if he were giving a child a great, mysterious treat, he took out a bunch of keys from some interior hidey-hole in his jacket—key after key, a key, he said, for every lock in the house. Keys of all kinds—huge, ancient things of black iron; others slender, delicate, almost baroque; wafer-thin Yale keys for safes and boxes. . . . Keys, keys, keys.

But, says Carter's Blue Beard:

> "Every man must have one secret, even if only one, from his wife," he said. "Promise me . . . you'll use all the keys on the ring except that last little one I showed you. . . . All is yours, everywhere is open to you—except the lock that this single key fits. Yet all it is is the key to a little room at the foot of the west tower.[16]

And Perrault, describing how Blue Beard discovers that his young wife visited the "little room" against his wishes:

La Barbe bleuë l'ayant considerée, dit à sa femme, pourquoy y a-t-il du sang sur cette clef ? je n'en sçais rien, répondit la pauvre femme, plus pasle que la mort : Vous n'en sçavez rien, reprit la Barbe bleuë, je le sçay bien moy, vous avez voulu entrer dans le cabinet ? Hé bien, Madame, vous y entrerez, & irez prendre vostre place auprés des Dames que vous y avez veuës. Elle se jetta aux pieds de son Mari, en pleurant & en luy demandant pardon, avec toutes les marques d'un vrai repentir de n'avoir pas esté obeïssante. Elle auroit attendri un rocher, belle & affligée comme elle estoit; mais la

*Figure 6.* Gustave Doré, ***Barbe bleue*** (Bluebeard), in ***Les contes de Perrault*** (Paris: Jules Hetzel, 1862).

> Barbe bleuë avoit un coeur plus dur qu'un rocher: Il faut mourir, Madame, luy dit-il, & toute à l'heure.[17]

This is the anonymous 1745 translation into English:

> *Having taken a view of it,* whence cometh, *says he,* the Blood I see here? I know not, *said she more dead then living.* You known not! *said he*; but I know it, you have attempted the opening of the Closet. Well, Madam, you'll go into it, & take your place amongst the Ladies you have seen there. *She threw herself att his Feet, cryed, Soe begg'd Pardon, with all the shew of a sincere sorrow for her fault. A Rock had been moved, such was her beauty, for her grief. Blue Beard's Heart was harder than a Rock.* You must die said He, Madam, & presently.[18]

"*Il faut mourir, Madame*," makes general what the English restricts to Blue Beard's addressee: "You must die said He, Madam, & presently." Let's follow the French original for now. Generally—or at least in the generality, in the circumstance, that Blue Beard seeks to install in his castle, as the condition of its closure—generally what is necessary for human species-beings, before even we are addressed in person, is what we first have in common: common necessities are what we have, even what we are, in common. In the world we who inhabit the castle share, common "necessities"—the common experience of finitude—lead to being-in-common. Death, for instance. It's the open secret that "every man must have," to which every woman and every man is destined; it's the shared and open secret whose content may not be known. We build our world, our culture, and our castle walls against it and hide our recollection of the secret in the last chamber, the bloody one, where the wilderness of finitude outside the castle finally lies. Blue Beard says: "You may not know that we will die, that my powers and yours will wane, my estate and yours fail. I hide our secret behind one locked door, and more deeply still by sending you to die in my place, all of you and all 'you' inasmuch as I address you, one after another, all moved by curiosity."

So it seems. Our topology is messy, though. Let's try to be clearer and a little less allegorical. Kit Fine calls the common experience of biological finitude a "scientific" necessity, and places it alongside metaphysical, normative, and "other forms of necessity." What he calls "modal pluralism" (following Whitehead's 1925 *Science and the Modern World*) results. Modal pluralism gathers all necessities into one world—"the universe," in Fine's words—where locked doors requiring different keys face "philosophers" as the row of closed chambers in Blue Beard's castle faces his wives.[19] To each lock, one and only one adequate key; behind every locked door, the same thing: "the universe." Like all pluralisms, the modal sort stands on a strongly unitarian base, on a single world subject to a plurality of views held by subjects similar to each other *in being holders of views*.

It would be nice, so nice, to be a modal pluralist: it means having a single world in common. It means having similarity and subjectivity.

Doors are locked for all sorts of reasons, and Fine's "philosophers" (and we, and Blue Beard's last wife) open locked doors for diverse ones as well—we open a door because we know what's behind the door and *require* it; because we don't know what the door hides and would like to find out (we are *curious*); because we are ordered to; because we just wish to, independently of knowing or not what the locked door hides; because it is our job to open doors ("philosophers" are sorts of doormen). All our keys—each addressing one of our necessities—are alike in this respect, and in this regard equivalent: they each serve to open a given door in the castle; they are to be used as means to address problems in the world or "universe" we have in common. (George Eliot's Casaubon might say: If mythologies are diverse ways of describing the unitary world or "universe," then that, that the world or "universe" is held in common and reflexively holds in common what is common to the plural views subjects hold on it—that is *their* key.) To put it differently: to the second-order question, why is it necessary that there be different forms of necessity? There is an answer, also a key: because "there are many locks" in the "universe" (which, for Fine, might be described as comprising the set of all possible "doors," and, for the more Spinozist Whitehead, "the one substance" of which "eternal possibility and modal differentiation into individual multiplicity are the attributes").[20]

The last key in Perrault's and in Angela Carter's Blue Beard stories is different from all the others—though not exactly and not only for its second-order function. It is the bloody key to a door guarding something that may not be known; it is a key to what ends the world of the woman who uses it, definitively locking all other doors in the sinister castle; *and* it figures what is often considered a primary, indeed a definitive, philosophical virtue: curiosity.[21] (A virtue not infrequently ranged opposite *necessity*. Here is the "Discours préliminaire des éditeurs," introducing D'Alembert and Diderot's *Encyclopédie*: "La curiosité est un besoin pour qui sait penser, sur-tout lorsque *ce desir inquiet* est animé par une sorte de dépit de ne pouvoir entierement se satisfaire. Nous devons donc un grand nombre de connoissances simplement agréables à l'impuissance malheureuse où nous sommes d'acquérir celles qui nous seroient d'une plus grande nécessité." [Curiosity is a need for anyone who knows how to think, especially when *this restless desire* is driven by a kind of spite at not being able to satisfy itself completely. We therefore owe a great deal of merely pleasant knowledge to our unfortunate inability to acquire that which would be of greater necessity (my emphasis and translation)].) We're safe where what's necessary is known or *may be known* and has just to be unlocked with the right key, but when curiosity's restless desire moves the woman—the philosopher, us—beyond what may be known in the world, then the world ends. Perrault offers this "Moralité" to Blue Beard's tale. (A second, immediately following, cheekily affirms that no violent, Blue Beard–esque men exist any longer to "demand the impossible": men now—no matter the color of their beard—submissively walk beside their wives):

> La curiosité, malgré tous ses attraits,
> Couste souvent bien des regrets;
> On en voit, tous les jours, mille exemples paroistre,
> C'est, n'endeplaise au sexe, un plaisir bien leger,
> Dés qu'on le prend, il cesse d'estre,
> Et toûjours il couste trop cher. (81)

> Curiosity, for all its attractions, often brings regret; of this, every day we see a thousand examples. It is (and I say this without meaning to displease the female sex) a very light pleasure: as soon as you take it, it ceases to be, and it always costs too much.

Perrault's philosophical, world-ending key is strung on the chain with all the others, with the "Keys, keys, keys" to all the world's domestic and philosophical secrets, with all the keys whose use locks the young wife into her instituted role, masking her subjection to that role in the subjective agency that the keys' use affords her and in the promise that neither subjection nor subjectivity will "cease to be." Only the last key, so like the rest and so different from them all, offers her another door, an alternative to a world of synonymous necessities. Of all the keys that Blue Beard offers his young bride, the last alone bears the indelible, bloody mark of finitude; it alone offers "slight pleasure," ephemerality, the right to know and not to know. The cost: always too high; once the key turns in that door light pleasure (Perrault) and restless desire (*Encyclopédie*) *cease to be*.

Or perhaps they just cease to be in and as expressions of the unitary and commonplace institution, of one same space or "substance"; of the *one* world; of the "universe"; of Blue Beard's castle.

What are the alternatives? Let's follow Freud, for whom necessities are not keys to different doors in one same space, and do not remit to a common world, or admit of analogy amongst themselves. Let's go back to my first, more or less self-evident affirmation that what is necessary for us as species-beings is what we first, primarily, ontogenetically, have in common: common necessities are what we have, even what we are, in common. I will be loose in my use of the terms "common" and "necessary" or "necessity." The words mean something slightly different on either side of the colon that separates the phrase "that which is necessary for us as species-beings, is what we first, primarily, have in common" from the phrase "common necessities are what we have, even what we are, in common." That this symptomatic looseness of expression is necessary to the production and definition of what we have in common, "life" or ontogenesis, "culture," or "civilization," is one of Freud's decisive discoveries.

Here's what I mean. Freud marshals two concepts of necessity in *Civilization and Its Discontents*, in 1929–1930. The first, explicitly addressed, called out by name, lines up with natural necessity (what Fine calls "the form of necessity that pertains to natural phenomena," and Freud calls "the compulsion to work . . . [or] external necessity"). It flows from *transcendental* sources; it bears the mythological name *Ananke*, "*Not-*" (hence *Notwendigkeit*, need/want/necessity) in German—and contrasts with the "equally immortal" principle of Eros on which the essay turns.[22] Blue Beard: "*Il faut mourir, Madame*."

The second concept of necessity that we find in *Civilization and Its Discontents* is implied and performed in the form of Freud's argument, and might be called analytic or syllogistic—"syllogistic," in a long tradition following Aristotle, at *Prior Analytics* 24b18–20: "A syllogismos is speech or reason [*logos*] in which, certain things being supposed, something other than the things supposed results of necessity [*ex anankes*] because they are so."[23] On this definition we line up the syllogistic necessities and contingencies in Freud's exposition—its formal structure; its evidentiary paradigms and rules of consequence and entailment; the embedded responses to objections to some of its historical and historicizing analogies; and so on. Here the antagonist of necessity is not Eros, but contradiction, imprecision, what does not persuade, and whatever it is about a state of affairs that remains unspeakable, *alogon*, or unanalyzable. Here, on the syllogistic side, we'll note the movement of Freud's essay—*from* considering the anecdotal claim that an "oceanic feeling" (more on this anecdotal claim in a moment) lies at the origins of religion, *to* the remarkable discussion of the analogy between his argument's levels—"between the process of civilization and the path of individual development." On this side, ana-logy is lent the force of the syl-logism.

Each concept of necessity in *Civilization and Its Discontents* corresponds to a concept of community, and to a concept of subjective identity supported by and supporting such community: on one hand a contingent community, ephemeral, the product of competing forces, illegible at heart; on the other a normative and norm-dependent community, structured, conventional, transparent. The sort of community we call a "culture," Freud maintains in his early work, should represent a compromise between these two figures of necessity, and between the two sorts of community they entail. But the position the late Freud occupies with respect to culture expresses the impossibility of maintaining that compromise. Instead, *Civilization and Its Discontents* lays the ground, for a defective form of association where concepts of necessity, identity, and community clash with each other violently. *Uncommonly*. That failure is manifest in the subjunctive tone that characterizes *Civilization and Its Discontents*; in the essay's abnegation; in its seeming humility; and, as I will show in a moment, in symptomatic lapses that disjoin natural from syllogistic or analytic necessity and disjoin the commonalities each seems to install.

"Uncommon necessities" are at work wherever what Freud calls "intellectual perceptions" arise, seemingly in response either to empirical sense-perceptions or to affective responses to physical and mental stimuli. "Uncommon necessities" cannot be "satisfied"; they are not "basic"; they do not furnish grounds for moving by analogical steps from some primary domain of needs and satisfactions that we'd commonly assent to call "nature" to a secondary or consequent domain we would commonly assent to call "culture." Freud's necessities do not provide grounds for drawing an analogy between the commonality of natural necessity and the commonalities of culture.[24] And yet these "uncommon necessities," and not the common necessities of nature, argument or culture, of physiology or safety, provide Freud's most far-reaching and controversial account of being-in-common—that being-in-common that takes place in the framework of defective institutions, like the institution of the family and of psychoanalysis; of defective subjectivities; and of cultures or civilizations.

Back to the beginning. I invited us to imagine the contingencies which, being necessary for us as species-beings and constituting, for us as species being, the realm of necessity, are what we first have in common. Common necessities are what we have, even what we are, in common. What is "necessary for us as species-beings" is something, a quality, that is analytically necessary: we are possessed of species-being if and only if we possess that quality. We will say: the necessity of responding to necessity or natural finitude is what every human animal has in common with every-other. Of course this is too broad. This condition is not unique to the human animal. Quite the contrary. In all animals necessity produces commonalities—species-groupings, packs, tribes, bands of brothers or of siblings collected with the goal of providing for each individual a minimal surplus-protection from threats, and a minimal surplus of access to resources. What does seem to be unique to and definitive of the human animal, Freud says as early as *Totem and Taboo*, is the *theoretical* nature of this response to finitude—that is, that for the human animal the response to natural necessity in its most extreme form, as the finitude of life, as physiological necessity, has a theoretical dimension. In the human animal the natural necessities that condition biological life and mark its limit also produce taboos; they produce spirits. Properly human animals are those who are compelled to become *nachdenklich*, after-thought-ly, at the encounter with natural necessity.

So how *does Civilization and Its Discontents* dis-join its necessities, and what sort of being-in-common do we imagine upon that disjunct? The essay does so *theoretically*, by making afterthoughliness, *Nachdenlichkeit*, a constitutive, even a *necessary*, part of *Civilization and Its Discontents*.

Back again to the beginning. It's an odd moment. Freud opens *Civilization and Its Discontents* addressing Romain Rolland's observation in a letter to him that the source of religion is a "peculiar," "oceanic feeling" "which he would like to call a sensation of 'eternity,' a feeling as of something boundless, unlimited."[25] Freud does not discount that others may have this "feeling," though he does not find it in himself, and further believes Rolland's "oceanic" feeling to be other than primary—it accompanies what Freud takes to be "something in the nature of an intellectual perception." The frame seems familiar: "intellectual perceptions" are secondary both to empirical sense-perceptions and to affective responses to physical and mental stimuli. "Primariness" and "secondariness" here are logical as well as chronological determinations; Freud's drive here is to establish what is genuinely "primary," and Rolland's expression fails that test. Freud sets out to understand this other-than-primary "feeling," and as is his custom he looks in a literary work for an analogue. The gesture's familiar: as when Freud turns to Sophocles or Shakespeare, the literary text is taken to express something that any human might have experienced, or dreamt, or felt. In *Civilization and Its Discontents* the gesture has greater force but is also much more fraught than (say) in the *Interpretation of Dreams*, precisely because in *Civilization and Its Discontents* the turn to a cultural product for an example is an argumentative trope that borrows its legitimacy, as it were, from the future, from the closing steps of the argument of *Civilization and Its Discontents*, where the analogy "between the process of civilization and the path of individual development" has become, as I wanted to put it, something of the order of a syllogism. The method, if we can call it that, of conceptual legitimation-after-the-fact has obvious and unsettling consequences for readers schooled in a classically syllogistical logic, but it seems entirely fit to Freud's analytic procedures, which move (as in his discussion of Rolland's little "oceanic" phrase) from phenomena that present themselves *as* primary, to prior consideration of the reason *for* their appearing as primary in the first place.

So let's say that this first moment sets the scene for what is to follow in *Civilization and Its Discontents*. Let's say that we consider it something like the primitive form of the production of "civilization." Here's how Freud addresses the "oceanic feeling":

> Where [it] is not possible [to describe the physiological signs of feelings]—and I am afraid that the oceanic feeling too will defy this kind of characterization—nothing remains but to fall back on the ideational content which is most readily associated with the feeling. If I have understood my friend rightly, he means the same thing by it as the consolation offered by an original and somewhat eccentric dramatist to his hero who is facing a self-inflicted death. 'We cannot fall out of this world.' [*Aus dieser Welt können wir nicht fallen*.] That is to say, it is a feeling of an indissoluble bond, of being one with the external world as a whole.[26]

*Civilization and Its Discontents* will now unfold this still-mute moment on three registers. In the first place, an ontogenetic register. Rolland's particular sense of the "oceanic" can be expressed by analogy. Freud rephrases Rolland's comment regarding the "oceanic feeling" in language from Christian Dietrich Grabbe's 1835 play *Hannibal*.[27] Grabbe's phrase thus provides the ideational content for the "feeling" that Rolland communicates to Freud.

In the second place, a phylogenetic register: a cultural product, Grabbe's play, discloses the *general* truth of a "feeling" that Rolland finds just in himself.

In the third place, a heuristic, disciplinary, institutional register: the analytic procedures of psychoanalysis that produce what is "primary" in both the expressed feeling and its ideational content permit us to move, as if by translation, thematically between the ontogenetic and the phylogenetic registers. The disciplinary devices—a strengthened, syllogistic *analogy* between those two registers, methodologically associating ontogeny with analysis and phylogeny with synthesis, which permits the analyst to translate between them.

Freud's essay unfolds in the pause between this first articulation of what may be "primary" in Rolland's "oceanic feeling," and the concept which will, by the close of the essay, catch up with it—the "intellectual perception" that will finally catch up with whatever it is that this primary example already exemplifies, though not yet clearly and distinctly.

It's an odd moment. Freud, recall, puts it like this: "If I have understood my friend rightly, he means the same thing by it as the consolation offered by an original and somewhat eccentric dramatist to his hero who is facing a self-inflicted death. 'We cannot fall out of this world.' [*Aus dieser Welt können wir nicht fallen.*] That is to say, it is a feeling of an indissoluble bond, of being one with the external world as a whole." Freud rephrases Rolland's comment regarding the "oceanic feeling," we said, in language taken from Grabbe's *Hannibal*. The line "We cannot fall out of this world" evidently struck Freud: he cites it once earlier that we know, in 1915, in an important letter to Lou Andreas-Salomé—though with a difference that I'll return to in brief. Grabbe's *Hannibal* is not especially well known today—though we can perhaps expect a sort of revival of interest in Grabbe's work, in the spirit of the "Grabbe-cult" that flamed under National Socialism in the mid 1930s. *Hannibal* was first performed in Munich in 1918 (so Freud was not, in 1915, recalling a production of the play), and then revived occasionally, finally reaching a sort of perverse fame (along with Grabbe's Napoleon play) in the hero-besotted years from 1935 to 1941 or so.[28] Freud himself, as he recalls, had "Hannibal-phantasies," and even felt an "enthusiasm for the Carthaginian general" during his school years, and he associated these fantasies and his enthusiasm "with [his] father's behavior toward the 'enemies of our people,'" toward Jews.[29] Here is Freud in *The Interpretation of Dreams*: "Hannibal, whom I had come to resemble in these respects [in having "formed a plan of going to Rome"], had been the favorite hero of my later school days . . . [*mit dem Ich diese Ähnlichkeit erreicht hatte*]."[30] A great deal that is of interest follows upon the recognition that this "resemblance," *Ähnlichkeit*, captures an earlier identification with the Carthaginian general's heroism: "And when in the higher classes I began to understand for the first time what it meant to belong to an alien race, and anti-semitic feelings among the other boys warned me that I must take a definite position, the figure of the semitic general rose still higher in my esteem. To my youthful mind Hannibal and Rome symbolized the conflict between the tenacity of Jewry and the organization of the Catholic church" (218).

More in brief on what follows. The scene that Freud remembers in 1915 and in 1929–1930 comes from the end of Grabbe's *Hannibal* play, where a defeated Hannibal and his friend and lieutenant, Turnu, resolve to kill themselves rather than be taken prisoner. Turnu wonders, "Do we have to?" and then, after Hannibal answers "You're not the one they're after—save yourself!" Turnu decides he will drink the poison. Here is a translation of Grabbe's lines.

TURNU We throw off the old skin, like snakes in springtime, and you'll see, we'll get another somewhere else.

HANNIBAL Yes, we won't fall out of this world. We are part of it. [*Ja, aus der Welt werden wir nicht fallen. Wir sind einmal darin.*] Drink!

TURNU *After drinking*. There, take the rest—It tastes strong—Devil, what's happening? Am I spinning around the world, or the world around me? [*Dreh' ich mich um die Welt, oder die Welt sich um mich?*] I'm sweating, and—*Weakly touching his forehead*.—it—is hot ice—commander—? *He dies*.

HANNIBAL You have conquered. Now, Romans, an exiled old man, before whom you have trembled even until his last breath, has eluded you—*He drinks the rest of the poison*. Poison to your health!—Isn't it working yet for me? It's taking so long!—Ha, there—it's coming—Black pilot, where are you?—
*He dies*.

At the origin of *Civilization and Its Discontents*, then, Freud indulges in a bit of translation—of Rolland's "oceanic feeling" into a literary scene that depicts, not the "feeling" that the facts of brute necessity or of being-in-the-world might induce, but rather the fantasy of mastery over necessity, of the conversion of Ananke, finitude and necessity, into a condition that one can "conquer," over which one can have power.[31] Even—especially—by ending their lives, Grabbe's characters "cannot fall out of this world," perhaps because (to use Freud's words from the letter to Lou Andreas-Salomé) "The unity of this world [*Die Einheit dieser Welt*] seems to me so self-evident as not to need emphasis." There is nothing beyond or outside of "this world" into which we *could* fall; no other world beckons, heavenly or hellish. Recall that Freud's *The Future of an Illusion*, published just three years earlier, describes and argues for abandoning an illusory "store of ideas . . . born of man's need to make his helplessness tolerable," ideas defending man "against the dangers of nature and Fate, and against the injuries that that threaten him from human society itself." The gist of these "ideas? To distinguish between *this* world and another, to which *this world* is subordinate. "Life in this world serves a higher purpose [*das Leben in dieser Welt*] . . . Everything that happens in this world [*Alles was in dieser Welt vor sich geht*] is an expression of the intentions of an intelligence superior to us." Grabbe's Turnu and Hannibal, like the Freud of *Future of an Illusion* and *Civilization and Its Discontents*, then, "cannot fall out of this world." With respect to the one-ness, to the this-here-ness, the *dieser*-ness of this world, the individual and the species are, indeed, analogous in the strong, syllogistic sense I am entertaining. My death and my drive to death are part of *this* world—that is what I assert in taking my life. My "my" here intends to designate, not Grabbe's Turnu or Hannibal in particular, but just what is common to all human animals inasmuch as they self-evidently participate in the "unity of this world." We might say: this is what constitutes the "resemblance," *Ähnlichkeit*, of all human animals to each other. Psychoanalysis is the disciplinary expression and the means of achieving understanding of our finite-being-in-common in relation to the one-ness of this world.

That, at any rate, is what we would expect to find here.

We do not. And of course I am moving much too quickly when I assert baldly that Perrault's "*Il faut mourir, Madame*" stands in for an ontogenetic universal, the universal condition of human mortality and finitude. At least the matter is controversial. Recall that Freud insists to Salomé in a letter of July 1915 that "The unity of this world seems to me so self-evident as not to need emphasis." Instead he has in mind, just because that unity can go unsaid, "the separation and breaking up into its component parts of what would otherwise revert to an inchoate mass." *Analysis* rather than *synthesis*, in short. He continues:

> Even the assurance most clearly expressed [*am schönsten*] in Grabbe's *Hannibal* that "we shall not fall out of this world" doesn't seem sufficient substitute for the surrender of the boundaries of the ego, which can be painful enough. In short, I am of course an analyst, and believe that synthesis offers no obstacles once analysis has been achieved. [*Kurz, ich bin offenbar Analytiker und meine, die Synthese macht keine Schwierigkeiten, wenn man erst die Analyse hat*].[32]

Two minimal economies are at work. The first compares the pain of the dissolution of the boundaries of the ego to the assurance, to the consolation, offered by Grabbe's beautifully expressive lines (*am schönsten*: most beautifully expressed). The second compares the movement from analysis to synthesis, to the synthetic drive or to the immediate desire for synthesis (this is where Rolland's "oceanic feeling" will enter on scene). Freud seems confident, in 1915, that the path of analysis rather than the immediate drive for synthesis offers the only way to address the pain of the dissolution of the boundaries of the ego—to a degree because analysis involves "separation and breaking up" and thus performs the ego's dissolution in the frame of the analytic encounter. "In short," he continues to Salomé, "I am of course an analyst, and believe that synthesis offers no obstacles once analysis has been achieved" (*Kurz, ich bin offenbar Analytiker und meine, die Synthese macht keine Schwierigkeiten, wenn man erst die Analyse hat*). The disaster of the First World War, just beginning, will mean, Freud says to Salomé in late November 1914, that "I and my contemporaries will never again see a joyous world. It is too hideous"—even this disaster tends to confirm, rather than put in question, that identity. He continues to Salomé: "And the saddest thing about it is that it is exactly the way we should have expected people to behave from our knowledge of psycho-analysis. Because of this attitude to mankind I have never been able to agree with your blithe optimism" (20–21). Freud's "sadness" at seeing the insights of psychoanalysis confirmed in war eventuates, two years later, in the analysis of "disappointment" (*Enttauschung*) in *Reflections on War and Death*—"disappointment" that the "white races," or "the state," or "the civilized world-citizen," or "the feeble morality of states in their external relations which have inwardly acted as guardians of moral standards, and the brutal behavior of individuals of the highest culture" (17). "Shall we not admit," Freud concludes, "that in our civilized attitude towards death we have again lived psychologically beyond our means? . . . Were it not better to give death the place to which it is entitled both in reality and in our thoughts and to reveal a little more of our unconscious attitude towards death which up to now we have so carefully suppressed? . . . To bear life remains, after all, the first duty of the living."[33]

To bring "life" within psychological means—not to live *über unserer Stand*, the grand economic metaphor: "above our station"—is the task of psychoanalysis: *Si vis vitam*, the *Remarks in War and Death* ends, *para mortem*.

By 1929–1930 Freud seems much less secure regarding the self-evident unity or oneness of this world, about the priority of analysis over synthesis, and—in consequence—regarding his professional identity as *offenbar Analytiker*. Is a "world" unified by war and pandemic "one"? Freud is moved to reject, explicitly and not just as mildly inadequate, the same oceanic "feeling" when Rolland, imagining death, expresses it ("being one with the external world as a whole"). Preparing for death seems, perhaps, a heavier task after world war and global pandemic: perhaps not even possible, even for an *Analytiker*. Now, a great deal, historically, changes between 1915 (a year so heavy with death in Europe) and 1929–1930 (when economic collapse, rather than the disaster of war, was at hand), so we would expect some differences in Freud's perspective on death and in his assurance regarding his own professional identity—but that these changes are, precisely, historical tells us that they are not *universal* and do not remit to ontogenetic laws or constants.

Rolland's "oceanic feeling" is excited by the contemplation of finitude: infinity, on offer as the *universal* experience of finitude. Just how "universal" the experience is seems not given—or (for Freud) not simply given:

> The savage, such as the Australian, the Bushman, or the inhabitant of Terra del Fuego, is by no means a remorseless murderer. . . . The savage fears the avenging spirit of the slain. But the spirits of the fallen enemy are nothing but the expression of his evil

> conscience over his blood guilt. . . . Such a powerful inhibition can only be directed against an equally strong impulse. What no human being desires to do does not have to be forbidden, it is self-exclusive. The very emphasis of the command, Thou shalt not kill, makes it certain that we are descended from an endlessly long chain of generations of murderers, whose love of murder was in their blood as it is perhaps also in ours.[34]

In general, the *anthropology* of "death" ("such as the Australian, the Bushman, or the inhabitant of Terra del Fuego") tends, perhaps for obvious reasons, to move very quickly either toward the register suggested by the faintly paradoxical expressions "thinking about" or "understanding" death, or to the more than faintly positivist register in which descriptions of individual or social "remembering," "grieving" or "celebrating" are set. We find on the *anthropological* side, as it were, arguments that enumerate and analyze the array of practices that respond to the fact of another's death; on the other, arguments that take as their starting point the general unthinkability of death (death, Wittgenstein says in the *Tractatus*, is not an event in life: "we do not live to experience death"; Freud on the "insincerity" of the "conventional attitude of civilized people" toward death: "Let us now leave primitive man and turn to the unconscious in our psyche. . . . Our unconscious therefore does not believe in its own death: it acts as though it were immortal.") Here, a condition of utter cultural particularism, and a turn toward the anthropology of everyday life; there, a universal limit to what can be known or spoken about, and an attendant turn to mysticism (in Wittgenstein's case), to speculation and metaphysics. Seldom are these two arguments, or strategies, put into conversation.

The face-off between cultural empiricism and speculative universalism ("*Il faut mourir*") could hardly be posed more starkly than in Freud's considerations of death's *necessity* in the last years of his life. (Remember the terrible last line of the 1913 essay "The Theme of the Three Caskets": "It is in vain that an old man yearns for the love of woman as he had it first from his mother: the third of the Fates alone, the silent Goddess of Death, will take him into her arms.") In an unexceptional *Via Sacra, y exercicios espirituales, y arte de bien morir* of 1619, Francisco Pérez writes: "*La muerte . . . es una puerta general de naturaleza. . . . Y aunque todas las otras criaturas cuando se corrompen, en su manera dezimos que mueren: mas propriamente se dize del hombre racional*" (Death . . . is a general door of nature, [and] although all creatures, when they decay, may be said to 'die' in their way; it is more properly said of rational man).[35] Pérez is making a broad, traditional claim not just about what "*la muerte*" is but about what sorts of creatures possess it (or are susceptible to it, or characterized by it).

It is the proper of the human, rational animal to die; other animals, unconscious of their end, soulless, die "*en su manera*," but not "*propriamente*." Man is the creature that *dies*. Among creatures, man is exceptional; qua human, no man is exceptional before or in respect to death, the universal condition, since man is only man inasmuch as he can die. (And anyone can die well—as the general Catholic principle, or fantasy, of deathbed conversion attests, and the abundance of *artes moriendi* tracts confirms.)

What is paradoxical about the matter makes up the heart of the phrase from Wittgenstein I cited. Although "Death is not an event in life," as he says in the *Tractatus*, not an event in my life inasmuch as it is not an experience that I can have (his German is stronger: "*Der Tod ist kein Ereignis des Lebens. Den Tod erlebt man nicht*"), it is also *not* something other than an event in life. My death is something you and I and Freud can discuss, in the way we discuss what lies over the horizon or the rising of the sun tomorrow—*ex hypothesi*. But what makes "my death" different from (say) the city of Paris (also a destination, also over the horizon), or the event of my birth, or a square circle, or the identity of the present king of France, is that, although it is not an event in my life, it is also, as "my death," Jacques's death, not an event in anyone else's life either—though this condition of "the-event-of-death-not-being-an-event-of-life" obtains for all others in an entirely different way from the way in which that event obtains for me. The most that we can say about "my death" and your own, in conversation, is that for each of us "my death" is not a part of "life," though this not being an event of life is not something that we *share* as experiences. When we give this not being an event of my life the same name, "my death" or "death" tout court, we act out of a communicative necessity, though in fact "my death" is the least translatable of terms, and perhaps the only genuinely untranslatable designation we have. (Whereas Paris is part of someone's life, and square circles and the identity of the present king of France are not part of anyone's life, but they are "defective," as Meinong might say, in exactly the same way for anyone.)

Still on the distinction between universalism and culturalism, but on the other side, we find a claim regarding cultural and historical particularism. Sure, "*La muerte . . . es una puerta general de naturaleza*," but when we consider death "*propriamente*," as it pertains to the creatures who can die, to human animals, this "*puerta general*" becomes many doors immediately. For the relation between "*naturaleza*" and what today we would call *cultura* or *sociedad* is not itself natural, if by that we mean given, inflexible, essential. Natural points of inflection are precisely where cultural and historical differences collect; death in the United States or Spain is different from death in France, in the Maghreb, in the Hispanic world; death in the early modern period is different among the Spanish and among the indigenous populations of New Spain. Death *then* was not what it is *now*; *that* death has passed away, though its ghostly traces remain, in the form of vestigial practices or unassimilated iterations of customs prevalent at other times. One could be even more forceful: these differences do not just merely collect at points of natural inflection (births, deaths, epidemics; the sharing of cooked or raw foods, the institution of taboos on incest, fratricide, etc.) but are constituted by them. The fact that "death" is different, or treated differently, in Freud's Vienna, in Spain and in the Andean societies, among Catholics in Cuenca, or the Inka in Cuzco, is what distinguishes these societies, and also what makes necessary a discipline devoted to the description of those distinctions. The classic study of the collective representation of death is Robert Hertz's "Contribution à une étude sur la représentation collective de la mort" of 1907. One is not surprised to find that Hertz's groundbreaking study is also importantly metadisciplinary, an inchoate effort to understand the limits of epistemologies that map cultures upon a developmental grid ("*les faits que présentent nombre de sociétés moins avancées que la nôtre*") or seek to enumerate their differences from a metropolitan norm or from other peripheral societies. The "representation of death" is where "collectivities" form, and where disciplines devoted to studying different "collectivities" also collect, differentiate themselves, form rules for their own subsistence, live, die.

This face-off between universalism and cultural particularism or cultural empiricism strikes me at first as a merely apparent disagreement. When we say "death" in this second sense we are generally referring to something a little different from what we mean in the first, universal or ontological sense. (I will get to the question of who "we" are in this phrase in just a moment.) There an organic fact, an event pertaining to one organism (and also to all organisms) is what we mean: creatures die, some properly (the rational ones: humans), all others merely "*en su manera*." Here, though, on the exceptionalist or culturalist side, "death" refers to the extensive collection of practices, technologies, rituals, and stories that surround and shape that fact. There is no need to make the distinction weaker than it need be: the cultural value of the term "death" extends to the shape, even the status, of the biological fact that it seems to surround. The (biological, ontological) fact of death is not just resemanticized by its (cultural, technological, social) shaping: its borders are shifted or redrawn, its characteristics and value changed, its time modified (think Karen Ann Quinlan or Terri Schiavo; time of death; legal death; zombie films; the Resurrection). Contemporary interest in biopolitics would be entirely ephemeral if the life of the *fact* were not at stake in the construction of death (Hertz: "*les faits que présentent nombre de sociétés*").

It is not clear that I can talk about death; it is not clear that I ever do anything but talk about it. This might be the paradoxical general shape that modern academic disciplines, including psychoanalysis, moral philosophy, sociology, and theology, have given the question of death, or more properly, of the experience of finitude. The paradox sounds pleasingly out of date, each of its elements somehow bypassed, so tightly linked to a historical moment as to appear, dare one say, ghostly, a sort of revenant from philosophical times past. It would seem that the only way to open that curious, last, terrible door, to talk about an event which is not part of life, entails destroying "life" and *exchanging* it for its analogue, its synonym: the institution.

And this is where the last matters comes in—the question of who "we" are in all this, "we" who act, *qua* subjects, first analytically and then synthetically to draw the analogy and assert the synonymy that allow us to exchange one necessity for another, as if we were trying out keys to locked doors (this key is like that one in being intended to open a lock: "Keys, keys, keys") or to a single, "general" door; or to exchange *institution* for *life*. I have been scaffolding my argument regarding modal pluralism on analogy: different necessities are like different keys; Fine's account of necessity may be drawn into analogy with Freud's; and so on. In what shape, and under the felicity conditions provided by what institutions, do we receive, then use, these terms—"analogy," "syllogistics," "equivalence," and "exchange"?

Today the four terms form a different system from the one they formed for Pythagoras and Proclus, the topic of my second chapter; it is different too from the one that Scholasticism builds in order to take up the proposition that knowledge of the divine must proceed by analogy; different still today than in 1915 or 1930. On what grounds do we stand the exchange of properties today, the assertion that properties of concepts are sufficiently alike to permit the concepts to be exchanged? Manifestly on different grounds from those to be found before "identity," "likeness," "analogy," "equivalence," and "exchange" assume roles in the imaginary of *Homo economicus* or laboring man, that is, before Mill and Marx. And on different grounds, too, in the age of cryptocurrency and global trade, than on those the system stood on when Marx and Mill offer their critiques of the political economy of industrial capitalism.

Take "equivalence" and "exchange" as keys to the question, "what system do these four terms form today?" Here is a quick, well-known definition of the concepts. My source is the "Chapter on Money" in Marx's *Grundrisse*. I am turning to it not necessarily because it is truer to the world we know than another definition, but because the "world we know" ("we," willy-nilly, knowingly or unknowingly, inheritors of Marx's lexicon) results in part *from* this definition.

> The exchange value of a commodity, as a separate form of existence accompanying the commodity itself, is money; the form in which all commodities equate, compare, measure themselves; into which all commodities dissolve themselves; that which dissolves itself into all commodities; thc universal equivalent.) Every moment, in calculating, accounting etc., that we transform commodities into value symbols, we fix them as mere exchange values, making abstraction from the matter they are composed of and all their natural qualities. On paper, in the head, this metamorphosis proceeds by means of mere abstraction; but in the real exchange process a real mediation is required, a means to accomplish this abstraction. In its natural existence, with its natural properties, in natural identity with itself, the commodity is neither constantly exchangeable nor exchangeable against every other commodity; this it is only as something different from itself, something distinct from itself, as exchange value. We must first transpose the commodity into itself as exchange value in order then to be able to compare this exchange value with other exchange values and to exchange it.[36]

A first approximation suggests that "equivalence" is not *just* the assertion that *X* and *Y* particulars, this key and that, the "primitive" peoples of Tierra del Fuego and the "civilized" Europeans Freud addresses, or flirting "Americans" and serious continentals, or this necessity and another, or "life" and "unitary institution," have the same value—it is a way of stipulating the rules and conditions under which *X* and *Y* can be compared in the first place. Before that still, to assert that *X* and *Y* are equivalent is to assert that there *are* such rules: that particularities can have in common this at least and minimally, that they have consistency *as* units, as singularities that can be counted (and counting is a rule) in the same way: equivalently. On this description, "general equivalence" is the device the market relies on to convert, or translate, differences of kind into differences of value. On this description, to take account of equivalence, local as well as "general," means taking account of the ideology and the effects of the market; it entails envisioning ways of disentangling other domains or spheres—private and secret ones as well as public ones—from the "dominant form of thought" and the dominant language for their expression. To take account of equivalence, local as well as "general," will mean marking the difference between *oikos*, the household, where my secret can be mine, and the *oikonomia*, the marketplace; it will mean being able to distinguish between political subjects and consumers of rhetorical tokens. Finally, and pertinently to those of us who work and think in the institution of the global university, to take account of equivalence will mean offering something other than academic institutions that admit only objects and means of study that can be evaluated *metrically*, comparatively, with reference to assessment standards into which any institution and any institution's objects and protocols of study can be translated.

This is compelling, but the claim is stronger still in Marx's work. What makes the economistic notion of equivalence more broadly useful today, what makes it the term organizing the four-way system of "analogy," "syllogistics," "equivalence," and "exchange"—is also what makes it problematical to imagine moving "beyond" it in any straightforward sense. I am referring to the dynamic tension that the concept of "equivalence" displays in Marx's description when we move to what he calls "the real exchange," and away from the "metamorphosis" of the commodity's value "On paper, in the head," where it occurs, he continues, "by means of mere abstraction." "In the real exchange process," though, " . . . we must first transpose [*umsetzen*] the commodity into itself as exchange value in order then to be able to compare this exchange value with other exchange values and to exchange it."[37]

A "real mediation," that is, the "transposition," *umsetzen*, of the commodity into itself *as exchange value* "in order then to be able to compare this exchange value with other exchange values and to exchange it." The claim is more complicated than it seems—and much of the work is carried out by the composite verb *umsetzen*, whose senses cover "to convert, "to exchange," "to transpose," "to carry out in practice," "to translate." To transpose something into itself *as exchange value* is not to bring into the commodity, from outside, a social value, the mark of its exchangeability imported from the public sphere of circulation to which it will be destined, but rather somehow, from within the commodity, to transpose it, to allow it to show itself to be different from itself, other than itself-alone, other than in "natural identity with itself" or better, in its natural likeness to itself [*in ihrer natürlichen Gleichheit mit sich*]. This allowing-the-commodity to disclose its un-likeness to itself reemerges in what a good, attentive reader of Marx like Patrick Dove calls the "negation of difference" and the mechanism that "establish[es] being" "*ad infinitum*."[38]

The difference between one key and another, or between two doors, or between a particular door and a "general" one; between your vote and mine; between an apple and a bale of cotton, or between *this* apple and *this other* apple, or between *this* product that I make and *that* one that you make; between the analysis of a poem or a film, and the research going into the development of a new polymer or a vaccine against a devastating disease: such differences are "negated" when both things I am pointing to or designating are asserted, or discovered, to be translatable into a single, same unit—initially, a unit like "labor-time," perhaps a more ideologically coded concept like "social utility" (as if one could say: "The analysis of a fable by Perrault or Carter is worth three social utility chits, and research leading to developing a new antibiotic or a strain of pest-resistant corn is worth three hundred social utility chits"), eventually their abstract equivalent, money. We call this process "abstraction," or "mathematization," and when we extend it generally, when we note that anything and all things produced are potentially, if not yet actually, equivalent in that they have consistency *as* units that can be counted in the same way (and counting is a rule), then we may speak of a "general equivalency," and of the "global logic of equivalence." Marx's example is notorious: "In the crudest barter," he says in the *Grundrisse*, "when two commodities are exchanged for one another, each is first equated with a symbol which expresses their exchange value, e.g. among certain Negroes on the West African coast, = x bars. One commodity is = 1 bar; the other = 2 bars. They are exchanged in this relation. The commodities are first transformed into bars in the head and in speech before they are exchanged for one another."

The standard example of the multiplication and exchangeability of commodities is the supermarket shelf, and the seemingly endless production of products for us to consume, whose identity is established differentially—this product rather than that, this thing *is* inasmuch as it is different from that thing. Only the primary value of "difference itself" is not defined this way. The trickiness of the matter comes when we try to ask what "difference itself" might mean—the "itself" of difference. We can only "extend" the process of abstraction by accepting that "difference" is both the device that produces being serially, *ad infinitum*; and also one of the beings, commodities, etc. produced, sold acquired, assessed in the *oikonomia*. I say that "we extend" the process of abstraction of value of this or that thing, but really, it's not up to *us* to extend it or not—not a subjective act. It's either a *historical* circumstance, a consequence of the mode of production that we call capitalism in its "global" form, and in this way it happens whether we like it or not ("we" are the abstract agents of that extension, of that mathematization of this-thing into something that can be of equivalent value to that-thing); it's either a *historical* circumstance, I say, or our "extending the process of abstraction" is the manifestation, as history, as historicity, of our forgetting an originary disposition toward the being of beings as they *cannot* be counted: as they are *ontologically* different.

Neither of these circumstances is set or stable. Anything and everything, no matter how singular, may become or be made equivalent to some-other-thing, countable, abstract, mathematizable—under the historical circumstance we call global capitalism (for instance, the "West African Negroes" of Marx's example are sufficiently equivalent to the European subjects so that their "barter economy" can serve as an analog, as having a degree of equivalence, to the European subject's economy). Anything, too, may flicker or be made to fade out of value and out of a position of equivalence once firmly held as well, *both* in ways that drive the logic of acquisition explicitly, technically, as when a fashionable item is rendered unfashionable in order to make place for further consumption; *but also* in ways that make intelligible the contingent, hence nontechnical or even antitechnical quality of consumer desire.

Take Perrault's story "La Barbe Bleuë." Its value in European culture—assessed by the gross number of rewritings, translations, reiterations, echoes, allusions, and so on—seems incontrovertibly high. In all these, something like a likeness to the original persists, and amongst them, that likeness *necessarily* draws each version into analogy with the rest: it's the property they have in common. This is the stuff of Propp's *Morphology of the Folk-Tale*, and of countless literary and anthropological historiographies. Carter's 1979 revision, "The Bloody Chamber," takes the tale's enduring cultural value as a second-order topic: at their peril, readers recognize the likeness of "The Bloody Chamber" to the tradition and implicitly acquiesce to the tale's cultural value. Even taking a stand against "La Barbe Bleuë"'s forming role in versions of European patriarchy requires that we assent to the authority and value of the tradition. This collusion, this structural assent to the antecedent value, this necessary likeness we assert between Carter and Perrault's tales, offers the tale its value as a cultural token or commodity. It is *also* the condition of felicity and of intelligibility of the reader's judgment with regard to both "The Bloody Chamber" and "La Barbe Bleuë." Carter marks this structural assent to the antecedent (to the antecedent marital convention), indelibly, upon her protagonist: a value symbol, in Marx's terms. Assuming for the moment the figure of the monstrous tradition whose name the story bears, Carter transfers the spot that the last, singular key bears onto the woman who used it out of curiosity:

> I knelt before him and he pressed the key lightly to my forehead, held it there for a moment. I felt a faint tingling of the skin and, when I involuntarily glanced at myself in the mirror, I saw the heart-shaped stain had transferred itself to my forehead, to the space between the eyebrows, like the caste mark of a brahmin woman. Or the mark of Cain. And now the key gleamed as freshly as if it had just been cut. . . . No paint nor powder, no matter how thick or white, can mask that red mark on my forehead; I am glad he cannot see it—not for fear of his revulsion, since I know he sees me clearly with his heart—but because it spares my shame. (90)

"Like the caste mark of a brahmin woman. Or the mark of Cain." Carter's narrator *likens* the value-symbol mark upon her forehead to others, Eastern and Western. Its function in the tale: it is a defect that conveys shame, the narrator's at her willingness to marry out of love for convention rather than "love" for her suitor, the reader's shame at rendering intelligible Carter's critique of the Blue Beard tradition only on condition of remaining within the world that tradition institutes. This function is determined by the mark's likeness to other marks, also culturally determined. Recall Marx: "Every moment, in calculating, accounting etc., that we transform commodities into value symbols, we fix them as mere exchange values, making abstraction from the matter they are composed of and all their natural qualities." From a common source, division, analysis, then synthesis: we're safe in the psychoanalytic institution Freud imagines in 1915, and in the professional identity he summarily seizes: "*Kurz, ich bin offenbar Analytiker*."

But other unread marks and defects, similar to these in different ways, intrude upon Perrault's scene of transformation and exchange. Nothing about my experience of subjection is immediate, I argued in my last chapter; so too nothing about my experience of *likeness* is immediate, or coherent. Unread marks and defects messily, unsystematically, unequally, intrude upon Perrault's scene. They divide it, distribute it, and jangle clashingly, like keys on a chain. Where the red mark's unique reference seemed *necessarily* and immediately impressed upon it, like a key upon a forehead, the wild and curious logic of unfettered likeness necessarily multiplies and divides the world of Perrault's senses. Birthmarks and scarlet letters rush in from the American tradition (Hawthorne: "'[The mark] has been so often called a charm that I was simple enough to imagine it might be so.' 'Ah, upon another face perhaps it might,' replied her husband, 'but never on yours. No, dearest Georgiana, you came so nearly perfect from the hand of Nature that this slightest possible defect, which we hesitate whether to term a defect or a beauty, shocks me, as being the visible mark of earthly imperfection'")[39]; brands and scars, from the European; stigmata, *maculae*, *nodae*, and *notae*; *lunares*, raspberries; assorted *gnorismata* or recognition-tokens like the birthmark that Heliodorus's *Historia aethiopica* sets on Chariclea's arm; from Mariolatry, the devotional figure of Mary as *speculum sine macula Dei majestatis*, the unblemished, immaculate, nondefective mirror of God's majesty.[40] Other Blue Beards, antagonistic to Perrault's, barge in—comic ones, women, musical; Blue Beards in which it is not curiosity but courage that leads the last wife to open the door; Blue Beards that transform the bloody mark into a swelling and enveloping song, as tell-tale as the mark but the emblem, this time, of liberation.

I am thinking of Paul Dukas's extraordinary 1906–1907 operatic adaptation of Maeterlinck's play *Ariane et Barbe-Bleue*. Here, in Maeterlinck/Dukas, Ariane, the sixth and last wife, *saves* Blue Beard *and* all the previous, unexecuted wives. She opens, exclaiming:

> They are not dead. . . . I felt doubtful of it there, but I am certain of it here . . .—He loves me, I am pretty and I'll know his secret. First, disobedience, that's the first duty when the order given one is threatening and inexplicable. . . . He gave me these keys, they open the bridal treasures he has locked away. The six silver keys I am allowed to use, but not the gold one. That is precisely the most important. I'll throw away the others and keep this one.[41]

Marks intrude and are transformed. Here, in Maeterlinck/Dukas, the bloody mark becomes the spreading, "ever louder" chant of the imprisoned wives that calls to Ariane and brings Blue Beard onstage: "*Le chant remplit la salle*," the Nurse exclaims to Ariane; "*il se répand partout*" (the chant fills the hall, it spills all over). Marks spill in, borrowed from antecedent and incompatible traditions and from traditions yet to come (the traditions that make up every imaginable reader's eventual worlds). The red mark thus insists—a sort of empty synthesis or gathering point for what cultures set on offer that is *like* the mark. Its reference value exceeds just Carter's world, and Perrault's, and Maeterlinck/Dukas's, and any possible given world. Overdetermined, unreadable, or only *over*-readable because referring to more marks than any chamber or world or institution can contain, "that red mark" does more than unlock a world of doors: its disaggregation and the spreading likeness that it occasions destroy the immediate, synthetic unity of Perrault's world (and Carter's, and any recognizable world). Which is to say as well: Blue Beard's spreading red mark destroys the institutional frames that make it possible to move between analytic and synthetic judgments regarding *a* mark and whatever it is to which it refers.

And yet "the unity of this world [*Die Einheit dieser Welt*] seems to [Freud] so self-evident as not to need emphasis." And yet, Freud says, "I am of course an analyst, and believe that synthesis offers no obstacles once analysis has been achieved" (*Kurz, ich bin offenbar Analytiker und meine, die Synthese macht keine Schwierigkeiten, wenn man erst die Analyse hat*).

In 1915 Freud finds, with Grabbe's Hannibal, nothing beyond or outside of "this world" into which we *could* fall: to "have" analysis "first" is to have the world in sum, and there is to be no difficulty in disclosing, from that divided and distributed world, syntheses which are also part of the world—that synthesis of syntheses, Fine's "universe" with many doors—in sum. Then, in 1915, with respect to the oneness of this world, the individual and the species are, indeed, analogous in the strong, syllogistic sense, as analytic and synthesis judgments regarding the marks comprising the world are alike. Psychoanalysis, as Freud understands it in or around 1915, is the institutional expression and the means of achieving understanding of our finite-being-in-common in relation to the oneness of this world.

So it seemed in or around 1915. Of course a great deal changes, we said, in the fifteen years between Freud's Hannibal letter to Salomé and the Hannibal reference of *Civilization and Its Discontents*: worlds end in war and pestilence; sudden death brings catastrophe. In 1915 Freud writes that "Our habit is to lay stress on the fortuitous causation of the death—accident, disease, infection, advanced age; in this way we betray an effort to reduce [*herabdrucken*] death from a necessity to a chance event [*von einer Notwendigkeit zu einer Zufälligkeit herabzudrucken*]." Sophie Halberstadt-Freud dies in 1920 of the Spanish influenza pandemic that moved across the world between 1918 and 1920; her son Heinz, "Heinerle" to Freud and the family, dies in June 1923 of tuberculosis. The logic of reduction-limitation fails Freud in both cases, and—now taking, he says, no "enjoyment in life"—he famously finds indifference.[42] "For me," Freud writes to Binswanger in 1926 (Binswanger had written to tell Freud of the death of Johannes Binswanger, his fifth child; this is Arnold J. Pomerans's translation), "that child took the place of all my children and other grandchildren, and since then, since Heinele's death, I have no longer cared for my grandchildren, but find no enjoyment in life either. This is also the secret of my indifference—it has been called courage—towards the threat to my own life."[43] In the period, the institutional frame that psychoanalysis provides *der Analytiker*—or seems to provide—for achieving understanding of finite-being-in-common in relation to the oneness of this world—fails as well, and perhaps for reasons Freud offers in his letter to Binswanger, mostly hidden in Pomerans's translation: exceptional child that he was, Freud's grandson Heinele doesn't only—to his famous grandfather—take "the place [*Stand*] of all my children and other grandchildren," but of *all* children and grandchildren. The function of standing-for is wrenching, pathetically devastating to the small institution of Freud's family: Heinele *stands for* Freud's other children and grandchildren, and having lost him Freud becomes indifferent to the others—knocking out one great leg on which the family-institution traditionally stands, the father's ambivalent, violent-nurturing, love for his children and grandchildren. The catastrophe extends voraciously, triumphantly: the indifferent "courage" of Freud's *Analytiker* position flows from it, from the passage from the individual child to *all* children and *all* grandchildren, all of them susceptible, qua species beings, *to* analysis as to death. This is indeed the more literal sense of Freud's *Mir stand es für alle Kinder and anderen Enkel*: *alle*, inclusive, not just "all my own children" but *all*, the class of children. The best, the highest example, can stand for all others. Therapy and technique, the very scientificity of psychoanalysis, demand of the *Analytiker* who proposes, with no difficulty, to move toward synthesis, this sacrifice of the *all* to the *one* and of the *one* who dies to the *all* who must die; of the loving attention felt for a being's singular characteristics, no matter how endearing the being, to the class-identity for which Freud's *Kerlchen*, his "little fellow of 3 or 4," *must stand*.

Shortly before writing to Salomé in 1915, Freud publishes "The History of the Psychoanalytic Movement," determining, by offering the discipline's authorized, first-person history—his own—the conceptual and institutional frame in which psychoanalysis may be practiced. Freud's story stands against Jung's practice and history, against Adler's, against those who would trace the practice to Breuer. Freud breaks definitively with Otto Rank in 1924 on the primacy of the Oedipus complex, and with the Medical Society of Vienna in 1925 over Reich on the matter of lay analysis. After the catastrophes—his own, the one he brings down upon the psychoanalytic institution's—psychoanalysis must be recomposed. No longer will it serve to diagnose the limits or delusion in reducing (*herabdrucken*) death from a necessity to a chance event. It will not protect finite-being-in-common in relation to the world's oneness, nor offer self-evident steps from analysis to synthesis. The analytic indifference it offers now spells loss of life, loss of pleasure, loss of desire: loss of the *thisness* of the world. Psychoanalysis will no longer offer and defend professional identities. Instead, psychoanalysis guards the simultaneous work that incompatible necessities do to show finite being to be *un*common, the synthetic oneness of the world a fantastic illusion rather than self-evident, the *event* to be *necessary*, and division everywhere at work.

The words of Grabbe's *Hannibal* play offer Freud just this view—and perhaps *because* they do Freud misremembers the lines he cites, both in 1915, writing to Lou Andreas-Salomé, and again in 1930, when *Civilization and Its Discontents* translates Rolland's "feeling" into the ideational content that *Hannibal* provides. "*Aus dieser Welt* werden *wir nicht fallen*," Freud writes in 1915: "We will not fall out of this world." In 1930 Freud writes: "*Aus dieser Welt* können *wir nicht fallen*," We *cannot* fall out of this world. But Grabbe's Hannibal, speaking to Turnu, says neither thing: "*Ja, aus der Welt* werden *wir nicht fallen. Wir sind einmal darin*," that is, "We *will not* fall out of *the* world: we're in it, well and truly in it." It's a subtle but decisive difference with both Freud's versions. Freud seems to come closer to the mark in 1915, when he has Hannibal merely refer to *this* world rather than *the* world. In *Civilization and Its Discontents*, though, Freud remembers the consolation of a statement about the future and about the world in general—we *will not* fall out of the world—as a statement regarding modality and about a particular world: necessarily, we *cannot* fall out of *this* world. No matter what we do, no matter how hard we try, we simply cannot fall out of *this* world—we are subject to this world's necessity, the necessity of the rules of the world. The *thisness* of Freud's world translates, incorrectly, Grabbe's indeterminate world: by *determining* it, Freud makes *the* world into *this* world to which the play, and his own phrases, refer: *this* world, our common world, the world that psychoanalysis describes. We recall that Pomerans's translation of Freud's letter obscures the devastating but scientifically necessary *quantification* it implies. Heinele stands for Freud's closest and dearest family; he was *like* them, only better, cleverer. He was different, but the difference served to characterize, rather than block or destroy, Freud's relation to his *other* children and grandchildren. But Heinele also stands for *all* children and all grandchildren—and *this* difference, that he alone was both a child in "this world," in the world of Freud's family, and the stand-in for all children of "the world" (borrowing Freud's Grabbe scene), was not of "this world"—rather, that standing-for constituted the world of institutional psychoanalysis. Yes, the standing of Freud's *Kerlchen* in "this world," the world of one particular family in 1923 or 1926, stands for the child's standing in "the world." On this similarity Freud bases his condolences to Binswanger. Thus the sacrificial, scientific representativity of the *Analytiker*'s position and professional commitment: "this world," the world of the languages of psychoanalysis, of the institution of psychoanalysis, leads, ineluctably, necessarily, to indeterminate, encompassing "the world," because the *thisness* of the world of one family suffering the death of one child can become, as the Christian tradition would have informed Freud, *the world*.

This is not Grabbe's position, however. Hannibal, the "semite," as Freud characterizes him, who for Freud "symbolized . . . the tenacity of Jewry" precisely against "the organization of the Catholic church," consoles Turnu, if that is indeed what he is doing, with a prediction, an effort to describe what's to come. But what *does* come hardly bears Hannibal out. "Am I spinning around the world," Turnu cries, poisoned, "or the world around me?" or even better, "Am I spinning myself around the world, or is the world spinning itself around me?" (*Dreh' ich mich um die Welt, oder die Welt sich um mich?*) Turnu, in the grip of the fatal poison, finds or feels himself out of place with regard *to* the world, unable to say which of the two is in motion, himself or *the* world, but in neither case from *within* the world; he carries out Hannibal's design, but his last words *disprove* the consoling Senecan fantasy that suicide will bring necessity under his sway and show the "oneness" of "this world" to include his drive to death as well as his death.

I am prepared to believe that Freud's two necessities can be linked by analogy—natural necessity, Ananke, is *like* the syllogistic necessities according to which we build the truth of our relation to the world of natural necessity. I would like to think that Freud imagines the sort of community we call a "culture" to exist in part as a compromise between these two figures of necessity, and between the two sorts of community they entail. I am ready to imagine, much more locally, that Freud intends only *his* children and grandchildren when he describes to Binswanger the "indifference" that his *Kerlchen* Heinele's death provokes, and that Freud simply gets Grabbe's line wrong—wrong, slightly, in 1915, when "the world" becomes "this world," and more mysteriously in 1930, when Freud's "*Aus dieser Welt* können *wir nicht fallen*" replaces a contingent prediction with an analytic necessity. I am ready to bet that Freud forgot that Grabbe's play immediately undercuts Hannibal's consoling phrase, if that is indeed what it is, when the dying Turnu finds himself not *falling* but spinning around a world he is no part of, or he finds the strange world spinning about him. I am almost certain that Freud's translation of Rolland's "feeling" into Grabbe's language did not seek to register the cryptic turn that the English word "turn" takes into Turnu's name just as Grabbe's play ends, as if, *nomen omen*, the strange undecidable turning of the character around the world, or of the world around the character, acted out the "turn" in Turnu's name. I am confident that the line of closed doors, German *Thüre, die Türe*, from Blue Beard's (French or English) castle barely informed Grabbe's choice of name—*Turnu*, who guards the door to Hannibal's life and death—for the character the play calls *ein Negerhäuptling*, an "African chieftain" or "faithful Negro leader," as Roger Nicholls refers to him.[44] The thought then comes to me that Freud's memory may turn away from Grabbe's lines on the door hinge of the proper name/word *Tur*. I recall the complicated, thematic and metathematic, even theoretical role that doors have in Freud's work. I remember the door between the father and the burning child, in Freud's decisive dream from the 1900 *Interpretation of Dreams*; I recall that already in *Studies on Hysteria*, five years before, Freud says that "the patient only gets free from the hysterical symptom by reproducing the pathogenic impressions that caused it and by giving utterance to them. . . . The situation may be compared with the unlocking of a locked door, after which opening it by turning the handle offers no further difficulty."[45] Now I remember that the case of "Little Hans" of 1909–10 turns on the figure of the door. I recall the contemporaneous use to which Freud puts the "comparison" (the word will again be *Gleichnis*) to the *door* in the second of the *Five Lectures on Psycho-analysis*:

> Perhaps I may give you a more vivid picture of repression and of its necessary relation to resistance, by a rough analogy derived from our actual situation at the present moment. Let us suppose that in this lecture-room and among this . . . there is nevertheless someone who is causing a disturbance and whose ill-mannered laughter, chattering and shuffling with his feet are distracting my attention from my task. I have to announce that I cannot proceed with my lecture; and thereupon three or four of you who are strong men stand up and, after a short struggle, put the interrupter outside the door [*und setzen den Störenfried nach kurzem Kampfe vor die Tür*]. So now he is 'repressed', and I can continue my lecture. But in order that the interruption shall not be repeated, in case the individual who has been expelled should try to enter the room once more, the gentlemen who have put my will into effect place their chairs up against the door and thus establish a 'resistance' after the repression has been accomplished [*rücken die Herren . . . ihre Stühle an die Türe*]. If you will now translate [*aufs Psychische übertragen*] the two localities concerned into psychical terms as the 'conscious' and the 'unconscious', you will have before you a fairly good picture of the process of repression.[46]

So Freud's necessities can be linked by analogy, then—natural necessity, Ananke, is *like* the syllogistic necessities according to which we build the truth of our relation to the world of natural necessity. Where that likeness is at work others intrude, clamorously beating at the door, so to speak, of that primary argumentative analogy. Now I am ready to set aside these intruding and unnecessary analogies, thoughts, recollections, and references. I tell myself that someone else would recall otherwise, or not at all; that the likeness of "door" in German to a fictional character's name, and of both of these to the likenesses that Freud finds to psychoanalytic practice and mechanisms, are not to be brought in, or translated into, the argument regarding the "likeness" Freud builds between his two necessities.

I am ready, but the grounds on which I am prepared to set aside this sort of intruding, mediating consideration are not clear to me: I can find no *necessary* way of excluding the range of references that intrude just here. And yet discipline, the discipline of psychoanalysis and the argumentative conventions to which I am hewing just now depend on it. Freud's essay unfolds in the pause between the first articulation of what may be "primary" in Rolland's "oceanic feeling," and the concept which will, by the close of *Civilization and Its Discontents*, catch up with it—the after-thoughtly, *nachdenklich*, "intellectual perception" that catches up with whatever it is that Freud's primary example of the experience of confronting common finitude offers (though not yet clearly and distinctly)—here, Rolland's "oceanic feeling." The clamoring, intrusive, and unnecessary likenesses that the work elicits and produces are the afterthoughts of "culture," and they will not be kept at the disciplinary door.

For Freud does not place his two necessities into a strict analogic relation or allow his reader to set them in a relation of exchangeability based in a commonality of properties. No term will *suture* Ananke, natural necessity, to analysis: no single, determinate door allows passage, or translation, or (Marx's term, recall) transposition (*Umsetzung*), or displacement (*Übertragung*) from one to the other. Yes, the unity of the world, like the suture of the two models of subjectivization I described in the previous chapter, the subject as constituted by denumerable empirical experiences, and as transcendentally, formally, responsible for every experience in the abstract—the unity of the world lies in the direction of analogy, exchange, and suture: a self-evident good in the war-turned and war-torn year of 1915 but by 1929–1930 unacceptable, perhaps incomprehensible. In its performance of the contingency of forgetting and remembering, in its (surely compensatory) introduction of the modality of analytic necessity in place of Grabbe's mere possibility, *Civilization and Its Discontents* destroys the unity of the world, along with the plural modalities that remit to it—along with the subject, a certain "Freud," whose autobiography, synonymous with "The History of the Psychoanalytic Movement," stands at the center of the institution of psychoanalysis. Suicide, in short: *Kurz*. Hannibal's fate, and Turnu's. Freud destroys his family, the family, and the world of institutional psychoanalysis in the years between 1915 and 1930 in order to destroy the self-evident unity of the world psychoanalysis describes—the great Roman synthesis of syntheses he first saw, toward which all analytic roads would lead, the "general" door proper to all humanity.

Destroys it, that is, in order to replace it with an indifferent, unitary, *theoretical*, institution working *nachdenklich* and after death, *nachträglich*, to regulate analogy, syllogistics, and exchange. The work of destruction-reuse that Carter does with the Blue Beard story, with the persisting cultural value-form of the Blue Beard story, Freud seeks to do with the institution of psychoanalysis when he shows the *im*possibility of imagining "culture" as a "world" unified or unifiable by analogy. Freud's destruction-work leading up to *Civilization and Its Discontents* lays the ground for the *contuberium*, for defective forms of subjectivity and "low," uncommon, defective ways of being-in-common, just where the position of the analyst *fails* to bring the "world's" necessities, identities, and corresponding communities into synthesis or even into relation, that is, gathered under the hazy sovereignty of a common term or analogon. Out of the cultural material into which it seeks to translate the physiology of "feeling" and passion, *Civilization and Its Discontents* produces the *theory* of low association and *un*common necessities. Just there, where we cannot decide whether we "spin around the world, or the world around us," the disciplinary protocols of psychoanalysis produce defective, low forms of commonality, association, and analogy, a defective institution in which necessity, identity, and community clash with each other as violently, as productively, and as eternally as Ananke and Eros are said to do.

# CONCLUSION

Fragonard, on the other hand, retained the idea of death; but he reversed the original moral. He depicted two cupids, probably spirits of departed lovers, clasped in an embrace within a broken sarcophagus while other, smaller cupids flutter about and a friendly genius illumines the scene with the light of a nuptial torch. Here the development has run full cycle. To Guercino's "Even in Arcady, there is death" Fragonard's drawing replies: "Even in death, there may be Arcady."

Erwin Panofsky

You often take refuge, perhaps for want of time and space, in this minute word "and."

Jacques Derrida

Incidentally do you know that you saved my life again the other day when with an infinitely forgiving movement you allowed me to tell you where the trouble [*le mal*] is, its return always foreseeable, the catastrophe coming in advance [*prevenante*, also "thoughtful," "warning"], called, given, dated. It is readable on a calendar, with its proper name, classified, you hear this word, nomenclatured. It wasn't sufficient to foresee or to predict what would indeed happen one day, /forecasting is not enough/, it would be necessary to think (what does this mean here, do you know?) what would happen by the very fact of being predicted or foreseen, a sort of beautiful apocalypse telescoped, kaleidoscoped, triggered off at that very moment by the precipitation of the announcement itself, consisting precisely in this announcement, the prophecy returning to itself from the future of its own to-come [*à-venir*, also "future," "writ of summons"]. The apocalypse takes place at the moment when I write this, but a present of this type keeps a telepathic or premonitory affinity with itself (it senses itself at a distance and warns itself of itself) which loses me on the way and makes me scared.

Jacques Derrida

D. reminds me that it is likely, almost certain, natural that I will die before she does—our ages tell on us and on me especially.[1] She's right, of course. Does acknowledging this change how I am disposed to her? To the world? But I can't imagine it; I can't envision it. She says I should, even that I *must* try to do both. For if I remember that it is natural that I should die, and that I should die first, then what I and we do now will be different; I and we will be more attentive to the world's here and now, more caring. The registers of obligation, demand, guilt, and impotence work me.

That's the idea: *memento mori*. It is general, it is traditional, and it forms the basis of Abrahamic moral culture. (Remember Ecclesiastes 12, here in the King James translation: "Remember now thy Creator in the days of thy youth, while the evil days come not, nor the years draw nigh, when thou shalt say, I have no pleasure in them. . . Then shall the dust return to the earth as it was: and the spirit shall return unto God who gave it. Vanity of vanities, saith the preacher; all is vanity." Sophie Ramond reminds us that the *Biblia Hebraica Stuttgartensia* suggests translating "thy Creator" by "thy grave."[2] So: "Remember now thy grave.") But it is an embarrassing formula: remember, it enjoins, that you will die. How can I have a memory of what I cannot imagine? Or even a memory of what will come to pass? Perhaps you are asking or demanding that I draw from what I have already seen the image of what will come, and keep that before my eyes, in my imagination. I have seen others die (my mother, just now; and I saw C. die; and J., many years ago). I will call that prefigurative torsion of what I have lived a metaphor, since it is *like* what I think will happen, *but* never the same. Or perhaps a catachresis, since whatever I bend toward my use in the present mismatches, does violence, is improper to the present. Not only is my death not an event in my life, as Wittgenstein wrote and as we have just seen, but the remembrance that there is, there has been, and there will be *my* death in and for *my* life is itself *not* a part of my life. Or rather—it is not a part of my life in the way that (say) visiting Antarctica is: I have never been that far south but could go, as I have gone north to Iceland or east to Paris. But there is no "as I have done, or gone" before in the world, when you remind me that it is likely that I will die before you, and demand that I remember that and envision it. No cardinal points help me step closer or farther. I will need to recall in a different sense; I will need to remember not what can be *determined*, but what has been *es*-terminated; to envision differently than when I imagine a trip to Antarctica; to *institute* differently.

Here are two things. Imagine the ends of the world, I ask you: the multi-fronted, accelerating apocalypse of climate change; the certainty that the next pandemic, or the next, or the following one, will not respect the habits and immunities we have developed in this confinement or the morbidities and relatively low mortalities of the current SARS-COVID pandemic—but will catastrophically combine the highest rates of transmission with the highest rates of mortality. Remember the renewed threat of nuclear annihilation. The death of the species, the death of all species as we, our species, know them. Am I asking you to imagine traveling to Antarctica, or asking you to envision the world after, or including, your death?

Now envision the world you would like to have instead of the one we do have, the one headed, apparently ineluctably, toward the apocalypse. Are you a part of the world you would like to have? What cardinal points or what stories orient you toward it? What is it like, what known markers and termini lead you there? You will immediately object: the end of our world isn't a matter of *natural* necessity; it is our artifact, what we have done and are doing; it could have been prevented or can yet be. What is to be gained from drawing the ecological end into analogy with my own? In the analogy we lose, certainly, our sense of *ability*, our agency, our how-to. If strategy, project, intention, and institution are conditioned to these, then we will lose them as well. If we cannot imagine our death or the end of the world, then we have nothing before us *but* our death and the end of the world. Does this entail, does it make possible, as D. has me think, that we enjoy more fully our this-worldiness? Fatalism.

Let's not exclude from the start the analogy I am suggesting but insist on it. I think it offers us a different and stronger description of the imaginative, rational and rhetorical work, the "discursive play," the work of torsion, allegory, and catachresis, of institution, that we must do to imagine (the word isn't right) or envision (also wrong) both disaster and other, alternative futures. There is nothing like the disaster in our experience—not because we, each of us, have not found finitude written into our life, but because analogues to finding finitude, or envisioning disaster, or facing a people's extermination, or imagining our death and our species death, are furnished everywhere by the great machine of global capital, immediately, in near lossless translation across markets, platforms, chronologies, and cultures. It is the singular disposition toward finitude that seems torn from us by the marketing of disaster. With it we lose the disposition and the means of caring for the present and for the becoming present of the future. For visions do not come immediately, they never have. They come to us in the lexicon on offer, valued, marshaled, by the world that conditions us. When it is this lexicon and this conditioning world that we would like to bring into question—because the lexicon is the condition of disaster and the disaster the condition of this lexicon, each proper and adequate to the other but also its product and the means of its perpetuation—then we must (again the register of obligation!) look elsewhere and look differently.

Here is what I mean.

"All great leaders have been visionaries," Donella Meadows said in 1994, addressing the third biennial meeting of the International Society of Ecological Economics in Costa Rica.

> Even the scientific, systems-analyst side of me has to admit that we can hardly achieve a desirable, sustainable world, if we can't even picture what it will be like. . . . So I invite you to join with me in building that vision. What kind of sustainable world do you WANT to live in? Do your best to imagine not just the absence of problems but the presence of blessings. . . . But what else? What else do YOU want, for yourself, your children, your grandchildren? The best way to find your answer to that question is to go to a quiet place, close your eyes, take a few deep breaths, and put yourself in the middle of that sustainable world. Don't push, don't worry, and don't try to figure it out. Just close your eyes and see what you see.[3]

"Close your eyes and . . . see what you see." Meadows is asking me to borrow from the possible future, the wished-for future, a "picture" of what I "want, for [my]self, [my] children, [my] grandchildren." I'm immediately on guard, put off. Whence this mistrust, and is it the same as—related to, even—the embarrassment that Meadows registers in herself and in others she has asked to envision alternatives to hunger, ecocide, nuclear war, and so on? As for me, I don't trust the demand she is making; I don't believe in vision, in what is immediately in-spired with the breath I take (the air I breathe isn't to be trusted for cleanliness; it's impure; traces of unhealthy substances mark it). I don't believe that the "charisma" with which vision endows individuals—even me, if it does so—is to be trusted. Even less do I trust the economy that sits beneath Meadows's vision of envisioning: I borrow images from the possible, wished-for future, use them now to guide me, and on arrival find myself rejoining the images, now literalized, now happily materialized. Nothing new, or frightful, or other, intrudes, if possible. The interest on my loan is paid in the time it takes me simply to fulfill the vision, in the time it takes me just to arrive. Debt and scheduled repayment smooth out the years before me; envisioning on this description is the institution we set in place to master time, economize it, subject it to the intuition of *dura-*

*tion*; instituting "envisioning" renders the time before and behind us a familiar, value-producing instrument. The value here: nothing less than the alternative world we can produce from our visions of it.

Before writing *Air and Dreams*, Bachelard published *L'intuition de l'instant*, a strong argument against the Bergsonian account, precisely, of the way the intuition of duration structures human time. It is also an argument against the smoothness of economized time. Bachelard says:

> 1. Duration has no direct force. Real time exists only through the isolated instant, which is to be found wholly in the act, in what is actual, in the present.
>
> 2. Being is nonetheless a site of resonance by virtue of the rhythms of instants. As such, one might say that being has a past, much as an echo has a voice. Yet this past is no more than a present habit, and this present state of the past is, again, but a metaphor. For us, in fact, habit is inscribed neither in matter nor in space. What is at issue is simply a resonant habit that, we believe, remains essentially relative. Habit, which in our view is thought, turns out to be too ethereal to become permanently recorded, too immaterial to sleep within matter. It is a movement that keeps playing, a musical phrase that must be taken up again, for it forms part of a symphony where it plays a role. At least, this is the way we will attempt to reconcile [*solidariser*] past and future, through habit.[4]

We seem to move away from the world that *Defective Institutions* has been describing: the necessarily musical *operetta*, the operetta of abolition. Bachelard offers rhythm rather than duration, the shocking and suspending duration of the hanging note disjoining the integrity of the work. Rhythm registered or recorded rather than intuited. *Habit*, a "present habit" or habit of the present, here is the means for bringing into one, of solidarizing, *solidariser* (Rizo-Patron's "reconciling" gets wrong the amphibian quality of the term *solidariser*, which works in states of *matter*, solids and liquids; but also in the world of *politics*) present and past; and of bringing together present and future, a future that is *also* a metaphor of the present, more attenuated because the rhythms of what is to come as instant are still not given. (Bachelard continues: "Rhythm is naturally less reliable on the side of the future. Between yesterday's nothingness and tomorrow's nothingness there is no symmetry. The future is but a prelude, a musical phrase that proceeds and tries itself out—a solitary phrase. It is only through such a brief overture that the world prolongs itself. In the symphony that is being created, the future is assured by but a few musical measures.")[5]

It is a difficult and unsatisfactory position. Bachelard, working from Gaston

Roupnel's 1927 novel *Siloë*, wants to find a way to synthesize accident and historical knowledge. On May 2, 1943, in Dijon, he writes, concluding *Air and Dreams*:

> As soon as we put language in its proper place, at the height of human evolution, it is revealed in its double effectiveness: it bestows on us the virtues of clarity and the powers of dream. Really knowing the images of words, the images that exist beneath our thoughts and upon which our thoughts live, would advance our thinking in a natural manner. A philosophy concerned with human destiny must not only admit its images, but adapt to them and continue their flow. It must be an openly living language. It must study the literary man candidly, because the literary man is the culmination of meditation and expression, the culmination of thought and of dream.[6]

"Admit . . . adapt to . . . continue," *avouer*, *s'adapter*, *continuer*. The "virtue" of clarity and the "force" of dreams, revealed or unveiled by language, "as soon as it's put in its proper place," *à la pointe même de l'évolution humaine*, when it is placed at the highest point of human evolution. Imagine writing these words in occupied France in 1943. The world war is at its most terrible just now; the horror of the camps is now universally known. What *is*, in 1943, the "highest point" of human evolution? Where does it lie, when? Is it continuous with the dreadful present? Can habit help us place it somewhere—in the past, in the future? Bachelard says, in Edith R. Farrell and C. Frederick Farrell's translation, that language "bestows on us the virtues of clarity and the powers of dream." "Bestows" is off: the gesture is less benevolent in the French, *il met en nous ses vertus*, "it places in us, it inserts in us its virtues." More important, though: Is "human language" the sort of thing that can be *placed*, or does it not rather emplace, differently, unevenly, violently inserting us in place or places?

It is 1932. Bachelard advocates for the intuition of the instant, for making habit the foundation on which that intuition can take the place of the governing intuition of duration Bergson advocated. By 1943, faced with disaster, in the midst of uncertainty, Bachelard seeks to place language in its proper place, in order to draw from it the metaphorical resources—clarity and power—required to describe the world around him: the worst. The compounding of metaphors is terrible: can language have a "place"? It is not an object (nor is "human evolution"); no "place" is proper to it, and no place can be its own. Bachelard seeks to ground metaphoric language in language's proper, that is, nonmetaphorical place—and to do so he makes both "human evolution" and "language" radically metaphorical. "Radically metaphorical" means: a figurative torsion that takes from past and future and abolishes the possibility of returning what has been taken, with or without interest, to its proper place. To tell the story of this torsion requires us—me—to think otherwise.

What follows? Putting into "discursive play" fiction and accident, fiction that imagines times future and past as continuous with the present (that is, as something over which we can have agency and from which the history and foundations of that agency can be derived), *and* as accidental (compounded of the unforeseeable, not susceptible of mathematization, aslant the laws of probability). It is fiction that reminds me to remember that my death is waiting, and thus reminds me to await it, to live this moment in the metaphor of what is naturally *and* accidentally to come. What follows, and what allows us to work (with) the catastrophe, is setting into discursive play (Wynter) stories that simultaneously suspend, abolish, withdraw, and offer the dream of political agency; stories whose clarity and force work where we want them to, on the matter of day-to-day disasters present and to come—*and* where we do not want them to, outside their proper place, to ends we do not and perhaps cannot know, or imagine, or envision. This is the "*and*" of defection and defectiveness; of vile, contubernial association; of what Kant calls *Beimischung*: the dragon's blood that falsifies the empirico-transcendental *doublet* of subjection that we have learned to desire from the classic institution. This weak "and" conjoins, *solidarizes*, accident and intention, substance and act, *and* makes room for a weakened, better yet: indecisive, analogy between my "remembrance" of my necessary death to come, and the finitude of merely human civilization.

Imagine a republic consisting of institutions each built on this weak "and" and all allied, each with each, by that weak "and." For now, it is a fiction, a radically allegorical fiction taking from future and past and returning nothing in exchange, or nothing that can be measured against what it takes. It will be nothing like either Rawls's "social union of social unions" or Searle's village of material safeguards become symbolic. For defection operates not just to suspend and eventually abolish this or that institution, the connubial family, the university, the first person, the police force, "race," the state—it works also where by play, accident, and design we build vile, contubernial association, where whatever it is that replaces each of these classic institutions con-sists with other such defective institutions. Defection works to mar the logic and the temporalities making the necessity of my death and the finitude of human histories into analogues of one another and into grounds, foundations on which to build a city sheltering us all. I note that my "other such" is marred as well or begs the question, if by it I intend that the republic's defective institutions entertain with one another the sort of antecedent similitude that serves to determine *one* concept or to identify *one* world, concept and world to be articulated with or even just made to stand next to others that resemble them. And then what would "consisting of" mean in the phrase, "A republic consisting of institutions built on this weak 'and'"? Guercino and Fragonard may intend for the skull each puts into a canvas's "discursive play" to become an object; just an inscription; or a commodity. Thus they foreclose the phrase's injunction that you and I *act*; that, remembering a finitude we can neither share nor tell together, we institute ways of standing together before the object, the inscription, or the commodity. To *consist* is, etymologically, to stand together, next to one another; to be together in one place; you *and* I. But defective institutions, like Bachelard's language, like the injunction *memento mori*, have no one "place." They are not *an* object; no one "place" is proper to them, no time. Just for this reason they offer ephemeral times and places where you and I, also alone and each not-one, may stand together. A defective institution is a *hapax*, a *unicum*, a singular that is not-one, an injunction just to me that *I* remember what *I* cannot imagine; *and yet* in its horizon, it is some not-yet-object that maybe you or perhaps I may be able to wrench into standing next to, if not into likeness with, another; for a moment; to an end; for me; for you. *Republicanism* is the name I give the violent disposition to abolish one life and produce ephemeral and low, even vile, *solidarities*, *associations*, between and among defective institutions. The *republic* is the incoherent form in which these solidarities consist.

# ACKNOWLEDGMENTS

My mother, Giggy Paull Lezra, died while *Defective Institutions* was in production. She was a writer and a teacher. She drew, she sang, she played Appalachian songs on a ukulele. I hope she would have liked this book.

Ten years ago a message from Tom Lay came with the news of Helen Tartar's death in a car accident. Helen published my first book, shepherding it from dissertation to monograph with long, handwritten comments. She and Tom published my second, by then at Fordham. She and Tom supported the idea of a book series that sought to push the extremes of critical expression—what turned out to be IDIOM. And some days ago I received a message from Tom Lay with the news that *Defective Institutions* would enjoy a press subvention from the Helen Tartar Memorial Fund at Fordham University Press. Helen Tartar was a friend—to so many and to so many ideas and books! This book, like many others that others have written and published since March 3, 2014, would have been impossible without her—without her early warm support, her intelligence, her resolve, her friendship to thought and to generations of young scholars. *Defective Institutions* is dedicated, in gratitude and admiration, to her memory and to her example.

I began thinking about the problems I touch on here many years before COVID-19 changed so very much for so many, but the traces of quarantine and confinement and the exhaustion of solitude run through *Defective Institutions*. I am grateful beyond telling to the friends who saw me through those grim months and months. This book is yours.

To the colleagues and doctoral students who listened online, in impromptu or formal seminars, as the argument came together: thank you.

I had the honor to be elected 2022 Chaire Internationale de Philosophie Contemporaine at Université de Paris-8. One of my seminars at Paris-8, on "Institution Abolition," became the conceptual backbone of the book. I am deeply in debt to the seminar's students and to the members of the committee who nominated me for the chair, in particular Éric Alliez, Étienne Balibar, and Barbara

Cassin. To Frédéric Rambeau, for his friendship and hospitality in Paris, my great thanks.

The College of Humanities, Arts, and Social Sciences at the University of California Riverside were generous and flexible. They made it possible for me to accept the chair.

Some portions of *Defective Institutions* appeared in print in earlier versions. They are “Keisatsu no shinkyu: Fukanzen na seido nitsuite” (Instance of the Police: On Defective Institutions), trans. Yuki Ueda, in *Shuken no sho jouken* (Conditions of Sovereignty) (Tokyo: University of Tokyo Press, 2022), 5–24; “The Schema of Institution,” *Philosophy Today* 66, no. 2 (2022): 385–404; “Defective Institutions, or, Critique,” in *Ends of Critique*, ed. Kathrin Thiele, and Birgit Kaiser (London: Rowland Littlefield, 2022), 201–218; “Insufficiency,” *Interfere* 1, no. 1 (2020), https://interferejournal.org/current-issue/; “Efeméride/institución,” in *Terror: La perspectiva hispana*, ed. José Luis Villacañas, Erin Graff Zivin, Jacques Lezra, and Alberto Moreiras (Madrid: Escolar, 2020), 161–168; *“Lacrimae rerum:* Institution of Grief,” in *Niobes: Antiquity Modernity Critical Theory*, ed. Mario Telo and Andrew Benjamin (Columbus: Ohio State University Press, 2024); and “‘[C]ounting your heads/As I’m making the beds’: Piratesthetics, Weill-Brecht to Simone,” in *Resonances Against Fascism: Modernist and Avant-Garde Sounds from Kurt Weill to Black Lives Matter*, ed. Laura Chiesa (Albany: SUNY Press, 2024), 35–50.

# NOTES

## PREFACE

1. The epigraphs are from Marianne Moore, "Black Earth," in *Observations: Poems* (New York: Farrar Straus, 1996), 44–45, and Victor Doublet, *Logic for Young Ladies* (New York: O'Shea, 1868), 103, unattributed translation of *Logique des demoiselles* (Tours: R. Pornin, 1842). Except as indicated, translations throughout are mine.

2. John Rawls, *A Theory of Justice: Revised Edition* (Cambridge, MA: Harvard University Press, [1971] 1999), 462. The bibliography on the relation between "social union" and "institution" in Rawls is rich. I have found especially useful works that approach Rawls from four directions: in the first place, contractualism following Thomas Scanlon's "Rawls's Theory of Justice," *University of Pennsylvania Law Review* 121 (1973): 1020–1069. In the second place, works that take on the troublesome notion (partly drawn, Rawls reminds his readers, from Wilhelm von Humboldt's *The Limits of State Action*), that a "well-ordered society . . . is a social union of social unions"; here see especially Joshua Cohen, "Democratic Equality." *Ethics* 99, no. 4 (July 1989): 727–751; Rex Martin, "Rawls's New Theory of Justice," 69 *Chicago-Kent Law Review* 737 (1994), https://scholarship.kentlaw.iit.edu/cklawreview/vol69/iss3/8; Paul Weithman, *Why Political Liberalism?: On John Rawls's Political Turn* (Oxford: Oxford University Press, 2010). Third, specifically deontological engagements with the steps leading between "justice" and institutions political, economic, or social. Here the work of Onora O'Neill, *Bounds of Justice* (Cambridge: Cambridge University Press, 2000) is fundamental. Finally, work elaborating the weak—underdeveloped, at least—"guarantee of the fair value of the political liberties" (150) in the political realization of justice as fairness: on what basis is this guarantee laid? Asserted? Does not a "guarantee" assume some sort of guaranteeing frame or device, minimally linguistic, flowing from, permitting, and sanctioning mutual recognition? A classically imagined institution, let's say? See Saint-Just's definition: "The object of institutions is to establish in fact all social and individual guarantees, in order to avoid dissension and violence; to substitute the ascendancy of morals for the ascendancy of men." See also the key text, John Rawls, *Political Liberalism* (New York: Columbia University Press, 1996; 2nd ed., 2005). On the requirement that what Jonathan Gingerich calls "semiotic justice"

afford equal and fair access to the *cultural* sphere and thus ground the "guarantee of the fair value of the political liberties" in the sort of sort of guaranteeing device called "culture," broadly construed as forms and histories of representation, shared or coordinable phenomenologies of enjoyment, and what he calls "spontaneous freedom," see Gingerich, "Spontaneous Freedom," *Ethics* 133, no. 1 (2022): 38–71. See also Gingerich, "Remixing Rawls: Constitutional Cultural Liberties in Liberal Democracies," *Northeastern University Law Review* 11, no. 2 (2019): 401–466.

3. David Graeber, *The Utopia of Rules: On Technology, Stupidity, and the Secret Joys of Bureaucracy* (New York: Melville House, 2015), 200–201.

4. Ibid., 204.

INTRODUCTION

1. The first epigraph comes from the *Economic and Political Manuscripts of 1844*, The second epigraph comes from Walter Benjamin, "Antiquity of the North: Statues," in *The Storyteller*, trans. and ed. Sam Dolbear, Esther Leslie, and Sebastian Truskolaski (New York: Verso, 2016), 122. I corrected their translation of "diese Niobiden des Meeres?," which they give as "Niobes of the Sea?" ?" The German is from Walter Benjamin, "Nordisch See," *Gesammelte Schriften* IV.1, ed. Tillman Rexroth (Frankfurt am Main: Suhrkamp, 1991), 387: "Sie alle das Antlitz von salzigen Tränen verwittert, die Blicke auszerstoßenen, hölzernen Höhlen nach oben gerichtet, die Arme, wenn sie noch da sind, beschwörend über die Brust gekreuzt—wer sind sie,—so unsagbar hilflos und aufbegehrend—diese Niobiden des Meeres? Oder seine Mänaden?"

2. Raimo Tuomela, *The Philosophy of Social Practices: A Collective Acceptance View* (Cambridge: Cambridge University Press, 2002), 17.

3. James G. March and Johan P. Olsen, *Rediscovering Institutions: The Organizational Basis of Politics* (New York: Free Press, 1989). For the now-standard tripartite division of the "new institutionalism," see Peter A. Hall and Rosemary C. R. Taylor, "La science politique et les trois néo-institutionnalismes," *Revue française de science politique* 47, nos. 3–4 (1997): 469–496; and, more recently, Ellen M. Immergut, "Historical-Institutionalism in Political Science and the Problem of Change," and John Harriss "Institutions, Politics and Culture: A Case for 'Old' Institutionalism in the Study of Historical Change," both in *Understanding Change: Models, Methodologies, and Metaphors* (New York: Palgrave-Macmillan, 2006), ed. Andreas Wimmer and Reinhart Kössler, 237–260 and 177–187, respectively. See, for a view from political science, Orfeo Fioretos, Tulia G. Falleti, and Adam Sheingate, "Historical Institutionalism in Political Science," in *The Oxford Handbook of Historical Institutionalism*, ed. Orfeo Fioretos, Tulia G. Falleti, and Adam Sheingate (Oxford: Oxford University Press, 2016); and Giovanni Capoccia, "When Do Institutions 'Bite'? Historical Institutionalism and the Politics of Institutional Change." *Comparative Political Studies* 49, no. 8 (2016), 1095–1127.

4. Émile Durkheim, *Bulletin de la Société française de philosophie*, 15 (1917):

57. In Émile Durkheim, *The Rules of Sociological Method*, ed. Steven Lukes, trans. W. D. Halls. (London: Macmillan, 1982), 248.

5. Tuomela, *The Philosophy of Social Practices*, 157. Tuomela says, though, "collectively—but not necessarily intentionally." Searle will dispute both the collective nature of the act of institutionalization and the nonnecessity of "intention," but he will agree on the balance that institutions are "made devices for creating order in a human community, typically society, and helping people to satisfy their basic needs, such as needs related to food and shelter, sexual relations and reproduction, sociality and social power." See also 10: "We-attitudes drive much of human life, because people are social in the sense they involve and tend to take into account in their thinking and acting what others think and do." For Searle's response to Tuomela's critique of his *The Construction of Social Reality* (New York: Free Press, 1995), see John R. Searle, "Responses to Critics of *The Construction of Social Reality*," *Philosophy and Phenomenological Research* 57, no. 2 (1997): 449–458. A review of the problems raised by Searle's work can be found in Joshua Rust, *John Searle and the Construction of Social Reality* (New York: Continuum, 2006).

6. John Locke, *An Essay Concerning Human Understanding*, ed. Peter Nidditch (Oxford: Oxford University Press, 1975), 335.

7. René Descartes, *Les passions de l'âme*, in *Oeuvres de Descartes*, ed. Victor Cousin (Paris: F. G. Levrault, 1824), 4:175. Locke tends to use "instruction" rather than "institution" as a synonym for "education." See John Locke, *Some Thoughts Concerning Education* (London: A. and J. Churchill at the Black Swan in Paternoster-row, 1693). Robert Ainsworth, Locke's contemporary, published a didactic manual titled *The Most Natural and Easie Way of Institution*, using "institution" where Locke (from whom he sought some distance despite their affinities and their similar rather mediated recollection of the precepts of Ascham's *Schole-Master*) used "education." See Robert Ainsworth, *The Most Natural and Easie Way of Institution* (London, 1698).

8. Guattari's engagement with institutional psychotherapy, as developed by Francesc Tosquelles and Jean Oury, was profound and decisive for his work, independent and in collaboration with Gilles Deleuze. Indeed much of the intellectual energy of the Revue Chimères group—founded in part to develop Guattari's approaches—was devoted to deepening and extending the notion that psychotherapy could indeed *have* an institutional setting (which would necessarily be much more than just the passive location for classic cures). For an overview of the psychiatric situation in France at the time of the foundation of the St. Alban clinic, see most recently Camille Robcis, *Disalienation: Politics, Philosophy, and Radical Psychiatry in Postwar France* (Chicago: University of Chicago Press, 2021). An earler treatment, in Marie-Laure Dimon, "La folie au risque des discours institutionnels," *Topique* 76, no. 3 (2001): 141–157. Guattari's relations with Oury and Tosquelles, in his *Psychanalyse et transversalité: Essais d'analyse institutionnelle* (Paris, Maspéro, [1974] 2003); *Pratique de l'institutionnel et politique* (interviews with Jean Oury, François Tosquelles and Félix

Guattari) (Vigneux: Matrice, 1985); and Félix Guattari, *De Leros à La Borde* (Paris: Lignes/IMEC, 2022).

9. Maurice Hauriou, *Principes de droit public* (Paris: Sirey, 1916), 48. For background on Hauriou and an important selection of texts, see *The French Institutionalists: Maurice Hauriou, Georges Renard, Joseph T. Delos*, ed. Albert Broderick, trans. Mary Welling (Cambridge, MA: Harvard University Press, 1970). On early twentieth-century juridical institutionalism more broadly, see Mariano Croce and Marco Goldoni, *The Legacy of Pluralism: The Continental Jurisprudence of Santi Romano, Carl Schmitt, and Costantino Mortati* (Stanford, CA: Stanford University Press, 2020); and especially Roberto Esposito's *Instituting Thought: Three Paradigms of Political Ontology*, trans. Mark William Epstein (Cambridge: Polity, 2021). For a review of juridical institutionalism from the perspective of the sociology of law, see Massimo La Torre, "Institutionalism as Alternative Constitutional Theory: On Santi Romano's Concept of Law and His Epigones," *Jurisprudence* 11, no. 1 (2020): 92–100.

10. Jonathan Turner, *The Institutional Order* (New York: Longman, 1997), 6.

11. Seumas Miller, *The Moral Foundations of Social Institutions* (Cambridge: Cambridge University Press, 2010), 12.

12. Searle, *The Construction of Social Reality*, 32–33.

13. Compare Searle on regress and institutions: "If institutional facts require language and language is itself an institution, then it seems language must require language, and we have either infinite regress or circularity. There is a weaker and a stronger version of my claim. The weaker is that in order to have institutional facts at all, a society must have at least a primitive form of a language, that in this sense the institution of language is logically prior to other institutions. On this view language is the basic social institution in the sense that all others presuppose language, but language does not presuppose the others: you can have language without money and marriage, but not the converse. The stronger claim is that each institution requires linguistic elements of the facts within that very institution." Searle, *The Construction of Social Reality*, 51.

14. Émile Benveniste, *Dictionary of Indo-European Concepts and Society*, trans. Elizabeth Palmer (Chicago: HAU Books, 2016), 11. The French original is at Émile Benveniste, *Vocabulaire des institutions indo-européennes* (Paris: Minuit, 1969), 9.

15. I am echoing Derrida's analysis of Kant's famous text on *The Conflict of the Faculties* in "Mochlos, or the Conflict of the Faculties," trans. J. Plug et al., in *Who's Afraid of Philosophy: Right to Philosophy 2* (Stanford, CA: Stanford University Press, 2004), 83–112.

16. René Descartes, *Meditations on First Philosophy*, ed. and trans. John Cottingham (Cambridge: Cambridge University Press, 1996), 40. The original Latin is in René Descartes, *Meditationes de Prima Philosophia*, ed. Artur Buchenau (Leipzig: Meiner, 1913), 67.

17. Charlton T. Lewis and Charles Short, *A Latin Dictionary* (Oxford: Clarendon

Press,1879); CNRTL, Centre National de Ressources Textuelles et Lexicales, https://www.cnrtl.fr/definition/; Sebastián de Covarrubias Horozco, *Tesoro de la lengua castellana, o española* (Madrid: Luis Sánchez, 1611).

18. See, for instance, David McLellan, *The Young Hegelians and Karl Marx* (New York: Macmillan 1969); Harold E. Mah, *The End of Philosophy, the Origin of "Ideology": Karl Marx and the Crisis of the Young Hegelians* (Berkeley: University of California Press, 1987); Warren Breckman, *Marx, the Young Hegelians, and the Origins of Radical Social Theory* (Cambridge: Cambridge University Press, 1999). In my own work I have generally followed Althusser's readings of Marx's Hegel, though what interests me in *On the Nature of Marx's Things* (New York: Fordham University Press, 2018) is Marx's earlier encounter with Lucretius, definitive for the young Marx's uses of Hegel.

19. Georg Wilhelm Friedrich Hegel, *Werke* (Frankfurt: Suhrkamp, 1979), vol. 9. See also *Hegels Kleine Logik: Nebst dem Kapitel über Raum, Zeit und Bewegung nach dem Texte der Encyklopädie in der Ausgabe seiner sämmtlichen Werke, für das akademische Studium mit einem Kommentar herausgegeben*, ed. G. J. P. J. Bolland (Leiden: Adriani, 1899), vol. 1; Marco Bormann, *Der Begriff der Natur: Eine Untersuchung zu Hegels Naturbegriff und dessen Rezeption* (Herbolzheim: Centaurus, 2000). The discussion of Marx's concept of nature till recently was shaped by Alfred Schmidt's *Der Begriff der Natur in der Lehre von Marx* (Frankfurt am Main: Institut für Sozialforschung, Europäische Verlagsanstalt, 1962). See the discussion of Schmidt in Paul Burkett, "Nature in Marx Reconsidered: A Silver Anniversary Assessment of Alfred Schmidt's Concept of Nature in Marx," *Organization & Environment* 10, no. 2 (June 1997): 164–183, and Noel Castree, "Marxism and the Production of Nature," *Capital & Class* 24, no. 3 (2000): 5–36. A useful but dated review of scholarship on the topic is Neil Smith and Phil O'Keefe, "Geography, Marx and the Concept of Nature," *Antipode* 12 (1980): 30–39. Other recent returns to the matter of nature in Marx include John Bellamy Foster, *Marx's Ecology: Materialism and Nature* (New York: Monthly Review Press, 2000), *The Return of Nature: Socialism and Ecology* (New York: NYU Press, 2020); and Kohei Saito, *Karl Marx's Ecosocialism: Capitalism, Nature, and the Unfinished Critique of Political Economy* (New York: Monthly Review Press, 2017).

20. The figure of the abstract thinker is hardly foreign to Hegel, though the satirical essay he devotes to it, "Who Thinks Abstractly?," contemporaneous with the *Phenomenology of Spirit*, is most often read as an indictment on class grounds of such a "thinker." In Walter Kaufmann, ed., *Hegel: Texts and Commentary* (Garden City, NY: Anchor Books, 1966), 113–118. The German is in Georg Wilhelm Friedrich Hegel, "Wer denkt abstrakt?" *Werke* (Frankfurt: Suhrkamp, 1979), 2:576–581.

21. Friedrich Kluge, *An Etymological Dictionary of the German Language*, trans. John Francis Davis (London: G. Bell, 1891), 226.

22. Karl Marx, *The Economic and Political Manuscripts of* 1844, trans. Martin Mil-

ligan (New York: Prometheus, 1988), 167. The German is in Karl Marx and Friedrich Engels, *Werke* (Berlin: Dietz Verlag, 1968), 40:588.

23. Georg Wilhelm Friedrich Hegel, *Aesthetics: Lectures on Fine Art*, trans. T. M. Knox (Oxford: Oxford University Press, 1975), 143–153. The German is in Georg Wilhelm Friedrich Hegel, *Werke 13: Vorlesungen über die Ästhetik I* (Frankfurt am Main: Suhrkamp, 1986), 190–202. Knox translates *Mangelhaftigkeit* as "deficiency."

24. Mary Wollstonecraft Shelley, *Frankenstein* (New York: Dover, 1994), 114.

25. Fyodor Dostoevsky, *Winter Notes on Summer Impressions*, trans. David Patterson (Evanston, IL: Northwestern University Press, 1997), 49.

26. Corey Robin, "American Institutions Won't Keep Us Safe from Donald Trump's Excesses," *The Guardian*, February 2, 2017, https://www.theguardian.com/commentisfree/2017/feb/02/american-institutions-wont-keep-you-safe-trumps-excesses.

27. Searle—writing about "institutional facts"—puts it like this: "Though there is no necessary connection between being an intentional state at a given time and being conscious then and there, nonetheless, there is an important necessary connection between the two, in that every intentional state that is unconscious is at least accessible to consciousness. It is the sort of thing that could be conscious. An unconscious intentional state has to be in principle accessible to consciousness." *Construction of Social Reality*, 7.

28. Jacques Derrida, *Rogues: Two Essays on Reason*, trans. Pascale-Anne Brault and Michael Naas (Stanford: Stanford University Press, 2005), 46. Derrida is commenting on a passage from Jean-Luc Nancy's *The Experience of Freedom*, trans. Bridget McDonald (Stanford, CA: Stanford University Press, 1993), 78–79.

29. Sylvia Wynter, "No Humans Involved: An Open Letter to My Colleagues." *Voices of the African Diaspora* 8, no. 2 (1992): 16.

30. Sylvia Wynter, "On Disenchanting Discourse: 'Minority' Literary Criticism and Beyond," *Cultural Critique* 7, no. 2 (1987): 243.

31. Ibid.

32. Sylvia Wynter, "The Ceremony Found: Towards the Autopoetic Turn/Overturn, Its Autonomy of Human Agency and Extraterritoriality of (Self-)Cognition," in *Black Knowledges/Black Struggles: Essays in Critical Epistemology*, ed. Jason R. Ambroise and Sabine Broeck (Liverpool: Liverpool University Press, 2015), 194.

33. Sylvia Wynter, "The Ceremony Must Be Found: After Humanism," *Boundary 2* 12, no. 3 (1984): 56.

34. Ibid., 44.

35. Ibid., 201.

36. Wynter, "On Disenchanting Discourse," 243.

37. Ibid.

38. Stefano Harney and Fred Moten, *The Undercommons: Fugitive Planning & Black Study* (New York: Minor Compositions, 2013), 20.

39. Stanislas Breton, "'Dieu est Dieu': Essai sur la violence des propositions tautologiques." In *Philosophie buissonnière*, ed. Stanislas Breton (Grenoble: Millon, 1989), 133–140. Translation by Jacques Lezra, "'God Is God': Essay on the Violence of Tautological Propositions." In "Allegory and Political Representation," *Yearbook of Comparative Literature* (2017): 203–211.

40. Walter Benjamin, *Selected Writings I*, ed. Marcus Bullock and Michael W. Jennings (Cambridge, MA: Harvard University Press, 2004), 245.

41. Harney and Moten, *The Undercommons*, 20.

42. Roger Brown and Helen Carasso, *Everything for Sale? The Marketisation of UK Higher Education* (Abingdon, UK: Routledge, 2013).

43. Wynter, "On Disenchanting Discourse," 243.

44. Bill Readings, *The University in Ruins* (Cambridge, MA: Harvard University Press, 1999), 16.

45. For reenvisionings of the university in the wake of Readings, Brown, and Carasso, see the collection of essays *La universidad (im)posible*, ed. Willy Thayer et al. (Santiago, Chile: Ediciones Macul, 2018).

46. Breton, "Dieu est Dieu," 139.

47. Wynter, "The Ceremony Must be Found," 56.

48. M. E. O'Brien, "To Abolish the Family: The Working-Class Family and Gender Liberation in Capitalist Development," *Endnotes* 5 (2020): 361–417.

49. Catharine Malabou, *Au voleur! Anarchisme et philosophie* (Paris: PUF, 2022).

50. A review of the term *contubernio*'s genealogy and uses, in J. A. Benimeli Ferrer, *El contubernio judeo-masónico-comunista: Del satanismo al escándalo de la P-2* (Madrid: ISTMO, 1982). A provocative and influential treatment of the role of freemasonry in the elaboration of European modernity is in Reinhart Koselleck, *Critique and Crisis: Enlightenment and the Pathogenesis of Modern Society* (Cambridge, MA: MIT Press, 2000). See, in Koselleck's wake, Tim Mehigan and Helene De Burgh, "'Aufklärung', Freemasonry, the Public Sphere and the Question of Enlightenment." *Journal of European Studies* 38, no. 1 (2008): 5–25.

51. Paul Preston, *The Spanish Holocaust: Inquisition and Extermination in Twentieth-Century Spain* (New York: Norton, 2012), 59, 132.

52. José Antonio Primo de Rivera, *Revolución nacional: Puntos de Falange* (Madrid: Ediciones Prensa del Movimiento, 1949), 132–133.

53. Ibid., 133.

54. *Diccionario de la Real Academia Española* (Madrid, 1925).

55. A lively, accurate historical account of the Rif campaign, in Comer Plummer, "The Bogeyman Cometh: The Annual Disaster," *Military History Online*, April 5, 2022, https://www.militaryhistoryonline.com/Modern/BattleOfAnnua. For the dreary, terrible history of the concentration camp at Zeluán, see María Elena Fernández Díaz, *Melilla 1931–1940, gritos y susurros: El campo de concentración de Zeluán* (Melilla: UNED 2020).

56. Michèle Barrett and Mary McIntosh, *The Anti-Social Family* (London: Verso Editions/NLB, 1982).

## 1. THE SCHEMA OF INSTITUTION

1. The epigraphs are from Jean-François Lyotard, "The Foundation Crisis," trans. Chris Turner, *Cultural Politics* 9, no. 2 (2013): 138; Hannah Arendt, *On Revolution* (New York: Penguin Books, 1990), 232; and Alexander Hamilton, https://guides.loc.gov/federalist-papers/text-61–70#s-lg-box-wrapper-25493452.

2. Jean-François Lyotard, *The Differend: Phrases in Dispute*, trans. Georges Van Den Abbeele (Minneapolis: University of Minnesota Press, 1988), 55. The original can be found at *Le différend* (Paris: Éditions de Minuit, 1983), 90.

3. This is how Dylan Sawyer glosses this claim: "Lyotard also believes that 'reality entails the differend' (D, § 92), that throughout history there are times when traditional models of cognition, and even representation itself, appear insufficient for bearing witness to the events that surround them" (2). Later this position becomes a "problem." Sawyer: "The problem is that while 'reality entails the differend' (D, § 92) and so is unavoidable, reality is nevertheless felt by Lyotard to 'always [be] the plaintiff's responsibility' (D, §10), despite being a designation perpetually at risk of dismissal since it is reliant upon external validation of its status . . . this . . . also raises the question of what is to happen to the victim/plaintiff in the meantime. Ultimately, I understand Lyotard's entire philosophy of *The Differend* to be structured more towards the response of others than to the predicament of those who suffer from the injuries of a wrong and as a result risks sustaining (or at least overlooking) the damage that it hopes to eventually displace" (177). Dylan Sawyer, *Lyotard, Literature and the Trauma of the Differend* (New York: Palgrave McMillan, 2014).

4. A clear, if brief, account of Lyotard on names in *The Differend* (including mention of §92) is in Bill Reading, *Introducing Lyotard: Art and Politics* (New York: Routledge, 1991), 89–93. An illuminating account of Lyotard's consideration of vengeance as an inadequate response to the "damning bind" arising because "differends cannot be avoided by avoiding the contact between heterogeneous genres of language because it is precisely by outside validation that sense is determined" and thus that "once more we are confronted by the unhappy damnation if one does and damnation if one does not" (124) is in Mélanie V. Walton, *Expressing the Inexpressible in Lyotard and Pseudo-Dionysius: Bearing Witness as Spiritual Exercise* (Plymouth, UK: Lexington Books, 2013), pp. 89–159, esp. 124–127.

5. The New Testament Greek reads in full *mē heautous ekdikountes, agapētoi, alla dote topon tē orgē, gegraptai gar Emoi ekdikesis, egō antapodōsō, legei Kurios*.

6. Anicius M. S. Boethius and Luca Obertello, *De Hypotheticis Syllogismis* (Brescia: Paideia, 1969) III:11:6, 389.

7. Thomas Aquinas, *Glossa ordinaria* (Romans 12), in *Glossae Scripturae Sacrae*

*electronicae*, ed. Martin Morard, IRHT-CNRS, 2016–2018, https://gloss-e.irht.cnrs.fr/php/editions_chapitre.php?id=liber&numLivre=60&chapitre=60_12.

8. An astute account of the problem of "linking" in *The Differend*, in Gérald Sfez, *Jean-François Lyotard: La faculté d'une phrase* (Paris: Galilée, 2000). See, for instance, 72: "C'est du lieu de ce tort général entre les enchainements des phrases que peut s'entendre, a l'inverse de ce qu'on se represente, le tort dit 'humain.'"

9. See, for instance, Stephen Hastings-King, *Looking for the Proletariat: Socialisme ou Barbarie and the Problem of Worker Writing* (Leiden: Brill, 2014).

10. J. L. Austin, *How to Do Things With Words* (Oxford: Oxford University Press, 1962), 23; Gilles Lane's French translation, *Quand dire, c'est faire* (Paris: Éditions du Seuil, 1970), 56.

11. Martha C. Nussbaum, *Anger and Forgiveness: Resentment, Generosity, Justice* (Oxford: Oxford University Press, 2014), 3.

12. Aeschylus, *Eumenides*, in *Aeschylus*, trans. Herbert Weir Smyth (Cambridge, MA: Harvard University Press, 1926), vol. 2, ll. 825–830.

13. Lyotard's most compact formulation, in "Judicieux dans le différend," is: "L'argument nommé dilemme, connu des Sophistes, de Protagoras notamment, donne son ressort à la maxime épicurienne : si la mort y est (à Auschwitz), vous n'y êtes pas; si vous y êtes, elle n'y est pas. Dans les deux cas il vous est impossible de prouver que la mort y est." Jean-François Lyotard, "Judicieux dans le différend," in Jacques Derrida et al., *La faculté de juger* (Paris: Minuit, 1985), 231.

14. Lyotard's views on the connection between Stalinism and bureaucracy and on Socialisme ou Barbarie's critique are in his "Pierre Souyri: Le marxisme qui n'a pas fini," *Esprit* n.s. 61, no. 1 (1982): 11–31.

15. The bibliography on *Marbury v. Madison* is extensive. I have found my way into the case through, among others, William E. Nelson, *Marbury v. Madison: The Origins and Legacy of Judicial Review*, 2nd ed. (Lawrence: University Press of Kansas, 2018); Richard Allen Epstein, *The Classical Liberal Constitution: The Uncertain Quest for Limited Government* (Cambridge, MA: Harvard University Press, 2014); Gerald Flood Leonard, *The Partisan Republic: Democracy, Exclusion, and the Fall of the Founders' Constitution, 1780s–1830s* (New York: Cambridge University Press, 2019); Mark A. Graber and Michael Perhac, *Marbury Versus Madison: Documents and Commentary* (Washington, DC: CQ Press, 2002); Paul W. Kahn, *The Reign of Law: Marbury v. Madison and the Construction of America* (New Haven, CT: Yale University Press, 1997); Charles A. Beard, *The Supreme Court and the Constitution* (New York: Macmillan, 1922); Alexander M. Bickel, *The Least Dangerous Branch*, 2nd ed. (New Haven, CT: Yale University Press, 1986); Edward S. Corwin, *The Doctrine of Judicial Review: Its Legal and Historical Basis, and Other Essays* (Princeton, NJ: Princeton University Press, 1914). I am in great debt to Gabriel Lezra for help with technical questions regarding *Marbury* and for broader conversation on the topics of this essay.

16. On the historical roots of mandamus writs, see Richard E. Flint, "The Evolving Standard for the Granting of Mandamus Relief in the Texas Supreme Court: One More Mile Marker down the Road of No Return," 39 *St. Mary's Law Journal* 1 (2007), esp. 5–48. On mandamus in the postrevolutionary period, see Jacques de Ville, "Spectres of Coke: Judicial Supervision as a Revolutionary Inheritance," *Law Critique* 18 (2007): 29–54.

17. Kahn, *The Reign of Law*, 11.

18. John Marshall, "*Marbury v. Madison*," in *The Constitutional Decisions of John Marshall*, ed. Joseph Potter Cotton (New York: G. P. Putnam's Sons, 1905), 1:37.

19. Thomas Jefferson, letter to William Smith, November 13, 1787, https://founders.archives.gov/documents/Jefferson/01–12–02–0348. Hannah Arendt's remarks on Jefferson's mistrust of the belief in the "unchangeable" quality granted the Constitution by "those who 'look at constitutions with sanctimonious reverence, and deem them like the ark of the covenant, too sacred to be touched,'" and on what she sees as the dangers of "recurring revolutions" (235), are in *On Revolution* (New York: Penguin Books, 1990), 232–281.

20. Oliver Wendell Holmes, "Natural Law," *Harvard Law Review* 40 (1918–1919): 42. See, among others, Robert P. George, "Holmes on Natural Law," 48 *Villanova Law Review* 1 (2003), https://digitalcommons.law.villanova.edu/vlr/vol48/iss1/1; and Charles Donahue, "'The Hypostasis of a Prophecy': Legal Realism and Legal History," in *Law and Legal Process: Substantive Law and Procedure in English Legal History*, ed. M. Dyson and D. Ibbetson (Cambridge: Cambridge University Press, 2013), 1–16. Holmes's "Natural Law" is particularly invested in maintaining the fact-value distinction.

## 2. INSUFFICIENT GROUND: THE INSTITUTION OF REASON

1. The epigraph is from Jacques Derrida, *Heidegger: La question de l'être et l'histoire* (Paris: Galilée, 2013), 57, my translation. Derrida's own treatment of the principle of sufficient reason, especially in Jacques Derrida, "The Principle of Reason: The University in the Eyes of Its Pupils," trans. Catherine Porter and Edward P. Morris, *Diacritics* 13, no. 3 (1983): 2–20; and in his seminar *The Death Penalty*, ed. Geoffrey Bennington and Marc Crépon, trans. Elizabeth Rottenberg (Chicago: University of Chicago Press, 2017), 2:136–160. This chapter—in this and previous versions—benefited immeasurably from Viktoria Huegel's astute critique and commentary.

2. Martin Heidegger, *Being and Time*, rev. ed., trans. Joan Stambaugh (New York: SUNY Press, 2010), 36; John Macquarrie and Edward Robinson, *Being and Time* (Oxford: Blackwell, 1962), 63. The German is from Martin Heidegger, *Sein und Zeit* (Tübingen: Max Niemeyer Verlag, 1967), 39.

3. See Walter Burkert, *Lore and Science in Ancient Pythagoreanism*, trans. E. Minar (Cambridge, MA: Harvard University Press, 1972), 409–415.

4. T. L. Heath, *The Thirteen Books of Euclid's Elements* (Cambridge: Cambridge

University Press, 1928). See also Proclus, *Commentary on the First Book of Euclid's Elements*, trans. Glen Morrow (Princeton, NJ: Princeton University Press, 1970).

5. Pappus of Alexandria, *Tafsīr Bābūs li-al-Maqālah al-ʿāshirah 'min kitāb Uqlīdis* (The Commentary of Pappus on Book X of Euclid's *Elements*, as translated into Arabic by Abu Uthman al-Dimishqi), trans. William Thomson and Gustav Junge (Frankfurt: Institute for the History of Arabic-Islamic Science at the Johann Wolfgang Goethe University, 1997), 64 (English), 2 (Arabic). I am delighted to acknowledge Jeannie Miller's help in correcting the translation. Here is Thomas Taylor's translation of *Iamblichus's Life of Pythagoras* (London: Watkins, 1818), 126–127: "It is said, therefore, that he who first divulged the theory of commensurable and incommensurable quantities, to those who were unworthy to receive it, was so hated by the Pythagoreans that they not only expelled him from their common association, and from living with them, but also constructed a tomb for him, as one who had migrated from the human and passed into another life. Others also say, that the Divine Power was indignant with those who divulged the dogmas of Pythagoras: for that he perished in the sea, as an impious person, who rendered manifest the composition of the *icostagonus*; viz. who delivered the method of inscribing in a sphere the *dodecahedron*, which is one of what are called the five solid figures. But according to others, this happened to him who unfolded the doctrine of irrational and incommensurable quantities. Moreover, all the Pythagoric discipline was symbolic, and resembled enigmas and riddles, consisting of apothegms, in consequence of imitating antiquity in its character; just as the truly divine and Pythian oracles appear to be in a certain respect difficult to be understood and explained, to those who carelessly receive the answers which they give. Such therefore, and so many are the indications respecting Pythagoras and the Pythagoreans, which may be collected from what is disseminated about them."

6. I cite from the most probing account of this story I have found, Jean-Luc Périllié's "La découverte des incommensurables et le vertige de l'infini," *Cahiers philosophiques* 91 (2002): 9–30, at 15.

7. Proclus, scholium on Cratylus. See Robbert Maarten Van den Berg, *Proclus' Commentary on the Cratylus in Context: Ancient Theories of Language and Naming* (Leiden: Brill, 2008), 104.

8. See the very useful account of *grounding* in Heidegger's reading of Leibnitz, in Paul M. Livingston, *The Logic of Being: Realism, Truth, and Time* (Evanston, IL: Northwestern University Press, 2017), 30–32.

9. A thorough and influential account of the relation between the principle of identity, or contradiction, and the principle of sufficient reason, is in Paul Davies's "This Contradiction," in *Futures: Of Jacques Derrida*, ed. Richard Rand (Stanford, CA: Stanford University Press, 2001), 18–64. Davies's essay is remarkable particularly for its careful juxtaposition of Priestian dialetheism with Derridean indeterminacy, esp. 33–40. What I conclude by calling "principial mediation" shares features with the latter.

10. *Aristotle Metaphysics: Books G, D, and E*, trans. Christopher Kirwan (Oxford: Clarendon Press, 1993).

11. Bertrand Russell and Alfred N. Whitehead, *Principia Mathematica*, 2nd ed. (Cambridge: Cambridge University Press, 1963), 37.

12. Martin Heidegger, *The Principle of Reason*, trans. Reginald Lilly (Bloomington: Indiana University Press, 1996), 101. *Der Satz vom Grund*, in *Gesamtausgabe* (Frankfurt: Vittorio Klosterman, 1997), 10:151.

13. "Function and Concept" (1891), in *Translations from the Philosophical Writings of Gottlob Frege*, ed. P. Geach and M. Black (Oxford: Blackwell, 1960), 24.

14. Matthew M. P. Muir, *A Treatise on the Principles of Chemistry* (Cambridge: Cambridge University Press, 1884), 129.

15. Johannes Wislicenus, *Über die Räumliche Anordnung der Atome in Organischen Molekulen und Ihre Bestimmung in Geometrisch-Isomeren Ungesättigten Verbindungen* (Leipzig: Bei S. Hirzel, 1887). "The Space Arrangement of the Atoms in Organic Molecules and the Resulting Geometrical Isomerism in Unsaturated Compounds," in *The Foundations of Stereo Chemistry*, trans. and ed. George M. Richardson (New York: American Book Company, 1901).

16. This might reasonably be said to correspond to the influential, even naturalized position that Sebastiano Timpanaro first describes, then subtly dismantles, in his *La genesi del metodo del Lachmann* (Florence: Le Monnier, 1963).

17. Derrida, *The Death Penalty*, 2:153.

## 3. THE OBJECT OF ALLEGORY

1. Lucius Annaeus Seneca, *Mad Hercules* I.1: 76–87, in *The Tragedies of Seneca*, trans. Elizabeth I. Harris (London: Oxford University Press, 1904), 5. The quotation from Plato is from *Thaetetus*, in *Plato, with an English Translation*, trans. Harold North Fowler, W. R. M.Lamb, Robert Gregg Bury, and Paul Shorey (Cambridge, MA: Harvard University Press, 1921), 119–120.

2. The bibliography on each of the terms that concern me—"object," "allegory," "politics," "representation"—is vast. The works that lie directly behind my argument are fewer. Centrally and manifestly is Walter Benjamin's *The Origin of German Tragic Drama*, trans. John Osborne (London: Verso, 2003). I have had in mind two of Paul de Man's essays, especially "Pascal's Allegory of Persuasion" and "The Concept of Irony," both in *Aesthetic Ideology*, ed. Andrzej Warminksi (Minneapolis: University of Minnesota Press, 1996). Another older work that is useful, though extremely different, is Angus Fletcher's *Allegory: The Theory of a Symbolic Mode*, rev. ed. (Princeton, NJ: Princeton University Press, [1964] 2012). An influential reading of the phrase from Freud that I center on, from the perspective of object-relations psychoanalysis, is in Christopher Bollas, *The Shadow of the Object* (New York: Routledge, [1987] 2018). Reviews of the philosophy of the object are Olivier Boulnois's "Objet," "Objet, être objectif," and "Ratitudo," in *Vocabulaire européen des philosophies*, ed. Barbara

Cassin (Paris: Seuil, 2004), 868–870. For a treatment that stresses the term's value in the Marxist tradition, see also Etienne Balibar's "Althusser's Object," trans. Margaret Cohen and Bruce Robbins, *Social Text* 39 (1994): 157–188. My own previous tack into the matter are in Jacques Lezra, *República salvaje: De la naturaleza de las cosas* (Santiago, Chile: Ediciones Macul, 2020) and *On the Nature of Marx's Things: Translation as Necrophilology* (New York: Fordham University Press, 2018).

3. Charles Sanders Peirce, *Collected Papers*, ed. Charles Hartshorne, Paul Weiss, and Arthur W. Burks (Cambridge, MA: Harvard University Press, 1931), 1:553. Classic reviews of Peirce on interpretants are James Jakób Lizska, "Peirce's Interpretant," *Transactions of Charles S. Peirce Society* 26, no. 1 (1990): 17–62, and Brendan J. Lalor, "The Classification of Peirce's Interpretants," *Semiotica* 114, nos. 1–2 (1997): 31–40. See also Risto Hilpinen, "On the Immediate and Dynamical Interpretants and Objects of Signs," *Semiotica* 228 (2019): 91–101.

4. Charles Sanders Peirce, Lowell Lecture XI, 1866. In *Writings of Charles S. Peirce, A Chronological Edition*, ed. Max H. Fisch et al. (Bloomington: Indiana University Press, 1982), 1:503.

5. José Ortega y Gasset, *Meditations on Quixote*, trans. Evelyn Rugg and Diego Marín (New York: Norton, 1961), 41–45. The original is José Ortega y Gasset, *Meditaciones del Quijote* (Madrid: Cátedra, 1995), 77. The classic study of Ortega's circumstantialism is Julián Marías, *Ortega: I. Circunstancia y vocación*(Madrid: Revista de Occidente, 1960). More recently, see Javier San Martín and José Lasaga Medina, eds., *Ortega en circunstancia* (Madrid: Biblioteca Nueva, 2005). A useful guide to the circumstances surrounding the Spanish reception of *Meditaciones*, in Gregorio Morán, *El maestro en el erial: Ortega y Gasset y la cultural del franquismo* (Madrid: Tusquets, 1998).

6. Linda Martin Alcoff follows work on epistemic violence by Boaventura de Sousa Santos and Eduardo Viveiros de Castro in her "Extractivist Epistemologies," *Tapuya: Latin American Science, Technology and Society* 5, no. 1 (2022), https://www.tandfonline.com/doi/full/10.1080/25729861.2022.2127231. Their arguments maintain, as Alcoff puts it, that "the colonial context of extractivism, in all its permutations, has generated certain types of practices and related ideas about epistemic justification that need to be rethought." "Most types of extractivist projects today," Alcoff maintains, "treat both land and peoples primarily as resources. Seen primarily as resources, land, timber, bio-rich plants, labor, and communities are subject to external reorganization, without participatory decision making, guided only by the desire for more profit" (2–3). My argument accepts but also inverts this scheme. The "colonial context of extractivism" is not just the circumstance determining that "land, timber, bio-rich plants, labor, and communities" are viewed by colonial reason as "resources" "generating . . . practices and related ideas," but also—like "colonial reason"—a concept produced (and not "generated") *institutionally*, from more or less abstract cultural "resources" found or poached unevenly and more or less violently, by subjects act-

ing according to different, often disaggregated norms, in the "North" as well as the "South."

7. "Recorrido migratorio: 30 años de muertes en el estrecho," Informe 1988–2018: 30 años de muertes en el Estrecho. Andalucía Acoge y Fundación por Causa, 2018. Online at https://acoge.org/wp-content/uploads/2018/11/30A%C3%B1osMuertesFSdf.pdf.

8. *Immanuel Kants Werke. B. IV. Schriften von 1783–1788*, ed. Artur Buchenau and Ernst Cassirer (Berlin: Bruno Cassirer, 191), 349–366 and 545–548.

9. Walter Benjamin, "Baudelaire, or the Streets of Paris," *The Arcades Project*, trans. by Howard Eiland and Kevin McLaughlin (Cambridge, MA: Harvard University Press, 1999), 10–11. The German original is in Walter Benjamin, *Gesammelte Schriften*, ed. Rolf Tiedemann (Frankfurt: Suhrkamp, 1991), 5:1.

10. These verses from "Out of the Cradle, Endlessly Rocking," with notes regarding the emendations and changes that Whitman introduces in different editions, can be found in Walt Whitman, *The Collected Writings of Walt Whitman*, vol. 2, *Leaves of Grass: A Textual Variorum of the Printed Poems, 1860–1867*, ed. Sculley Bradley et al. (New York: NYU Press, 1980), 343–351.

11. Charles Baudelaire, *Flowers of Evil*, trans. Richard Howard (Boston: Godine, 1982), 91.

12. Gayatri Spivak, *A Critique of Postcolonial Reason* (Cambridge, MA: Harvard University Press, 1999), 153.

13. Freud adds to his term *Instanz* the modifier "special," *besondere*, in all editions after the first 1917 version. The expression *besondere Instanz* crops up elsewhere—in "Das Unheimliche" of 1919, in *Gesammelte Werke* vol. 12. (Frankfurt: Fischer Verlag, 2006), 229–271; in *Das Ich und das Es* (1923), in *Gesammelte Werke* vol. 13 (Frankfurt: Fischer Verlag, 1998), 237–293; in *Die Frage der Laienanalyse* (1926), in *Gesammelte Werke* (Frankfurt: Fischer Verlag, 1991), 14:209–287; in "Der Humor" (1928), *Gesammelte Werke*, 14:383–389; in "Dostojewski und die Vatertötung" (1928); in *Gesammelte Werke*, 14:399–421; and in the *Neue Folge der Vorlesungen zur Einführung in die Psychoanalyse* (1933), in *Gesammelte Werke*, 15:75. See also Etienne Balibar's entry/essay on "*Instanz*/Agency" in *Dictionary of Untranslatables: A Philosophical Lexicon*, ed. Barbara Cassin, Emily Apter, Jacques Lezra, and Michael Wood (Princeton, NJ: Princeton University Press, 2014), 23–24.

14. I am using the notions of "grief" and "grievability" in a way that is consonant with Judith Butler's in her *Precarious Life: The Powers of Mourning and Violence*: "To grieve, and to make grief itself into a resource for politics, is not to be resigned to inaction, but it may be understood as the slow process by which we develop a point of identification with suffering itself. The disorientation of grief—"Who have I become?" or, indeed, "What is left of me?" "What is it in the Other that I have lost?"—posits the "I" in the mode of unknowingness. But this can be a point of departure for a new understanding if the narcissistic preoccupation of melancholia can be moved

into a consideration of the vulnerability of others.Then we might critically evaluate and oppose the conditions under which certain human lives are more vulnerable than others, and thus certain human lives are more grievable than others. From where might a principle emerge by which we vow to protect others from the kinds of violence we have suffered, if not from an apprehension of a common human vulnerability?" Judith Butler, *Precarious Life: The Powers of Mourning and Violence* (New York: Verso, 2004), 30. I take the phenomenon of "grief" more broadly than Butler does (it embraces the *tout* in Baudelaire's poem: everything that becomes allegory). This in turn means understanding melancholia perhaps differently from Butler: not as a "narcissistic preoccupation," not even as primarily concerning the self, the subject, the individual psyche, but rather concerning relations of and among objects. This in turn brings the question of moving "melancholia . . . into a consideration of the vulnerability of others," partly out of the realm of human decisions.

15. Sigmund Freud, *Mourning and Melancholia*, in *The Standard Edition of the Complete Works of Sigmund Freud*, ed. and trans. James Strachey et al. (London: Hogarth Press and the Institute of Psychoanalysis, 1953–1974), 14:249. The German original is Sigmund Freud, "Trauer und Melancholie," in *Gesammelte Werke* (London: Imago, 1991), 10:428–446.

16. Jean Genet, *The Thief's Journal*, trans. Bernard Frechtman (New York: Grove Press, 1964), 70.

17. Genet, *The Thief's Journal*, 104–107. The original is in Jean Genet, *Journal du voleur* (Paris: Gallimard, 1949), 78–80.

18. Juan Goytisolo, *Count Julian*, trans. Helen Lane (New York: Viking Press, 1974),

19. Tahar Ben Jelloun, *Leaving Tangier: A Novel*, trans. Linda Coverdale (New York: Penguin Books, 2009), 7–8.

20. The most complete treatment I know of the iconography of the columns/pillars is Earl Rosenthal, "*Plus Ultra, Non plus Ultra*, and the Columnar Device of Emperor Charles V," *Journal of the Warburg and Courtauld Institutes* 34 (1971): 204–228.

21. Juan de Horozco, *Emblemas morales* (Madrid: Juan de la Cuesta, 1589). On Charles's use of the columns/pillars, see Fernando Moreno Cuadro, "La visión emblemática del gobernante virtuoso," *Goya* 187 (1985): 17–26.

## 4. *LACRIMAE RERUM*, OR, THE INSTITUTION OF GRIEF

1. The epigraphs are from Ovid, *Metamorphoses* VI, 299–300, trans. Arthur Golding, in *Shakespeare's Ovid, being Arthur Golding's translation of the Metamorphoses*, ed. W. H. D. Rouse (New York: Norton, 1966); and *Aeschylus II: Agamemnon, Libation Bearers, Eumenides, Fragments*, trans. Herbert Weir Smyth (London: Heinemann, 1926), 434. For a more recent edition of the "Fragments," see *Tragicorum Graecorum Fragmenta*, ed. Stefan Radt (Göttingen: Vandenhoeck and Ruprecht, 1985), 5:276.

2. Roberto Esposito, *Istituzione* (Bologna: Il Mulino, 2021), my translation. See also his *Instituting Thought: Three Paradigms of Political Ontology*, trans. Mark William Epstein (Cambridge: Polity, 2021).

3. See Colin Starger, "The Dialectic of *Stare Decisis* Doctrine," in *Precedent in the United States Supreme Court*, ed. Christopher J. Peters (Dordrecht: Springer, 2014), 19–47.

4. *Kimble v. Marvel Entertainment, LLC*, 576 U.S. 446 (2015)

5. Sergio Chejfec, *Los incompletos* (Buenos Aires: Alfaguara, 1994), 142.

6. Callimachus, *Hymns and Epigrams, Lycophron, Aratus*, trans. A. W. Mair and G. R. Mair (London: William Heinemann, 1921), 50–51.

7. Statius, *Silvae* 5, ed. and trans. Bruce Gibson (Oxford: Oxford University Press, 2006), 42–43.

8. Andrea Alciato ("Alciatus"), *Emblemata* (Padua: Petro Paulo Tozzi, 1621), Embl. 67.

9. Juan de Arguijo, "A una estatua de Niobe, que labró Praxíteles, de Ausonio," in *Sonetos* (Madrid: Biblioteca Virtual Digital Miguel de Cervantes, 2011).

10. Jean Hardouin, *Apologie d'Homère* (Paris: Rigaud, 1716); Anne Dacier, *Homère défendu contre l'apologie du R. P. Hardouin, ou suite des causes de la corruption du Goust* (Paris: Jean Baptiste Coignard, 1716). See also Anne Dacier, *Des causes de la corruption du goust, par Madame Dacier* (Paris, Rigaud, 1714). On the "querelle d'Homère" resulting from Hardouin's "retranslation" of *The Iliad*, see most recently David D. Reitsam, *La querelle d'Homère dans la presse des lumières: L'exemple du "Nouveau Mercure galant"* (Tübingen: Narr Francke Attempto Verlag, 2021).

11. Nietzsche: "Envy of the gods.—The 'envy of the gods' arises when he who is accounted lower equates himself with him who is accounted higher (as Ajax does) or who is made equal to him by the favour of fortune (as Niobe is as a mother too abundantly blessed)." In Friedrich Nietzsche, *Human, All Too Human*, trans. R. J. Hollingdale (Cambridge: Cambridge University Press, 1991), 315.

12. Walter Benjamin, "Toward a Critique of Violence," in *Reflections: Essays, Aphorisms, Autobiographical Writings*, ed. Peter Demetz, trans. Edmund Jephcott (New York: Schocken Books, 1978), 295. See also Walter Benjamin, *Toward the Critique of Violence: A Critical Edition*, ed. Peter Fenves and Julia Ng (Stanford, CA: Stanford University Press, 2021), 55. For a clear and incisive discussion of Benjamin's use of Niobe in the essay, see 33–34.

13. Judith Butler, *Parting Ways: Jewishness and the Critique of Zionism* (New York: Columbia University Press, 2012), 89.

14. Aulus Gellius, *The Attic Nights of Aulus Gellius*, trans. John C. Rolfe (Cambridge, MA: Harvard University Press, 1927), 443.

15. Neusner's translation of Sanhedrin Mishnah 4.5J–K, in *The Mishnah: A New Translation*, trans. Jacob Neusner (New Haven, CT: Yale University Press, 1991): "Therefore man was created alone, (1) to teach you that whoever destroys a single Israelite soul is deemed by Scripture as if he had destroyed a whole world. And whoever

saves a single Israelite soul is deemed by Scripture as if he had saved a whole world." The controversy Israelite/any human is not just editorial, of course, but it is that as well. Here is Morton Smith on the ways in which Jacob Jervell's *Imago Dei: Gen 1,26f. im Spatjudentum, in der Gnosis und in den Paulinischen Briefen* of 1960 seeks "to prove that 'man' means 'Israelite,'" Smith says, "Jervell uses Mishnah Sanhedrin 4.5, which he reads as saying, 'the Biblical text indicates that anyone who destroys one Israelite life is as guilty as if he destroyed a whole world.' In n. 46 (p. 82) he remarks that Beer-Holtzmann, in their edition of the Mishnah, said that some MSS omitted the word "Israelite" and preferred this reading. This preference, Jervell says, was a mistake, due to the fact that they did not understand that "man" means "Israelite." "Thus the reading proves the principle and the principle determines the reading (and the circle is the most elegant form of argument)." Morton, "On the Shape of God and the Humanity of Gentiles," in *Religions in Antiquity: Essays in Memory of Erwin Ramsdell Goodenough*, ed. Jacob Neusner (Leiden: E. J. Brill, 1970), 325.

16. Lucretius, *On the Nature of Things*, trans. Martin Ferguson Smith (Indianapolis: Hackett, 1969), 18–19.

17. On the political philosophy entailed in *terminus* in Lucretius, see Jacques Lezra, *República salvaje: De la naturaleza de las cosas* (Santiago, Chile: Ediciones Macul, 2020), esp. 40–73.

18. Lucretius, *The Nature of Things: A Philosophical Poem, in Six Books*, trans. John Selby Watson, with a "poetical version" by John Mason Good (London: Bohn, 1851), 28 (note to I. 599–605). Watson is citing from Denis Lambin ("Lambinus"), *Titi Lucretii Cari De rerum natura libri sex* (Paris, 1563) and John Evelyn, *An Essay on the First Book of T. Lucretius Carus De rerum natura: Interpreted and Made English Verse* (London: Gabriel Bedle and Thomas Collins, 1656).

19. Lucretius, *On the Nature of Things*, trans. William Ellery Leonard (Mineola, NY: Dover, 2004), 18.

20. David J. Furley, *Two Studies in the Greek Atomists. 1. Indivisible Magnitudes* (Princeton, NJ: Princeton University Press, 1967).

21. Lucretius, *The Nature of Things*, I:647–655: "Know, too, each seed, each substance is composed / Of points extreme no sense can e'er detect: / Points that, perforce, minutest of themselves, / To parts can ne'er divide: nor self-educed, / Nor, but as formed, existing, else destroyed. / Parts such can hold not: each the first, pure part, / Itself, of other substance: which, when joined / Alone by kindred parts, in order due, / Forms, from such junction, the prime seeds of things . . ."

And I:665–667: "Did no such points exist, extreme and least, / Each smallest atom would be, then, combined / Of parts all infinite."

22. Henry James, "The Altar of the Dead," in *Terminations* (London: Heinemann, 1895), 212–213.

23. Jorge Luis Borges, "El Testigo," in *Nueva antología personal* (Mexico City: Siglo XXI, 2000), 57.

24. Jorge Luis Borges, "The Witness," in *Collected Fictions*, trans. Andrew Hurley (New York: Penguin Books, 1999), 311. Compare with Norman Thomas di Giovanni's translation: "Before daybreak he will die, and with him will die—never to come back again—the final first-hand images of heathen rites. . . . Some thing—or an endless number of things—dies with each man's last breath. . . . What will die with me when I die, what poignant or worthless memory will be lost to the world? The voice of Macedonio Fernández, the image of a brown horse grazing in an empty lot at the corner of Serrano and Charcas, a sulphur candle in the drawer of a mahogany desk?" In *The Maker: Prose Pieces 1934–1960*, trans. Norman Thomas di Giovanni, https://libraryofbabel.info/Borges/themaker.pdf, 47.

25. John Duns Scotus, *Ordinatio*, in *Five Texts on the Mediaeval Problem of Universals: Porphyry, Boethius, Abelard, Duns Status, Ockham*, trans. and ed. Paul Vincent Spade (Indianapolis: Hackett, 1994), 69. Scotus is arguing against Henry of Ghent's theory of individuation. "Haecceity" is used most recently in so-called object-oriented ontology, partly out of Scotus, but largely from Peirce, who returns to the term in the context of his own semiotics. An excellent review is Jeffrey R. DiLeo, "Peirce's Haecceitism," *Transactions of the Charles S. Peirce Society* 27, no. 1 (Winter 1991): 79–109.

26. "El Aleph," in Jorge Luis Borges, *Obras completas, 1923–1972* (Buenos Aires: Emecé, 1974), 625. The English is from Jorge Luis Borges, *The Aleph and Other Stories*, trans. Norman Thomas di Giovanni (New York: Dutton, 1970), 26–27. The reading of "El Aleph" that I have learned most from is Erin Graff Zivin, "Exposición, experimento, exapropiación: Después del sujeto (latinoamericano)," in *Sujetos del latinoamericanismo*, ed. Florencia Garramuño, Héctor Hoyos, and Romina Wainberg (Pittsburgh: University of Pittsburgh Press, 2021), 37–56, esp. 41–42.

27. A detailed reading of the Niobe boundary stone problem is in M. Ty, "Benjamin on the Border," *Critical Times* 2, no. 2 (2019): 306–319.

28. "Statues," trans. Sam Dolbear and Antonia Grousdanidou, is in Walter Benjamin, *The Storyteller*, trans. and ed. Sam Dolbear, Esther Leslie, and Sebastian Truskolaski (New York: New York Review Books, 2016), 113°114. The drafting of this cycle was concluded on August 15, 1930, and published in the *Frankfurter Zeitung* on September 18, 1930. *Gesammelte Schriften*, ed. Rolf Tiedemann and Hermann Schweppenhäuser (Frankfurt: Sührkamp, 1991), 4:383–387.

29. Benjamin, *Gesammelte Schriften*, 6:792. My translation.

## 5. ALL COPS ARE BASTARDS

1. The epigraphs are from Antonio Gramsci, *Prison Notebooks*, ed. Joseph Buttigieg, trans. Joseph Buttigieg and Antonio Callari (New York: Columbia University Press, 1992), §150, 1:361; and August Vollmer, *The Police and Modern Society* (Berkeley: University of California Press, 1936), 185. I have corrected the Gramsci translation, which was flawed.

2. The bibliography on "a few bad apples" is appropriately large. Much recent academic work on the topic, and a great deal of the nonacademic as well, takes O'Brien's words as its point of departure. See Jomills H. Braddock II, Rachel Lautenschlager, Alex R. Piquero, and Nicole Piquero, "How Many Bad Apples? Investigating Implicit and Explicit Bias among Police Officers and the General Public." *Contexts* (2020), https://contexts.org/articles/how-many-bad-apples-investigating-implicit-and-explicit-bias-among-police-officers-and-the-general-public/. An excellent study of the extent of systemic racism is Vincent J. Roscigno and Kayla Preito-Hodge, "Racist Cops, Vested "Blue" Interests, or Both? Evidence from Four Decades of the General Social Survey," *Socius* 7 (2021), https://journals.sagepub.com/doi/10.1177/2378023120980913. An older study, focusing on the figure's effects in civil rights law, is Chiraag Bains, "'A Few Bad Apples': How the Narrative of Isolated Misconduct Distorts Civil Rights Doctrine," *Indiana Law Journal* 93, no. 1 (2018), https://www.repository.law.indiana.edu/ilj/vol93/iss1/3.

3. An excellent collection exploring contemporary conceptualizations of the police is *The New Police Science: The Police Power in Domestic and International Governance,* ed. Markus D. Dubber and Mariana Valverde (Palo Alto, CA: Stanford University Press, 2006). A critique of the uses of Foucault's work in studies of social order and policing is in Mark Neocleous, *The Fabrication of Social Order: A Critical Theory of Police Power* (London: Pluto, 2000), and his *War Power, Police Power* (Edinburgh: Edinburgh University Press, 2014). Neouclous's fundamental work seeks to show how "the whole logic of 'security' underpinning bourgeois modernity" (*War Power*, 5), that is, "the liberal identification of security with liberty and property in fact masks an underlying insecurity at the heart of the bourgeois order—the insecurity of property—which is deeply connected to the question of class" (*Fabrication of Social Order*, 44). This is Neouclous's great insight: "The recognition of the insecurity of the class system of private property meant that security came to be thought of as something to be achieved rather than merely conflated with liberty and property and left at that. Writers who recognized this . . . did so because they understood that security is imposed on civil society by the state through the exercise of police power. In some fundamental sense then, security is the concept of police, as Marx puts it. Security is part of the rationale for the fabrication of order. In terms of the demand for order in civil society, it is under the banner of 'security' that police most often marches" (*Fabrication of Social Order*, 44).

4. Seumas Miller, *The Moral Foundations of Social Institutions* (Cambridge: Cambridge University Press, 2010), 12.

5. My emphasis. See John L. Worrall, "The Politics of Policing," in *The Oxford Handbook of Police and Policing*, ed. Michael D Reisig and Robert J. Kane (Oxford; Oxford University Press, 2014), 55. See also Gene E. Carte and Elaine H. Carte, *Police Reform in the United States: The Era of August Vollmer, 1905–1932* (Berkeley: University of California Press, 1974).

6. On the history of the *universal* in relation to racialization, I have been particularly influenced by Charles Mills, *Blackness Visible: Essays on Philosophy and Race* (Ithaca, NY: Cornell University Press, 1998), esp. ch. 3; by Sylvia Wynter's work, very much apposite to the relation between racialization and universalism, which I discuss in my introduction; and by Étienne Balibar's publications on the topic, including his collaborative publication with Immanuel Wallerstein, *"Race," Nation, Class: Ambiguous Identities*, trans. Chris Turner (New York: Verso, 1991), and his "Racism as Universalism", in *Masses, Classes, Ideas: Studies on Politics and Philosophy Before and After Marx* (New York: Routledge 1994), 191–205; "Ambiguous Universality," in *Politics and the Other Scene* (London: Verso 2002); and *On Universals: Constructing and Deconstructing Community*, trans. Joshua David Jordan (New York: Fordham University Press, 2020). For a more specifically literary treatment, see Ronald Judy, *DisForming the American Canon: African-Arabic Slave Narratives and the Vernacular* (Minneapolis: University of Minnesota Press, 1993), esp. ch. 3.

7. Sigmund Freud, "The Uncanny," in *The Standard Edition of the Complete Psychological Works of Sigmund Freud* (London: Vintage Books, 1999), 17:242.

8. Lev Tolstoy, "The Death of Ivan Ilyich," trans. Louise and Aylmer Maude (New York: New American Library, 1960), 148.

9. The German is in Bertolt Brecht, *Gesammelte Werke* (Frankfurt: Suhrkamp, 1967), 1:416–417. My translation.

10. W. V. Quine, "Natural Kinds," in *Ontological Relativity and Other Essays* (New York: Columbia University Press, 1969), 134, 138. A still useful but now rather dated review of "kinds" in philosophy is Ian Hacking, "A Tradition of Natural Kinds," *Philosophical Studies* 61, nos. 1–2 (1991): 109–126.

11. James Baldwin, "A Report from Occupied Territory," *The Nation*, July 11, 1966. A convincing examination of the ways in which "recognition" was framed politically by African American writers of Baldwin's generation—especially Hughes, Wright, Himes, and Ellison—through the modified universalist claims of the Communist Party, in Cathy Bergin, *"Bitter with the Past but Sweet with the Dream": Communism in the African American Imaginary—Representations of the Communist Party, 1940–1952* (Leiden: Brill, 2015). Less specifically regarding "recognition," Cedric Robinson's *Black Marxism: The Making of the Black Radical Tradition* (Chapel Hill: University of North Carolina Press, [1983] 2000) is indispensable to understanding the political as well as historical limits of this universalism, even in the modified form it takes in (say) Baldwin's "All." Richard Wright is Robinson's example of a writer who "evoked in his writings the language and experience of 'ordinary' Black men and women [and thus] pressed home the recognition that whatever the objective forces propelling a people toward struggle, resistance, and revolution, they would come to that struggle in their own cultural terms. . . . From the measured discourse of a Black culture he illustrated the limits of a socialist movement that persisted in too many abstractions, too far removed, and was prey to the arrogance of racial paternalism" (315).

12. Baldwin is using Truman Nelson's *The Torture of Mothers* (Newburyport, MA: Garrison Press, 1965), 19–21. Nelson's book is based on reporting by the *New York Times* (Nelson shows its bias) and on taped interviews with Stafford and a number of others made by Nelson himself and by Willie Jones for Harlem Youth Opportunities Unlimited.

13. For the background of Nelson's *The Torture of Mothers*, see Carl Suddler, "The Color of Justice without Prejudice: Youth, Race, and Crime in the Case of the Harlem Six." *American Studies* 57, nos. 1–2 (2018): 57–78. For Steve Reich's use of the taped material furnished him by Nelson, see Sumanth Gopinath, "The Problem of the Political in Steve Reich's *Come Out* (1966)," in *Sound Commitments: Avant-Garde Music and the Sixties*, ed. Robert Adlington (New York: Oxford University Press, 2009), 121–144. On the political and social context for Baldwin's "Report," see Themis Chronopoulos, "Police Misconduct, Community Opposition, and Urban Governance in New York City, 1945–1965," *Journal of Urban History* 1, no. 26 (April 2015): 16.

14. Baldwin, "A Report," *The Nation*, July 11, 1966. For a close reading of Baldwin and policing focusing on *The Fire Next Time* and *No Name in the Street*, see Jesse A. Goldberg, "James Baldwin and the Anti-Black Force of Law: On Excessive Violence and Exceeding Violence," *Public Culture* 31, no. 3 (2019): 521–538.

15. Robert Penn Warren, *Who Speaks for the Negro?* (New Haven, CT: Yale University Press, [1965] 2014), 413.

16. Frank B. Wilderson III, *Afropessimism* (New York: Liveright, 2020).

17. Alex S. Vitale, *The End of Policing* (London: Verso, 2018); Khalil Gibran Muhammad, *The Condemnation of Blackness: Race, Crime, and the Making of Modern Urban America* (Cambridge, MA: Harvard University Press, 2019).

18. Axel Honneth, *The Struggle for Recognition: The Moral Grammar of Social Conflicts* (Cambridge, MA: MIT Press, 1995). The bibliography on the problem of recognition includes Nancy Fraser and Alex Honneth, *Redistribution or Recognition? A Political-Philosophical Exchange* (New York: Verso, 2003). My take on it is in *Wild Materialism* (New York: Fordham University Press, 2010), 16–18.

19. Saidiya Hartman, *Scenes of Subjection: Terror, Slavery, and Self-Making in Nineteenth Century America* (New York: Oxford University Press, 1997), 5. Zakiyyah Iman Jackson also comments on the passage, laying stress on the role played by *recognition* in the scene Hartman describes: "Hartman contends that the recognition of the enslaved's humanity did not redress slavery's abuses nor the arbitrariness of the master's power since in most instances the acknowledgment of the humanity of the enslaved was a 'complement' to the arrangement of chattel property rather than its 'remedy' (6). She demonstrates that recognition of the enslaved's humanity served as a pretext for punishment, dissimulation of chattel slavery's violence, and the sanction given it by the law and the state (Hartman 5). What's more, rather than fostering 'equality,' this acknowledgment often served as an instantiation of racial hierarchy, as the slave is 'recognized' but only as a lesser human in (pre)evolutionist discourse or

criminalized by state discourses. In other words, objecthood and humanization were two sides of the same coin, as ties of affection could be manipulated and will was criminalized." Zakiyyah Iman Jackson, *Becoming Human: Matter and Meaning in an Antiblack World* (New York: New York University Press, 2020), 27–28.

20. Frantz Fanon, *Black Skin, White Masks*, trans. Charles Lam Markham (New York: Grove Press, 1967).

21. As do Jackson in *Becoming Human* and Wilderson in *Afropessimism*.

22. Arendt, "What Is Authority?" In Hannah Arendt, *Past and Future*. (New York: Viking Press. 1968), 227–264. Revised edition. Portions first published as "What Is Authority?" in *Nomos I: Authority*, ed. Carl J. Friedrich for the American Society of Political and Legal Philosophy (1958). For an exploration of the distinction between authority and authoritarianism, see Viktoria Huegel, "From Authority to Authoritarianism and back again: Max Weber, Carl Schmitt, and Hannah Arendt," 2022, PhD diss., Centre for Applied Philosophy, Politics and Ethics (CAPPE), School of Humanities, University of Brighton.

23. Affirming this does not commit me to assenting to the truth of Arendt's thesis regarding the vanishing of authority.

24. Hannah Arendt, "Freedom and Politics," *Chicago Review* 14, no. 1 (1960): 41.

25. The version of "What Is Freedom?" was published as "Freedom and Politics" in *Freedom and Serfdom* (The Hague: Springer Netherlands, 1961), 191–217. It has instead: "Under the conditions of human society, then, which are governed by the fact that society is formed not of man, the individual, but man, the collective species, that it is organised not as one people but as many peoples, freedom and sovereignty have so little in common that they cannot even exist side by side. Wherever men, either as individuals or when grouped in communities, seek to gain sovereignty, they must first abolish freedom. But if they wish to be free, they must renounce their aspirations to sovereignty" (205). The 1960 version, published in the *Chicago Review*, is the one picked up in *BPF* (41).

26. A review of an edition of Shakespeare's (attributed) *1 Richard II*, by Ramon Jiménez, is "[S]elf-Pitying, Self-Dramatizing Masochist," https://shakespeareoxfordfellowship.org/review-of-tragedy-of-richard-ii-part-one-edited-by-michael-egan/.

27. The decision in *Pierson v. Ray* reads: "The common law has never granted police officers an absolute and unqualified immunity, and the officers in this case do not claim that they are entitled to one. Their claim is, rather, that they should not be liable if they acted in good faith and with probable cause in making an arrest under a statute that they believed to be valid. Under the prevailing view in this country, a peace officer who arrests someone with probable cause is not liable for false arrest simply because the innocence of the suspect is later proved. . . . A policeman's lot is not so unhappy that he must choose between being charged with dereliction of duty if he does not arrest when he has probable cause and being mulcted in damages if

he does. Although the matter is not entirely free from doubt, the same consideration would seem to require excusing him from liability for acting under a statute that he reasonably believed to be valid, but that was later held unconstitutional, on its face or as applied."

28. An exceptionally lucid account of the conceptual function of modern police, in Markus Dirk Dubber, "A Political Theory of Criminal Law: Autonomy and the Legitimacy of State Punishment," in "Legitimating Criminal Law," *SSRN Research Journal* (March 15, 2004), https://ssrn.com/abstract=529522. For the historical frame: "Law and police reflect two ways of conceptualizing the state. From the perspective of law, the state is the institutional manifestation of a political community of free and equal persons. The function of the law state is to manifest and protect the autonomy of its constituents in all of its aspects, private and public. From the perspective of police, the state is the institutional manifestation of a household. The police state, as *pater familias*, seeks to maximize the welfare of his—or rather its—household." See also Dubber, "'The Power to Govern Men and Things': Patriarchal Origins of the Police Power in American Law," 52 *Buffalo Law Review* 1277 (2004). An approach from the perspective of normative ethics is Emmanuel Melissaris, "Toward a Political Theory of Criminal Law A Critical Rawlsian Account." *New Criminal Law Review: An International and Interdisciplinary Journal* 15, no. 1 (Winter 2012): 122–155.

29. Lucid, statistically driven recent accounts of modern police tactics and the effects of militarization—especially the rise in use of SWAT teams—in the United States are in Jonathan Mummolo, "Modern Police Tactics, Police-Citizen Interactions, and the Prospects for Reform," *Journal of Politics* 80, no. 1 (2018): 1–15; and Jonathan Mummolo, "Militarization Fails to Enhance Police Safety or Reduce Crime but May Harm Police Reputation," *PNAS* 115, no. 37 (September 11, 2018): 9181–9186.

30. Brecht, "Literarization of the Theatre (Notes to the *Threepenny Opera*)," in Bertolt Brecht, *The Plays* (London: Methuen, 1960), 1:182–183.

31. The original French is in Louis Althusser, "Idéologie et appareils idéologiques d'État (Notes pour une recherche)," *La pensée* 151 (June 1970), collected in Louis Althusser, *Positions (1964–1975)* (Paris: Éditions sociales, 1976), 67–125, here at 113.

32. Judith Butler, *The Psychic Life of Power* (Stanford, CA: Stanford University Press, 1997), 5. See Noela Davis, "Subjected Subjects? On Judith Butler's Paradox of Interpellation," *Hypatia* 27, no. 4 (Fall 2012): 881–897.

33. Pras and kris Ex, *Ghetto supastar* (New York: Pocket Books, 1999), cited in Fred Moten, *Black and Blur* (Durham, NC: Duke University Press, 2017), 32–33. See Shahidha Bari, "The Insistent Poetics of Relation," *New Formations: A Journal of Culture/Theory/Politics* 99 (2019): 127–130.

34. For the very complicated publication history of Althusser's essay, and for an attentive interpretation seeking to establish Althusser's ultimate concern, in the extended version of the essay, with "the question of practice, a common name for the idea of an 'organization without organization' that would make the revolution

conceivable; and also for the idea of a 'counterinterpellation of the subject'" (xviii), see Étienne Balibar, "Althusser and the 'Ideological State Apparatuses,'" in Louis Althusser, *On Reproduction*, trans. M. Goshgarian (New York: Verso, 2014). See also Warren Montag, "Althusser's Empty Signifier: What is the Meaning of the Word 'Interpellation'"? *Mediations* 30, no. 2 (2017): 63–69. This is Brewster's translation. I have modified it a bit, and as soon as we switch into the section from *Sur la réproduction* the translation is mine. "Ideology," says Althusser, "functions in such a way that it recruits subjects among the individuals, it recruits them all, or transforms individuals into subjects, it transforms them all by that very precise operation, which I have called interpellation or hailing, in which can be imagined along the lines of the most commonplace everyday police or other hailing, 'Hey, you there . . .' It is all the same, a strange phenomenon not explained only by the feeling of guilt, notwithstanding the large number of people who have 'something to blame themselves for.' Unless, that is, everyone has, in fact, something to blame him or herself for incessantly, and thus that everyone feels confusedly that at the very least, and in every instance, she has an account to give, that is [*c'est-à-dire*], duties to respect, even if only the duty to answer to every interpellation. Strange."

35. Judith Butler, *The Psychic Life of Power* (Stanford, CA: Stanford University Press, 1997), 3.

36. Michel Foucault, *The Order of Things: An Archaeology of the Human Sciences*, trans. Alan Sheridan (New York: Routledge, 2004), 418: "If the question of formal languages gives prominence to the possibility or impossibility of structuring positive contents, a literature dedicated to language gives prominence, in all their empirical vivacity, to the fundamental forms of finitude. From within language experienced and traversed as language, in the play of its possibilities extended to their furthest point, what emerges is that man has 'come to an end', and that, by reaching the summit of all possible speech, he arrives not at the very heart of himself but at the brink of that which limits him; in that region where death prowls, where thought is extinguished, where the promise of the origin interminably recedes. It was inevitable that this new mode of being of literature should have been revealed in works like those of Artaud or Roussel—and by men like them; in Artaud's work, language, having been rejected as discourse and re-apprehended in the plastic violence of the shock, is referred back to the cry, to the tortured body, to the materiality of thought, to the flesh."

37. Louis Althusser, "The '*Piccolo Teatro*': Bertolazzi and Brecht," in *For Marx*, trans. Ben Brewster (London: Verso, 1969; 2005), 144.

38. Antonin Artaud, "The Theatre of Cruelty: First Manifesto," in *Antonin Artaud: Collected Works*, trans. Victor Corti (London: John Calder, 1974), 4:76.

39. The encounter of Althusserian interpellation and Foucauldian subjectivization, most searchingly in Butler, *Psychic Life*. See also Warren Montag, "'The Soul is the Prison of the Body': Althusser and Foucault, 1970–1975," *Yale French Studies* 88 (1995): 53–77. My direction into the *doublet* of Althusser/Foucault is a bit different

from both Butler and Montag's but is deeply indebted to both. I approach Althusser's scene through Foucault, whose terms seem to me to accompany the ones we find in Althusser's essay. A principle of translation or translatability moves me, necessarily: there must be a degree of synonymy between Foucault and Althusser's terms. No doubt I am making the two figures and their lexicon into my own *doublet*—noting the different uses to which the terms have been put, and to which the two signatures are assigned. I tell a little story: perhaps one of the two reads the work of the other; revising for publication the manuscript that results, he erases the obvious trace of that encounter, left symptomatically bare. Guided by some symptoms, following protocols of research and argumentation sanctioned by my discipline, I restore the encounter. An institution—or a collection of institutions, and their protocols—pulls my *doublet* of Althusser and Foucault together, disclosing on this point their synonymy. What is it about the scene that calls to me, today, in just this way, and swings the boom of my argument about Althusser around into Foucault's path? Something like the value added to one name by another, today, in an institutional setting that makes me *want* or *need* to authorize one by means of the other, and both eventually by means of a reflection like this on the conditions of their ephemeral synonymy in the late 1960s; something like the value I will derive (and will accrue to my name) from that synonymy and that reflection, today, as an object formed to and intelligible in the university-institution in 2021.

40. Michel Foucault, *The Order of Things* (London and New York, 2005), 347.

41. See Étienne Balibar, "'Ego sum, ego existo': Descartes on the Verge of Heresy," in *Citizen Subject*, trans. Steven Miller. (New York: Fordham University Press, 2016), 55–73.

## 6. THE SCHEMA OF ABOLITION

1. The epigraphs to this chapter are from Simone Weil, *The Iliad: The Poem of Force*, trans. Mary McCarthy (Wallingford, PA: Pendle Hill Press, 1991), 9; Theodor W. Adorno, *Minima Moralia*, trans. E. F. N. Jephcott (New York: Verso, 1978), 25; and Christina Sharpe, *In The Wake: On Blackness and Being* (Durham, NC: Duke University Press, 2016), 20.

2. Fred Moten & Stefano Harney, "The University and the Undercommons: Seven Theses," *Social Text* 79, no. 22 (2004): 114.

3. Maurice Hauriou, "Theory of the Institution," in *The French Institutionalists: Maurice Hauriou, Georges Renard, Joseph T. Delos*, ed. Albert Broderick, trans. Mary Welling (Cambridge, MA: Harvard University Press, 1970), 94. I have slightly modified the translation. The French original is at Maurice Hauriou, "La théorie de l'institution et de la fondation," in *La nouvelle journée (La cité moderne et les transformations du droit)* 4 (1925): 90; reprinted in *Aux sources du droit* (Paris: Bloud & Gay, 1933). So Hauriou's jurisprudence, despite attacking "objectivism" in "La théorie de l'institution," is associated with legal objectivism in Léon Duguit's important *Traité*

*de droit constitutionnel* (Paris: Fontemoing, 1927), 22–42. On Hauriou's views on institutions, see Éric Millard, "Hauriou et la théorie de l'institution," *Droit et société* 30–31 (1995): 381–412; see also Maria Lucia Tarantino, "La concezione istituzionale fra filosofia e teoria generale: Georges Renard e Maurice Hauriou," *Eunomia. Rivista semestrale del Corso di Laurea in Scienze Politiche e delle Relazioni Internazionali Eunomia* n.s. 2 (2013): 29–62.

4. See Gilles Deleuze's introduction to his edited volume *Instincts et institutions* (Paris: Hachette, 1953), viii–xi. Note Deleuze's conclusion: "Intégrer les circonstances dans un système d'anticipation et les facteurs internes, dans un système qui règle leur apparition, remplaçant l'espèce. C'est bien le cas de l'institution. Il fait nuit parce qu'on se couche; on mange parce qu'il est midi. Il n'y a pas de tendances sociales, mais seulement des moyens sociaux de satisfaire les tendances, moyens qui sont originaux parce qu'ils sont sociaux. Toute institution impose à notre corps, même dans ses structures involontaires, une série de modèles, et donne à notre intelligence un savoir, une possibilité de prévision comme de projet. Nous retrouvons la conclusion suivante : l'homme n'a pas d'instincts, il fait des institutions" (xi) ("Every institution imposes a series of models on our body, even in its involuntary structures, and provides our intelligence with knowledge and the possibility of forecasting and planning. We come to the following conclusion: man does not have instincts, he makes institutions." My translation).

5. Claude Gauvard, "Pardonner et oublier après la guerre de Cent Ans : le rôle des lettres d'abolition de la chancellerie royale française," in Reiner Marcowitz and Werner Paravicini, *Vergeben und Vergessen? Pardonner et oublier?: Vergangenheitsdiskurse nach Besatzung, Bürgerkrieg und Revolution—Les discours sur le passé après l'occupation, la guerre civile et la révolution* (Munich: Oldenbourg Wissenschaftsverlag, 2014), 27.

6. A sophisticated account of the concept of pirating is in Daniel Heller-Roazen, *The Enemy of All: Piracy and the Law of Nations* (New York: Zone Books, 2009). My own thoughts on pirates are in Jacques Lezra, *Unspeakable Subjects: The Genealogy of the Event in Early Modern Europe* (Stanford, CA: Stanford University Press, 1997), and "Ragozine's Beheading: Dramatic and Civil Logics of the European State-Form," in *Transnational Connections in Early Modern Theatre*, ed. M. A. Katritzky and Pavel Drábek (Manchester: Manchester University Press, 2019), 242–259.

7. A useful synthesis of the uses to which the Brecht/Weill *Moritāt* was put in popular U.S. song culture is at https://www.steynonline.com/7344/mack-the-knife. See also Kim H. Kowalke, "The *Three Penny Opera* in America," in *Kurt Weill, The Three Penny Opera*, ed. Stephen Hinton (Cambridge: Cambridge University Press, 1990), 78–120.

8. Ernst Bloch, "The Song of Pirate Jenny in *The Threepenny Opera*," in *Literary Essays*, trans. Andrew Joron et al. (Stanford, CA: Stanford University Press, 1998), 347.

9. The German is from Bertolt Brecht, *Die Dreigroschenoper* (Frankfurt: Suhr-

kamp, 1986), 40. Blitzstein's translation is in Bertolt Brecht and Kurt Weill, *The Threepenny Opera*, trans. Marc. Blitzstein (New York: Tams-Witmark Music Library, 1956). The Willett-Manheim translation is in Bertolt Brecht and Kurt Weill, *The Threepenny Opera*, translated from the German by Ralph Manheim and John Willett (New York: Arcade, 1994).

10. Martin Heidegger, *Being and Time:* "The everyday possibilities of being of *Dasein* are at the disposal of the whims of the others. These others are not definite others. On the contrary, any other can represent them. What is decisive is only the inconspicuous domination by others that *Dasein* as being-with has already taken over unawares. One belongs to the others oneself, and entrenches their power. 'The others,' whom one designates as such in order to cover over one's own essential belonging to them, are those who *are there* initially and for the most part in everyday being-with-one-another. The who is not this one and not that one, not oneself and not some and not the sum of them all. The 'who' is the neuter, *the they* [German, *das Man*; lit.: the One; as in: one does this or that]." Trans. Joan Stambaugh (New York: State University of New York Press, 2010), 126.

11. Walter Benjamin, "The Work of Art in the Age of Its Technological Reproducibility," in *The Work of Art in the Age of its Technological Reproducibility and Other Writings on Media*, ed. Michael W. Jennings, Brigid Doherty, and Thomas Y. Levin (Cambridge, MA: Harvard University Press, 2008), 42.

12. See Russell Berman's "Sounds Familiar? Nina Simone's Performances of Brecht/Weill Songs," in *Sound Matters: Essays on the Acoustics of German Culture*, ed. Nora M. Alter and Lutz Koepnick (New York: Berghahn Books, 2004), 181. A careful argument in favor of Simone's Brechtianism (a version of it, at any rate), and specifically contra Berman, in Rafael do Nascimento Cesar's "A Fragata Negra: Tradução e vingança em Nina Simone," *MANA* 24, no. 1 (2018): 39–70, esp. 56–59.

13. Hannah Arendt, *Totalitarianism* (San Diego and New York: Harcourt, 1968), 33.

14. Bloch, "The Song of Pirate Jenny," 349.

15. See the discussion of Bernard Nicolas's 1977 short "Daydream Therapy" in *L.A. Rebellion: Creating a New Black Cinema*, ed. Allyson Field, Jacqueline Najuma Stewart, and Jan-Christopher Horak (Berkeley: University of California Press, 2015), 211–212, esp. 236–241, where Samantha Sheppard expresses in the strongest, clearest terms the affirmative-therapeutic sense Nicolas's film can have: "In this case, the woman's transformation is marked in color, literally, where she represents a return to a Black Pan-African nationalism symbolized as more natural and authentic for the African diaspora than America's capitalist and patriarchal society. In waking up from her militant dream to this revolutionary reality, she is liberated and transformed into an activist. Nicolas's film explores the notion of personal awakening but also connects the individual experience of one Black woman with Pan-African struggles for equality. *Daydream Therapy*'s protagonist uses her mind not only to dissociate herself from her oppressive social environment but also to free-associate to her global community" (241).

16. Portuguese lyrics from https://www.letras.mus.br/chico-buarque/77259/. My translation.

## 7. ABOLISH THE FAMILY!

1. The epigraphs are from Jacques Derrida, "Letter to Francine Loreau," in Jacques Derrida, *The Work of Mourning*, ed. Pascale-Anne Briault and Michael Naas, trans. Pascale-Anne Briault and Michael Naas (Chicago: University of Chicago Press, 2001), 95; Sigmund Freud, *Reflections on War and Death*, trans. A. A. Brill and Alfred B. Kuttner (New York: Moffat, Yard & Co., 1918), 5; and Kit Fine, "The Varieties of Necessity," in *Modality and Tense: Philosophical Papers* (Oxford: Oxford University Press, 2002), 260.

2. Leo Tolstoy, *Anna Karenina*, trans. Marian Schwartz (New Haven, CT: Yale University Press, 2014), 1. Compare Constance Garnett's "Happy families are all alike; every unhappy family is unhappy in its own way," in Leo Tolstoy, *Anna Karenina*, trans. Constance Garnett (Philadelphia: George Jacobs, [1900] 1919), 5; and Richard Pevear and Larissa Volokhonsky's 2002 version: "All happy families are alike; each unhappy family is unhappy in its own way" (New York: Penguin Books, 2002), 12.

3. Lew Tolstoi, *Anna Karenina*, trans. Rosemarie Tietze (Munich: Carl Hanser Verlag, 2009), 7.

4. For the Russian, I have consulted Vladimir Dal, *Explanatory Dictionary of the Living Great Russian Language* (1882, in Russian), https://slovardalja.net/, and Anna A. Zaliznyak, "*Happiness* and *Pleasure* in the Russian Language Picture of the World," in *Klyuchevye idei russkoi yazykovoi kartiny mira* [Key Ideas of the Russian Language Picture of the World], ed. Anna A. Zaliznyak, I. B. Levontina, and A. D. Shmelev (Moscow: Yazyki slavyanskoi kul'tury, 2005), 152–174.

5. Léon Tolstoï, *Anna Karénine* (Paris: Hachette, 1885), 1. For a wonderful riff on this French translation of the opening line, which he renders as "All happinesses are alike but every unhappiness has its own features," see Michael Wood, "Dear Poochums," *London Review of Books*, October 23, 2014.

6. Ludwig Wittgenstein, *Philosophical Investigations*, trans. G. E. M. Anscombe (Oxford: Blackwell, [1958] 1986), 31e–32e. The literature on "family resemblances" in Wittgenstein is particularly rich. Useful overviews are in Hans Sluga, "Family Resemblance," *Grazer Philosophische Studien* 71, no. 1 (2006):1–21; Hjalmar Wennerberg, "The Concept of Family Resemblance in Wittgenstein's Later Philosophy," *Theoria* 33, no. 2 (2008): 107–132; Michael Forster, "Wittgenstein on Family Resemblance Concepts," in *Wittgenstein's Philosophical Investigations: A Critical Guide*, ed. Arif Ahmed (Cambridge: Cambridge University Press, 2010), 66–87; and a more technical, rather controversial approach, in Raymond E. Jennings and Dorian X. Nicholson, "An Axiomatization of Family Resemblance," *Journal of Applied Logic* 5 (2007): 577–585.

7. My earlier treatment of Wittgenstein and translation is in "Two Dogmas of Trans-

lation," in my *Untranslating Machines: A Genealogy for the Ends of Global Thought* (London: Rowman & Littlefield, 2017), 25–53.

8. Melinda Cooper, *Family Values: Between Neoliberalism and the New Social Conservatism* (New York: Zone Books, 2017).

9. Ibid., 61.

10. John Rawls, *A Theory of Justice*, rev. ed. (Cambridge, MA: Harvard University Press, [1971] 1999), 405–415.

11. Sophie Lewis, *Full Surrogacy Now: Feminism against Family* (New York: Verso, 2019), 151; and M. E. O'Brien, "To Abolish the Family: The Working-Class Family Liberation in Capitalist Development," *Endnotes* 5 (2020): 417.

12. O'Brien, "To Abolish the Family," 417.

13. Ibid., 209.

14. Maurice Maeterlinck and Paul Dukas, *Ariane and Blue Beard: A Lyric Story in Three Acts* (New York: Rullman, 1910), 6.

15. Casie E. Hermansson, *Blue Beard: A Reader's Guide to the English Tradition* (Jackson: University Press of Mississippi, 2014).

16. Angela Carter, "The Bloody Chamber," in *The Bloody Chamber and Other Stories* (New York: Penguin, 1987), 41–42.

17. Charles Perrault, *Histoires ou Contes du temps passé* (Paris: Claude Barbin, 1697), 72–73.

18. Charles Perrault, *Contes de ma mère l'Oye / Mother Goose's Tales* (The Hague: Chez Jean Neaulme, 1745).

19. This is how Whitehead puts it. Note the crucial concept of "antecedent limitation": "Eternal possibility and modal differentiation into individual multiplicity are the attributes of the one substance. In fact each general element of the metaphysical situation is an attribute of the substantial activity. Yet another element in the metaphysical situation is disclosed by the consideration that the general attribute of modality is limited. This element must rank as an attribute of the substantial activity. In its nature each mode is limited, so as not to be other modes. But, beyond these limitations of particulars, the general modal individualisation is limited in two ways: In the first place it is an actual course of events, which might be otherwise so far as concerns eternal possibility, but is that course. This limitation takes three forms, (i) the special logical relations which all events must conform to, (ii) the selection of relationships to which the events do conform, and (iii) the particularity which infects the course even within those general relationships of logic and causation. Thus this first limitation is a limitation of antecedent selection. So far as the general metaphysical situation is concerned, there might have been an indiscriminate modal pluralism apart from logical or other limitation. But there could not then have been these modes, for each mode represents a synthesis of actualities which are limited to conform to a standard. We here come to the second way of limitation. Restriction is the price of value. There cannot be value without antecedent standards of value, to discriminate the acceptance

or rejection of what is before the envisaging mode of activity. There is an antecedent limitation among values, introducing contraries, grades, and oppositions." Alfred North Whitehead, *Science and the Modern World* (New York: Free Press, [1926] 1967), 177–178.

20. Ibid., 178.

21. For a recent treatment of *curiosity*, both as a virtue in interpersonal relations and as a philosophical operator, see Daniela Dover, "Two Kinds of Curiosity," *Philosophy & Phenomenological Research* (2023), https://onlinelibrary.wiley.com/doi/10.1111/phpr.12976.

22. The most cogent analysis I know of necessity in Greek tragedy is Jean-Pierre Vernant and Pierre Vidal Naquet, *Myth and Tragedy in Ancient Greece*, trans. Janet Lloyd (New York: Zone Books, 1990), 70: "Aristotle's distinction between the two categories of action does not oppose constraint to free will but rather a constraint imposed from outside to a determination that operates from within. And even if this internal determination is different from external constraint, it is nevertheless something that is necessary. When the subject follows the disposition of his own character or ethos he is reacting necessarily, *ex anankes*, but his action nevertheless emanates from himself. Far from being constrained to make the decision that he does, he shows himself to be the father and cause of what he is doing and so bears full responsibility for it."

23. See Fine: "I suspect that many philosophers, in response to these questions, might be attracted to some version of modal monism. They would maintain that there was a single underlying modal notion in terms of which all others could be defined or understood. However, philosophers of this persuasion might well be tempted to adopt different views of what that underlying notion was. Many philosophers of the 'old school' would take it to be that of logical necessity in the narrow sense. This is the sense in which it is necessary that anything red is red, though not necessary that nothing red is green or that I am a person. The philosophers of the 'new school', on the other hand, would take the single underlying notion to be that of logical necessity in the broad sense or what is sometimes called 'metaphysical' necessity. This is the sense of necessity which obtains in virtue of the identity of things (broadly conceived). Thus in this sense not only is it necessary that anything red is red or that nothing is both red and green, but also that I am person or that 2 is a number." "Varieties of Necessity," 2.

24. Here, the fine distinction that Deleuze draws in his introduction to the collection *Instincts et institutions* (Paris: Hachette, 1955) is especially pertinent: "Ce qu'on appelle un instinct, ce qu'on appelle une institution, désignent essentiellement des procédés de satisfaction. Tantôt en réagissant par nature à des stimuli externes, l'organisme tire du monde extérieur les éléments d'une satisfaction de ses tendances et de ses besoins; ces éléments forment, pour les différents animaux, des mondes spécifiques. Tantôt en instituant un monde original entre ses tendances et

le milieu extérieur, le sujet élabore des moyens de satisfaction artificiels, qui libèrent l'organisme de la nature en le soumettant à autre chose, et qui transforment la tendance elle-même en l'introduisant dans un milieu nouveau; il est vrai que l'argent libère de la faim, à condition d'en avoir, et que le mariage épargne la recherche d'un partenaire, en soumettant à d'autres tâches. C'est dire que toute expérience individuelle suppose, comme un *a priori*, la préexistence d'un milieu dans lequel est menée l'expérience, milieu spécifique ou milieu institutionnel. L'instinct et l'institution sont les deux formes organisées d'une satisfaction possible." This is Michael Taormina's translation: "What we call an instinct and what we call an institution essentially designate procedures of satisfaction. On the one hand, an organism reacts instinctively to external stimuli, extracting from the external world the elements which will satisfy its tendencies and needs; these elements comprise worlds that are specific to different animals. On the other hand, the subject institutes an original world between its tendencies and the external milieu, developing artificial means of satisfaction. These artificial means liberate an organism from nature though they subject it to something else, transforming tendencies by introducing them into a new milieu. So money will liberate you from hunger, provided you have money; and marriage will spare you from searching out a partner, though it subjects you to other tasks. In other words, every individual experience presupposes, as an a priori, the existence of a milieu in which that experience is conducted, a species-specific milieu or an institutional milieu. Instinct and institution are the two organized forms of a possible satisfaction." "Instincts and Institutions," in Gilles Deleuze, *Desert Islands and Other Texts, 1953–1974*, ed. David Lapoujade and trans. Michael Taormina (New York: Semiotext(e), 2004), 19.

25. On the possible sources of this seemingly-monist "oceanism," see Henri Vermorel, "The Presence of Spinoza in the Exchanges between Sigmund Freud and Romain Rolland," *International Journal of Psychoanalysis* 90 (2009):1235–1254.

26. Sigmund Freud, *Civilization and Its Discontents*, trans. James Strachey (New York: Norton, 1962), 12.

27. Hans Christian Grabbe, *Hannibal* (Düsseldorf: Schreiner, 1835). Some historical notes are in Sean Armstrong, "Freud's Hannibal: New Light on Freud's Moses—In Memory of David Bakan, 1921–2004," *Psychoanalytic Review* 95 (2008): 231–257.

28. See Detlev Kopp, ed., *Grabbe im Dritten Reich: Zum nationalsozialistischen Grabbe-Kult* (Bielefeld, Germany: Aisthesis Verlag, 1986; and Margaret Anne Sutherland, *The Reception of Grabbe's 'Hannibal' in the German Theatre* (New York: Peter Lang, 1984).

29. Freud returns to a series of symptomatic errors he commits in *The Interpretation of Dreams* regarding Hannibal. See Sigmund Freud, *The Psychopathology of Everyday Life*, trans. A. A. Brill, in *The Basic Writings of Sigmund Freud* (New York: Modern Library, 1995), 230–232.

30. Sigmund Freud, *The Interpretation of Dreams*, trans. James Strachey (New York: Basic Books, [1955] 2010), 218.

31. See Sigmund Freud, "Letter from Freud to Lou Andreas-Salomé," July 30, 1915, *International Psycho-Analytical Library* 89 (1915): 32–33. "Dear Frau Andreas . . .Every time I read one of your letters of appraisal I am amazed at your talent for going beyond what has been said, for completing it and making it converge at some distant point. Naturally I do not always agree with you. I so rarely feel the need for synthesis. The unity of this world seems to me so self-evident as not to need emphasis. What interests me is the separation and breaking up into its component parts of what would otherwise revert to an inchoate mass. Even the assurance most clearly expressed in Grabbe's *Hannibal* that 'we shall not fall out of this world' doesn't seem sufficient substitute for the surrender of the boundaries of the ego, which can be painful enough. In short, I am of course an analyst, and believe that synthesis offers no obstacles once analysis has been achieved." On Freud's citing Grabbe, and on the "oceanic feeling," see Kaja Silverman, *Flesh of My Flesh* (Stanford, CA: Stanford University Press, 2009), 30: "Once again, though, something within Freud keeps affirming what he is trying to negate. We learn from a footnote that the text from which he takes this quotation is Christian Dietrich Grabbe's *Hannibal* and that the passage in question reads: 'Indeed we shall not fall out of this world. We are in it for once and for all' (63). Far from proving that the oceanic feeling is nothing but infantile narcissism, this passage helps us to see how little the two resemble each other. The narcissist seeks to include everything (good) within himself. Grabbe consoles his hero by reminding him that the opposite is true: the world contains us. The quotation from *Hannibal* also defies the other use to which Freud puts it. If we do not leave the world when we die, then it is all that we can ever experience; the oceanic feeling must consequently be something we access through our finitude."

32. Freud to Salomé, July 31, 1915, in *Sigmund Freud and Lou Andreas-Salomé, Letters*, ed. Ernst Pfeiffer, trans. William and Elaine Robson-Scott (New York: Harcourt Brace Jovanovich, 1972), 32.

33. Sigmund Freud, *Reflections on War and Death*, trans. A. A. Brill (Durham, NC: Duke University Press, 2014), 54–55. See also Grimm, *Wörterbuch*: *Stand*, sb. status, ordo, "handlung, ort, art des stehens."

34. Freud, *Reflections*, 60–61.

35. Francisco Perez Carrillo, *Via Sacra y exercicios espirituales, y arte de bien morir* (Zaragoza, 1619), 154r–v. For an overview of *artes moriendi*, see Juan Manuel Castro-Carracedo, "La evolución del Ars Moriendi post-tridentino en España e Inglaterra," in *Proceedings of the 29th AEDEAN Conference*, ed. Alejandro Alcaraz-Sintes, Concepción Soto-Palomo and María de la Cinta Zunino-Garrido (Jaén, Spain: Servicio de Publicaciones de la Universidad de Jaén, 2006), 39–49.

36. Karl Marx, *Grundrisse: Foundations of the Critique of Political Economy*, trans. Martin Nicolaus (New York: Penguin Books/NLR, 1973), 142.

37. Karl Marx and Friedrich Engels, *Werke* (Berlin: Dietz Verlag, 1983), 42:77.

38. Patrick Dove, *Literature and "Interregnum": Globalization, War, and the Crisis of Sovereignty in Latin America* (Albany: State University of New York Press, 2016), 220.

39. Nathaniel Hawthorne, "The Birth-Mark," In *Mosses from an Old Manse* (Boston: Houghton Mifflin, 1883), 48.

40. See Erwin Panofsky, *Early Netherlandish Painting* (Cambridge, MA: Harvard University Press, 1966), 148.

41. Maeterlinck and Dukas, *Ariane and Blue Beard*, 6–7. Olivier Messiaen, in a wonderful review from 1936, reads Dukas's Ariane as a figure of truth and enlightenment and his Blue Beard as a figure for the World. See "Ariane et Barbe-bleue de Paul Dukas," *La Revue musicale* 166 (1936): 79–86. In Stephen Broad, ed., *Olivier Messiaen: Journalism, 1935–1939* (Farnham, UK: Ashgate, 2012), 15–21.

42. On Derrida and these two deaths in Freud's life, see David Farrell Krell, *The Cudgel and the Caress: Reflections on Cruelty and Tenderness* (Albany: SUNY Press, 2019), 128–129.

43. Letter from Freud to Ludwig Binswanger, October 15, 1926, in *The Sigmund Freud-Ludwig Binswanger Correspondence 1908–1938*, ed. Gerhard Fichtner, trans. Arnold J. Pomerans (New York: Other Press, 2003), 50:184.

44. For the English translation of descriptions of Turnu, Grabbe's *Negerhäuptling*, see Grabbe, *Hannibal*, in *The Dramas of Hans Christian Grabbe*, trans. Roger Nicholls (Mouton: The Hague, 1969).

45. Freud, *Interpretation of Dreams*, 535–550; Sigmund Freud and Joseph Breuer, *Studies in Hysteria*, trans. Nicola Luckhurst (New York: Penguin Books), 285.

46. Sigmund Freud, *Five Lectures on Psycho-analysis*, trans. James Strachey, in *The Standard Edition*, ed. James Strachey (London: Hogarth Press, 1957), 11:25.

## CONCLUSION

1. The epigraphs are from Erwin Panofsky, "'*Et in Arcadia Ego*': On the Conception of Transience in Poussin and Watteau," in *Philosophy and History: Essays Presented to Ernst Cassirer* (Oxford: Clarendon Press, 1936), 319; Jacques Derrida, "Et Cetera," in *Deconstructions: A User's Guide*, ed. Nicholas Royle (New York: Palgrave, 2000), 299; and Jacques Derrida, "Telepathy," *Oxford Literary Review* 10, no. 1 (1988): 4.

2. In Sophie Ramond, "Comme on pense la mort, on vieillit—Une lecture de *Qohélet* 12,1–8," *communio* 44, no. 4 (2019): 27–37. See 29: "Les propositions de corrections du texte [of Ecclesiastes 12] sont nombreuses, parmi lesquelles celle d'une note de *Biblia Hebraica Stuttgartensia* qui propose de lire en place du participe du verbe *br'* l'expression *bôreka*, 'ta citerne, ta fosse'. Le terme *bôr* ('fosse') est particulièrement employé dans des expressions qui nomment ceux qui descendent dans la fosse, c'est-à-dire les moribonds."

3. Donella Meadows, "Envisioning a Sustainable World/Down to Earth," Third Biennial Meeting of the International Society of Ecological Economics, Costa Rica, 1994, https://donellameadows.org/wp-content/userfiles/Envisioning.DMeadows.pdf.

4. Gaston Bachelard, *Intuition of the Instant*, trans. Eileen Rizo-Patron (Evanston, IL: Northwestern University Press, 2013), 30. The French original is at Bachelard, *L'intuition de l'instant* (Paris: Éditions Gonthier, 1932), 43.

5. Bachelard, *Intuition of the Present*, 31.

6. Gaston Bachelard, *Air and Dreams: An Essay on the Imagination of Movement*, trans. Edith R. Farrell and C. Frederick Farrell (Dallas, TX: Dallas Institute of Humanities and Culture, 2002), 266. The original is at Bachelard, *L'air et les songes: Essai sur l'imagination du mouvement* (Paris: Librairie José Corti, [1943] 1990), 306.

# BIBLIOGRAPHY


Adorno, Theodor W. *Minima Moralia*. Trans. E. F. N. Jephcott. New York: Verso, 1978.

Aeschylus. *Eumenides*. Trans. Herbert Weir Smyth. Cambridge, MA: Harvard University Press, 1926.

Ainsworth, Robert. *The Most Natural and Easie Way of Institution*. London, 1698.

Alciato, Andrea ("Alciatus"). *Emblemata*. Padua: Petro Paulo Tozzi, 1621.

Alcoff, Linda Martin. "Extractivist Epistemologies." *Tapuya: Latin American Science, Technology and Society* 5, no. 1 (2022). https://www.tandfonline.com/doi/full/10.1080/25729861.2022.2127231.

Althusser, Louis. "Idéologie et appareils idéologiques d'État (Notes pour une recherche)." In *Positions (1964–1975)*, 67–125. Paris: Les Éditions sociales, 1976.

——. "The '*Piccolo Teatro*': Bertolazzi and Brecht." In *For Marx*. Trans. Ben Brewster. London: Verso, [1969] 2005.

Aquinas, Thomas. *Glossa Ordinaria* (Romans 12). In *Glossae Scripturae Sacrae electronicae*, ed. Martin Morard, IRHT-CNRS, 2016–2018. https://gloss-e.irht.cnrs.fr/php/editions_chapitre.php?id=liber&numLivre=60&chapitre=60_12.

Arendt, Hannah. *Freedom and Serfdom*. The Hague: Springer Netherlands, 1961.

——. *The Origins of Totalitarianism*. New York: Harcourt, 1968.

——. *On Revolution*. New York: Penguin Books, 1990.

Arguijo, Juan de. *Sonetos*. Madrid: Biblioteca Virtual Digital Miguel de Cervantes, 2011.

Aristotle. *Metaphysics: Books G, D, and E*. Trans. Christopher Kirwan. Oxford: Clarendon Press, 1993.

Armstrong, Sean. "Freud's Hannibal: New Light on Freud's Moses—In Memory of David Bakan, 1921–2004." *Psychoanalytic Review* 95 (2008): 231–257.

Artaud, Antonin. *Collected Works*. Trans. Victor Corti. London: John Calder, 1974.

Aulus Gellius. *The Attic Nights of Aulus Gellius*. Trans. John C. Rolfe. Cambridge, MA: Harvard University Press, 1927.

Austin, J. L. *How to Do Things With Words*. Oxford: Oxford University Press, 1962.

——. *Quand dire, c'est faire*. Trans. Gilles Lane. Paris: Éditions du Seuil, 1970.

Bachelard, Gaston. *Air and Dreams: An Essay on the Imagination of Movement*.

Trans. Edith R. Farrell and C. Frederick Farrell. Dallas, TX: Dallas Institute of Humanities and Culture, 2002.

——. *Intuition of the Instant*. Trans. Eileen Rizo-Patron. Evanston, IL: Northwestern University Press, 2013.

——. *L'air et les songes: Essai sur l'imagination du mouvement*. Paris: Librairie José Corti, [1943] 1990.

Bachelard, Gaston. *L'intuition de l'instant*. Paris: Éditions Gonthier, 1932.

Baldwin, James. "A Report from Occupied Territory." *The Nation*, July 11, 1966.

Balibar, Étienne. "Althusser and the 'Ideological State Apparatuses.'" Foreword to Louis Althusser, *On Reproduction*. Trans. M. Goshgarian. New York: Verso, 2014.

——. "Althusser's Object." Trans. Margaret Cohen and Bruce Robbins. *Social Text* 39 (1994): 157–188.

——. *Citizen Subject*. Trans. Steven Miller. New York: Fordham University Press, 2016.

——. "Instance/Agency." In *Dictionary of Untranslatables: A Philosophical Lexicon*, ed. Barbara Cassin, Emily Apter, Jacques Lezra, and Michael Wood, 23–24. Princeton, NJ: Princeton University Press, 2014.

——. *Masses, Classes, Ideas: Studies on Politics and Philosophy Before and After Marx*. New York: Routledge, 1994.

——. *On Universals: Constructing and Deconstructing Community*. Trans. Joshua David Jordan. New York: Fordham University Press, 2020.

——. *Politics and the Other Scene*. London: Verso 2002.

Balibar, Étienne, and Immanuel Wallerstein. *"Race," Nation, Class: Ambiguous Identities*. Trans. Chris Turner. New York: Verso, 1991.

Bari, Shahidha. "The Insistent Poetics of Relation." *New Formations: A Journal of Culture/Theory/Politics* 99 (2019): 127–130.

Barrett, Michèle, and Mary McIntosh. *The Anti-Social Family*. London: Verso Editions/NLB, 1982.

Baudelaire, Charles. *Las flores del mal*. Trans. Eduardo Marquina. Madrid: Librería de Fernando Fé, 1906.

——. *Las flores del mal*. Trans. M. J. Santayana. Madrid: Vaso Rotos, 2023.

——. *Les fleurs du mal*. Trans. Richard Howard. Boston: Godine, 1982.

Beard, Charles A. *The Supreme Court and the Constitution*. New York: Macmillan, 1922.

Benimeli Ferrer, J. A. *El contubernio judeo-masónico-comunista: Del satanismo al escándalo de la P-2*. Madrid: ISTMO, 1982.

Benjamin, Walter. *The Arcades Project*. Trans. Howard Eiland and Kevin McLaughlin. Cambridge, MA: Harvard University Press, 1999.

——. *Gesammelte Schriften*. Frankfurt: Suhrkamp, 1991.

——. *The Origin of German Tragic Drama*. Trans. John Osborne. New York: Verso, 1998.

——. *Reflections: Essays, Aphorisms, Autobiographical Writings*. Ed. Peter Demetz, trans. Edmund Jephcott. New York: Schocken Books, 1978.

——. *Selected Writings*, vol. 1. Ed. Marcus Bullock and Michael W. Jennings. Cambridge, MA: Harvard University Press, 2004.

——. *The Storyteller*. Trans. and ed. Sam Dolbear, Esther Leslie, and Sebastian Truskolaski. New York: Verso, 2016.

——. *Toward the Critique of Violence: A Critical Edition*. Ed. Peter Fenves and Julia Ng. Stanford, CA: Stanford University Press, 2021.

——. *The Work of Art in the Age of Its Technological Reproducibility and Other Writings on Media*. Ed. Michael W. Jennings, Brigid Doherty, and Thomas Y. Levin. Cambridge, MA: Harvard University Press, 2008.

Benveniste, Émile. *Dictionary of Indo-European Concepts and Society*. Trans. Elizabeth Palmer. Chicago: HAU Books, 2016.

——. *Vocabulaire des institutions indo-européennes*. Paris: Minuit, 1969.

Bergin, Cathy. *"Bitter with the Past but Sweet with the Dream": Communism in the African American Imaginary—Representations of the Communist Party, 1940–1952*. Boston: Brill, 2015.

Berman, Russell. "Sounds Familiar? Nina Simone's Performances of Brecht/Weill Songs." In *Sound Matters: Essays on the Acoustics of German Culture*, ed. Nora M. Alter and Lutz Koepnick, 171–182. New York: Berghahn Books, 2004.

Bickel, Alexander M. *The Least Dangerous Branch*. 2nd ed. New Haven, CT: Yale University Press, 1986.

Boethius, Anicius M. S., and Luca Obertello. *De Hypotheticis Syllogismis*. Brescia: Paideia, 1969.

Bollas, Christopher. *The Shadow of the Object: Psychoanalysis of the Unthought Known*. New York: Columbia University Press, 1987.

Borges, Jorge Luis. *The Aleph and Other Stories*. Trans. Norman Thomas di Giovanni. New York: Dutton, 1970.

——. *Collected Fictions*. Trans. Andrew Hurley. New York: Penguin Books, 1999.

——. *The Maker: Prose Pieces 1934–1960*. Trans. Norman Thomas di Giovanni. https://libraryofbabel.info/Borges/themaker.pdf.

——. *Nueva antología personal*. Mexico City: Siglo XXI, 2000.

——. *Obras completas, 1923–1972*. Buenos Aires: Emecé, 1974.

Bormann, Marco. *Der Begriff der Natur: Eine Untersuchung zu Hegels Naturbegriff und dessen Rezeption*. Herbolzheim: Centaurus, 2000.

Boulnois, Oliver. "Objet." In *Vocabulaire européen des philosophies*, ed. Barbara Cassin, 867–869. Paris: Seuil, 2004.

Brecht, Bertholt. *Die Dreigroschenoper*. Frankfurt: Suhrkamp, 1986.

——. *Die Dreigroschenoper: Der Erstdruck 1928*. Berlin: Suhrkamp, 2013.

——. *Gesammelte Werke*. Frankfurt: Suhrkamp, 1967.

Brecht, Bertholt, and Kurt Weill. *The Threepenny Opera*. Trans. Marc Blitzstein. New York: Tams-Witmark Music Library, 1956.

——. *The Threepenny Opera*. Trans. Ralph Manheim and John Willett. New York: Arcade, 1994.

Breckman, Warren. *Marx, the Young Hegelians, and the Origins of Radical Social Theory*. Cambridge: Cambridge University Press, 1999.

Breton, Stanislas. "'Dieu est Dieu': Essai sur la violence des propositions tautologiques." In *Philosophie buissonnière*, 133–140. Grenoble: Millon, 1989.

——. "'God Is God': Essay on the Violence of Tautological Propositions." Trans. Jacques Lezra. *Yearbook of Comparative Literature* (2017): 203–211.

Broderick, Albert, ed. *The French Institutionalists: Maurice Hauriou, Georges Renard, Joseph T. Delos*. Trans. Mary Welling. Cambridge, MA: Harvard University Press, 1970.

Brown, Roger, and Helen Carasso. *Everything for Sale? The Marketisation of UK Higher Education*. Abingdon, UK: Routledge, 2013.

Buarque, Chico. "Geni e o Zepelim." https://www.letras.mus.br/chico-buarque/77259/.

Burkert, Walter. *Lore and Science in Ancient Pythagoreanism*. Trans. E. Minar. Cambridge, MA: Harvard University Press, 1972.

Burkett, Paul. "Nature in Marx Reconsidered: A Silver Anniversary Assessment of Alfred Schmidt's *Concept of Nature in Marx*." *Organization & Environment* 10, no. 2 (1997): 164–183.

Butler, Judith. *Parting Ways: Jewishness and the Critique of Zionism*. New York: Columbia University Press, 2012.

——. *Precarious Life: The Powers of Mourning and Violence*. Verso, 2004.

——. *The Psychic Life of Power*. Stanford, CA: Stanford University Press, 1997.

Callimachus. *Hymns and Epigrams, Lycophron, Aratus*. Trans. A. W. Mair and G. R. Mair. London: William Heinemann, 1921.

Capoccia, Giovanni. "When Do Institutions 'Bite'? Historical Institutionalism and the Politics of Institutional Change." *Comparative Political Studies* 49, no. 8 (2016): 1095–1127.

Carte, Gene E., and Elaine H. Carte. *Police Reform in the United States: The Era of August Vollmer, 1905–1932*. Berkeley: University of California Press, 1974.

Castree, Noel. "Marxism and the Production of Nature." *Capital & Class* 24, no. 3 (2000): 5–36.

Castro-Carracedo, Juan Manuel. "La evolución del *Ars Moriendi* post-tridentino en España e Inglaterra." In *Proceedings of the 29th AEDEAN Conference*, ed. Alejandro Alcaraz-Sintes, Concepción Soto-Palomo, and María de la Cinta Zunino-Garrido, 39–49. Jaén, Spain: Servicio de Publicaciones de la Universidad de Jaén, 2006.

Centre Nationale de Ressources Textuelles et Lexicales (CNRTL). https://www.cnrtl.fr/definition/.

Cesar, Rafael do Nascimento. "A fragata negra: Tradução e vingança em Nina Simone." *MANA* 24, no. 1 (2018): 39–70.

Chejfec, Sergio. *Los incompletos*. Buenos Aires: Alfaguara, 1994.

Chronopoulos, Themis. "Police Misconduct, Community Opposition, and Urban Governance in New York City, 1945–1965." *Journal of Urban History* 1, no. 26 (2015): 643–668.

Cohen, Joshua. "Democratic Equality." *Ethics* 99, no. 4 (1989): 727–751.

Cooper, Melinda. *Family Values: Between Neoliberalism and the New Social Conservatism*. New York: Zone Books, 2017.

Corwin, Edward S. *The Doctrine of Judicial Review, Its Legal and Historical Basis, and Other Essays*. Princeton, NJ: Princeton University Press, 1914.

Covarrubias Horozco, Sebastián de. *Tesoro de la lengua castellana, o española*. Madrid: Luis Sánchez, 1611.

Croce, Mariano, and Marco Goldoni. *The Legacy of Pluralism: The Continental Jurisprudence of Santi Romano, Carl Schmitt, and Costantino Mortati*. Stanford, CA: Stanford University Press, 2020.

Dacier, Anne. *Des causes de la corruption du goust, par Madame Dacier*. Paris: Rigaud, 1714.

——. *Homère défendu contre l'apologie du R. P. Hardouin, ou suite des causes de la corruption du Goust*. Paris: Jean Baptiste Coignard, 1716.

Dal, Vladimir. *Explanatory Dictionary of the Living Great Russian Language* (1882) (in Russian). https://slovardalja.net/.

Davies, Paul. "This Contradiction." In *Futures: Of Jacques Derrida*, ed. Richard Rand, 18–64. Stanford, CA: Stanford University Press, 2001.

Davis, Noela. "Subjected Subjects? On Judith Butler's Paradox of Interpellation." *Hypatia* 27, no. 4 (2012): 881–897.

De Man, Paul. *Aesthetic Ideology*. Minneapolis: University of Minnesota Press, 1996.

——. *Allegory and Representation: Selected Papers from the English Institute, 1979–1980*. Ed. Stephen Greenblatt. Baltimore: Johns Hopkins University Press, 1981.

Deleuze, Gilles. *Instincts et institutions*. Paris: Hachette, 1955.

Derrida, Jacques. *The Death Penalty*. Vol. 2. Ed. Geoffrey Bennington and Marc Crépon, trans. Elizabeth Rottenberg. Chicago: University of Chicago Press, 2017.

——. "Et Cetera." In *Deconstructions: A User's Guide*, ed. Nicholas Royle, 282–305. New York: Palgrave, 2000.

——. *Heidegger: La question de l'être et l'histoire*. Paris: Galilée, 2013.

——. "The Principle of Reason: The University in the Eyes of Its Pupils." Trans. Catherine Porter and Edward P. Morris. *Diacritics* 13, no. 3 (1983): 2–20.

——. "Telepathy." *Oxford Literary Review* 10, no. 1 (1988): 3–41.

——. *Who's Afraid of Philosophy: Right to Philosophy 2*. Trans. Jan Plug et al. Stanford, CA: Stanford University Press, 2004.

———. *The Work of Mourning*. Ed. and trans. Pascale-Anne Briault and Michael Naas. Chicago: University of Chicago Press, 2001.

Descartes, René. *Les passions de l'ame*. In *Oeuvres de Descartes*, vol. IV. Ed. Victor Cousin. Paris: F. G. Levrault, 1824.

———. *Meditationes de Prima Philosophia*. Ed. Artur Buchenau. Leipzig: Meiner, 1913.

———. *Meditations on First Philosophy*. Ed. and trans. John Cottingham. Cambridge: Cambridge University Press, 1996.

de Ville, Jacques. "Spectres of Coke: Judicial Supervision as a Revolutionary Inheritance." *Law Critique* 18 (2007): 29–54.

*Diccionario de la Real Academia Española*. Madrid, 1925.

DiLeo, Jeffrey R. "Peirce's Haecceitism." *Transactions of the Charles S. Peirce Society* 27, no. 1 (1991): 79–109.

Dimon, Marie-Laure. "La folie au risque des discours institutionnels." *Topique* 76, no. 3 (2001): 141–157.

Donahue, Charles. "'The Hypostasis of a Prophecy': Legal Realism and Legal History." In *Law and Legal Process: Substantive Law and Procedure in English Legal History*, ed. M. Dyson and D. Ibbetson, 1–16. Cambridge: Cambridge University Press, 2013.

Dostoevsky, Fyodor. *Winter Notes on Summer Impressions*. Trans. David Patterson. Evanston, IL: Northwestern University Press, 1997.

Doublet, Victor. *Logic for Young Ladies*. New York: O'Shea, 1868.

———. *Logique des demoiselles*. Tours: R. Pornin, 1842.

Dove, Patrick. *Literature and "Interregnum": Globalization, War, and the Crisis of Sovereignty in Latin America*. Albany: State University of New York Press, 2016.

Dover, Daniela. "Two Kinds of Curiosity." *Philosophy & Phenomenological Research*. 2023. https://onlinelibrary.wiley.com/doi/10.1111/phpr.12976.

Dubber, Markus D. "A Political Theory of Criminal Law: Autonomy and the Legitimacy of State Punishment." *SSRN Research Journal*, March 15, 2004. https://ssrn.com/abstract=529522.

———. "'The Power to Govern Men and Things': Patriarchal Origins of the Police Power in American Law." 52 *Buffalo Law Review* 1277 (2004). https://hdl.handle.net/1807/88536.

Dubber, Markus D., and Mariana Valverde, eds. *The New Police Science: The Police Power in Domestic and International Governance*. Palo Alto, CA: Stanford University Press, 2006.

Duns Scotus, John. *Ordinatio*. In *Five Texts on the Mediaeval Problem of Universals: Porphyry, Boethius, Abelard, Duns Status, Ockham*. Ed. and trans. Paul Vincent Spade. Indianapolis: Hackett Publishing, 1994.

Durkheim, Émile. *The Rules of Sociological Method*. Ed. Steven Lukes, trans. W. D. Halls. New York: Macmillan, 1982.

Epstein, Richard Allen. *The Classical Liberal Constitution: The Uncertain Quest for Limited Government*. Cambridge, MA: Harvard University Press, 2014.

Esposito, Roberto. *Instituting Thought: Three Paradigms of Political Ontology*. Trans. Mark William Epstein. Cambridge: Polity, 2021.

——. *Istituzione*. Bologna: Il Mulino, 2021.

Euclid. *The Thirteen Books of Euclid's Elements*. Trans. T. L. Heath. Cambridge: Cambridge University Press, 1928.

Evelyn, John. *An Essay on the First Book of T. Lucretius Carus De Rerum Natura. Interpreted and Made English Verse*. London: Gabriel Bedle and Thomas Collins, 1656.

Fanon, Frantz. *Black Skin, White Masks*. Trans. Charles Lam Markham. New York: Grove Press, 1967.

Fernández Díaz, María Elena. *Melilla 1931–1940, Gritos y susurros: El campo de concentración de Zeluán*. Melilla: UNED, 2020.

Field, Allyson, Jacqueline Najuma Stewart, and Jan-Christopher Horak, eds. *L.A. Rebellion: Creating a New Black Cinema*. Berkeley: University of California Press, 2015.

Fine, Kit. *Modality and Tense: Philosophical Papers*. Oxford: Oxford University Press, 2002.

Fioretos, Orfeo, Tulia G. Falleti, and Adam Sheingate. "Historical Institutionalism in Political Science." In *The Oxford Handbook of Historical Institutionalism*, ed. Orfeo Fioretos, Tulia G. Falleti, and Adam Sheingate, 3–28. Oxford: Oxford University Press, 2016.

Fletcher, Angus. *Allegory: The Theory of a Symbolic Mode*. Ithaca, NY: Cornell University Press, 1964.

Flint, Richard E. "The Evolving Standard for the Granting of Mandamus Relief in the Texas Supreme Court: One More Mile Marker down the Road of No Return." 39 *St. Mary's Law Journal* 1 (2007). https://ssrn.com/abstract=2891824.

Forster, Michael. "Wittgenstein on Family Resemblance Concepts." In *Wittgenstein's Philosophical Investigations: A Critical Guide*, ed. Arif Ahmed, 66–87. Cambridge: Cambridge University Press, 2010.

Foster, John Bellamy. *Marx's Ecology: Materialism and Nature*. New York: Monthly Review Press, 2000.

——. *The Return of Nature: Socialism and Ecology*. New York: NYU Press, 2020.

Foucault, Michel. *The Order of Things: An Archaeology of the Human Sciences*. Trans. Alan Sheridan. New York: Routledge, 2004.

Fraser, Nancy, and Alex Honneth. *Redistribution or Recognition? A Political-Philosophical Exchange*. New York: Verso, 2003.

Frege, Gottlob. "Function and Concept." In *Translations from the Philosophical Writings of Gottlob Frege*, 130–148. Ed. P. Geach and M. Black. Oxford: Blackwell, 1960.

Freud, Sigmund. *Gesammelte Werke*. Berlin: Fischer Verlag, 1991–2006.

——. "Letter from Freud to Lou Andreas-Salomé," July 30, 1915. *The International Psycho-Analytical Library* 89 (1915): 32–33.

——. *The Interpretation of Dreams*. Trans. James Strachey. New York: Basic Books, [1915] 2010.

——. *The Psychopathology of Everyday Life*. Trans. A. A. Brill. In *The Basic Writings of Sigmund Freud*. New York: Modern Library, 1995.

——. *Reflections on War and Death*. Trans. A. A. Brill. Durham, NC: Duke University Press, [1918] 2014.

——. *Standard Edition of the Complete Psychological Works of Sigmund Freud*. Ed. and trans. James Strachey. London: Hogarth Press, 1953–1999.

Freud, Sigmund, and Joseph Breuer. *Studies in Hysteria*. Trans. Nicola Luckhurst. New York: Penguin Books, 2004.

Furley, David J. *Two Studies in the Greek Atomists. 1. Indivisible Magnitudes*. Princeton, NJ: Princeton University Press, 1967.

Genet, Jean. *Journal du voleur*. Paris: Gallimard, 1949.

——. *The Thief's Journal*. Trans. Bernard Frechtman. New York: Grove Press, 1964.

George, Robert P. "Holmes on Natural Law." 48 *Villanova Law Review* 1 (2003): 1–11.

Gingerich, Jonathan. "Remixing Rawls: Constitutional Cultural Liberties in Liberal Democracies." *Northeastern University Law Review* 11, no. 2 (2019): 401–466.

——. "Spontaneous Freedom." *Ethics* 133, no. 1 (2022): 38–71.

Goldberg, Jesse A. "James Baldwin and the Anti-Black Force of Law: On Excessive Violence and Exceeding Violence." *Public Culture* 31, no. 3 (2019): 521–538.

Golding, Arthur. *Shakespeare's Ovid, Being Arthur Golding's translation of the Metamorphoses*. Ed. W. H. D. Rouse. New York: Norton, 1966.

Gopinath, Sumanth. "The Problem of the Political in Steve Reich's *Come Out* (1966)." In *Sound Commitments: Avant-Garde Music and the Sixties*, ed. Robert Adlington, 121–144. New York: Oxford University Press, 2009.

Goytisolo, Juan. *Count Julian*. Trans. Helen Lane. New York: Viking Press, 1974.

——. *Reivindicación del Conde don Julián*. Madrid: Cátedra 1985.

Grabbe, Hans Christian. *The Dramas of Hans Christian* Grabbe. Trans. Roger Nicholls. The Hague: Mouton, 1969.

——. *Hannibal*. Düsseldorf: Schreiner, 1835.

Graber, Mark A., and Michael Perhac. *Marbury Versus Madison: Documents and Commentary*. Washington, DC: CQ Press, 2002.

Graeber, David. *The Utopia of Rules: On Technology, Stupidity, and the Secret Joys of Bureaucracy*. New York: Melville House, 2015.

Graff Zivin, Erin. "Exposición, experimento, exapropiación: Después del sujeto (latinoamericano)." In *Sujetos del latinoamericanismo*, ed. Florencia Garramuño, Héctor Hoyos, and Romina Wainberg, 37–56. Pittsburgh: University of Pittsburgh Press, 2021.

Gramsci, Antonio. *Prison Notebooks*. Ed. Joseph Buttigieg. Trans. Joseph Buttigieg and Antonio Callari. New York: Columbia University Press, 1992.

———. *Quaderni del Carcere*. Ed. Valentino Gerratana. Torino: Einaudi, 1972.

Guattari, Félix. *De Leros à La Borde*. Paris: Lignes/IMEC, 2022.

———. *Pratique de l'institutionnel et politique*. Vigneux: Matrice, 1985.

———. *Psychanalyse et transversalité: Essais d'analyse institutionnelle*. Paris: Maspéro, [1974] 2003.

Hacking, Ian. "A Tradition of Natural Kinds." *Philosophical Studies* 61, nos. 1–2 (1991): 109–126.

Hall, Peter A., and Rosemary C. R. Taylor. "La science politique et les trois néo-institutionnalismes." *Revue française de science politique* 47, nos. 3–4 (1997): 469–496.

Hamilton, Alexander. Federalist No. 65 (1788). https://guides.loc.gov/federalist-papers/text-61–70#s-lg-box-wrapper-25493452.

Hardouin, Jean. *Apologie d'Homère*. Paris: Rigaud, 1716.

Harney, Stefano, and Fred Moten. *The Undercommons: Fugitive Planning & Black Study*. New York: Minor Compositions, 2013.

Harriss, John. "Institutions, Politics and Culture: A Case for 'Old' Institutionalism in the Study of Historical Change." In *Understanding Change: Models, Methodologies, and Metaphors*, ed. Andreas Wimmer and Reinhart Kössler, 77–187. New York: Palgrave-Macmillan, 2006.

Hartman, Saidiya. *Scenes of Subjection: Terror, Slavery, and Self-Making in Nineteenth Century America*. New York: Oxford University Press, 1997.

Hastings-King, Stephen. *Looking for the Proletariat: Socialisme ou Barbarie and the Problem of Worker Writing*. Leiden: Brill, 2014.

Hauriou, Maurice. *Principes de droit public*. Sirey: Paris, 1916.

Hawthorne, Nathaniel. *Mosses from an Old Manse*. New York: Modern Library, 2003.

Hegel, Georg Wilhelm Friedrich. *Aesthetics: Lectures on Fine Art*. Trans. T. M. Knox. Oxford: Oxford University Press, 1975.

———. *Hegels Kleine Logik: Nebst dem Kapitel über Raum, Zeit und Bewegung nach dem Texte der Encyklopädie in der Ausgabe seiner sämmtlichen Werke, für das akademische Studium mit einem Kommentar herausgegeben*. Vol. 1. Ed. G. J. P. J. Bolland. Leiden: Adriani, 1899.

———. *Werke*. Frankfurt: Suhrkamp, 1979–1986.

———. "Who Thinks Abstractly?" In *Hegel: Texts and Commentary*, 113–118. Ed. Walter Kaufmann. Garden City, NY: Anchor Books, 1966.

Heidegger, Martin. *Being and Time*. Trans. Joan Stambaugh. Albany: State University of New York Press, 2010.

———. *Der Satz vom Grund*. Frankfurt: Vittorio Klosterman, 1997.

———. *The Principle of Reason*. Trans. Reginald Lilly. Bloomington: Indiana University Press, 1996.

——. *Sein und Zeit*. Tübingen: Max Niemeyer Verlag, 1967.

Hermansson, Casie E. *Blue Beard: A Reader's Guide to the English Tradition*. Jackson: University Press of Mississippi, 2014.

Holmes, Oliver Wendell. "Natural Law." *Harvard Law Review* 40 (1918–1919): 40–44.

Honneth, Axel. *The Struggle for Recognition: The Moral Grammar of Social Conflicts*. Cambridge, MA: MIT Press, 1995.

Horozco y Covarrubias, Juan de. *Emblemas morales*. Madrid: Juan de la Cuesta, 1589.

Huegel, Viktoria. "From Authority to Authoritarianism and back again: Max Weber, Carl Schmitt, and Hannah Arendt." PhD dissertation, Centre for Applied Philosophy, Politics and Ethics, School of Humanities, University of Brighton, 2022.

Iamblichus. *Iamblichus's Life of Pythagoras*. Trans. Thomas Taylor. London: Watkins, 1818.

Immergut, Ellen M. "Historical-Institutionalism in Political Science and the Problem of Change." In *Understanding Change: Models, Methodologies, and Metaphors*, ed. Andreas Wimmer and Reinhart Kössler, 237–260. New York: Palgrave-Macmillan, 2006.

Jackson, Zakiyyah Iman. *Becoming Human: Matter and Meaning in an Antiblack World*. New York: New York University Press, 2020.

James, Henry. *Terminations*. London: Heinemann, 1895.

Jefferson, Thomas. "Letter to William Smith, November 13, 1787." https://founders.archives.gov/documents/Jefferson/01–12–02–0348.

Jennings, Raymond E., and Dorian X. Nicholson. "An Axiomatization of Family Resemblance." *Journal of Applied Logic* 5 (2007): 577–585.

Jiménez, Ramon. "Review of *Tragedy of Richard II, Part One,* Edited by Michael Egan." *Shakespeare Oxford Fellowship*, June 20, 2006. https://shakespeareoxfordfellowship.org/review-of-tragedy-of-richard-ii-part-one-edited-by-michael-egan/.

Judy, Ronald. *DisForming the American Canon: African-Arabic Slave Narratives and the Vernacular*. Minneapolis: University of Minnesota Press, 1993.

Kahn, Paul W. *The Reign of Law: Marbury v. Madison and the Construction of America*. New Haven, CT: Yale University Press, 1997.

Kant, Immanuel. *Immanuel Kants Werke*. Ed. Artur Buchenau and Ernst Cassirer. Berlin: Bruno Cassirer, 1913.

Katritzky, M. A., and Pavel Drábek, eds. *Transnational Connections in Early Modern Theatre*. Manchester: Manchester University Press, 2019.

Kluge, Friedrich. *An Etymological Dictionary of the German Language*. Trans. John Francis Davis. London: G. Bell, 1891.

Kopp, Detlev, ed. *Grabbe im Dritten Reich: Zum nationalsozialistischen Grabbe-Kult*. Bielefeld, Germany: Aisthesis Verlag, 1986.

Koselleck, Reinhart. *Critique and Crisis: Enlightenment and the Pathogenesis of Modern Society*. Cambridge, MA: MIT Press, 2000.

Kowalke, Kim H. "The *Three Penny Opera* in America." In *Kurt Weill, The Three Penny Opera*, ed. Stephen Hinton, 78–120. Cambridge: Cambridge University Press, 1990.

Krell, David Farrell. *The Cudgel and the Caress: Reflections on Cruelty and Tenderness*. Albany: SUNY Press, 2019.

La Torre, Massimo. "Institutionalism as Alternative Constitutional Theory: On Santi Romano's Concept of Law and His Epigones." *Jurisprudence* 11, no. 1 (2020): 92–100.

Lambin, Denis ("Lambinus"). *Titi Lucretii Cari De rerum natura libri sex*. Paris, 1563.

Leonard, Gerald Flood. *The Partisan Republic: Democracy, Exclusion, and the Fall of the Founders' Constitution, 1780s–1830s*. Cambridge: Cambridge University Press, 2019.

Lewis, Charlton T., and Charles Short. *A Latin Dictionary*. Oxford: Clarendon Press,1879.

Lewis, Sophie. *Full Surrogacy Now: Feminism against Family*. New York: Verso, 2019.

Lezra, Jacques. *On the Nature of Marx's Things*. New York: Fordham University Press, 2018.

——. *República salvaje: De la naturaleza de las cosas*. Santiago, Chile: Ediciones Macul, 2020.

——. *Untranslating Machines: A Genealogy for the Ends of Global Thought*. London: Rowman & Littlefield, 2017.

——. *Wild Materialism*. New York: Fordham University Press, 2010.

Littré, Émile. *Dictionnaire de la langue française*. https ://www.littre.org/.

Livingston, Paul M. *The Logic of Being: Realism, Truth, and Time*. Evanston, IL: Northwestern University Press, 2017.

Locke, John. *An Essay Concerning Human Understanding*. Ed. Peter Nidditch. Oxford: Oxford University Press, 1975.

——. *Some Thoughts Concerning Education*. London: A. and J. Churchill at the Black Swan in Paternoster-row, 1693.

Lucretius. *The Nature of Things: A Philosophical Poem, in Six Books*. Trans. John Selby Watson. London: Bohn, 1851.

——. *On the Nature of Things*. Trans. William Ellery Leonard. Mineola, NY: Dover, 2004.

——. *On the Nature of Things*. Trans. Martin Ferguson Smith. Indianapolis: Hackett, 1969.

——. *Titus Lucretius Carus De Rerum Natura Libri VI*. Ed. Mark Deufert. Berlin: de Gruyter, 2019.

Lyotard, Jean-François. *The Differend: Phrases in Dispute*. Trans. Georges Van Den Abbeele. Minneapolis: University of Minnesota Press, 1988.

——. "The Foundation Crisis." Trans. Chris Turner. *Cultural Politics* 9, no. 2 (2013): 117–143.

——. "Judicieux dans le différend." In Jacques Derrida et al., *La faculté de juger*, 195–236. Paris: Minuit, 1985.

——. *Le différend*. Paris: Les Éditions de Minuit, 1983.

——. "Pierre Souyri: Le marxisme qui n'a pas fini." *Esprit* n.s. 61, no. 1 (1982): 11–31.

Maeterlinck, Maurice, and Paul Dukas. *Ariane and Blue Beard: A Lyric Story in Three Acts*. New York: Rullman, 1910.

Mah, Harold E. *The End of Philosophy, the Origin of "Ideology": Karl Marx and the Crisis of the Young Hegelians*. Berkeley: University of California Press, 1987.

Malabou, Catharine. *Au voleur! Anarchisme et philosophie*. Paris: PUF, 2022.

March, James G., and Johan P. Olsen. *Rediscovering Institutions: The Organizational Basis of Politics*. New York: Free Press, 1989.

Marcowitz, Reinerm, and Werner Paravicini, *Vergeben und Vergessen? Pardonner et oublier?: Vergangenheitsdiskurse nach Besatzung, Bürgerkrieg und Revolution. Les discours sur le passé après l'occupation, la guerre civile et la révolution*. Munich: Oldenbourg Wissenschaftsverlag, 2014.

Marías, Julián. *Ortega: I. Circunstancia y vocación*. Madrid: Revista de Occidente, 1960.

Marshall, John. "Marbury v. Madison." In *The Constitutional Decisions of John Marshall*, vol. 1. Ed. Joseph Potter Cotton. New York: G. P. Putnam's Sons, 1905.

Martin, Rex. "Rawls's New Theory of Justice." 69 *Chicago-Kent Law Review* 737 (1994): 737–761.

Marx, Karl. *The Economic and Political Manuscripts of 1844*. Trans. Martin Milligan. New York: Prometheus, 1988.

——. *Grundrisse: Foundations of the Critique of Political Economy*. Trans. Martin Nicolaus. New York: Penguin Books/NLR, 1973.

Marx, Karl, and Friedrich Engels. *Werke*. Berlin: Dietz Verlag, 1968–1983.

McLellan, David. *The Young Hegelians and Karl Marx*. New York: Macmillan 1969.

Meadows, Donella. "Envisioning a Sustainable World/Down to Earth." Third Biennial Meeting of the International Society of Ecological Economics, Costa Rica. 1994. https://donellameadows.org/wp-content/userfiles/Envisioning.DMeadows.pdf.

Mehigan, Tim, and Helene De Burgh. "'Aufklärung,' Freemasonry, the Public Sphere and the Question of Enlightenment." *Journal of European Studies* 38, no. 1 (2008): 5–25.

Melissaris, Emmanuel. "Toward a Political Theory of Criminal Law: A Critical Rawlsian Account." *New Criminal Law Review: An International and Interdisciplinary Journal* 15, no. 1 (2012): 122–155.

Messiaen, Olivier. "Ariane et Barbe-bleue de Paul Dukas." In *Olivier Messiaen: Journalism, 1935–1939*, 15–21. Ed. Stephen Broad. Farnham, UK: Ashgate, 2012.

Miller, Seumas. *The Moral Foundations of Social Institutions*. Cambridge: Cambridge University Press, 2010.

Mills, Charles. *Blackness Visible: Essays on Philosophy and Race*. Ithaca, NY: Cornell University Press, 1998.

MMAA. *The Mishnah: A New Translation*. Trans. Jacob Neusner. New Haven, CT: Yale University Press, 1991.

Montag, Warren. "Althusser's Empty Signifier: What Is the Meaning of the Word 'Interpellation'?" *Mediations* 30, no. 2 (2017): 63–69.

——. "'The Soul Is the Prison of the Body': Althusser and Foucault, 1970–1975." *Yale French Studies* 88 (1995): 53–77.

Moore, Marianne. *Observations: Poems*. New York: Farrar Straus Giroux, 1996.

Morán, Gregorio. *El maestro en el erial: Ortega y Gasset y la cultura del franquismo*. Madrid: Tusquets, 1998.

Moreno Cuadro, Fernando. "La visión emblemática del gobernante virtuoso." *Goya* 187 (1985): 17–26.

Moten, Fred. *Black and Blur*. Durham, NC: Duke University Press, 2017.

Muhammad, Khalil Gibran. *The Condemnation of Blackness: Race, Crime, and the Making of Modern Urban America*. Cambridge, MA: Harvard University Press, 2019.

Muir, Matthew M. P. *A Treatise on the Principles of Chemistry*. Cambridge: Cambridge University Press, 1884.

Mummolo, Jonathan. "Militarization Fails to Enhance Police Safety or Reduce Crime but May Harm Police Reputation." *PNAS* 115: 37 (2018), 9181–9186.

——. "Modern Police Tactics, Police-Citizen Interactions, and the Prospects for Reform." *Journal of Politics* 80, no. 1 (2018): 1–15.

Nelson, Truman. *The Torture of Mothers*. Newburyport, MA: Garrison Press, 1965.

Nelson, William E. *Marbury v. Madison: The Origins and Legacy of Judicial Review*. 2nd ed. Lawrence: University Press of Kansas, 2018.

Neocleous, Mark. *The Fabrication of Social Order: A Critical Theory of Police Power*. London: Pluto, 2000.

——. *War Power, Police Power*. Edinburgh: Edinburgh University Press, 2014.

Nicolas, Bernard, dir. *Daydream Therapy*. UCLA School of Film and Television, 1977.

Nietzsche, Friedrich. *Human, All Too Human*. Trans. R. J. Hollingdale. Cambridge: Cambridge University Press, 1991.

——. *Kritische Studienausgabe: Menschliches, Allzumenschliches I und II*, vol. II. Ed. Giorgio Colli and Mazzino Montinari. Munich: Deutscher Taschenbuch Verlag/de Gruyter, 1980.

Nussbaum, Martha C. *Anger and Forgiveness: Resentment, Generosity, Justice*. Oxford: Oxford University Press, 2014.

O'Brien, M. E. "To Abolish the Family: The Working-Class Family and Gender Liberation in Capitalist Development." *Endnotes* 5 (2020): 361–417.

O'Neill, Onora. *Bounds of Justice*. Cambridge: Cambridge University Press, 2000.

Ortega y Gasset, José. *Meditaciones del Quijote*. Madrid: Cátedra, 1995.

——. *Meditations on Quixote*. Trans. Evelyn Rugg and Diego Marín. New York: Norton, 1961.

Palissy, Bernard. *Oeuvres complètes de Bernard Palissy*. Paris: Éditions du Seuil, 1844.

Panofsky, Erwin. *Early Netherlandish Painting*. Cambridge, MA: Harvard University Press, 1966.

——. "'*Et in Arcadia Ego*': On the Conception of Transience in Poussin and Watteau." In *Philosophy and History, Essays Presented to Ernst Cassirer*, ed. R. Klibansky and H. J. Paton, 295–320. Oxford: Clarendon Press, 1936.

Pappus of Alexandria. *Tafsīr Bābūs li-al-Maqālah al-'āshirah min kitāb Uqlīdis (The Commentary of Pappus on Book X of Euclid's Elements*, as translated into Arabic by Abu Uthman al-Dimishqi). Trans. William Thomson and Gustav Junge. Frankfurt: Institute for the History of Arabic-Islamic Science at the Johann Wolfgang Goethe University, 1997.

Pérez Carrillo, Francisco. *Via sacra y exercicios espirituales, y arte de bien morir*. Zaragoza, 1619.

Périllié, Jean-Luc. "La découverte des incommensurables et le vertige de l'infini." *Cahiers philosophiques* 91 (2002): 9–30.

Perrault, Charles. *Contes de ma mère l'Oye/Mother Goose's Tales*. The Hague: Jean Neaulme, 1745.

——. *Histoires ou Contes du temps passé*. Paris: Claude Barbin, 1697.

Plato. *Thaetetus*. Trans. Harold North Fowler, W. R. M. Lamb, Robert Gregg Bury, and Paul Shorey. Cambridge, MA: Harvard University Press, 1914.

Plummer, Comer. "The Bogeyman Cometh: The Annual Disaster." *Military History Online*. 2022. https://www.militaryhistoryonline.com/Modern/BattleOfAnnual.

Pras and kris Ex. *Ghetto Supastar*. New York: Pocket Books, 1999.

Preston, Paul. *The Spanish Holocaust: Inquisition and Extermination in Twentieth-Century Spain*. New York: Norton, 2012.

Primo de Rivera, José Antonio. *Revolución nacional: Puntos de Falange*. Madrid: Ediciones Prensa del Movimiento, 1949.

Proclus. *Commentary on the First Book of Euclid's Elements*. Trans. Glen Morrow. Princeton, NJ: Princeton University Press, 1970.

Quine, Willard Van Orman. *Ontological Relativity and Other Essays*. New York: Columbia University Press, 1969.

Ramond, Sophie. "Comme on pense la mort, on vieillit: Une lecture de *Qohélet* 12,1–8." *communio* 44, no. 4 (2019): 27–39.

Rawls, John. *Political Liberalism*. 2nd ed. New York: Columbia University Press, 2005.

——. *A Theory of Justice: Revised Edition*. Cambridge, MA: Harvard University Press, [1971] 1999.

Readings, Bill. *Introducing Lyotard: Art and Politics*. New York: Routledge, 1991.

——. *The University in Ruins*. Cambridge, MA: Harvard University Press, 1999.

Reitsam, David D. *La querelle d'Homère dans la presse des lumières: L'exemple du 'Nouveau Mercure galant.'* Tübingen: Narr Francke Attempto Verlag, 2021.

Robcis, Camille. *Disalienation: Politics, Philosophy, and Radical Psychiatry in Post-war France*. Chicago: University of Chicago Press, 2021.

Robin, Corey. "American Institutions Won't Keep Us Safe from Donald Trump's Excesses." *The Guardian*, February 2, 2017. https://www.theguardian.com/commentisfree/2017/feb/02/american-institutions-wont-keep-you-safe-trumps-excesses.

Robinson, Cedric. *Black Marxism: The Making of the Black Radical Tradition*. Chapel Hill: University of North Carolina Press, [1983] 2000.

Rosenthal, Earl. "Plus Ultra, Non Plus Ultra, and the Columnar Device of Emperor Charles V." *Journal of the Warburg and Courtauld Institutes* 34 (1971): 204–228.

Russell, Bertrand, and Alfred N. Whitehead. *Principia Mathematica*. 2nd ed. Cambridge: Cambridge University Press, 1963.

Rust, Joshua. *John Searle and the Construction of Social Reality*. New York: Continuum, 2006.

Saito, Kohei. *Karl Marx's Ecosocialism: Capitalism, Nature, and the Unfinished Critique of Political Economy*. New York: Monthly Review Press, 2017.

San Martín, Javier, and José Lasaga Medina, eds. *Ortega en circunstancia*. Madrid: Biblioteca Nueva, 2005.

Sawyer, Dylan. *Lyotard, Literature and the Trauma of the Differend*. New York: Palgrave McMillan, 2014.

Scanlon, Thomas. "Rawls's Theory of Justice." *University of Pennsylvania Law Review* 121 (1973): 1020–1069.

Schmidt, Alfred. *Der Begriff der Natur in der Lehre von Marx*. Frankfurt: Institut für Sozialforschung, Europäische Verlagsanstalt, 1962.

Searle, John R. *The Construction of Social Reality*. New York: Free Press, 1995.

——. "Responses to Critics of *The Construction of Social Reality*," *Philosophy and Phenomenological Research* 57, no. 2 (1997): 449–458.

Sfez, Gérald. *Jean-François Lyotard, La faculté d'une phrase*. Paris: Galilée, 2000.

Silverman, Kaja. *Flesh of My Flesh*. Stanford, CA: Stanford University Press, 2009.

Sluga, Hans. "Family Resemblance." *Grazer Philosophische Studien* 71, no. 1 (2006): 1–21.

Smith, Morton. "On the Shape of God and the Humanity of Gentiles." In *Religions in Antiquity: Essays in Memory of Erwin Ramsdell Goodenough*, ed. Jacob Neusner, 315–426. Leiden: E. J. Brill, 1970.

Smith, Neil, and Phil O'Keefe. "Geography, Marx and the Concept of Nature." *Antipode* 12 (1980): 30–39.

Spivak, Gayatri Chakravorty. *A Critique of Postcolonial Reason*. Cambridge, MA: Harvard University Press, 1999.

Statius. *Silvae*. Ed. and trans. Bruce Gibson. Oxford: Oxford University Press, 2006.

Steyn, Mark. "The Mark Steyn Club: Mack the Knife: Sinatra Song of the Century #95, by Kurt Weill, Bertolt Brecht and Marc Blitzstein." *Steyn's Song of the Day*. December 8, 2015. https://www.steynonline.com/7344/mack-the-knife.

Suddler, Carl. "The Color of Justice without Prejudice: Youth, Race, and Crime in the Case of the Harlem Six." *American Studies* 57, nos. 1–2 (2018): 57–78.

Sutherland, Margaret Anne. *The Reception of Grabbe's "Hannibal" in the German Theatre*. New York: Peter Lang, 1984.

Thayer, Willy, et al., eds. *La universidad (im)posible*. Santiago, Chile: Ediciones Macul, 2018.

Timpanaro, Sebastiano. *La genesi del metodo del Lachmann*. Florence: Le Monnier, 1963.

Tolstoy, Leo. *Anna Karenina*. Trans. Constance Garnett. Philadelphia: George Jacobs, [1900] 1919.

——. *Anna Karenina*. Trans. Richard Pevear and Larissa Volokhonsky. New York: Penguin Books, 2002.

——. *Anna Karenina*. Trans. Marian Schwartz. New Haven, CT: Yale University Press, 2014.

——. *Anna Karenina*. Trans. Rosemarie Tietze. Munich: Carl Hanser Verlag, 2009.

——. *Anna Karénine*. Paris: Hachette, 1885.

Tuomela, Raimo. *The Philosophy of Social Practices: A Collective Acceptance View*. Cambridge: Cambridge University Press, 2002.

Turner, Jonathan. *The Institutional Order*. New York: Longman, 1997.

Ty, M. "Benjamin on the Border." *Critical Times* 2, no. 2 (2019): 306–319.

Van den Berg, Robbert Maarten. *Proclus' Commentary on the Cratylus in Context: Ancient Theories of Language and Naming*. Leiden: Brill, 2008.

Vermorel, Henri. "The Presence of Spinoza in the Exchanges between Sigmund Freud and Romain Rolland." *International Journal of Psychoanalysis* 90 (2009): 1235–1254.

Vernant, Jean-Pierre, and Pierre Vidal Naquet. *Myth and Tragedy in Ancient Greece*. Trans. Janet Lloyd. New York: Zone Books, 1990.

Vitale, Alex S. *The End of Policing*. London: Verso, 2018.

Vollmer, August. *The Police and Modern Society*. Berkeley: University of California Press, 1936.

Warren, Robert Penn. *Who Speaks for the Negro?* New Haven, CT: Yale University Press, [1965] 2014.

Weil, Simone. *The Iliad: The Poem of Force*. Trans. Mary McCarthy. Wallingford, PA: Pendle Hill Press, 1991.

Weithman, Paul. *Why Political Liberalism?: On John Rawls's Political Turn*. Oxford: Oxford University Press, 2010.

Wennerberg, Hjalmar. "The Concept of Family Resemblance in Wittgenstein's Later Philosophy." *Theoria* 33, no. 2 (2008): 107–132.

Whitehead, Alfred North. *Science and the Modern World*. New York: Free Press, [1926] 1967.

Whitman, Walt. "Out of the Cradle, Endlessly Rocking." In *The Collected Writings of Walt Whitman, vol. II: Leaves of Grass: A Textual Variorum of the Printed Poems, 1860–1867*. Ed. Sculley Bradley, Harold W. Boldgett, Arthur Golden, and William White. New York: New York University Press, 1980.

Wilderson III, Frank B. *Afropessimism*. New York: Liveright, 2020.

Winnicott, D. W. "Transitional Objects and Transitional Phenomena: A Study of the First Not-Me Possession." *International Journal of Psycho-Analysis* 34 (1953): 89–97.

Wislicenus, Johannes. "The Space Arrangement of the Atoms in Organic Molecules and the Resulting Geometrical Isomerism in Unsaturated Compounds." In *The Foundations of Stereo Chemistry*, trans. and ed. George M. Richardson, 61–132. New York: American Book Company, 1901.

——. *Über die Räumliche Anordnung der Atome in Organischen Molekulen und Ihre Bestimmung in Geometrisch-Isomeren Ungesättigten Verbindungen*, 1–77. Leipzig: Bei S. Hirzel, 1887.

Wittgenstein, Ludwig. *Philosophical Investigations*. Trans. G. E. M. Anscombe. Oxford: Blackwell, [1958] 1986.

Wood, Michael. "Dear Poochums." *London Review of Books*, October 23, 2014.

Worrall, John L. "The Politics of Policing." In *The Oxford Handbook of Police and Policing*, ed. Michael D Reisig and Robert J. Kane, 49–68. Oxford: Oxford University Press, 2014.

Wynter, Sylvia. "The Ceremony Found: Towards the Autopoetic Turn/Overturn, Its Autonomy of Human Agency and Extraterritoriality of (Self-) Cognition." In *Black Knowledges/Black Struggles: Essays in Critical Epistemology*, ed. Jason R. Ambroise and Sabine Broeck, 184–252. Liverpool: Liverpool University Press, 2015.

——. "The Ceremony Must Be Found: After Humanism." *boundary 2* 12: 3 /13: 1 (1984), 19–70.

——. "*No Humans Involved*: An Open Letter to My Colleagues." *Voices of the African Diaspora* 8, no. 2 (1992): 238–279.

——. "On Disenchanting Discourse: 'Minority' Literary Criticism and Beyond." *Cultural Critique* 7, no. 2 (1987): 207–244.

Zaliznyak, Anna A. "*Happiness* and *Pleasure* in the Russian Language Picture of the World." In *Klyuchevye idei russkoi yazykovoi kartiny mira* [Key Ideas of the Russian Language Picture of the World], ed. Anna A. Zaliznyak, I. B. Levontina, and A. D. Shmelev, 152–174. Moscow: Yazyki slavyanskoi kul'tury, 2005.

# INDEX

**Jacques Lezra** is Distinguished Professor in the Departments of English and Hispanic Studies at the University of California, Riverside. His most recent publications are *República salvaje* (2019), *On the Nature of Marx's Things* (2018), *Untranslating Machines: A Genealogy for the Ends of Global Thought* (2017), and *Contra todos los fueros de la Muerte* (2016).

IDIOM: INVENTING WRITING THEORY

Jacques Lezra and Paul North, series editors

Werner Hamacher, *Minima Philologica*. Translated by Catharine Diehl and Jason Groves

Michal Ben-Naftali, *Chronicle of Separation: On Deconstruction's Disillusioned Love*. Translated by Mirjam Hadar. Foreword by Avital Ronell

Daniel Hoffman-Schwartz, Barbara Natalie Nagel, and Lauren Shizuko Stone, eds., *Flirtations: Rhetoric and Aesthetics This Side of Seduction*

Jean-Luc Nancy, *Intoxication*. Translated by Philip Armstrong

Márton Dornbach, *Receptive Spirit: German Idealism and the Dynamics of Cultural Transmission*

Sean Alexander Gurd, *Dissonance: Auditory Aesthetics in Ancient Greece*

Anthony Curtis Adler, *Celebricities: Media Culture and the Phenomenology of Gadget Commodity Life*

Nathan Brown, *The Limits of Fabrication: Materials Science, Materialist Poetics*

Jay Bernstein, Adi Ophir, and Ann Laura Stoler, eds., *Political Concepts: A Critical Lexicon*

Willy Thayer, *Technologies of Critique*. Translated by John Kraniauskas

Julie Beth Napolin, *The Fact of Resonance: Modernist Acoustics and Narrative Form*

Ann Laura Stoler, Stathis Gourgouris, and Jacques Lezra, eds., *Thinking with Balibar: A Lexicon of Conceptual Practice*

Nathan Brown, *Rationalist Empiricism: A Theory of Speculative Critique*

Gerhard Richter, *Thinking with Adorno: The Uncoercive Gaze*

Kevin McLaughlin, *The Philology of Life: Walter Benjamin's Critical Program*

Alenka Zupančič, *Let Them Rot: Antigone's Parallax*

Adi M. Ophir, *In the Beginning Was the State: Divine Violence in the Hebrew Bible*

Ronald Mendoza-de Jesús, *Catastrophic Historicism: Reading Julia de Burgos Dangerously*

www.ingramcontent.com/pod-product-compliance
Lightning Source LLC
Chambersburg PA
CBHW031141020426
42333CB00013B/464
* 9 7 8 1 5 3 1 5 0 6 9 1 9 *